The Concise Encyclopedia of

SYMBOLISM

The Concise Encyclopedia of
SYMBOLISM

Jean Cassou

OMEGA BOOKS

Translated by Susie Saunders

This edition published 1984 by Omega Books Ltd,
14 Greville Street London EC1N 8SB
under licence from the proprietor.

Reprinted 1986, 1988
Copyright © 1974 by Editions Aimery Somogy, Paris
Illustration copyright © S.P.A.D.E.M. an A.D.A.G.P.

ISBN 0 907853 23 4

Printed an bound in GDR

(00 29912 48 T

Contents

The Spirit of Symbolism

The creative dream

'An habitual dreamer has come here today to talk to you about another who is dead.' It was with this sentence that Stephane Mallarmé opened the conference which in 1880, at the Arts Circle and the Groupe des XX in Brussels, and later in various other Belgian towns, he dedicated to his friend Villiers de l'Isle-Adam who had died the previous year. He stood up to pronounce these words, then sat down and began to read a text for ever famous for its beauty and emotive power.

The solemnity of the opening phrase directs our attention to the essential word — *dream*. There is an underlying complicity here between the speaker and his subject. Both give this word a special significance. Certainly the public of that time — and maybe of all time — used it in everyday speech to denote a roving and unlimited emotional vision, a type of romantic oleography which fitted in perfectly with the popular conception of poets and artists, and to which they accorded an obliging indulgence. But for Mallarmé and Villiers, as for those of their contemporaries for whom the quality of poet or artist was absolute reality rather than equivocal fallacy, the dream is something different, something precise. it is also different from the scholar's imagination which starts from fact in order to seek truth, and finds it by using reason and experience. Knowledge makes use of imagination, we might even say of dreams, but with a view to dealing with essentials rather than with contingencies or chances.

It must of course be understood that the dream of which we speak has nothing to do with the dreams of sleep which have always intrigued humanity and which are studied by psychoanalysis.

Here, then, is the simplest form of the meaning of the mysterious word dream. It is, as already mentioned, something precise. Among those who called themselves dreamers, among the authentic poets and artists of this period at the end of the nineteenth and beginning of the twentieth centuries, which we call Symbolism, it was in effect a certain deep, intimate relationship which they maintained with their creative imagination. The word imagination is used here on purpose, because it conveys the fullness of its power when applied to the idea of freedom which the term 'dream' implies. The imagination of a creator takes no notice of established rules or hallowed principles. One can, of course, affirm that it has always been the essential factor in artistic creation; but in Symbolism, in its spirit and its aestheticism, we should see a fully conscious and insistent assertion of this predominant quality.

Symbolism burst upon Europe, including Russia, upon both Anglo-Saxon and Spanish America, and even upon French-speaking America. I repeat 'including Russia', for Russia was living through a time of positive and active civilization. It was open to what was happening abroad in the world of artistic creativity. It had had its Symbolic poets, and every day more importance is attached in the field of music to the role played by Scriabin, whose clever tonal and rhythmic innovations animate what could be said to be his favourite theme: the theme of fire.

Thus, the whole epoch spoke the language of Symbolism. It was spoken in all the different ways of human expression, obviously that of language in the first place; in the alterations it brought about in both poetry and prose, in unorthodox combinations and mixtures of the two, in theatrical innovations, and in new views in the field of philosophical speculation, as well as in other forms of expression, such as painting, sculpture, drawing, decoration, printing, furnishing, architecture and music. It is possible to see here just how removed the spiritual whole, formed gradually during a certain moment in the universal history of human genius, is from the peaceful and routine mechanism to which the society of that time claimed to have reduced the undertakings and practices of those restless and habitual dreamers. It is quite likely that the ridiculous echoes which the masses heard in the word 'dream' came from the wealth of subjective experience which the creators wittingly put into it. It was only this subjective experience which was not shrouded in a cocoon of mist, something which should have admirably suited those good souls so determined to confuse 'dream' with 'reverie' — the stupid and sterile reverie, which manifests itself as a constant art in every art.

An artificial society of remarkable personalities

The dream invents. The dream was the creative and imaginative faculty of the Symbolist. Every one of them cultivated, developed and used it to his own creative ends, following his own individuality and his own personal adventure. The Symbolists certainly formed groups, cliques; they connived in cafès, in little reviews, in dissident salons. All this tended to be coloured by a feeling of subversion, by an asocial and antisocial spirit, so that although the community of these artists maintained an air of mystery it was in fact a community of lawless individualism.

This apparent contradictory connivance was made up of customs, that is to say communal habits. There was a society within a society; it was a separate little society with its somewhat provocative manners which were bohemian, avant-garde, and only just acceptable. Its members had a very elevated idea of what constituted art and poetry outside a way of life which was firmly rooted in its bourgeois assurance, its order, its financial and industrial power, and the comforts which the unchangingly academic productions of its licensed and famous trades-men procured for it. It was thus possible to recognize as totally separate from this solidly constructed society a different community which, although a disparaged minority, was the creative reality which wrote its name under the historical heading of Symbolism.

It is, however, an essential fact that this little artificial society was made up of individual personalities, who took their originality as far as they could, even sometimes as far as scandal. And it is on these personal originalities that the accent must be put.

Each of the great Symbolist figures has been distinguished by a quality of inherent destiny, even if this has not been marked by outstanding events. In this way Symbolism resembles Romanticism, at least the particular chapter of Romanticism which has been illustrated by certain touchingly human figures in German music, and certain strange and tragic figures in the school of poetry for which the name 'German Romanticism' was coined. Nevertheless, that was only one part, without doubt sublime, but limited in the universal sense of Romanticism. It must be recognized that the great Romantic figures were more conditioned by the times in which they lived. They very often played a prestigious and guiding role in the history and events of their era.

With the advent of the Symbolist era, history suffered the sort of rupture which can only be brought about by great human figures. Each of those who created the rupture admitted with pride the part he had played in its creation, affirmed the originality of his own personality, and emphasized this originality without help, without affectation and with the deep conviction that it was vital to him and rooted in his being. The value of a great historical movement is measured not only by the outstanding characteristics of its products and style, but by the people who have principally illustrated it, who have represented it, and whose nature and energy have given them an unusual individuality. Younger generations refer to them, follow

Ferdinand Hodler *The Dream.* 1897-1903

their example and take their inspiration from them. We are faced here by a dialectic according to which an ensemble on the one hand defines itself by common characteristics, on the other it is due to those men who were prompted by their deep vocations to distinguish themselves as individuals.

Baudelaire, Rimbaud, Gauguin, van Gogh and Toulouse-Lautrec must not be seen as historic figures, that is to say characters integrated with the continuity and logic of history, but more as characters in the break-up. And it was a totally unforeseen, ridiculous and explosive break-up. Here I must note in parentheses that I use the term Symbolism as indicating a vast period which cannot be enclosed in too strict an exactitude of dates and names, but which achieves its full significance if the figure of Baudelaire is included for his value as a precursor, as I have done. Baudelaire was not a Romantic, and if it is not appropriate to speak of him as a Symbolist either, at least he heralded the full meaning of Symbolism. He was typically representative of this new concept of genius as a particular individuality condemned to struggle pathetically against its fate. So much can be said of the three painters mentioned together with Baudelaire: one finished his life in the geographical antipodes of the world, Tahiti and the Marquesas Islands; the second in the mental antipodes — madness and suicide; the third lived in the social antipodes — the brothels. These lonely prophets reached a conscious self-awareness strong enough to be expressed in an aggressive and open revolt. Take, for example, Jarry's *La Chanson de Decervelage*, a comic and enraged Marseillaise of the war on stupidity; this work was later praised by a society at the height of its totalitarian powers of restraint. And the Symbolists, at the instigation of one of their keenest critical minds, Remy de Gourmont, interpreted the mysterious *Maldoror* as a universal blasphemy. Later the Surrealists put the same interpretation on it; this arose out of ignorance of where they stood, or still stand, with regard to the profound aims of this book, which progresses at a pace both bubbling and solemn and was written by an adolescent who soon disappeared. Efforts were made to interrogate the families of his student friends in order to find out about him. But the essential interest which this problem of literary history inspires resides in the problem itself and in the taste awakened by Symbolism for everything which, in the world of the imagination, appears as problematical or extremely problematical. This applies particularly when the object of the problem clothes its form in a furious and satanic invective against society, humanity, life, nature, God. In the same spirit account must be taken of the injurious and stinging buffoonery of Tristan Corbière who, with his *Amours jaunes* opened the way to poetic soliloquies.

Thus the creative minority, who saw themselves as the protagonists of an 'accused art' and extracted from it a code of ethics and a point of honour, replied with sarcasm to the rejection of society. Likewise they deluded themselves that the prosperous society was composed solely of 'decadents'. In Paris, the left bank despised the right bank, the bank of the Boulevard. The 'Tuesdays' in the Rue de Rome, which numbered among their habitués so many of the young men destined to be the finest geniuses of the century, inspired literary analogues such as the *Kreis* of Stefan George. The poet Albert Saint-Paul, who had introduced George to the world of the Parisian Symbolists, and in particular to Mallarmé, once told me of the enthusiasm which such meetings had engendered in the heart of his German friend. To George, poetic finesse (and he pushed his own to a point of extreme perfection) necessitated a rigorous isolation. This discipline showed in the exterior presentation of his work: the use of unusual print, the suppression of capital letters. George remained faithful to his belief in an ordering of principles and details which he imposed on himself and on his circle. Such a willing aestheticism appeared to be fairly new in German literature and conferred a great honour on it. There was the same selective solicitude among the Pre-Raphaelite and the various English groups which had found, besides, a traditional British tendency to assert their differences, an aestheticism, a dandyism or what the French, borrowing a term from the English (particularly Thackeray) who understand it differently, call snobbery. What this sort of fashion cost Oscar Wilde is well known. But it must be noted that the happy little world where the brazen disports of Wilde took place was still part of the 'gentry', whose authority, prestige and manners lived in harmony with what was common in the unshakeable English community. What a contrast with the French aristocracy of the same period, who had no connection at all with either a

EDOUARD MANET *Portrait of Stéphane Mallarmé.* 1876

financial or a political power which from then on was in the hands of the ascending middle class. The aristocrats confined themselves to the fashionable salons, and to the friendly spontaneity of academic elections and brilliant conversation. They were 'the world'. They were totally marginal. It sometimes happened that one of the personalities on the fringe of this marginality would stretch out a hand towards the edge of the Symbolist group. I would like to speak here of Count Robert de Montesquiou-Fezensac. This great titled man of the world, this model for Huysmans' *Des Esseintes* and Proust's *Monsieur de Charlus*, and whose dashing impression was left to us in the portrait by Boldini, wrote reports and art criticisms using affectations and mannerisms of the most extreme Symbolist sort. He also wrote poems in the same style, of which some, and I underline the world 'some', achieved a melodious and grandiose nobility. Certainly such behaviour gave rise to a certain amount of scandal among his friends, but this never went too far, nor did it cause him very much trouble. He had sworn a passionate allegiance to Verlaine, and he followed his funeral without hestitating to mix with the unwholesome mob of the neighbourhood where the poor Lélian had finally ended his squalid struggle. If I take as an example this representative of a class which was itself dying, who was so concerned to honour another fringe group, it is only to make the relief and impact of this marginality and the brilliance it brought more understandable, as he understood it.

The outstanding characteristic of these European literary groups at that time appeared in a taste which they shared for a certain past era, which was definitely not the Antiquity of the classics, nor the German, Spanish or Italian Middle Ages of the Romantics. This was another Middle Ages, less historic and on the contrary imprecise, irregular and legendary. Every cultural era furnishes itself with a past, and takes its ideas and examples from it. The Symbolists only needed a confused past, and they were fascinated with the confusion. This fanciful and muddled nostalgia has often been conjured up, by poets as diverse in the poetic spectrum as Swinburne, Hofmannsthal and D'Annunzio.

Symbolism and idealism

All this went with a leaning towards mysticism. Without doubt there were at this time strong adherences to the Catholic faith and worship: Verlaine, Francis Jammes — and also Claudel who on certain points, for example his prosody, seemed to be an heir of Symbolism. But, looked at from a little further away, it is possible to perceive a vaguely mystic and virginal feeling among certain Symbolist poets, in particular the French and Flemish-speaking Belgians, and the German poets such as Rainer Maria Rilke. In fact, a particularly important way in which all this European lyricism had marked its individuality had been the desire to return to primitive sources, that is to say to naive drawings and carvings, to popular art, to the cheap prints of the itinerant booksellers, to the romance of the countryside and town, to the *Volkslied*, to oral expression. Whence came Gauguin's quest in Brittany and the South Sea Islands? Whence came the creation of *vers libre* in which Jules Laforgue played a big part, and the delightfully absurd art with which he put the most difficult metaphysical thought into Chat Noir style couplets? It is not surprising that he was one of the first, in the Old World, to discover Walt Whitman, and he could not have failed to exercise influence over the later schools. Besides, the United States must not be forgotten in this effort to synthesize Symbolism. The figure of Edgar Allan Poe, successively translated by Baudelaire and Mallarmé, has ensured them an eminent position in its beginning. And now the moment has come to speak of the other America, the Spanish one.

Symbolism, without doubt, had some effect on the poetic enthusiasm of that continent, if only by certain aspects of Juan Ramón Jiménez and Valle Inclán. But it burst on Spanish America with prodigious force thanks to the Nicaraguan Rubén Darío, who had lived in Paris in the time of Verlaine and the *Mercure de France*, had come under the influence of French Symbolism, and had transplanted the Symbolist spirit into the Spanish tongue. The Spanish language was destined to produce in the tropics certain prestigious and nostalgic music, such as would never have been expected of it. The genius of Rubén Darío made him the great representative of a whole rich collection of original Spanish-American poets. And in return, this tropical Spanish harmony, like the baroque music of the past, enriched the poetry of the Peninsular with its magic. It is the luck of the imperial languages such as Spanish, Portuguese and English that they are able to extend their influence outside their mother country, beyond the oceans, into countries where nature and the native people appear in a completely different light, and where, very often, they are astonished to find fully structured civilizations who have themselves attained a very high degree of originality. From these meetings arise the most marvellous opportunities for enrichment and renewal of the metropolitan tongue. This is what happened with Latin-American Symbolism. It constituted a truly original phenomenon. It had personalities with a social and intellectual *milieu*, with feelings, anxieties, hopes and passions of an order totally different from the cultural tradition of the conquering nations, but which opened to this tradition strangely fascinating new paths. The works of comparative literature do not give enough importance to the influential figure of Rubén Darío, an extraordinarily gifted poet, an inspired lyricist, irresistibly fascinating, who was not only a great Spanish poet, a successor to Gongora or Lope de Vega, but one of the prime movers of a completely new movement of experience and emotional expression.

HENRI FANTIN-LATOUR *Corner of a table*. 1872

All these crises, this whole critical aspect of Symbolism shows why its contemporaries reproached it above all for its isolation and segregation. Other critics, in the course of time, have toned down this aspect. The isolation and segregation were necessary to mark that which separated a new expression, a *frisson nouveau*, from previous ways of feeling, of writing, of painting. Already the Impressionists had been spurned, their successors were not received much better, and people were whistling Debussy. Mallarmé was pronounced obscure, which in fact he was. By means of reading his works and studying them in depth, a simplicity can be found in him. But the difficulties continued to exist, and simplicity was perhaps one of these, and even the greatest. Rimbaud also was obscure, but in a different way: his was a deliberately

GUSTAVE MOREAU *The Apparition* 1876

harsh and injurious desire to translate the happenings of a very individual personal adventure into a series of crazy mental pictures; from these came an astonishing beauty to which the poet declared that he alone possessed the key.

A Rebours of K.J. Huysmans (1884) can be taken as dating the rupture precisely. Huysmans broke with his friends of Médan, and put forward through the medium of his character Des Esseintes an outrageous doctrine of tastes, sensual pleasures and aspirations. He exalted the strangeness of Mallarmé, Gustave Moreau and Redon. A little later he performed one of his returns to the Catholic faith which, as has already been suggested, implied in its irrefutable and passionate sincerity a way of hurling maledictions at prosaic contemporary society. It is necessary, however, to come back to the great break with Naturalism in order to understand fully the essence of the originality of Symbolism. There was certainly a revolutionary spirit in the literary naturalism of Zola, as there had been in the plastic realism of Courbet. Leaving aside the political opinions of both Courbet and Proudhon, their friendship and the part it played in the Commune, as much as the strong and generous action of Zola in the Dreyfus affair, made these two men the *bêtes noires* of the thinking community of their time. But this opposition had even deeper reasons: it did not stop at historical conjuncture. It valued the same artistic spirit of which this painter and this writer had been theorists and exponents at the same time. This was because the description of the truth gave offence to a society who wished to see in it a criticism not only of matters of propriety, but in fact of itself. Nevertheless, maybe it found itself even more upset and ill at ease when art disdained reality to the point of clinging to ideas alone. But according to the vocabulary of philosophy, Symbolism was essentially an idealism.

Gauguin had cultivated the symbol and its synthesis as a reaction against the Impressionists, whom he considered had a 'low ceiling' and in whose works 'thoughts did not dwell'. In reality the vital foundation of their art and its strength was the preponderant part played by feeling. This covered every aspect of naturism or realism to be found in it. Odilon Redon described nothing, showed nothing — except, at the end of his life, humble flowers, the supreme mystery. He evoked dreams, among them the most terrifying nightmares. His notebook was entitled *A soi-même* which did not fail to astonish those who believed painters to be people for whom the outside world existed solely when the painter in question was a habitual dreamer. His senior, Gustave Moreau — at this time still more of an illustrator than a Symbolist — made the severed head of John the Baptist appear before the eyes of Salome just as she, in her whim of depraved little girl, had wished it. But, in his *Cantique de Saint Jean*, Mallarmé abolished representation, and identified his words with the subjectivity of the head:

Je sens comme aux vertèbres	I feel, as if in my bones
S'éployer des ténèbres.	The darkness spreading out.

I correct this absolute assertion in favour of Laforgue, heir of German metaphysics. Into the cruelly brief fragment of existence accorded to this young genius, he concentrated a Schopenhauer-like view of the cosmos, of its games, its illusions, its derisory daily occurrences, its nothingness; there are only two ways out: one towards the sincere warmth of love, the other to music. This could be the taunting music of the old café-concerts, music of the street, music of *vers libre*.

Vers libre is capable of saying everything, including even the most subtle of ambiguities. It created a revolution as great as did the invention of the rhyme at a time of 'mystic Latin', so dear to Gourmont, and the prosody of our modern languages. The melodic line of this shatters in moments, and these moments condense themselves into an intrinsic life like as many rich and powerful monads. Poetry thinks of itself quite differently from the way in which it has been accepted through the centuries — as shocking, surprising, and syncopating, and totally separate from the generally understood meaning of inspiration. People tried to believe that here was escapism, abandonment to a passing whim, which was both facile and soft, a feeling of *laisser-faire*. This was a grave error, and an ironic one, for the opposite applied: it was an awakening and attention of the spirit, a perpetual concern with minute detail. This new freedom involved a new science and a new discipline, another 'book of rules';

those secret and personal rules which the poet imposed on himself according to the demands of the occasion, and where a different occasion might necessitate the substitution of different obligations.

These technical difficulties which escaped the old conventions corresponded to the affective difficulties which had so far not expressed themselves. Thus *vers libre* became the language of a state of mind which was like twilight landscapes of nature, its most furtive half-seasons. It was neither clear-cut nor eloquent, and it settled nothing. But it followed the meanderings of a way of speaking which could run through the meanderings of whispering, of confidence and of digressions. In short it was a very special kind of prose: a prose which neither analyzed nor reasoned. At the very most it related. To tell the truth, it sang. The pictures of James Abbott

ODILON REDON *The Origins*   ODILON REDON *Dreams*

McNeill Whistler, the American in Paris, (the Symbolist Paris was very cosmopolitan) realized admirably the deep desire of this feeling. Their titles transpose in musical modes the mobile and cloudy impressions of atmospheric changes. Whistler was of course one of the regular attendants at Mallarmé's Tuesdays, and one of his dearest friends.

It is impossible not to keep returning to the celebrated precept of Verlaine of music above all. It inspired the whole of Symbolist poetry which made itself enclosed and apart in order to study itself more intimately. The remarks of Eugenio d'Ors about the preference which each period has for a predominant art are well known. One period makes painting, spatial art, its favourite and driving art, and this preference gives a special tonality to that particular age. Another period gives the palm to music: this was the case with Symbolism. The whole poetic quality of Symbolism, all its humour, its entire climate is in the realm of temporality. Impressionist painting had, without doubt, been a changing and forward-moving art: thus it had conceived the surprising project of introducing the time factor into its technique which was, on the contrary, the technique of space. There still remains in Impressionist painting a certain fugitive quality, a certain melancholy which enchants us. But this melancholy is a secondary effect in Impressionist painting, which moves and charms us because it is contradictory. It was

Paul Gauguin *Vairumati*. 1897

not essential to it as to the poetic works of Symbolism. And as the Impressionist paintings are principally outdoor paintings, the idea, obviously sad in itself that natural things are always transitory, is absorbed into a great and luminous cosmic joy. As for the Impressionist pictures of towns, those which have as subject scenes illuminated by the enchantment of gaslight would doubtless convey a certain element of sadness to their beholder on second viewing. But at first glance he would see in them what they are — entertainment. The moment would come later to ask himself what remained of the balls and the spectacles, the whole character of which had been transitory. But the root of the problem is not there, and it would not be right to read into the Impressionist works more affective meanings than they put into them. The important thing for them was the power and universe of the eye, the sensorial, the spatial. This can be said without reticence, ambiguity or contradiction. The Symbolists showed how to integrate with the secrets of the temporal and the subjective. The need for expression no longer agreed with that which was happening outside. It was no longer satisfied with exteriority, but retreated into a halting language which consented willingly to being understood in terms of pure suspense, anticipation, or even imperceptible, perhaps soundless sighs. Thus the art which appeared as the most influential in the whole epoch, the one which best responded to its inclinations and aspirations was, in fact, music.

Wagner and Debussy

Whence came the fervent enthusiasm with which the Symbolists saluted 'the god, Richard Wagner irradiating a consecration'? This imperious and complete sovereignty could have inspired jealousy among the exponents of verbal or plastic expression. Their devotion can be explained by realizing that Wagner brought to so many 'failures' the compensation of seeing their lonely métiers come together at collective meetings, at public festivities, at what Mallarmé called 'offices'. It can also be explained by considering the place which ideas, in the form of symbols or leitmotifs, occupied in the vast Wagnerian system: the ceremonies at Bayreuth attracted pilgrims from the whole world. The early reticences which finally raised Wagner to glory stopped only at an appropriate level, if one sees in him, above all, a powerful dramatic and philosophical genius. He was essentially a man of expression and of theatrical thought, endowed with a decisive feeling for the theatre and theatrical language. He was a great poet, capable of arranging in his colossal compositions surprises of character and passion, of putting them into action and staging them. For this sort of personality, with so resolute a vocation, music must have been a means rather than an absolute end. Certainly this music, in very many great moments, becomes sublime. It can throw us into confusion by a cosmic joy of the most exalted kind as well as by the accent it puts on the gloomy and the funereal. But very often it loses itself and stretches out into one orchestral and vocal body. Finally, it is possible to accord full justice to Wagner in acknowledging that although his prestigious power is certainly of a musical order, it is excelled by the power of another order, a power which is equally rare and equally important: the ability to create a myth.

Naturally pure music, that is to say the exclusive art of sound, could not fail to react. Replying to Wagner and equally to the virulent attacks by Nietzsche who had previously been one of his most ardent partisans, Debussy accomplished one of the greatest revolutions in the history of music and invented a musical language. The public, surprised to start with, thought they would discover in it the deliquescence and half-tints which they saw as the principal attribute of Symbolist poetry. This was a primary and superficial view. It was in fact, as is every new language, concerned with mathematics, and this mathematics was no less scholarly or less bold than its precedents. As with every new musical mathematics, indeed as with the whole of Symbolism, this did not consist solely of technical propositions. It also showed itself capable of expressing the most private mysteries of the soul. Debussy, by *Le Prélude à l'après-midi d'un faune* and by *Pelléas et Mélisande*, has associated himself eternally with two great Symbolist poets, and it would be unjust to think of him merely as their musical illustrator. In the two masterpieces which I have just named, this ballet and this opera, a dramatic idea is staged by different means of expression: words, dancing, music. The gesture, the voice, the poetic imagination, the theatrical order, the mastership of the orchestra and its instruments, combine to form a whole which must never be taken just as poetry set to music, or given other treatments, but as a whole which appears in an organic and living fashion. Without doubt the critic, on the occasion of such and such a presentation, takes into account the particular roles of the dancers, the singers and the instrumentalists. In the same way art can be analyzed and broken down into component parts, each of which forms a whole. This collusion does not consist of addition. To the work of the two poets the musician did not add his own invention; he quite simply executed his own work, which was the work of a musician. And this work was characteristic of Symbolism as indeed were the works of the two poets. Under each of the titles of *Prélude à l'après-midi d'un faune* and *Pelléas et Mélisande*, two masterpieces of Symbolist poetry, we find a double masterpiece of Symbolist music. There had of course to be a profound accord between the genius of the musician and that of the two poets. From their encounter in the text of the two poems and the two musics arose two third masterpieces, each one intrinsic in itself

HENRI DE TOULOUSE-LAUTREC
Loïe Fuller at the Folies-Bergère. 1893

GIOVANNI BOLDINI
Portrait of the Count Robert de Montesquiou. 1898

ODILON REDON *The Chariot of the Sun*

AUGUSTE RODIN *Danaïde.* 1885

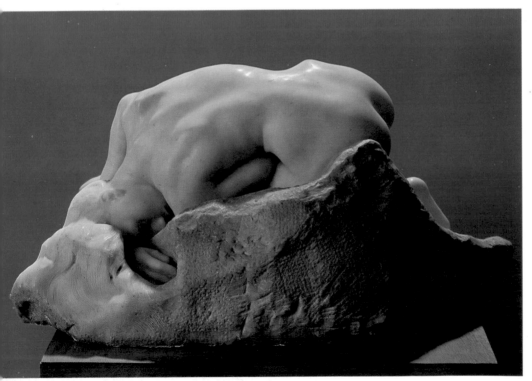

and identified with itself, each one an absolutely individual creation. Having put this, it is possible to halt for a moment to look at the particular art of the musician who created so perfect a miracle, and to realize that this is Symbolism in its finest form of music. Here, perhaps, is its purest definition in its most essential affirmation. For everything that can be said of the innovations of Symbolism in the different arts is shown at its most vivid in the music of Debussy. This especially applies to what has been said about the basic characteristics of the poetry of that time, and of *vers libre*. This is why, as has been said already, it is so pleasing to rediscover in the titles of certain of Debussy's works such deliciously shaded images of this poetry. The public was in fact wrong to adopt an air of disdainful disapproval about them, but it was not mistaken: the analogies between this music and this poetry were striking. They were actually so vivid that the poetry, in its principle, referred to the music; it was only natural that it should admire the decisive assurance with which the clear genius of Debussy risked and experimented with the most subtle divisions of tone, and used them to organize the associations, the combinations and the sliding together of unaccustomed harmonies.

It is stupefying to recall that this beauty, invented with an authority so constant and so luminous, and capable of such enchantment, was able on its first appearance to produce so grating an effect. The 'misunderstandings' of the ear with music are old history and one which repeats itself. Are they more acute, and worthy of more reflection and observation than the quarrels of the eye with painting? This has always been a subject for debate for those physiologists and sociologists who are interested in the history of tastes.

Symbolism is a humanism

Maeterlinck insisted that we pause at a complete section of Symbolist poetry: that is the Symbolist poetry of Belgium. Maeterlinck, together with Max Elskamp and very many others, produced a literary marvel of powerful orginality which could be called Franco-Belgian. It was poetry in the French language, but of Flemish inspiration. The extraordinary reanimation which their transplant to the New World gave to old European cultures has already been mentioned. Similar regeneration was brought to French literature by foreign countries where the same language was in use. One of the most successful revivals was due to Belgian Symbolist poetry. It was with its inflexions, its turns of phrase, its lexical repertoire of a quite novel charm that this poetry emphasized a very individual choice of spiritual themes: the search, the intimate relationships of the solitary soul with nature and the town, the striking of the hours from the belfry and the *beguinage*, hidden innocence, popular songs.

In the plastic arts the Flemish genius was no less fertile, and the prodigious fantasy of James Ensor made its first appearance at the same time as the pathetic adventure of van Gogh. The lyrical fierceness of his scenes and their titles, as much as his written or spoken words, made him a legendary character, and those who knew him never forgot him.

Maeterlinck, among other devices, thought of a theatre made of silences. In a general manner it can be said that for Symbolists an action was not necessarily a sequence of concrete facts, however dramatic, but that it revealed a 'wrong side' still more dramatic because it was enigmatic and because it re-awakened the conflicts and aspirations of the unconscious. Very different from the theatre of Maeterlinck, but likewise going in the direction discussed above was the brilliant and important dramatic work of Ibsen. It equalled in dimensions and abundant richness the work of Shakespeare, and painted in the same way by its burning truth a whole human reality, indeed a whole society, at the same time as it staged and started strange spiritual energies which were extremely alive although often phantom-like. This harmony of cruel commonplaceness with its multiple imaginary meanings lingers in us like an excruciating discord.

Henri Fantin-Latour *Daughters of the Rhine*

In the work of Ibsen one can find the whole Scandinavian spirit which exercised its fascination over the European restlessness. Paris in particular was imprinted with it and the Théâtre de l'Oeuvre was the centre from which this fashion emanated. But Ibsen exercised no less influence in the rest of Europe, just as the Norwegian, Swedish and Danish novelists did. A dreamy and melancholic feeling was spreading out, the origin of which could be attributed to the Protestant introspectiveness even if, in many aspects of its moral and social revolt, it rose violently against the sectarianism of the pastors, that hypocritical prop of bourgeois conservatism. Strindberg, the writer and painter, a kind of brother to Gauguin found in his neurosis the motives for transmitting the detestable reality of loneliness into an infernal unreality. The painter Munch, with his images of anguish and his whole career of struggle against madness, is characteristic of the anxiety of Symbolism to portray the 'other side' of the portrayable.

Is it possible to rediscover the same anxiety in the work of the sculptor Rodin? Sculpture is the most directly figurative of all the arts. It does not transpose reality on to abstract plans, but reconstructs it in its own proportions. It allows one to go around its works as around natural objects. Sculpture then, goes further than its own completion — and this is to its advantage and its glory — when not confined by the reproduction of reality in space, it is forced to

EDVARD MUNCH *Peer Gynt.* 1896

explain the idea of this reality. This is what Rodin did in giving us the meaning, in his blocks of stone, of the strength of thought, of the creative urge, of the vital force.

The synthesis of a great moment of human genius reassembles facts which, to start with, seem dissimilar, and attempts to specify convergent intentions in them. This work is all the more delicate when the moment in question is complex, and has been manifested in many countries and in many cultures.

It is essential to recognize in certain areas of Symbolism the persistence of earlier influences, for example Impressionism, encounters with German Romanticism (as previously mentioned), and finally the signs of a counter-movement close at hand, such as Expressionism. Gauguin, van Gogh, Ensor and Munch had already introduced Expressionism, which also provided the points of contact and accord between Symbolism and some aspects of the art of the *Nabis*: their taste for the street, for posters, for nocturnal pleasures, for popular crafts. There are also subtle relationships to be noted between Symbolism and the different *fin de siècle* arts which were then flourishing on the two continents. None of this coming together and mingling can be neglected; it goes out again into the richness of life: analyses, as much aesthetic as historical and sociological, can be made of it. But the essential fact remains, and it is that which must be reached in its radical contrast. It would be easy to pinpoint this contrast in two personalities who seemed to define the concept of Symbolism in its absolute form: Mallarmé and Rimbaud. The former was, since his night at Tournon, no longer set on producing a true likeness of the universe, but on absorbing it into a purely imaginary and invented resemblance. This was an outrageous metaphysical attempt, and one which gave the tone to the dreams of all the creative art of the era. We will retain as the essential formula for the other great experiment, that of Rimbaud, the title given to one part of his work *Alchimie du verbe*. Here light is thrown on another contrast: that which separated a new category of artists from their predecessors. They were the Parnassians who put their ambition into becoming perfect goldsmiths, and into the delicate finishing of enamels, cameos, trophies and other works or ornamentation. But their successors, perfect chemists and alchemists, were devoted to changing these same metals, worldy and artistic materials, into materials for the philosopher's stone. By these two adventurous extremes, and all that they created or discovered, Symbolism was affirmed as a marvellous chapter in the history of the spirit.

Such supreme consideration encourages a return to various earlier observations relevant to a sociological summary of Symbolism. The uneasiness which this had provoked obviously originated from the contrivances and peculiarities which people claimed to see in its creative originality and the works of its exponents. These appeared to be outside the human. But the human never materializes more humanly than when it steals away into irreducible personal strangeness. What is more moving than to ponder other destinies, or more revealing of the possible mystery of one's own? A figure not less representative of the struggle with life, if not indeed more sorrowful and more terrible still, was that of Verlaine. It would not be possible to share his downward spiral of misfortune more intimately than by reading again the first quatrain of the *Tombeau* which Mallarmé dedicated to him. To my way of thinking it is the most beautiful of the *Tombeaux* which were written by Mallarmé, poet of death and glory.

> Le noir roc courroucé que la bise le roule
> Ne s'arrêtera ni sous des pieuses mains
> Tâtant sa ressemblance avec les maux humains
> Comme pour en bénir quelque funeste moule.

> The black angry rock which is rolled by the blast
> Will not stop, nor under the devout hands
> Which feel its resemblance to human woes
> As if to bless some deadly mould with them.

Understand. Understand that this was a peak of moral thought. The lowest levels of ignominy, the most rapturous heights, the amorous adventures of Arthur Rimbaud, the pistol shot in Brussels, the prison at Mons from whence came such saintly elevations of the spirit — none

JAMES ENSOR *Self-portrait with masks.* 1899

of all this, neither the absinthe, nor the hospitals, nor the lodging-houses, nor any part of these extremes of accumulated horror is worse than those ordinary faults and miseries which are ours, and ours alone. The judgement of Mallarmé puts us in the same category as these sinful downfalls. And this lonely man whose most subtle enigmas had horrified the riddle-solvers of the Boulevard and the world, pronounced then words of humility and charity. Was it understood, this utterance of a soul? What distance there was between it and the disdainful insults of the era on an art produced by artists who were capable of speaking such words on the arrival of another amongst them — and he the most pitiable as well as the most admirably inspired.

It must also be said that this inscrutable Mallarmé was in his behaviour the simplest and the best of men, enjoying the pleasures of luminous irony, of friendship, the ballet, music and women. A no less exemplary model of good behaviour was his artistic ally, Redon, who was supposed to have been haunted by devils and terrors, but who was basically only worried by the anxieties of that most learned of techniques — engraving. This great stoic spirit confined himself entirely to his art and his affections. He asked for nothing more. He declined the temptation of the conversion towards which his two friends, Huysmans and Jammes, albeit very dear to him, tried to push him, and clung to a spirituality based on the images of Christ and Buddha, which he saw, without unnecessary proclamation, as a good deal more true than any confessional theology.

It is again of wisdom that one must speak when considering Maeterlinck, one of the spirits who had never been far from the scene. He, in the whole richness of his work, the mysteries of his poetry and theatre as much as his books of nature and moral essays, touched in his

EDVARD MUNCH *The Cry.* 1895

depth the very essence of the most simple daily moment as well as that of his personal destiny and the cosmic life.

The tragedy of Oscar Wilde has already been mentioned. The downfall of this dazzling aesthete from the heights of his success produced some of the most rending sobs ever torn from the heart by disaster or fraternally shared shame. But if, in the tableau of humanity, there was a case for particular devotion, was it not that of van Gogh, as he tells it in his incomparable work and in his disturbing letters? His was an epic adventure, at the beginning of which came the evangelical encounter with *Sien*, the poor alcoholic and pregnant prostitute. The lithograph *Sorrow*, which leaves to us her most pathetic image, accompanies Michelet's question, a question without reply, without echo: 'How is it that there is on earth one woman alone and abandoned?'

It has been said of another eminent epoch — the Elizabethans — that it had a 'smell of man'. It would be possible to say the same about this modern epoch of our age, taking of course the different conditions into account. These are, however, negligible in comparison with the strong, vital and accented meaning of the term 'man'. In such examples of its history it is not just the genius of man which is concerned, but the whole man, body and soul. It is the whole man who achieves his fullness from lowly misery up to supreme ascension. Symbolism revealed itself in its essential truth to those who knew how to recognize humanism in themselves.

VINCENT VAN GOGH *Sorrow*. 1882

Painting, engraving and sculpture

The spirit surpasses matter

Contrary to Impressionism which was an essentially pictorial movement, Symbolism in the plastic arts was the visual expression of a literary and intellectual current which sustained diverse inspirations. Symbolist aesthetics took the most unexpected forms induced by its research into little explored fields: the world of the dream and the imaginary, the fantastic and the unreal, the world of magic and esotericism, of sleep and death.

In France, contact between painters and poets had seldom been closer. They loved to meet each other, to discuss, to absorb the same philosophical and social influences. It was the era of science and positivism, of naturalism and realism. In literature, the Symbolist poets, as they were called after the publication of the *Manifeste du symbolism* by Moréas, were opposed to Zola and the Naturalist school. They referred to Baudelaire, and took Mallarmé as their leader. Their names, Verlaine, Rimbaud, Laforgue, Viélé-Griffin, Maeterlinck and Verhaeren among others, were often cited alongside those of painters such as Gustave Moreau, Redon, Puvis de Chavannes, Carrière and Gauguin who, with their friends, exhibited at the Rose + Croix salons organized by the Sâr Péladan, an unusual character who represented the esoteric *fin de siècle* movement.

The realism of Courbet and the landscape artists of his school, together with the Impressionism of Monet, renounced imagination and took as their only task the representation of the real. In the brilliant light of some and the chiaroscuro of others, subjectivity is totally lacking, whether in the sensitivity of Sisley or Pissarro, the expansive vision of Monet or the bursting passion of Manet.

But, as René Huyghe so clearly expressed it, art was at that time no more than the reflection of the materialistic which weighed so heavily on civilization. In opposing the scientific and technical society, in particular the invention of photography which had recently been discovered, Symbolism wanted to return priority to the spiritual rather than the material. In order to do this the experts called on the forces which animate the conscious — the intuition, the imaginary, the unexplained — when it fights against the influence of matter and the laws governed by physics.

Imagination is opposed to both rationalist and positivist doctrines as much in the field of literature as in that of the plastic arts. Delacroix, the great romantic, had already spoken of it in this lyrical fashion: 'Silent power which at first speaks only with the eyes, and which gains and takes over all the faculties of the soul!' Böcklin defines his thoughts thus: 'A picture must say something, give the spectator something to think about, as does a poem, and leave him an impression as does a piece of music.' Again, Odilon Redon, about his master, Bresdin: 'Does not art draw all the force of its eloquence, its impact, its grandeur, from the things which leave to the imagination the problem of defining them?' The Symbolist artist untiringly follows the intangible, everything which hides behind the appearance of reality, the whole world which escapes him, the universe of fairy creatures, demons, mythological beings, the world of legend and the beyond, of mysticism and eroticism. Already in 1818 Coleridge wrote in his *Essays on Fine Art*: 'The artist must copy what is inside the object, that which exercises its action by the

EDVARD MUNCH *The Vampire.* 1893

intermediary of the form and figure and addresses itself to us by means of symbols: the spirit of Nature.' This was to open the way to Romanticism and foretell Symbolism by defining it, according to Hans H. Hoffstätter, as 'the fundamental duty of pictorial art: the comprehension of ideological problems whose penetration and representation in image form complete the purely intellectual analysis.' The dream, the vision and the hallucination permit a deeper penetration into the world of the invisible in order to follow the endless search for reality. For Nietzsche, the artistic world of the dream was the world of Apollo, and the artistic world of rapture the world of Dionysus. Thus certain Symbolists found their inspiration in *Naissance de la tragédie* published in 1873, where they read: 'The nature of the Dionysiac world is best revealed by the analysis of rapture. These Dionysiac pulses, in the advancement of which the subjective fades into a total forgetfulness of self, awaking either by the influence of a narcotic beverage praised by men and peoples since their origins, or by the powerful approach of Spring, which fills up the whole of Nature... Something which he has never experienced takes him outside himself, the rending of the Maia's veil, the likening of himself to the genius of the species or even to nature itself. Henceforth the essence of nature will be explained symbolically: a new world of symbols is therefore necessary.' The lure of death and the occult, the confusion of the erotic and the mystic were primarily a need to run away from a material-istic society. Women, love and death were no longer approached according to realistic criteria, but in the perspective of a spiritual fusion of two beings, and in the fear of the other world. Munch and Klimt were the painters who best expressed the mystical union of a man with a woman. The woman embodies the fatal beauty which carries the man along to death, flowers appear as the symbols of Good and Evil; according to Grandville the animals tend to dis-quieting metamorphoses, the countryside projects us into a visionary world, and the Symbolist artist could make this phrase of Nietzsche his own: 'One can see how, through works of art, it is possible to drag the ill and the moribund off the long funerary road of humanity for a tiny moment of pleasure.' And is this not the essential?

The precursors

After the end of the eighteenth century, three great visionary artists, Goya, Blake and Füssli, laid the foundations on which was built an art that again gave priority to the spiritual over the material.

In his engravings and his drawings, as in his painting of the home for the deaf, Goya (1746-1828) translated his nightmares and his hallucinations, gave birth to monsters, called up sorcerers and opened the door to madness. He tamed 'the forms which only exist in the imagination of men', and, cloistered in his deafness, relieved the anguish of loneliness by tracking down with pencil and paintbrush the demons who assaulted and defied him.

Goya's whole world was brought together in his painting of the house of the deaf: the Maia and the bearded old man who, leaning on his stick, does not hear the demon howling in his ear, Saturn devouring his son, Judith decapitating Holophernes, the *romeria* of San Isidro, the women gathered round the billy-goat and, crowning the whole, the fantastic vision of two people sailing in the air above an enormous rock and a fabulous city. Strange symbols arose from the inner world of the artist who fled the horrors of war to shut himself into those of his own obsessions.

Poet, painter and engraver, Blake (1757-1827) spent his whole life in London. He pro-foundly despised nature and reality, and lived entirely in the imaginary, in a 'Platonic paradise' which corresponded to his role of privileged intermediary between the eternal and the tem-poral, his works only being transpositions of his celestial visions. His first hallucination came at the age of four, when he saw the face of God appear at his brother's window. At school he mastered techniques of ancient and Gothic art at the same time, and this allowed him to pursue his visionary art, nourished by his relationships with supernatural powers. He received visits from the angels and from characters out of the past, when he was not too concerned with 'the horrible phantom of a flea.' His 'Prophetic Books', his *Marriage of Heaven and Hell* expressed his revolutionary beliefs which were as unexpected as the graphic works which mirrored them. Whether he illustrated Milton, Dante or *Night Thoughts* by Young, Blake introduced us to a world of fantasy and the supernatural, a universe where the spirit is embodied in the sublime or fearful forms which have been born in the unconscious.

The art of Heinrich Füssli (1741-1825) was no less strange. It evolved, as did that of Goya and Blake, from the world of dreams and the supernatural. Young women asleep are prey to terrifying visions peopled with monsters; a skeleton holds them prisoner; two naked women are frightened by a beast, straddled by a devil, which is jumping through a window. In his drawings the erotic factor is even more striking; here are shown female insects, praying mantises ready to devour their males. Füssli's lascivious women, spied on by voyeurs, are not only in the vanguard of Symbolism but also of Surrealism.

In England, William Turner (1775-1851), if he was a direct forerunner of Impressionism, also opened the way to Symbolism. In fact he did not limit himself, as did the Impressionists, to the representation of a real landscape transfigured by light; he also used the intervention of the imaginary and the fantastic. He ventured into a world where the whirling of colours, especially in his later works, escaped the constraints of reality.

ODILON REDON *Birth of Venus*

HEINRICH FÜSSLI *The kiss.* 1819

RODOLPHE BRESDIN *Peacocks.* 1869

VICTOR HUGO *My destiny*

Of course France also contributed to the flowering of Symbolism, with the drawings of Victor Hugo, the engravings of Meryon, Bresdin and Gustave Doré. Meryon (1821-68) at first appeared, with his precise strokes, like a romantic Realist, but from the earth, the caves and the air arose strange monsters which added to the life of those engraved plates by giving them a soul — even when they only depicted stones. If Victor Hugo was dazzled by Meryon, Baudelaire wrote in his *Salon* of 1859: 'By the harshness, the finesse and the certainty of his drawing, M. Meryon recalls the old and excellent etchers...the majesty of the accumulated stones; the steeples pointing their fingers at the sky; the obelisks of industry belching

33

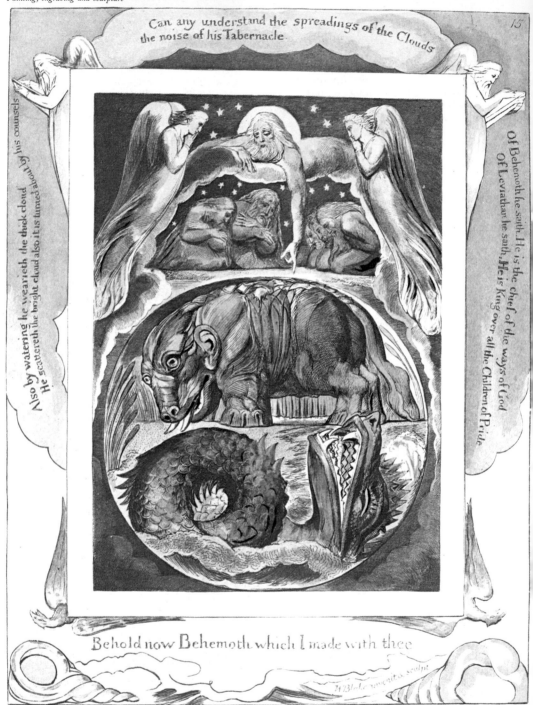

WILLIAM BLAKE *The Book of Job*: God shows Job the Earth on which Behemoth and Leviathan face each other. *c.*182⁵

their conspiracy of smoke into the firmament; the prodigious scaffolding of the monuments under repair adding to the solid body of the buildings their up-to-date architecture of such paradoxical beauty; the tumultuous sky charged with anger and malice; the depth of perspective augmented by the thought of all the dramas contained therein — not one of these complex elements which make up the sorrowful and glorious decor of civilization has been forgotten.' Attracted by painting to start with, Meryon devoted himself to nitric acid etching, a technique which has since been abandoned. His visionary side haunted him throughout his life, but his mental health could not tolerate these onslaughts and he died in a bout of extreme madness.

This state of hallucination, the solitude, the minute details of execution, the mysterious forms, all the incomprehensibility hidden behind appearances brought the engravings of Bresdin (1825-85) nearer to those of Meryon. Incapable of drawing from life, it was in a precarious shelter that Bresdin reconstituted from his obsessed imagination a world of tribes in flight, legions on the march, hermits, all the animals of the creation, and communicated to us the shock of the fantastic. In *A soi-même* Odilon Redon, who was his pupil and his admirer, wrote, in speaking of his master: 'What one finds throughout is a man in love with solitude,

GUSTAVE DORE
The errant Jew. 1856

Francisco Goya *Meeting of Sorcerers*. 1819-23

madly fleeing under an alien sky, in the anguish of hopeless and endless exile...Sometimes it is a whole family, a legion, an army, a whole people fleeing, always fleeing from civilized man.' Gustave Doré, (1832-83) whether illustrating the knights of the Round Table, a ship in perdition, or the *Contes drolatiques*, plunged into the fantastic and the imaginary, and sometimes, as in his engravings for *The Divine Comedy* into a symbolism of extraordinary beauty. Victor Hugo also, in his drawings, his washes and his water-colours, suggested mystery with a visionary art which followed the evolution of his poetic work. Beyond his medieval villages, his boats in the mist, his ghostly towns, his grimacing faces, it is possible to see a certain tell-tale Symbolism.

It would be wrong to think that it was only the Symbolist engravers who used themes and techniques which bore a close relationship to the research of the Symbolist artists. Two great French painters, Delacroix and Chassériau, can also be counted among the forerunners of the Symbolist movement. Gustave Moreau was directly influenced by Delacroix (1798-1863) and communicated his admiration for the great Romantic to his pupils, including Khnopff who remained a Symbolist throughout his career. In the works of Delacroix, Biblical subjects abound, especially those which have death as their central theme. Baudelaire wrote: 'Delacroix — a lake of blood haunted by horrid angels.' He illustrated Faust, the satanic poems of Byron, and took pleasure in scenes of carnage, massacres and burnings when he was not painting bloodthirsty Arabs chasing lions also eager for blood. His heroines were morally and physically tormented: Ophelia drowns herself, Rebecca, naked, is bound prisoner on a horse in *Les Massacres de Scio*, concubines are slaughtered on the funerary couch of Sardanapalus, Angelica and Andromeda are chained to a rock.

The Symbolists were attracted to the type of woman depicted by Chassériau (1819-56), who represented their feminine ideal. Gustave Moreau and Puvis de Chavannes, who frequented his studio, were especially influenced by his style and choice of subject. Moreau resumed the theme of Sappho who, throwing away her lyre before jumping from the top of a rock, is the

EUGENE DELACROIX *Death of Sardanapalus*. 1827 ▶

very image of the tragic destiny of those souls incapable of reconciling themselves to the loss of their love.

In Germany, the Nazarenes can be mentioned together with Caspar David Friedrich (1774-1840), Philip Otto Runge (1777-1810), and Gustav Carus (1789-1869) inasmuch as they were all precursors of Symbolism. With their romantic temperaments they blended the aspirations of the Impressionists and the Symbolists. Friedrich, who came from Pomerania, and was a friend of the poets Kleist and Novalis and of the painters Carus and Dahl, gave his pictures a symbolic religious flavour. In his landscapes he put his own phantasms, always marked by sadness or melancholy. Another native of Pomerania, Runge associated with the writers Tieck, Kleist, Goethe and Klopstock and wished to revive Christian art. He saw in the cosmic landscape a poetic 'hieroglyph' of religious meaning. He explained his theories on the metaphysics of light and the symbolism of colour in a work which found echo in the painters of the Jugendstil and the Blaue Reiter. After his scientific studies, Carus gave himself up to painting and drawing. He was influenced by his friend Friedrich, and his landscapes seemed to be the link between him and the next generation.

CARL GUSTAV CARUS *Homage to Goethe*. 1832

CASPAR DAVID FRIEDRICH
Cliffs at Rügen. c.1818

PHILIP OTTO RUNGE *Morning*. 1803

Parallel to the artists from north Germany, a group of young painters left the Academy in Vienna to set themselves up in Rome. They did not find the German countries a cultural centre matching their ideal. They gathered around Johann Friedrich Overbeck (1789-1869) and Franz Pforr (1788-1812), and in 1810 withdrew into the disused convent of Sant'Isidoro on Monte Pincio where they founded a new community and took the name of Nazarenes. Their aim was the renewal of German art following the example of the Italian Renaissance

THEODORE CHASSERIAU *The toilet of Esther*. 1841

GUSTAVE MOREAU *Orpheus.* 1865

artists. Their masters were Raphael and Perugino whom they admired as representatives of the simple piety to which they were trying to return. They took their subjects from both the Old and New Testaments and applied themselves to the historic *genre* by multiplying the characters as did the masters of the Quattrocento. Certain of their number remained attached to the German traditions and took their inspiration from the old German legends, the Niebelungen.

This group left the convent of Sant'Isidoro, but new enthusiasts gave the movement a second wind. Peter von Cornelius (1783-1867) worked at first on the illustrations for *Faust* and the *Song of the Niebelungen*, and then with Overbeck, he undertook a series of frescoes destined for the Casa Bartholdy, residence of the Prussian consul-general in Rome. They were inspired by the frescoes of Raphael and Pinturicchio in the Vatican and the Farnese villa which they had always in front of them. This impressive decoration is the origin of the great historic frescoes of Schnorr von Carosfeld, the most representative of the Nazarenes, of Alfred Rethel and Wilhelm Schadow.

If mural painting was the favourite medium of expression of the Nazarenes, certain of them, faithful to neo-classicism, painted idyllic landscapes enlivened by conventional and idealized characters. Thus Rudolph Friedrich Wasmann (1805-86), having collaborated on the decoration of the Casa Bartholdy, withdrew to a secluded corner of the Tyrol there to paint his lovely landscapes of the Adige Valley.

Although the work of the Nazarenes tended towards an academic and official art, the spirit which inspired them, notably when they evoked the Niebelungen and the haunted forests which had already inspired Altdorfer, found an echo in the historical painters with spiritualist preoccupations such as E.J. Steinle (1803-86) and Moritz von Schwind (1804-71) who executed romantic decorations in the Hohenschwangau castle. This spirit, characteristic of the Nazarenes, appeared again in artists of succeeding generations who had a joint desire to offer something different from the submission to a reality with no attraction. They called into question the meaning of the work of art which they wanted to be the translation, in visual

RUDOLPH FRIEDRICH WASMANN
Young Tyrolean girl with crucifix. 1865

JOHANN FRIEDRICH OVERBECK
Christ on the Mount of Olives. 1833

ALFRED RETHEL *Death. c.*1845

JAKOB EDWARD VON
STEINLE *Adam and Eve after
the Fall.* 1867

terms, of a thought. Influenced by the Wagnerian myth, they drew their inspiration from the ancient German legends and, liberating the hidden powers of the soul, they sought a fusion between creatures and humanity. Thus Böcklin strove to evoke an ideal world of antiquity where he mixed mythology with a mysterious atmosphere. Max Klinger, too, dreamed of an art which would realize the synthesis of heathenism and Christianity. he aspired to the Symbolism of Nietzsche which was often declamatory.

The influence of the Nazarenes extended also to certain artists whose literary preoccupations and Symbolist tendencies prepared the Jugendstil. The Symbolist spirit was clear in the first number of the review *Jugend* which appeared in Munich in 1896, and the following year in *Pan*, published in Berlin and founded by the German art critic, Meier-Graefe, a friend of Bing and Van de Velde. The Jugendstil was marked by the 'Sezessionen' principally in Vienna and Munich. These secessions were the signs of rupture with the official academic societies. That of Munich, constituted in 1892, comprised artists such as Uhde, Trübner and Stuck, who were all influenced by Böcklin. Of the Vienna Secession, which was closer to decorative Symbolism, Gustave Klimt was the most original representative.

DANTE GABRIEL ROSSETTI *La Ghirlandata*. 187

Pre-Raphaelism and the roots of Symbolism

Art historians agree today to consider the Pre-Raphaelites as the direct precursors of the Symbolists, even to the extent of sometimes bracketing them together. Proof of this statement was provided by the exhibition 'Symbolism in Europe' which from November 1975 to July 1976 travelled from Rotterdam to Paris passing through Brussels and Baden-Baden. The exhibition took as its starting point 1848, the year of the foundation of the Pre-Raphaelite Brotherhood. English Pre-Raphaelism is incontestably one of the sources of Symbolism. How is it possible, then, to understand Gustave Moreau without knowing the ambitions and aspirations of the Pre-Raphaelites?

In 1848, William Hunt, John Everett Millais and Dante Gabriel Rossetti, strongly influenced by the writings of Ruskin, decided to form a sort of brotherhood to which they gave the name of 'The Pre-Raphaelite Brotherhood', and which, as its name implied, drew its inspiration from the painters of the first Italian Renaissance. This brotherhood originated from Rossetti's friendship for Hunt whom he met at the time of the Royal Academy exhibition in 1848. It was during the discussions that took place afterwards with Millais, in the studio which they shared, that the idea of this association was born. Rejecting the academic tradition, they wished to draw nearer to the art of the Gothic and the Quattrocento, and their preoccupations were not without similarity to those of the Nazarenes. The whole pictorial technique was called into question: the colours became more brilliant, the style specified attention to the most minute detail. They took the inspiration for their subjects directly from nature, or borrowed them from history, the Bible, legends, themes which they loaded with literary intentions and mystical allusions.

This new way of painting was adversely received by the critics. Speaking of Millais' *Christ in the house of his parents*, which had been shown at the Royal Academy, the art critic of *The Times* called it 'revolting' while Hunt's style was qualified as 'grotesque and bizarre'. In spite of these ungracious comments, the Pre-Raphaelites persisted in their research, and expressed their theories in a review, *Germ*, founded by themselves, which only had four issues but which gained numerous sympathisers for them. Moreover, John Ruskin, in the face of the attacks against them, rose to their defence and sounded their praises in several articles in *The Times*. In spite of

ARNOLD BÖCKLIN *The Island of the Dead.* 1880

GUSTAVE KLIMT *Danae. c.*1907

a more favourable reception, following several exhibitions at the Royal Academy, and the success obtained at the Universal Exhibition of Paris in 1855, the brotherhood slowly began to dissolve, each member going his own way. Rossetti concluded: '...now the round table is dissolved'; but Pre-Raphaelism was not dead and continued to inspire numerous Symbolists.

The Pre-Raphaelites, and the artists who had contributed to the renaissance of the decorative arts in referring to the Quattrocento or to Gothic art and in employing a technique of absolute exactitude, wished to harmonize the noble feelings which animated them with the reality of an object to which the invention of photography gave a burning actuality. This fidelity made the legendary, historic or Biblical scenes more credible. How could the veracity of Ophelia, the magician Merlin, or Christ be in doubt when they were represented without omitting the smallest detail of their outward appearance? Pre-Raphaelism directly influenced a whole generation of painters which extended from the esoteric symbolism of Gustave Moreau to the more classic art of Puvis de Chavannes.

The artists and the great themes of Symbolist painting

A new fact strikes us as we approach the works of the Symbolist artists: the communion of ideas between painters and men of letters had never been more real than during this era. They held discussions in cafés, such as the Café Voltaire, or in their studios; they submitted to the same philosophical and social influences. The society which the painters frequented was that of Jean Lorrain, Robert de Montesquiou, of Rachilde's *Monsieur Vénus* where an aristocratic lady takes a beautiful youth as a toy, of Remy de Gourmont and his good genius Miss Barney who presided over a literary salon patronized by the elite of Tout-Paris, notably by the poetess Renée Vivien and Liane de Pougy. They read the Marquis de Sade and *English sadism* found an echo in Barbey d'Aurevilly and the Sâr Péladan. The antithesis of vice and virtue, a driving force of Symbolism, was born in the writings of de Sade who opposed 'Juliette' to 'Justine', and who attempted to prove that virtue leads to misery and ruin while vice leads to prosperity. If sapphism was visible in the novels of Jean Lorrain, incest was exalted in the *Crépuscule des dieux* of Elémir Bourges, and homosexual tendencies praised by Oscar Wilde, who inspired Beardsley.

The actresses and the demi-mondaines of the era, their beauty pure but their morals scandalous, dressed as princesses from remote countries, with their affected manners brought to life the ideal so dear to the Symbolists. They evolved from the hazy, unreal atmosphere which was that of gilded canopies and fairy-tale gardens. This atmosphere is as easily recognizable in the canvases of the painters as in the prose or poems of the writers.

However, other Symbolists fled the world, preferring an intimate or solitary life, walks with a kindred spirit, evenings by lamplight. The Belgian artists who had played a major role in the evolution of Symbolism often turned to familiar reality and to *intimist* scenes. Poets fraternized with painters. Verhaeren inspired Henry de Groux and Spilliaert, Grégoire Le Roy Degouve de Nuncques, Gustave Kahn and Khnopff.

The articles by Robert de Montesquiou brought Moreau, Whistler and Bresdin to a 'snob' public while Jean Lorrain in his reports acclaimed the artists who corresponded to his own aestheticism.

This 'correspondence' between painters and writers was apparent in their choice of subjects and in the attraction which they felt for similar myths. If the painters found their sources of inspiration in the novel or in poetry, the writers borrowed their subjects from painting. Thus *La Princesse des chemins* by Jean Lorrain is an interpretation in prose, Mario Praz tells us, of Burne-Jones' painting *King Cophetua and the Beggarmaid* 'with a particular emphasis on the blood-flecked ivory of the bare feet of the young girl, whose eyes burnt with a vigilant and sad blue flame'. Gustave Moreau inspired the same writer with the bloodthirsty scene *La fin du jour* which tells of a Byzantine revolt, with the severed head of an empress, covered in jewels, hanging like a pendant and strangely resembling Orpheus in the painting *Woman with the head of Orpheus*. On the other hand, when looking at the *Perseus invested with his mission* by Burne-Jones, one thinks of Swinburne's poem *Hermaphroditus*.

After the optical truth so praised by Naturalism and Impressionism, one needed to show the aspirations of the inner life, and not to be satisfied with the impact of a single look. This introspective search led the artist towards his own unconscious: the visual image learns to become the sign of the inexpressible. Redon was the first to attempt to translate these messages: 'In art', he wrote, 'everything happens by submitting docilely to the coming of the unconscious.'

In order to express this internal language with the brush or the graving-tool, the Symbolists resorted to the same themes: woman in all her aspects — deadly woman, impure or decadent woman, idealized woman, *femme fleur*; the flower in all variations and stylizations which Art Nouveau gave to it; eroticism; Satan and Satanic perversions; sadism; lust.

This Symbolist era was dominated by woman. There were two opposing schools of thought: one presented her as idealized, pure, chaste, motivated by religious sentiments or simply remote; the other put forward the view of woman as depraved, damned, dragging man down to vice and decadence.

The innocent nakedness of Puvis de Chavannes' women brings to life *l'Espérance*, the country life, the protective virtues. Those of Maurice Denis, animated by religious sentiments, take pleasure in their family life. Gauguin looked for his ideal woman in the Marquesas islands, and in Tahiti among the natives with their simple, primitive life. The Breton women of Paul Sérusier, inhaling the scent of flowers or occupied with their toilette, incarnate this idealistic beauty in the same way as do the dreamy and meditative women of Aman-Jean and those of Le Sidaner who walk in groups in the country. If the flower-girls of Fantin-Latour, the lyre players of Ménard, and the shepherdesses of Osbert are reassuring, the heroines of Lévy Dhurmer and Maxence are more disquieting and resemble those of Gustave Moreau, who are the personifications of eternal woman as understood by the majority of Symbolist artists.

During a period of about thirty years the evolution of this ideal type of woman continued, passing from the melancholy of Rossetti's *Beatrice* to the fatal beauty sung about by Baudelaire and easily recognizable in the paintings of Gustave Moreau, whose favourite theme was that of Evil and Death, incarnate in feminine beauty. Marked throughout his life by the influence of an abusive mother, he thought of women as naturally corrupt and unwholesome, possessed of the ambiguous beauty of a hermaphrodite as in, for example, *Oedipus and the sphinx*, where the sphinx with the head and the breast of a woman, grips the chest of the young man with its lion's claws and feet, and offers him its lips. Moreau found this theme of Satanic beauty in primitive mythology. Salome, Helen and the sphinx are not the only incarnations of the cruel feminine 'Eternal' as the artist saw it. His predilection covered subjects of morbid sensuality and mournful beauty, and of monstrous love. Dalida, Galatea, Pasiphae, Semele, Leda and Europa are the personification of the cold beauty necessary to seduce the decadents of the era such as Des Esseintes, the hero of *A Rebours*. Huysmans, describing Moreau's two paintings of Salome which Des Esseintes acquired, saw in this Jewish princess the same type of femme fatale, 'the symbolic deity of indestructible Lust, goddess of immortal Hysteria, accursed Beauty chosen above all others by the catalepsy which hardens the flesh and stiffens the muscles, the monstrous beast, indifferent, irresponsible, unfeeling, which poisons, as did Helen in olden times, everything which approaches her, everything which touches her, everything which sees her.'

All these mythical heroines corresponded to the visionary universe of Gustave Moreau who had retreated as far as possible from the outside world: 'Only my inner feelings are eternal and incontestably sure' he stated.

The artists near to Art Nouveau transformed the female figure into a type dominated by provocation and corruption. Only *The Bathers* by Maillol reflects innocence and purity, while the creations of Beardsley show immodesty and lewdness. He practises exhibitionism, and exaggerated ariapic cult. The women of Klimt and Mucha, without attaining this degree of indecency, are nevertheless stimulating, provocative and morbid, as are those of Georges de Feure. With Khnopff, who was directly influenced by the Pre-Raphaelites, the leopard-woman was born, the seductress who dominates the entire man whilst abandoning herself to sensual pleasure.

The whole life of Munch bears the imprint of the tragedy of his early years, and his pessimism marks the anaemic and deluded expression of the faces he paints. To him woman is a 'vampire'; she devours, she is the image of Death even at the moment of conception (*Madonna*), imposing it on man by her bestiality and sensuality.

Odilon Redon chose a more mysterious art, marked by uneasiness. This need for mysticism, this search for imaginary worlds conceived in the unconscious, attributed to woman attitudes which were bewitching and terrifying at the same time; she draws us towards the mystery of the unknown.

Félicien Rops was less visionary. Goncourt said in *Le Journal*: 'He is really eloquent in painting the cruel aspect of contemporary woman, her steely look, the ill-will she bears man which is not hidden, not dissimulated, but shown obviously throughout her whole person'. Rops takes us nearer to Satanism; Huysmans wrote: 'He has penetrated and summarized Satanism in excellent plates which are like inventions, like symbols, in an art which is incisive and vigorous, fierce and distressing, really unique'.

If Rops represented one of the aspects of a *fin de siècle* era, Ensor showed another which was

JOHN EVERETT MILLAIS *Autumn Leaves*. 1856

grimacing and caustic with his Masques and his Christ betrayed to the abuses of a delirious crowd.

We are introduced to the vampire woman in the canvases of Franz von Stuck, as she offers her nakedness to the coils of the serpent, and again in the fiancées of Toorop, who permit all forms of desire, desire which lends itself to all forms of gratification.

With Böcklin we glide towards *The Island of the Dead*, penetrate the secret world of shadows, and take the road which others such as Keller took after him. On the other hand, Derkinderen, Gallén-Kallela, Klinger, von Marées drew their inspiration from history and old legends in order to plunge us into the tumult of massacres or apocalyptic scenes such as *Le Chambardement* by Henry de Groux.

The theories of Symbolist painting

In the *Manifeste du Symbolism* the poet Jean Moréas discussed the tendencies and general theories of the movement. The great theorists of the plastic art in particular were Albert Aurier, Paul Sérusier and Maurice Denis who explained clearly the pursuits and directional aims of the Symbolist painters.

In February 1982 an article by Albert Aurier entitled *Paul Gauguin ou le Symbolisme en peinture* appeared in the *Mercure de France*. In this he defined the five fundamental rules for the Symbolist work of art: 'The work of art must first be idealist, since its only aim is the expression of an idea; secondly it must be symbolist because this idea must be expressed through forms; thirdly it must be synthetic, because these forms, these symbols, must be arranged in a manner suitable for general comprehension; fourthly it must be subjective, because the object will never be considered as an object but as the symbol perceived by the subject; fifthly, the work of art must be (as a natural consequence) decorative, because painting which is properly called decorative, such as the Egyptians and probably the Greeks also understood it, is nothing other than the manifestation of art which is subjective, synthetic, symbolist and idealist at the same time'. In order for the artist to be 'the expresser of absolute beings' he must 'simplify the language of signs'. He defines two tendencies in the history of art which depend 'one on clairvoyance, and the other on blindness, that interior eye of man of which Swedenborg spoke, the realistic tendency and the deistic tendency.' Rejecting the scientific criticism of Taine, he referred to Baudelaire, to Swedenborg, and a phrase from Plotin sums up his thoughts: 'We attach ourselves to the outside of things, unaware that inside them is hidden that which moves us.' Like Gauguin, he wanted to 'return to the creative artists of the Assyrian and Egyptian myths', to see the Symbolists compete with the Japanese, and he supported them each time they rejected academics.

Directly related to the Symbolist artists, the Nabis had Paul Sérusier and Maurice Denis as their theorists. With a feeling for synthesis, and a perceptive intelligence, Sérusier explained his ideas and his advice in *ABC de la Peinture*. He dreamed of an ideal brotherhood, that of the Nabis (prophets), which collected his friends together, including Maurice Denis, Vallotton and Ranson. During their meetings, they discussed the problems of art which Maurice Denis codified in a famous article, published in 1890 by *Art et Critique*. Taking Puvis de Chavannes as a subject to think on, he concluded that the role of artist is not slavishly to copy nature, but to 'visualize' his dreams, an idea already expressed by the Symbolists.

After a long period of purgatory, during which time inspiration was monopolized by constant artistic revolutions — Expressionism, Cubism, Surrealism, Abstract Art, Pop Art amongst others — a movement, which was one of the most profound metamorphoses, not just of art but of taste and a certain way of life, was returned to its place. Painting had been the best way of transmitting Symbolist thought since, in easily understood visual terms, it allowed the symbol, by form and by colour, to be made more easily legible than in poetry or music.

By reacting against the positivist spirit of its time, Symbolism found the way to discover the right language for man to recover his faith in the imaginary and the unreal.

Fernand Khnopff *Memories.* 1889

Pierre Puvis de
Chavannes *Hope.*
*c.*1871

51

PAUL GAUGUIN *Te Ave no Maria: the month of Mary.* 18

AMAN-JEAN Edmond (Chevry-Cossigny, Seine-et-Marne 1859 — Paris 1936). He enrolled at the School of Fine Arts in 1880, became a pupil of Lehmann, and made the acquaintance of Seurat with whom for many years he shared a studio situated on the Rue de l'Arbalète in Paris. He then joined Puvis de Chavannes and worked with him on the decoration of the *Bois Sacré* which the master exhibited at the Salon of 1884. In 1885 he obtained a travel scholarship which allowed him to go to Rome with Henri Martin and Ernest Laurent. In 1891 he met Léonce de Larmandie and the Sâr Péladan, who offered to publish a Journal, *La Revolte*, in which they allowed him to write the art reviews. He frequented the Symbolist literary milieu, Mallarmé's 'Tuesdays', and became close friends with Verlaine whose portrait he painted in 1892. He exhibited at the Salons of the Rose + Croix, and the poster he produced for their exhibition in 1893 had as its theme Dante

EDMUND AMAN-JEAN *Young girl with peacock.* 1895

Portrait of Aman-Jean by Georges Seurat

and Beatrice, inspired by Rossetti. Having contributed to the official Salon, he became a member of the Salon of the National Society, showed works in Munich, with the Vienna Secession, and in the autumn Salon of 1903. Much later, in 1924, he and Albert Besnard founded the Salon des Tuileries.

Because of his delicate health, Italy was his favourite holiday country; he stayed there several times, which had some influence on his painting. From 1895 he gradually abandoned dull colours in favour of clearer tones, a gentle luminosity which was especially sensitive in his pastels. It was also the period where, as a 'painter of the soul', he produced faces which were secret and meditative in the harmony of their delicate and subtle effects. Léonce Bénédite said of him: 'This artist with his northern temperament which is so different from the southern temperament of M. Henri Martin, has found with the help of his chosen masters, the gentle warmth which brought his poetic thoughts delicately into bloom. At the outset he willingly became involved with the world of imagination and legend, of history and fable, but little by little he broke away from Saint Julien l'Hospitalier, Sainte Geneviève, Joan of Arc, and the Muses in order to evolve in a more modern sense, and to realize, with elements borrowed from daily life, a method of decoration which was both dreamlike and deeply moving, with an enveloping and persuasive charm that speaks to the eyes and the soul at the same time.'

If the Symbolist period of Aman-Jean was without doubt his most important, it would be wrong to ignore the influences such as that of Bonnard which affected him after 1910. His decorative work must also be remembered: the six panels executed for the Museum of Decorative Art, as well as *Les quatre éléments* for the amphitheatre of the chemistry school at the Sorbonne.

53

BEARDSLEY, Aubrey Vincent (Brighton 1872 — Menton 1898). A subtle draughtsman, frequently considered the artist most representative of Art Nouveau, Beardsley was revealed as a young prodigy as gifted in music and literature as in design. Influenced by the Pre-Raphaelites and William Morris, he showed a great refinement of talent. When he was hardly twenty a publisher commissioned him to illustrate a new edition of Malory's *Morte d'Arthur*. Two years later he was artistic director and illustrator of the review *Yellow Book* which supported Art Nouveau, but after publication of four issues it was discontinued because of his very stormy private life.

SICKERT *Portrait of Aubrey Beardsley*

AUBREY BEARDSLEY *I kissed your mouth Johann.* 1893

A friend of Oscar Wilde, for whom he illustrated *Salome*, he was one of the princes of dandyism of the era, which brought him close to Baudelaire. He led a worldly life and encouraged scandal. His workroom, papered in black, was lit only by candles, and when he sat at his piano a skeleton sat beside him. A regular attendant at the hedonists' club, he wore a faded rose in his buttonhole and, having become involved with black magic, he received his friends in a room the walls of which were covered by erotic Japanese prints, adapted to the English taste.

'He is a born graphist' said Bernard Champigneulle, 'he expresses himself in two dimensions. He ignores space. His posters have the same affectations as the ornamentation of his books. When he uses, exceptionally, colour, he limits it to two or three subtle tones without relief. He

obviously thinks highly of the Japanese, but his figures are closely connected to those on Greek vases. He remains, however, completely individual.' Having contractd tuberculosis he left Great Britain for the south of France, where he died at the age of twenty-six.

BERNARD Emile (Lille 1868 — Paris 1941). Emile Bernard, who was both poet and art critic, arrived in Paris in 1881, and joined the studio of Cormon in 1885. There he met Toulouse-Lautrec and van Gogh. Dismissed in 1886 for insubordination, he travelled through Normany and

Brittany where he got to know Emile Schuffen-ecker. In 1887 he first attempted cloisonnism, a theory which Gauguin adopted and which was in at the birth of synthetic Symbolism. In August 1888 he joined Gauguin at Pont-Aven, formed a close friendship and worked with him. From their collaboration was born the aestheticism of the Nabis. But the two friends fell out in 1891. Emile Bernard exhibited at the Indépendants, and later with the Nabis at Le Barc de Boutteville where, in 1893, he organized the first exhibition of the works of van Gogh, whose faithful friend he had been. But by then he had given up the style of the Nabis, and was inspired by religious art as is shown by the canvas he exhibited in the first Salon of the Rose + Croix. He frequented a literary Symbolist milieu and illustrated *Les Cantilènes* by Moréas, *L'Ymagier* by Remy de Gourmont, and *Les Fleurs du Mal* by Baudelaire.

Later he went to Italy, Spain and Egypt from where he brought back numerous studies. After

EMILE BERNARD *Madeleine in the Bois d'Amour.* 1888

that he turned towards classicism, and his admiration for the Venetian school made him disown his Breton period. His role has remained

EMILE BERNARD *The Poet*

important in the world of aesthetics. He was one of the first to recognize the genius of Redon, and Francis Jourdain praised him 'as an artist, a poet of the highest class, a true art-lover and one of those who has done most to promote the current renaissance of Symbolism.'

BESNARD Albert (Paris 1849 — Paris 1934). Pupil of Jean Brémond, later of Cabanel, Besnard

was awarded the Grand Prix de Rome for his painting *Death of Timophanos, tyrant of Corinth*, which was exhibited at the School of Fine Arts. He spent four years in Rome, boarding at the Villa Medici. On his return from Italy, after a brief stay in Paris, he went to London where he remained two years; this gave him a chance to admire the work of the Pre-Raphaelites which influenced his own. On returning to France, he was commissioned to decorate the vestibule of the Ecole de Pharmacie in 1883, and the *salle des mariages* in the town hall of the *1er arrondissement* in 1886. Numerous other works followed. Some of them were Symbolist inspired, such as the ceiling of the science room in the Hotel de Ville in Paris (1890), the amphitheatre of the chemistry department at the Sorbonne, and the cupola of the Petit Palais. Other compositions were inspired with a lyrical and ornamental quality such as the celebrated panel of *L'Ile heureuse* for the Museum of Decorative Arts (1900) and the ceiling of the Comedie Française.

Apart from these great decorations, Besnard was a portraitist, and his travels to Algeria in 1893 and India in 1910 produced paintings which confirmed his ability as a colourist and brought him considerable acclaim. 'His love of the picturesque' wrote Michel Leroy, 'his clear vision, his knowledge of colour and composition served him very well in his interpretation of the sights he saw. He did numerous drawings, sketches and various notations; on his return he extended them, and created great paintings which ensured lasting and deserved success for him'.

He exhibited in various salons, notably that of the National Society of Fine Arts, of which he was one of the founder members in 1890.

BÖCKLIN Arnold (Basle 1827 — San Domenico, Fiesole 1901). Having completed his courses at Basle, Böcklin finished his artistic studies at the Fine Arts Academy of Düsseldorf where he became firm friends with Feuerbach. In 1846 he travelled through Switzerland, and the following year went to Brussels, Antwerp, and later Paris in 1848. He only stayed there a short time, leaving France at the start of the revolution. On the advice of Jacob Burckhardt, in 1850 he went to Rome where he discovered Italian Renaissance art and the Roman countryside. Until then he had only been a landscape artist. This contact with the Italian masters helped to enrich the treatment of his subjects. His Symbolism, noticeable around 1870, was interpreted in many works by the

ALBERT BESNARD *The happy island.* 1900

ARNOLD BÖCKLIN *Self-portrait with Death playing the violin* 1872

introduction of creatures from the world of mythology: mermaids, tritons, naiads, unicorns, satyrs and centaurs. An air of mystery cloaked his landscapes and made his works pictures of dreams as much as pictures of reality. Jules Laforgue wrote on this subject in 1886: 'One is constantly amazed at the unity in the dream, this blindness in the fantastic, this faultless naturalness in the supernatural.' His painting, *The Island of the Dead*, painted in 1880, of which five versions are known, is an isle in another world where Charon arrives with his barge of departed souls. With its high rocks and funereal cypresses, the atmosphere is one of isolation and despair, which appears again in *Villa by the sea*, where a thoughtful woman leans against a ruined wall, or again in the *sacred wood*, where the characters kneeling in front of the sacrifical altar contribute to the majesty of the great trees which shelter them. All his landscapes are imprinted with a deep lyrical quality which is born of this confrontation between the vain efforts of man and the impassiveness of nature.

Arnold Böcklin *War.* 1896

BORISSOV-MOUSSATOV Victor Elpidifo-rovitch (Saratov 1870 — Taroussa, near Moscow 1905). He started his studies at the school of painting, sculpture and architecture in Moscow, then entered the Academy of Arts at St. Petersburg. From 1895 to 1898 he wintered in Paris where he was a pupil of Cormon. He came under the influence first of the Impressionists, later of Puvis de Chavannes and the Nabis. Around 1903, in Moscow, he struck up a friendship with the poets Briussov and Andreï Biely. He presented to the real world an image which was idealized, transfigured by interior analysis and the dream, a world in which the past became reassuring. He had a great influence on the young Russian Symbolist painters, especially the 'Rose Bleue' group, and on the avant-garde artists such as Goncharova and Larionov.

BRULL VIÑOLES Juan (Barcelona 1863 — Barcelona 1912). Studied at the Fine Arts School in Barcelona, and took courses in Paris with Raphaël Collin who was also Lévy-Dhurmer's

JUAN BRULL VIÑOLES *Dream.* 1898

Portrait of Juan Brull Viñoles.

BURNE-JONES Sir Edward (Birmingham 1833 – London 1898). Born of a modest family — his father was a picture framer and gilder — Burne-Jones began his studies at King Edward's school

P. BURNE-JONES *Portrait of Edward Burne-Jones.* 1898

master. Between 1887 and 1889 he exhibited *genre* paintings and historical tableaux at the Salon of French artists. The painters were sent to the National Exhibition of Madrid in 1892, and then to the Exhibition of Fine Arts in Barcelona in 1894. Gradually his style became more idealistic; his female figures, taken from legend and often only shown to the waist were called Calypso or Ophelia. His most beautiful Symbolist works were executed between 1898 and 1900, such as *The Dream* which was loaded with distant Pre-Raphaelite memories and which recalled the poetry of the canvases of Aman-Jean and Ernest Laurent.

in Birmingham. A gifted draughtsman, in 1848 he attended evening courses at the Government School of Design. In 1853 he decided to take holy orders and enrolled at Exeter College at Oxford where he met William Morris who became his best friend. They shared the same passion for the arts. After a visit to Thomas Combe, director of the

EDWARD BURNE-JONES *The Golden Staircase*. 1898

EDWARD BURNE-JONES *The Beguiling of Merlin*. 1878

Clarendon Press in Oxford, and the discovery of the works of Rossetti, the two students decided to abandon theology for painting. At the beginning of 1856, Burne-Jones met Ruskin and Rossetti, and in May of the same year he was admitted to the latter's studio as a pupil. The following year he helped Rossetti with his project for the mural decoration in the hall of the Oxford Debating Society. Apart from this work he gave himself up entirely to pen or wash drawings, executed with great attention to detail. After his marriage in 1860, he began to paint watercolours to which he added gouache made from the bile of a cow on a brown base. From this period date the two portraits of the sorceress *Sidonia von Bock*, and her cousin *Clara von Dewitz* inspired by the Italian Renaissance and influenced by Rossetti. The same year he executed several versions on the theme of the ballad of the beautiful Rosamund and Queen Eleanor, as Rossetti and Hughes had both done before him.

In 1861 William Morris opened a shop in London where everything to do with furnishing a house was sold: furniture, glazed windows, ceramics, furnishing fabrics, objet d'art. His faithful friends Philip Webb, Rossetti and Burne-Jones joined him, and thus shared out the work of this little group.

Between 1859 and 1873 Burne-Jones made many trips to Italy which enabled him to learn more about Mantegna, Botticelli and Michelangelo. His style from that time on was marked by this influence.

Elected in 1864 a member of the Old Watercolour Society, he exhibited with the society in 1870. In 1877 he showed seven works at the first exhibition of the Grosvenor Gallery where he participated in every subsequent showing until 1887. His reputation was still growing and became international. In 1894 he received the title of baronet, the crowning of a period of glory and recognition.

During the last part of his life he devoted himself to large compositions the subjects of which were taken from literature.

EDWARD BURNE-JONES *Sponsa da Libano*. 1891

CARRIERE Eugène (Gournay, Seine-et-Marne 1849 — Paris 1906). Carrière started as a lithographer in Strasbourg, then came to Paris, where he was a pupil of Cabanel at the School of Fine Arts until 1876. He discovered the works of

EUGENE CARRIERE *Self-portrait. c.*1900

Rembrandt during a visit to Dresden in 1871. After his marriage in 1877 he went to London where he was very impressed by the work of Turner whose influence can be recognised in the soft atmosphere of some of his works.

61

On his return to Paris he exhibited for the first time, in the Salon of 1879, his *Motherhood*, a theme which he often returned to during his life. He placed his models in a cotton-wool atmosphere where he faded out the exterior details in order to concentrate on the feeling inside their beings. Jean Dolent, in 1885, defined his art as 'realities having the magic of a dream.'

If these scenes of domestic intimacy, bathed in a half-light, are immersed in a blur which becomes light mist, it is also due to the fact that sight no longer allowed him to grasp all the details of things but to encompass them in the whole.

In 1890 he founded, with Puvis de Chavannes, the *Societé National des Beaux Arts*, where he exhibited regularly. An assiduous attendant at Mallarmé's Tuesdays, he became involved in the Symbolist movement and declared that 'the eye depends on the spirit'. He painted the portrait of numerous artists and prose writers of the era, including Verlaine, Mallarmé, the Goncourt brothers, Anatole France, not forgetting Gauguin who painted him as well.

Admired in France, his exhibitions at the Libre Esthétique of Brussels in 1896, the Munich Secession and the Vienna Secession in 1898, made him known abroad. From 1895 he devoted his art to

EUGENE CARRIERE *The sick child.* 1884

JULES CLAIRIN *The distant Princess.* 1899

large compositions for the Hotel de Ville in Paris, for the Sorbonne, and for the town hall of the XIIe arrondissement. He was a sensitive artist and knew how to express in his own realm the pure sentiments which inspired him in a manner which was both serene and melancholy.

CLAIRIN Georges-Jules-Victor (Paris 1843 — Belle-Ile-en-Mer, Morbihan, 1919). He went to the School of Fine Arts where he attended courses given by the artist Pils. With Henri Regnault he travelled through Spain and Morocco. This journey inspired one of his principal works, *Après la victoire ou les Maures en Espagne*. He was a portrait painter and many personalities of the age sat for him, notably Madame Krauss and Sarah Bernhardt, which created a sensation. He was also known for the numerous decorations he executed for public buildings: panels and ceiling for the Opéra in Paris, Monte Carlo, the Bourse du Commerce, the Sorbonne, the Hotel de Ville, two ceilings for the Eden-Théâtre. Certain critics reproached him for too great a facility.

CRANE Walter (Liverpool 1845 – London 1915). Collaborator and faithful disciple of William Morris, Walter Crane played a primary role in the evolution of Symbolism, in bringing together the social preoccupations and the spiritualist aspirations of the Pre-Raphaelites. He came from a family of artists and was trained by his father, and then by W.J. Linton, the painter and engraver. A great admirer of the masters of the Quattrocento, he became an enthusiastic expert of the Pre-Raphaelite movement, and contributed with William Morris to the renewal of the decorative

art of his time. He designed wallpaper, illustrated numerous books, and expounded his theories in works such as *Decorative Book Illustration, Bases of Design* and *The Need for a Decorative Art*. As a decorative painter he tried to realize a harmony between ordinary objects and the larger lines of decorative art, a harmony based on a knowledge

G.F. WATTS *Portrait of Walter Crane.* 1891

WALTER CRANE *The Horses of Neptune.* 1892

of anatomy and the necessities of life, as much as the research of line and colour. To illustrate his books he used manuscripts and illuminations of the Middle Ages. Together with Burne-Jones he engraved plates for works by Shakespeare, Spencer and Perrault.

WILLIAM DEGOUVE DE NUNCQUES *The Peacocks.* 1898

DEGOUVES DE NUNCQUES William (Montherme, Ardennes 1867 — Stavelot, Belgium 1935). He was born in the French Ardennes of an old aristocratic family. His parents took up residence in Belgium, first in Spa and later in Brussels, shortly after the war of 1870. A cultivated and well-bred man, he became the first confidant and friend of Henry de Groux. In 1883, at Machelen

JAN TOOROP *Portrait of William Degouve de Nuncques.* 1891

near Vilvorde, he shared a studio with Jan Toorop; this was a very important relationship which influenced his painting. Some years later in 1891, Toorop painted a striking portrait of his friend. It was a portrait typical of a Symbolist artist: elongated face, nostalgic expression as if inclined towards the depths of the soul, lit by bright eyes. Degouve de Nuncques read Edgar Allan Poe, was enthusiastic over his writings, and *The House of Usher* inspired him to paint *The Blind House or the Pink House* (1892). In 1894 he married Juliette Massin, a young painter, sister-in-law of Emile Verhaeren. He then frequented the literary

scene, especially that of the Jeune Belgique. He did the decor for Maeterlinck's play *Intérieur* which was produced at the Théâtre de l'Oeuvre. He exhibited many times in Paris thanks to the support of Rodin and Thaulow, and was encouraged by Puvis de Chavannes and Maurice Denis.

The Low Countries attracted him: he showed his works at Groningen where he took refuge from the First World War. It is in the Kröller-Müller Museum at Otterlo that the best collection of his works can be seen.

A tireless traveller, he was always in search of new landscapes and sights which would suit his state of mind. He made prolonged trips to Austria, Switzerland and Italy. From Majorca he brought back fairy landscapes bathed in mystical light. In 1919 he rediscovered the soft, blurry atmosphere which was better suited to his artistic temperament.

WILLIAM DEGOUVE DE NUNCQUES *The Angels.* 1894

Some people considered him beyond Symbolism, a precursor of Surrealism, and compared *The Pink House* with *The Empire of Lights* by Magritte. Degouves de Nuncque penetrated a magic world where 'there is no place for man, not even for his feelings.'

WILLIAM DEGOUVE DE NUNCQUES *Boy with an owl.* 1892

WILLIAM DEGOUVE DE NUNCQUES *The Pink House.* 1892

DELVILLE Jean (Louvain 1867 — Forest-lez-Bruxelles 1953). This master of philosophic Symbolism, a disciple of Péladan, was equally well known as a writer and painter. He struggled tirelessly in his capacity of initiate to awaken the world to the knowledge of ancient esoteric tradition. He spent four years in Rome, then went

JEAN DELVILLE *Parsifal*

to live in Paris where he studied under Barbey d'Aurevilly, Villiers de l'Isle-Adam, and the Sâr Péladan, whose faithful disciple he became. He took part in the Salons of the Rose + Croix. Later he became a convinced theosophist under the influence of Scriabin, and then a disciple of Krishna Murti.

JEAN DELVILLE *Angel of Splendour*. 1894

JEAN DELVILLE *Portrait of Mrs Stuart Merrill*. 1892

artists such as Armand Point and Séon exhibited. After being a professor at the School of Fine Arts in Glasgow from 1900 to 1905, he taught at the Royal Academy of Fine Arts in Brussels. He executed some large decorative compositions in a cold and impersonal style. But in his drawings and paintings he tried to express his ideas on philosophy. Inspired by a spirituality in which Beauty is dragged into the abyss of the fantastic, as in Satan's Treasures (where Satan appears as a ballet dancer, crowned with a halo of thick red hair, bounding over swooning sirens whose entangled naked limbs float wherever the water takes them), his works captivate us by their fantastic symbolism which is near to magic.

JEAN DELVILLE *Satan's Treasures*. 1895

After 1892, he was one of the moving spirits of the 'Pour l'Art' Salon, for which he designed a sphinx as an emblem, and in 1896 he created the Salon of Idealist Art in Belgium, in which French

DENIS Maurice (Granville 1870 — Paris 1934) His parents left Normandy shortly after his birth – they used to go back there for their holidays – to live near Paris in St. Germain-en-Laye, where the

young Denis began his studies which he continued at the Lycée Condorcet. From the age of thirteen he began to keep a diary, and the following year he recorded his decision to become an essentially religious painter. After his bachelor's degree, his father allowed him to go to the Académie Julian where he prepared for his admission to the School of Fine Arts. At the Julian he became friends with Sérusier, Ranson and Bonnard, and met again Vuillard and Roussel whom he had known at Condorcet. These young artists formed the Nabis group, in close relationship with the Symbolist poets, composers and the avant-garde theatre. In 1891 Maurice Denis designed the decor for the play *Théodat* by Rémy de Gourmont.

Two important factors determined his future style: his meeting with Redon and his discovery of the work of Gauguin at the Volpini exhibition. In 1890 he published the manifesto of the Nabi movement, exhibited at the Le Barc gallery in Boutteville, and at the Salon des Indépendants. For the Théâtre de l'Oeuvre, recently formed by his friend Lugné-Poe, he designed both the décor and the costumes, as well as the cover of the programme for *Pelléas et Mélisande* by Maeterlinck

MAURICE DENIS *Self-portrait.* 1896

MAURICE DENIS *The Adoration of the Magi.* 1904

MAURICE DENIS *The Muses*. 1893

measurements'. With K.X. Roussel in France he made the acquaintance of Cézanne and Renoir. In Rome he went walking with André Gide while they discussed classic art.

In 1908 he joined, as professor, the Ranson academy where he taught until 1919, the year of the foundation of the Studios of Sacred Art. he shared his time between painting large religious compositions (Le Vésinet, Vincennes) decorations for public buildings (Champs-Elysées theatre) and private houses, (those of Ernest Chausson, of Count Kesslier in Weimar, and of Morosov in Moscow, among others). However, he did not forsake his easel paintings in which *intimist* scenes alternated with portraits of members of his family in the style of those by Carrière. He undertook other journeys to Canada, to the United States, to Greece and the Holy Land. In 1932 he entered the Institute. In 1943 he died, knocked down by a lorry.

Although he painted secular scenes, Maurice Denis was an artist of essentially religious inspiration, perceptible even in his portraits. He respected womanhood, and showed such purity in his idealized and timeless female figures that he could be compared to Fra Angelico.

MAURICE DENIS *The Sacred Wood. c.* 1900

with music by Debussy. 1895 marked the beginning of his numerous journeys, starting with Italy where he often returned. In 1903 Sérusier went with him to Germany, to the convent of Beuron, where they studied the technique of Benedictine art which was based on geometry and the 'sacred

His work as a painter was complemented by his work as a writer. He was the theorist of Symbolism, and published numerous articles which were collected in *Théories* (1912) and later *Nouvelles Théories* (1922), and a *Histoire de l'art religieux* (1943).

DERKINDEREN Antonius Johannes (Bois-le-Duc 1859 — Amsterdam 1925). Derkinderen attended his first art courses at Bois-le-Duc and then Delft. He enrolled at the Rijksacademie in Amsterdam, and in 1883-84 he became a fellow-pupil of Toorop in the Brussels Academy. While still young he discovered the operas of Wagner which made him understand the possibilities which might be found in a marriage of different art forms, plastic, literary and musical. He read Ruskin, Morris and Viollet-le-Duc which helped him to consolidate his idea of an art where the fusion of arts animates a collective life. In Italy he discovered Giotto, and in Paris he met Puvis de Chavannes, both of whom inspired his decorations of public buildings, such as the chapel of the beguinage in Amsterdam. This search for a new style linked to the great compositions of Renaissance art in Italy is also expressed in his work as an illustrator.

DORE Gustave (Strasbourg 1832 — Paris 1883). Three designers and engravers had a determining influence on the Symbolist painters: Gustave Doré, Bresdin and Victor Hugo. How many dreams gave birth to Doré's illustrations where the fantastic mixes with the symbolic, from the castle of the Sleeping Beauty, surrounded by creepers, and the virgin forests of Atala, to the knights of *Orlando Furioso* and the phantom ship in the *Rime of the Ancient Mariner*? His illustrations for the works of Coleridge, Tennyson and Edgar Allan Poe could be those of a Symbolist. His engravings for *Le Corbeau* are perhaps his masterpiece, as Philippe Jullian says. How can his illustrations for *The Divine Comedy* be qualified? Marcel Briton wrote in *l'Art fantastique*: 'Dante's poem found in Doré an interpreter who was aware of all the grandeur, all the majesty and all the sacred horror which is exuded from the "canticles" of the three parts: it is in the infernal fantastic that Doré excels, and if he is

GUSTAVE DORE *Don Quixote*

incapable of raising himself to the crystalline spirituality of Paradise it is because Paradise, by its very essence, makes very difficult any plastic interpretation of a text which is so hard to illustrate.' And what can be said of *Don Quixote* other than to echo Marcel Brion: 'This character of Doré's is exaggerated and raised to the level of a myth; he sheds the irony with which Cervantes has burdened him, acquiring on the other hand, in his shattering innocence, in his choice of visionary world and vital illusion, an incomparable majesty which the drawings of Doré have admirably preserved.'

If his pictorial work is less important and often forgotten, he was nevertheless able, in certain compositions such as *Ship among the icebergs* to produce the hallucinatory atmosphere of a nightmare.

MAGNUS ENKELL *Self-portrait.* 1891

EGEDIUS Halfdan (Drammen, Norway 1877 — Oslo 1899). He showed an exceptional gift for draughtsmanship at a very early age. When eight years old he joined the classes taken by Knud Bergslien at the School of Painting in Oslo, and later he was a pupil of Harriett Backer and Kristian Zahrtmann. He was inspired by the landscapes of southern Norway, especially those of Telemark. He interpreted them according to his own instinct, in an atmosphere of rustic feasts both diurnal and, more especially, nocturnal. These were bathed in a mysterious atmosphere in which appeared female figures animated by love and passion for the dance. Carried away by his fantasies he devoted the last two years of his short life to illustrating the nordic sagas which corresponded well to his dreamy and chimeric personality.

MAGNUS ENKELL *Fantasy.* 1895

ENCKELL Magnus (Hamina, Finland 1870 — Stockholm 1925). During his long stay in Paris he came under the influence of the mysticism of Edouard Schuré and the Sâr Péladan, and that of Puvis de Chavannes and Carrière in the world of painting. Around 1892 all his works, whether in oils, pencil, or charcoal, represented adolescents, entrenched in their loneliness, who foreshadowed the hermaphrodite so dear to Péladan, the 'complete type of new man with a higher destiny' as Ernest Raynaud wrote. But soon the mysticism of Paris could teach him no more, and he went in 1894 to Italy, travelling through Germany and Switzerland. He was fascinated by Böcklin's vision of antiquity which was 'melancholy and joyous at the same time'. In 1900 he renounced Symbolism to go back to the clear, bright brush strokes of the Impressionists which he imprinted from time to time with the mysticism of his first period.

AMES ENSOR *Skeletons warming themselves at a stove.* 1889

ENSOR James (Ostend 1860 - Ostend 1949). For those who knew him the memory is Ensor is linked to his studio at Ostend, situated above the family shellfish shop. An amazing bric-à-brac

JAMES ENSOR *Self-portrait*. 1885

of dolls and fetishes surrounded the swarming crowd of his *The entry of Christ into Brussels*. His visionary gift had been born, according to him, one night when he was asleep in his cradle, his windows wide open to the sea, with the appearance of a big sea-bird which came battering into his room and knocked against the cradle. If one adds to the bird the shellfish of the family shop and the Balinese masks relegated to the loft, all the elements are present to nourish the imagination of the painter.

Few artists have been endowed with as precocious a genius as Ensor. For three years he attended classes at the Academy in Brussels where Stallaert and de Portaels freely gave him their advice.

From this time date his portraits painted in a very individual Impressionist style, both in their subject matter and in their chiaroscuro of vaporous nuances and deep blacks. He was not slow to return to Ostend, and in that lively town of beaches swarming with people and celebrated for its balls and carnivals, he gave free reign to his fantasies: 'I was born in Ostend on a Friday, the day of Venus. On the dawn of my birthday, Venus came to me, smiling, and we looked for a long

time into each other's eyes. She smelt pleasantly of the salt sea'. The ordinary life of Ostend inspired compositions impregnated with this mood and with his liking for the Flemish village fairs which characterized his art. Already he was starting to use the masks which became for him both a source of plastic invention and symbols of social hypocrisy. It was in *The entry of Christ into Brussels* in 1888 that he gave free rein to his enthusiasm and his talent. At the same time he applied himself to engraving. Ensor was, in certain respects, a Symbolist, and in his way of expressing himself he joined forces with the Impressionists. His Flemish dash, his mocking humour, are very much in the tradition of Bosch and Bruegel. A faithful successor to Daumier, it was with a ferocious joy that he ridiculed the constitutional bodies, the doctors, the judges, the police, the politicians. He caricatured himself. In spite of his renown, he was not always accepted in the Salons where he exhibited, even in the Groupe des XX in Brussels, of which he was a founder member; in Paris, in 1898, his exhibition at *La Plume* was a failure. He withdrew into himself and went back to themes which were dear to him rather than looking for new ones.

JAMES ENSOR *Skeletons in the Studio*. 1900

But at last fame came to him and, in 1929, following a brilliant retrospective exhibition in the Palais de Beaux Arts in Brussels, he received the title of baron.

FABRY Emile (Verviers 1865 — Brussels 1966). Painter, decorator and lithographer, he was a pupil of Portaels at the Fine Arts Academy in Brussels. He was very strongly influenced by Symbolist poetry and theatre, and for a while his art was clearly pointing towards Symbolism. His style was influenced by Blake and Füssli. In 1892 he founded, with Jean Delville and Xavier Mellery, the *Pour l'Art* circle, to which he painted the

During his Symbolist period, Emile Fabry elaborated the allegoric tales of human destiny and yet, he who lived to become a hundred years old, always dreaded death and stove to interpret the passing of time. The titles of his works are also significant: *The Angels of Life, Autumn, Gestures, Stages and Gestures, The Fates.*

Fabry's style is entirely peculiar to him: he shows stiff figures, solidly modelled, which conjure up statues rather than flesh and blood beings. The enigmatic or deluded silhouettes stand out strongly from their backgrounds, giving the pictures a strange and fascinating effect. Even after his hundredth birthday, Fabry worked right up to his last day, marvellously aware of all that went on around him.

MILE FABRY *Initiation*. 1890

FANTIN-LATOUR Henri (Grenoble 1836 — Bure, Orne 1904). His father came from a family of Italian origin and his mother was Russian. When he was very young he lived in Paris and went to the studio of Lecocq de Boisbaudran where the teaching was based on the education

HENRI FANTIN-LATOUR *Self-portrait*. 1858

osters. Later he exhibited in the Rose + Croix alons in Paris in 1893 and 1895, and brought the lealist painters together. In 1900 he took on the uties of professor at the Academy in Brussels, nd gave up a large part of his time to projects for ural decoration. He collaborated with the architect Horta in Brussels, and conceived the decorations for the villa of his friend Philippe Wolfers t la Hulpe; from 1905 to 1925, he painted ecorative frescoes for the Theatre Royal de la Monnaie in Brussels, and for different official hambers in the town halls of Saint-Gilles, Laeken nd Woluwe-Saint-Pierre where he lived. During te 1914-1918 war, he took refuge in England.

of the memory to encourage the painting of the imaginary. He had as fellow-students Cazin and Legros who remained his friends. Together with Whistler he went to London where he was deeply influenced by Pre-Raphaelite art. From 1801 he exhibited in the Salon paintings of still life, allegories and portraits, and contributed to the

73

Salon des Refusés in 1863 because Manet was a friend of his. He often went to the café Guerbois and thus became involved with the Impressionists. He then painted the series of *Hommages* which are a valuable testimony to the literary and artistic life of the era: *Homage to Delacroix*, around whom are grouped Manet, Whistler, Legros, Duranty,

Wagner with his flower-girls of the Rhine and his Valkyries who appear out of the surrounding mist, and whose languid figures rise from the bluish undergrowth. His fondness for this type of subject, together with the blurred imprecision of the atmosphere he creates, marked the evolution of his Symbolist vision.

HENRI FANTIN-LATOUR *The Reading*. 1877

Champfleury, Baudelaire and Fantin himself; *Homage to Manet* where it is possible to recognize Bazille, Manet, Renoir and Zola; *Homage to Baudelaire*, which figures Verlaine, Rimbaud, Jean Aicard and Pelletan; and finally *Homage to Wagner* where Chabrier, Vincent d'Indy and Adolphe Julian appear. However, it was the compositions which had musical themes as their subjects which connected him most strongly to the Symbolist stream. Thrilled by Wagner, he took the subjects of his operas for such paintings as *Prélude to Lohengrin*, and *Scenes from Tannhäuser*. He collaborated on *La Revue Wagnérienne* in which appeared numerous pastels and drawings, all relating to the great master of Bayreuth. He evoked the music of

FEURE Georges de (Paris 1868 — Paris 1928) Born in France of a Dutch father and a Belgian mother, he represented the type of artist dedicated to the cult of Art Nouveau and the flower girls. In 1884, he worked with Cheret, and his watercolours attracted attention at the two first Salons of the Rose + Croix. He met Bing who commissioned him to decorate the façade of his pavilion at the universal Exhibition of 1900, and to design the furniture. De Feure seemed to be the spiritual heir to Beardsley by his delicate and subtle eroticism in imagining a very sophisticated type of woman, the Parisienne of 1900. He created the decor of everything around her in the dressing-room and the boudoir, using the most precious materials — onyx, ivory, silver, crystal, not forgetting gilded wood — all sparkling in their harmony of delicate colours in which grey played the greatest part.

De Feure was involved in the world of the theatre, he was a friend of Debussy, he designed patterns for tapestry such as *La Fée Caprice* and he executed numerous illustrations in watercolour for *La Porte des rêves* by Marcel Schwob. He contributed a great deal to the diffusion of posters.

FILIGER Charles (Thann 1863 — Brest 1928). Having worked in Paris in the Colorassi studio, Filiger went in 1889 to Brittany which he never left again. He stayed at Le Pouldu to start with, where he met Gauguin, Emile Bernard, Schuffenecker, Sérusier and Count Antoine de la Rochefoucauld, who bought his works and paid him an annuity of twelve hundred gold francs. He exhibited at the Salon des Indépendants in 1889 and 1890. At this time, Emile Bernard, in an article which appeared in *La Plume*, spoke of

GEORGES DE FEURE *In Search of the Infinite. c.*1897

GEORGES DE FEURE *Voice of Evil. c.*1895

CHARLES FILIGER *Self-portrait. c.*1903

The Sleeping Saint as 'a truly Giottoesque dream'. In 1891 Filiger joined the Groupe des XX in Brussels, thanks to the support of Gauguin who had recommended him to Maus in these terms: 'A friend of mine, Monsieur Filiger, who is in some degree one of my pupils. I think very highly of his personality, his art is his own and very modern.' In 1892 he was one of the exhibitors in the first Rose + Croix Salon. There he showed mystic gouaches inspired by the Byzantine icons, which were worthy of the following review by Alfred Jarry: 'It is the work of God which remains static, soul without animal movement, canvas or cork,

CHARLES FILIGER *Symbolic figure*

where the artist pins down and collects the arrested flash from one of the faces of a revolving lighthouse.' He then devoted himself to the illustration of two pieces of work at the request of Rémy de Gourmont, and of *l'Ymagier*, a review which he edited with Alfred Jarry. He was a disciple of Gauguin and the Pont-Aven school, but left in 1900 to concentrate on research into a geometric style which took him away from Symbolism. He became more and more solitary and finally retired to paint in an inn in Tregunc.

GALLEN-KALLELA Axel (Pori, Finland 1865 — Stockholm 1931). Following a youth devoted to romanticism, he went to Paris in 1889 in order to study better the new artistic tendencies. At the time, he represented the realist movement which was dominant in the Scandinavian countries. After his period in Paris, he became interested in the Symbolist movement without, however, linking it up to his own ideas. In 1893 he met a friend of Munch, the writer Adolf Paul, and under his influence he took up Symbolism. From 1895 he interpreted, in a very stylized and decorative way,

the national legends of the Kalevala. His efforts corresponded to those which Sérusier was making at the same time in France. Adolf Paul initiated Gallén-Kallela into the metaphysical concepts of the modernists who had met in Berlin. He exhibited in this town at the same time as Edvard

AXEL GALLEN-KALLELA *Problems*. 1894

Munch. He then adopted the style of Art Nouveau and spent several months in England in order to study the graphic and decorative arts. In his later period he went back to the themes of the Kalevala.

AXEL GALLEN-KALLELA *The Virgins of Tapio*. 1895

and interpreted them with no realism at all, in a manner which was purely Symbolist, and where the stories were coloured by mysticism.

GAUGUIN Paul (Paris 1848 — Atuana, Marquesas Isles 1903). His mother, Aline, was the daughter of Flora Tristan, famous for the action she took in the women's liberation movement, and a Spaniard who died shortly after her birth. In 1846 Aline married Clovis Gauguin, who after the coup d'etat of 1851, became a political suspect, left with his family for Peru, and died before reaching the country. Aline and their two children reached Lima, and went back to France in 1855. The

PAUL GAUGUIN *Self-portrait.* 1889

young Paul's ambition was to become a sailor. In 1865 he sailed as an apprentice pilot in a three-master bound for Rio. He did his service in the navy and was demobilized in 1871. His mother had died in 1867.

His tutor, Gustave Arosa, was an art lover, a shrewd collector, who was interested in the Impressionists and especially Pissarro, and he made Gauguin share his passion for painting. He entered him as agent with the stockbrokers Bertin. In the pension where he took his meals, Paul met a young Danish girl, Mette-Sophie Gad, whom he married. This was a time of prosperity for Gauguin. His home life was happy, he had many

PAUL GAUGUIN *Oviri (the savage) Self-portrait.* c.1893

children. He speculated on the Stock Exchange, and managed to make forty thousand gold francs a year, which enabled him to start a wonderful collection of paintings by contemporary artists who were mostly Impressionist. He met Pissarro, who encouraged him to paint himself. First as an amateur, later as an impassioned artist, he gave himself more and more to his art, frequented the Nouvelle Athènes *cénacle* and exhibited with the Impressionist group until 1882. He also discovered the Japanese prints which were to inspire his future paintings, and which he showed in some of his still lifes. In 1883, he used the economic crisis as a pretext for giving up finance, left Bertin and dedicated himself completely to his painting. He joined Pissarro, while Mette, disappointed, returned to her family in Copenhagen with the children. Gauguin accompanied them, but his in-laws were hostile to him, and he had no choice but to go back to France, taking his son Clovis with him.

Henceforth he led a life which was difficult, bordering on misery. He was an eternal wanderer, and in 1886 he went to Pont-Aven in Brittany for the first time. His friends told him that life there cost nothing: sixty francs per month at the

PAUL GAUGUIN *Nevermore.* 1897

PAUL GAUGUIN *Nave Nave Moe: the Joy of rest.* 1894

pension Gloanec. In the group of habitués the artist cut a revolutionary figure. he was getting further away from Impressionism, his colours were becoming brighter, his lines stronger, his landscapes more precise. But with the approach of winter, his thoughts turned to departure. He dreamed of the sunshine, of exotic lands beyond the seas. He embarked for Panama with his friend Laval. It was a failure. On the way back he stopped at Martinique, but his state of health obliged him to return to France, and he went back to Pont-Aven in 1888. There he met Emile Bernard who shared in his studies. They painted almost the same pictures, and with the help of emulation, evolution was accelerated. With the approach of

wards himself and cut off his own ear. Gauguin went back to Paris, frequented the café Voltaire, and joined the Symbolist literary scene. He joined the discussions of the writers and artists of the movement: Aurier, Morice, Redon Carrière, Moréas, Mirbeau. Mallarmé admired him and supported him. But he could not settle, and return to Pont-Aven for the third time before going to live in Le Pouldu.

However, he still kept alive the idea of a country where he could live with no constraints, and having mobilized his friends and organized a sale of his works, he left in 1891 on the great adventure to Tahiti, on the other side of the world. In 1893 he went back to France for the death

PAUL GAUGUIN *Te Rerioa: the dream.* 1897

winter Gauguin responded to the call of van Gogh who was begging him to come to Arles. The two men, in spite of their mutual admiration, were hardly made to live together. One evening van Gogh lost all control and threw himself upon Gauguin with a razor in his hand, turned it to-

of his uncle from whom her inherited, organized a great exhibition which did not have the success he expected, and paid a last visit to his wife and children in Copenhagen without finding the understanding he had hoped for in Mette. He made another trip to Brittany, had a disappointing sale, but relying on new payments of money he sailed again for Tahiti in 1895. The natives did not disappoint him, the *vahinés* were always sweet and tender, but he found in the French the same meanness which had made him flee the metropolis. He wanted to be a righter of wrongs, but he was exposed to administrative vexations. The money he awaited from France was slow to arrive, he experienced a very difficult period and tried to kill himself. Finding that Tahiti had lost its mystery, he went to the Marquesas Islands. He sailed for Atuana, on the isle of Fatu-Iva. In July 1901, he wrote to Charles Morice: 'I am going to make a last effort next month to establish myself in Fatu-Iva, which is still nearly cannibal. I believe that there, this completely wild element, this total solitude, will give me before I die one last spark of enthusiasm, which will rejuvenate my imagination and bring my talent to a conclusion.' He had more disputes with the gendarmes and the representatives from the Catholic mission. He defended the natives against the Europeans more and more furiously, which put him endlessly into conflict with the authorities. Exhausted, exposed to the pesterings, even the hatred of some, he died alone in his cabin on May 8, 1903.

fever.' All the studies of his later years are summed up here. 'It will be' said Georges Boudaille 'the sum of all his ideas, all his feelings, all his anxieties. At the same time it is a great question which will live on for ever without reply, and a philosophy of life.' This long painting of unusual dimensions — 4.50 metres long and 1.70 metres high — is a desperate meditation on human destiny, and the denial of existing civilization. Gauguin was rebelling against his era as much as against our Graeco-Roman civilization and our rationalism. He wished to be a barbarian, the 'good savage' dear to Rousseau, and his return to the primitive life foreshadowed the disgust which many among us now have for an industrial civilization which in Gauguin's time was still embryonic.

The second picture, *Breton Village in the snow*, was found after his death by Victor Segalen, on the easel in his cabin. It was thus possible to deduce that the artist, before dying, felt a longing for the European countries, and a desire to make them come alive. But for Germain Bazin the truth was something different: he said 'Gauguin never painted except from life. But this painting is directly analogous to others painted in Brittany during his visit on his return from Tahiti, from

PAUL GAUGUIN *Where do we come from? What are we? Where are we going?* 1897

Two key pictures illuminate the anxieties and the longing of Gauguin. One, painted in 1897, *Where do we come from? What are we? Where are we going?* is his pictorial testament, the last creation which he pursued relentlessly before dying, and then, at the beginning of 1898, he tried to poison himself. 'I wished', he said, 'to paint before I died one great picture which I had in my head, and during the whole month I worked on it in a tremendous November to December 1894...there were several

heavy falls of snow in November and December 1894 in Brittany...But Gauguin must have retouched this painting in Atuana; one can in fact see in the sky a grey-blue and pinkish tone which are found on the palette of the Marquesas.'

Painting, for Gauguin, radically altered the subject. Instead of trying to describe the outside world, it turned towards the world inside the artist. He summarized his doctrine in some concise phrases: 'you can see in graphology the

PAUL GAUGUIN *Mahana No Atua: the day of God.* 1894

characteristics of sincere or untruthful men; why... do lines and colours not also give us the more or less grandiose life of an artist?...The straight line gives infinity, the curve limits creation.' Imagination resumes its rightful place, and the lesson of Cézanne and the example of Emile Bernard prove that the new way he chose for himself was justified. Besides, as he was not content with what he could see, he turned towards the sacred. He was sensitive to the mystery of another reality and, in Tahiti, he gave a Maori interpretation to Christian iconography. In *Noa-Noa* he referred himself to Tahitian beliefs.

It is possible to conclude, with René Huyghe, that 'rarely has a man, in breaking away from his era, in boldly asserting an adventurous but necessary backward step, been able to feel the future as did Gauguin: separating painting from the imitation of the visible in order to show its true nature...he prepared the way for an immense stream which went from Cubism to Abstract Art; wanting painting to renounce description in favour of suggestion and thus foreknow the mysteries of the soul..., he worked towards the development of a current of expression which

passed from Fauvism and Expressionism to Surrealism while it was trying to go beyond the bounds of the unconscious.'

GRASSET Eugène (Lausanne 1841 — Sceaux 1917). This Swiss, naturalized French, first studied architecture under the direction of Viollet-le-Duc before devoting himself entirely to the graphic arts. But he also showed a rare virtuosity in many diverse spheres: glass, furnishing, fabrics, wallpaper and printing. He studied passionately the Japanese engravings which were fashionable at that time. Ukiyo-e had an important influence on his style: interlaced arabesques appeared in his illustrations for *La Légend des quatre fils d'Aymon* in 1883. In 1892 he exhibited at the Rose + Croix Salon, and at the Libre Esthétique in Brussels. A professor at the School of Design in Paris, and a great nature lover, he joined forces with Gallé, and in 1897 published *La Plante et ses applications ornementales* which showed the plant as an essential element of Art Nouveau. His windows, too, were always inspired by woman and flowers. He

Eugene Grasset *Young girl in a garden*

specialized more and more in printing, posters and book illustration; he designed covers and emblems.

'Like Guimard, like van de Velde and many others' wrote Bernard Champigneulle, 'the attraction of art does not inhibit him from declaring himself to be a functionalist. Contrary to the English, the preachers of craftsmanship, he realizes that industry is progressively invading the world, and that, artist though he be, the decorator must come to terms with it.'

GROUX Henry de (Brussels 1867 — Marseilles 1930). Painter, sculptor and lithographer, he exhibited at l'Essor and then with the Groupe des XX established in Brussels by Octave Maus. His earliest works stirred up fervent admiration and violent criticism, which contributed to his notoriety. In 1888 he painted *Christ being insulted* which met with great success but also some virulent attacks. First shown in Brussels, this painting was presented in Paris in 1892 where numerous artists

Henri de Groux *Lohengrin*. 1908

and writers came to admire it. He was considered one of the painters who had best incarnated the tragic character of his era. After his allegorical, religious and historical compositions he became an inspired witness of the 1914-1918 war as much in his big canvases as in his vivid pastels: he showed terrifying scenes of pillage, fire, fleeing refugees, peopled with dead bodies and skeletons. He engraved numerous series of lithographs, did illustrations for *Le Livre secret de Péladan* and carved busts of Baudelaire and Wagner.

GUAL QUERALT Adria (Barcelona 1872 — Barcelona 1944). Symbolism numbers few experts in the Iberian countries, and only Catalonia has produced an artist who could claim to belong to the movement.

Having attended classes at the Barcelona School of Fine Arts, where he was a pupil of Pedro Borell, he went to the studio of lithography

He tried to reform the theatre, and imposed himself as one of the most original renovators of the stage. He was so successful that he could be compared, for his work in Barcelona, to Jacques Copeau. In fact he is numbered among the European stage designers who, in freeing the theatre from Naturalism, started a systematic simplification of décor and of the expressive methods of the actors. His efforts were inseparable from the Symbolist movement. Not only was he enthusiastic about Wagner, but he knew the experiments of Paul Fort at the Théâtre des Arts, and of Lugné-Poe at the Théâtre de l'Oeuvre. The theatrical reform which he undertook started with Maeterlinck; he was the first in Spain to stage *L'Intruse*, in the Catalan translation by Pompeu Fabre. He pursued this fidelity to Maeterlinck for several years. Thanks to him and his drama group, the Catalans also discovered *L'Intérieur* and *Monna Vana*. On 30 January 1899, the Théâtre Intime, a theatrical organization which he had founded, gave at Sitges a series of demonstrations entitled

ADRIA GUAL QUERALT *The rose bush.* 1897

founded by his father, and directed it up till 1901. Attracted first of all by the theatre, he was the author of *Nocturn, andante morat* which he illustrated with drawings of Pre-Raphaelite inspiration. He founded the 'teatro intimo' and installed himself during the last years of the nineteenth century as stage designer and professor of dramatic art.

Bataille pour Maeterlinck, with a performance of *L'Intérieure* and a play by Gual himself entitled *Blancaflor*.

Considered a dramatic author, Gual was directly inspired by Symbolism: his first play, *Silenci* (1898) strongly recalls *L'Intruse*.

For about thirty years Gual worked to hoist

Catalan art up to the European level. He supported a theatre school and a company in Barcelona,
opening the Spanish world to Ibsen, D'Annunzio
and Pirandello. His importance declined after
1930, but his name has remained in Catalonia
as the standard-bearer of modern theatre. It
must also be noted that he was one of the first in
Barcelona to become actively interested in the
cinema. In 1914 he established a production
studio with the industrialist Lorenzo Mata. Four

In a similar manner he was also at the forefront
of the modernist Catalan movement with his
painted and graphic work which is recorded in the
Art Nouveau stream of his time. He took part in
the Fine Arts exhibitions in Barcelona in 1894 and
1896, and in the competition for posters, organized in 1898 by the same town. Articles were
written about him by Leon Deschamps in *La Plume*.
He designed publicity posters and continued to
paint pictures where dreamy young girls, seen in
profile, seemed, like those of Aman-Jean, to be
awaiting the coming of Prince Charming to turn
their lives upside down.

HAWKINS Louis Welden (Esslingen, Württem-
berg 1849 — Paris 1910). Born near Stuttgart of
English parents he took French nationality in

Portrait of Adria Gual Queralt

films were made under his direction, including the
cinematographic adaptation of *El Alcade de Zalamea*
by Calderon.

ADRIA GUAL QUERALT *Sketch for a theatre design*

LOUIS WELDEN HAWKINS *Séverine.* 1895

1895. Hawkins studied in Paris where he was a
pupil of Bouguereau, Jules Lefebvre and Gustave
Boulanger. These academic painters taught him a
scholarly technique and the well-finished and
polished workmanship which was at that time the
hallmark of classic painting. A cousin of the writer
George Moore, Hawkins met Whistler, turned

towards Impressionism, and was able to reconcile the two tendencies. He exhibited in the Salon of French artists, contributed later to that of the Rose + Croix, and until his death sent pictures to the National Society of Fine Arts.

In general, his subjects were landscapes or genre paintings of a sentimental realism, but he showed more originality in certain portraits of Pre-

Louis Welden Hawkins *Self-portrait*

Antoine-Auguste-Ernest Hebert *Ophelia*

Raphaelite inspiration, such as that of *Séverine* 'Apostle of pity and social solidarity', earnest feminist, who is shown like a Byzantine virgin against a background of gold.

He was involved with the literary milieu of the era, and met Mallarmé, Laurent, Tailhade, Paul Adam, Jean Lorrain and Robert de Montesquiou. He was also a friend of the Symbolist-inspired painters such as Carrière, Rodin and Puvis de Chavannes, who thought of him as one of themselves.

HEBERT Antoine-Auguste-Ernest (Grenoble 1817 — 1909). A pupil first of David Augers and then Paul Delaroche, he became the winner of the Grand Prix de Rome at the age of twenty-two, having obtained an early success with his *Le Tasse en prison (A cup in prison)* exhibited in the 1839 Salon. But it was his painting *La Malaria*, in the 1850 Salon, which brought him fame. This suffering young woman represented an ideal of the era. If Hébert was principally a classic painter, he deserves, however, to figure among the Symbolists because he strove during his whole career to conjure up the sylphs, the concubines, and the Ophelias, all sorts of wistful and discouraged female figures in a lyrical and passionate atmosphere.

HENNER Jean-Jacques (Bernviller 1829 — 1905). Of Alsatian origin, he started at the age of twelve in the studio of Gutzwiller, a painter of Altkirch. He then went to Gabriel Guérin in Strasbourg. In 1847 he went to Paris and entered the studios of Drolling and Picot at the School of Fine Arts. In 1858 he won the Prix de Rome with *Adam and Eve discovering the body of Abel*. He soon obtained success with his particular manner of making faces appear out of the mist, or nude figures disport themselves in broad daylight. His thoughtful young girls, his nymphs at the edge of a fountain, his languorous Madeleines, link him by their wistful dispositions to the Symbolist movement.

HODLER Ferdinand (Bern 1853 — Geneva 1918). He came from a modest family; his father was a carpenter and his mother a cook at the Prison in Bern. Hodler was only seven years old when his father died, and fourteen at the death of his mother. He then left Bern for Geneva where he had as his master Barthélemy Menn, who had been a pupil of Ingres and a friend of Corot. Under his tuition Hodler studied for six years at the School of Fine Arts in Geneva. During these years, he had to struggle against wretchedness, hostility, and lack of understanding. He won the

FERDINAND HODLER *Self-portrait*

forms which can be seen in his representation of historic and Symbolist subjects such as *Disappointed souls*, which was shown in the Rose + Croix Salon, and *Tired of life* where five personages, clothed in white, are seated side by side on a bank.

Apart from his great mural works, Hodler painted numerous portraits including that of his friend James Vibert with whom he was, in 1914, the initiator of the protest signed by the Swiss artists following the fire of the cathedral at Rheims. His landscapes were almost exclusively Swiss. He knew, better than anyone, how to evoke the mountains, the lakes and the trees in flower. 'No one since Turner', said François Fosca, 'knows better than Hodler how to show the structure of the mountains, the accumulation of the massive rocks, the way the peaks stand out against the sky, the grandeur and extra-human permanence of the

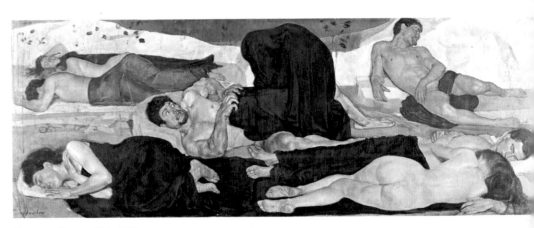

FERDINAND HODLER *Night*. 1890

Calame prize and the Diday prize in turn. A trip to Spain enabled him to discover new horizons, and to give more depth to his ideas. He admired the paintings of Velasquez, Holbein and Raphael, who influenced him. In 1884 he made the acquaintance of the Symbolist poet of Geneva, Louis Duchosal, a great lover of Wagner and Baudelaire. This meeting influenced the development of his studies. Until then he had painted landscapes where lighting took precedence over colour, and genre scenes inspired by the craftsmen he knew: carpenters, watchmakers and cobblers.

Gradually he abandoned naturalist realism, in order to perfect a very personal Symbolist style. His Symbolist ideas were assimilated into an art where symmetry reigned in a rigorous order. This new style appeared for the first time in *Procession of wrestlers* 1884. But *Night* (1890) was his great Symbolist work; in it he realized fully his theory of parallelism, based on the repetition of identical

summits...if Hodler knows so well how to evoke them it is because his whole life, all his untiring efforts, have been an incessant struggle against lack of comprehension, misery, ill-will and petty jealousies.' His art was essentially Swiss; he wanted to show forcefully the grandeur and the virtues of his country, to praise them by taking his inspiration from the masters of the Middle Ages and the Renaissance. So he showed warriors and pikemen as in *Retreat from Marignano*, and described celebrations such as *Procession of Wrestlers*. On the other hand, his mystic compositions take us into the world of dreams by their pantheist idealism which is especially noticeable in *Communion with the Infinite* 1892, in which a naked woman extends her arm in a gesture of oblation.

In conclusion, there is the judgement of Jean Rudel in *L'Art et le monde moderne*: 'Hodler's pictures introduce us to a pictorial world where the persistent play of the lines transforms the characters into real puzzles: this corresponds to his anxiety to establish firmly a correct form, and to define a style which is already leading towards Art Nouveau whilst remaining partially attached to the preoccupations of the Symbolist of Pont-Aven.'

HOFMANN Ludwig von (Darmstadt 1861 — Pillnitz 1945).
He started his studies at the Academy of Dresden with his uncle, Heinrich Hofmann, the historical painter, as his master. He completed his artistic knowledge at Munich and finally at Karlsruhe under the teaching of Ferdinand Keller. In 1889 he went to Paris where he met Puvis de Chavannes and Albert Besnard whose influence can be seen in his work. In 1890 he established himself in Berlin, and there became member of the Groupe des XI which was run by Max Liebermann in opposition to the Union of Berlin Artists (Verein Berliner Kunstler), of which Anton von Werner was president. In 1892, in Munich, he was very attracted by the work of Hans von Marées which also had some influence on his style. The themes of his paintings are those often found in Symbolism: rustic and idyllic landscapes inhabited by unreal people, a mythological world. Aspiring to formal beauty Hofmann looked towards Art Nouveau for inspiration to give his subjects a misty, erotic atmosphere. Thus he set some of his paintings in decorated frames where the ensemble of motifs produced an erotic climate. His ambiguous female figures are influenced by a symbolism which is marked by sensuality impregnated with dreams and nostalgia.

In 1903 he was made professor of the Academy of Fine Arts in Weimar. He was then asked to undertake large projects such as the decoration of the theatre and the rooms in the museum at Weimar. He was also, like many painters of his era, a designer and engraver. He illustrated the books of his friends, Stefan George and Theodor Daübler.

HUNT William Holman (London 1827 — London 1910).
Nothing destined Hunt to take up an artistic career. He was the son of a warehouse director, and his family's ambition was to train him for commerce and especially for the City of London. And so, in 1841, he found himself employed in a London office. However, he painted in his spare time, and in 1844 he was admitted to the Royal Academy school for a trial period. He made friends with John Everett Millais then aged sixteen. In 1848 he showed *The Eve of*

LUDWIG VON HOFMANN *Pastoral scene*

J. BALLANTYNE *Portrait of William Holman Hunt*

St. Agnes at the Royal Academy, a painting which was conceived according to the new theories of Ruskin, with models taken from nature. Rossetti visited the exhibition, was thrilled with what he saw, and asked Hunt to become his pupil. This decision was very important for what was to follow, since the lessons became a pretext for discussions which led, under the influence of the writings of Ruskin, to the rejection of academic principles and the creation by Rossetti, Millais and

Hunt of the Pre-Raphaelite Brotherhood. Hunt continued to work in the way which he had marked out for himself; like the other Pre-Raphaelites he took his subjects from nature which he idealized, as did the Symbolists. Later, around 1855, he devoted himself to sacred art. *The Light of the World* became the religious symbol of his era. In order that the models for his Biblical themes should be 'true to life' he went to the Holy Land on three different occasions. His work remained dominated by religious themes, laden with symbols, as in *The Shadow of Death*. Towards the end of his life he went back to his early sources of inspiration, themes such as the *Lady of Shalott* and *Isabella*, which were more literary.

In 1905 he published a book, *Pre-Raphaelism and the Pre-Raphaelite Brotherhood*, which is the principal source of information on the movement.

KELLER Ferdinand (Karlsruhe 1842 — Baden-Baden 1922). From his childhood he showed precocious tendencies for the arts, and did sketches and studies from life. At the age of twenty, he often visited the Academy of Fine Arts in Karlsruhe where he studied, like Hans Thoma, under Johann Wilhelm Schirmer. In 1866 he travelled to Switzerland and France, and then spent two years in Rome, from 1867 to 1869, where he met Anselm Feuerbach. He brought back from Italy numerous studies of landscapes and people, which he later used in his great historical compositions. Being above all a painter of history, he was nicknamed the 'Makart badois' after the Austrian artist Hans Makart, who was celebrated in this field.

It was only in 1900 that he was influenced by

WILLIAM HOLMAN HUNT *Claudio and Isabella*. 1850

FERDINAND KELLER *Self-portrait*. 1889

Böcklin and, like him, inspired by themes taken from ancient mythology. His landscapes, romantic in spirit, were animated by rustic characters who played the flute by the edge of a lake on which floated swans, and which was surrounded by thick forests. A magical atmosphere emanates from these evocations of the myth of Narcissus or the cult of the dead, like that which he called *The Tomb of Böcklin*, where a mysterious door, surrounded by black cypress trees, appears in a misty valley enveloped in melancholy. It is a transposition of *The Island of the dead* by Böcklin, and a token of the admiration he had for this master.

FERDINAND KELLER *The Tomb of Böcklin.* 1901-02

FERNAND KHNOPFF *The Caresses*. 1896

FERNAND KHNOPFF *The Temptation of St. Anthony*. 1883

KHNOPFF Fernand (Grembergen-lez-Termonde 1858 — Brussels 1921). The critics of the time thought of him as the great Belgian Symbolist artist. Khnopff was born into a rich family of the Ardennes, originally from Heidelberg. He spent his childhood in Bruges which left him with a certain melancholy. He left the faculty of law to enter the Academy of Fine Arts in Brussels where he was a pupil of Zavier Mellery. During a short period in Paris he admired the works of Delacroix and became passionately interested in the imagination of Gustave Moreau. But it was the Pre-Raphaelites — Burne-Jones, Rossetti and Watts — who had the greatest influence on his style. 'He is' said Philippe Jullian 'one of those rare decadents who are both artist and aesthete.' His character

FERNAND KHNOPFF *A Recluse*. 189

was that of a worldly dandy; '...two very sharp, steely eyes, a slightly pointed chin, a scornful mouth...; a stiff bearing, correct behaviour, a simple nature. A horror of slovenliness. A clergyman in process of becoming a dandy.' So Verhaeren saw him.

In 1883 he was one of the founder members of the Groupe des XX in Brussels, but he exhibited mainly in Paris and showed some works at the first Rose + Croix Salon. Péladan became his friend and his admirer; he found in him his herm-aphrodite ideal, and asked him to design the frontispiece for his novel *Le Vice suprême*. In the introduction to the second Salon the Sâr wrote: 'I consider you the equal of Gustave Moreau, of Burne-Jones, of de Chavannes and Rops. I look upon you as an admirable master.' Khnopff mingled with the Symbolists and became a friend of the poets George Rodenbach and Grégoire Le Roy, for whom he illustrated several books. He returned in his paintings to the themes dear to the Symbolist writers: solitude, the sphinx, the chimera, deserted towns. Sometimes he calls Redon to mind, for example in *The Sleeping Muse*, and sometimes almost rejoins Moreau such as when evoking the ambiguous charm of a woman with the body of a tigress in *The Caresses*.

Painting was not his only interest; he also practised sculpture, pastel, colour wash, design, engraving, and executed some large decorations for the Théâtre de la Monnaie in Brussels.

If a large number of his contemporaries con-curred in praising him, some of them accused him of too much facility. Albert Aurier called him the 'Bouguereau of painting' in his report of the first Rosicrucian Salon, and Félix Fénéon wrote: 'No one will ever make M. Fernand Khnopff nor a number of his co-exhibitors understand that a painting must attract first of all by its rhythm, that a painter is giving proof of excessive humility by choosing subjects which are already rich in literary meaning.' However, he still remains the most characteristic master of the Belgian Symbolists.

KLIMT Gustav (Vienna 1862 — Vienna 1918). Klimt was without argument the most original personality at the Viennese Secession. He studied at first, from 1876 to 1883, at the School of Plastic Art in Vienna and in 1880 went to work with his brother Ernest and Frantz Matsch on the great mural decorations destined for the Burgtheater in Vienna. On the death of his brother, he ceased to collaborate with Matsch and decided to open his own studio. With some other artists, including Olbrich and Hofmann, he staged in 1897 the Vienna Secession, of which he was the first president until 1899. Until 1903 he collaborated actively on the review *Ver Sacrum*.

GUSTAV KLIMT *Red fish*. 1901-2

91

GUSTAV KLIMT *The Kiss.* 1907

If he was influenced in his early stages by Makart, and attracted to historical composition, he soon interpreted Symbolism to his own very individual concept, and devoted his attention to an ornamental stylization based on constant observation of nature. Bernard Champigneulle wrote of him: 'He is the darling of the ladies of Viennese society. Woman is the subject of his strange paintings, a subject which is constantly repeated, always renewed; the silhouette appears like a heap of vividly contrasting ornaments, inspired by Egyptian civilization and Byzantine mosaics. There is not the slightest relief, it is pure iridescent decoration, where he frequently introduces gold and silver. At the top of this stiffly composed garment a face, sometimes half a face, is drawn like a portrait stamped with voluptuous and morbid rapture. He has a rather excessive and decadent side which would be almost gaudy if it were not supported by a very sure taste. These paintings, where one finds nothing unoriginal, obtained, while he was still young, a success which gushed out over the whole of the Secession. It was from Ravenna, where he went in 1903, that Klimt drew his Byzantine inspiration.

Next to the statue of Beethoven by Klinger he exhibited his *Beethoven Frieze*, a free interpretation of the Ninth Symphony, on the theme of the evolution of mankind. He refused the job of professor which he was offered by the Academy of Vienna, and stayed in Brussels, London and Paris where he compared his work and style with that of Bonnard, Vuillard and Vallotton. After this confrontation he tempered his artistic language somewhat; he abandoned the gilded style, which had made his reputation, in favour of a new choice of colours and a less heavily accented style. On this subject José Pierre wrote: 'By different routes his portraits and his landscapes discover the same lack of depth as Gauguin; they could both be considered as the only artists of the era to have confused the act of painting with the immediacy of amorous delights.'

KLINGER Max (Leipzig 1857 — Grossjena bei Naumburg 1920). This artist, considered by some as a precursor of the Jugendstil, was a painter, an

fantasy. Böcklin was the only artist with whom he felt any affinity, so he turned to the painters of the past: Rembrandt, Goya and Menzel were all masters whose engravings especially he had admired. In fact his own first years of work had been devoted to etching. In 1882, he received a commission for a mural painting to decorate the villa Albers near Berlin. In 1883 he executed his first sculpture, a bust of Schiller. He then spent three years in Paris, during which time he started the statue of Beethoven which he finished at a later date. He went to Italy, spent a long time in Rome (1889-1893) and discovered the Italian works of the fifteenth century which were a revelation to him. He studied the nude, anatomy and the representation of volume. During this period he worked very hard and returned with the study for his last painting: *Christ on Olympus* where he tried to reconcile his pagan aspirations with those of Christianity.

After 1897 he devoted himself exclusively to sculpture and finished the statue of Beethoven which was exhibited at the Vienna Secession in 1902, with the seven panels which Gustav Klimt dedicated to the Ninth Symphony, a kind of homage of Symbolism to the great composer.

Klinger explained his ideas on art in a book entitled *Painting and Design*.

MAX KLINGER *Discovery of a glove: the theft.* 1878

engraver and a sculptor. A pupil of the School of Fine Arts in Karlsruhe, he followed his master, Gussow, whose advice had a determining influence on his style, to the Academy of Fine Arts in Berlin. There the Realist movement was in full swing, but this did not correspond to Klinger's feelings towards the dream, the imagination, or

KOUSNETSOV Pavel Warfolomeivitch (Saratov 1878 — Moscow 1968). With his fellow-students Sarlan and Petrov-Vodkine, he attended the classes of Korovin and Serov from 1897 to 1904, at the School of Painting, Sculpture and Architecture in Moscow. He was deeply influenced by the art of Borissov-Moussatov. After 1902 he

Portrait of Pavel Kousnetsov. c.1912

became the ringleader of the young Symbolist painters in Moscow, who were grouped together under the name 'Blue Rose'; this movement was started to oppose Russian academicism at the end of the last century. After 1906 Kousnetsov stayed many times in Paris, where he became a member

PAVEL KOUSNETSOV *A Kurdish woman.* 1914

of the Society of Fine Arts and a juror of the Autumn Salon. He discovered Gauguin and was influenced by his work. But after 1910 he broke gradually away from Symbolism and started to search for a way of interpreting in the simplest possible manner the impressions which he had experienced when travelling through the steppes of the Volga and central Asia. Towards the end of his life he painted only landscapes and still lifes.

KUBIN Alfred (Leitmeritz, Bohemia 1877 — Château de Zwickledt, Wernstein am Inn 1959). Having been interested in photography he went to Munich to attend the Academy, and worked in the studio of Schmidt-Rottluff. He was interested in the study of the work of 'visionary' painters such as Bosch, Goya, Munch, Ensor and Rops. A disciple of Schopenhauer, he expressed his pessimistic conception of the world in fantastic and demoniacal drawings of which H. von Weber published a collection in 1903. He discovered

Portrait of Alfred Kubin

Klinger whose painting was a revelation to him and he created works where the subjects seemed to issue from his subconscious mind, following the contemporary theories of Freud. In 1905 he met Odilon Redon while staying in Paris. Under the latter's influence, he tried watercolour and

tempera techniques which he soon abandoned to come back to his pen, which he preferred for its vigour. Some years later, in 1908, he wrote his novel *Die andere Seite* where he gave free rein to his penchant for fantasy and hallucination, and described the imaginary world of the dream where all the anxieties and torments of the real world mingle. He illustrated his text with numerous drawings. In 1909 he became involved with the Nouvelle Association of young artists, founded by Kandinsky, and in 1911 he participated in the Blaue Reiter movement. He then worked with Marc, Klee, Feininger and Kandinsky. He illustrated works of writers such as Poe, Nerval, Hauff, d'Aurevilly, Strindberg, Wilde and Thomas Mann.

ALFRED KUBIN *Lot's Wife*

FRANZ KUPKA *Woman picking a flower*

In 1912, in his book *Über das Geistige in der Kunst*, Kandinsky wrote, speaking of Kubin, 'he ranks in the front line of those lucid spirits who reflect the great obscurity which manifests itself.' And again: 'An irresistible force pitches us into the horrible atmosphere of nothingness. This force issues from the designs of Kubin as it does in his novel.' Until the end of his life he followed his search into the fantastic and the imaginary, immersing us in an oppressive atmosphere in which dreams and nightmares take on a symbolic value.

KUPKA Frank (Opocno, Bohemia 1871 — Puteaux 1957). He went to classes at the School of Fine Arts in Prague from 1886 to 1889. In 1891 he went to Vienna, read the philosophers and the German poets, and took an interest in astronomy and the occult. Art Nouveau was then at its highest point, which naturally influenced Kupka

whose tendency towards mysticism was favourable terrain for the acceptance of Symbolist aestheticism. He established himself in Paris in 1895 and devoted himself above all to humorous drawings in journals and numerous book illustrations. At the beginning of his stay in France his work was marked by Fauvism and later Cubism. From 1911 he pursued his studies 'to liberate colour from form' and his art became more abstract. He was a Symbolist during his figurative period, when his visionary talent presented a certain similarity to the decorative style of Art Nouveau.

LACOMBE Georges (Versailles 1868 — Alençon 1916). Born of a well-to-do family, he had a cultivated mother who was herself artistically talented and who encouraged her son's penchant for painting, and considered that 'one never sells a work of art.' The young Georges led a worldly life and welcomed his friends the Nabis at Madame Wengner's receptions. She was a pretty widow from Versailles, who was a friend of his mother and who gave dinner parties following concerts. In 1897 he married one of her daughters, Marthe, then eighteen.

Having been a regular attendant at the Roll studio, Lacombe went to the Académie Julian. From 1888 to 1897 he returned each summer to Camaret in Finisterre, where he discovered a little circle of artists and writers. Thus, in 1892, he made the acquaintance of Sérusier, and from the following year joined in the exhibitions of the

GEORGES LACOMBE *Self-portrait*

Autumn have come down to us. In *The Spring*, the artist represents the various stages of life in the middle of a forest. He was himself a wood carver, and was influenced by Gauguin. He gave full measure to this art in a bed, where the different panels symbolized copulation, birth, death and the dream. It is a fascinating work which, according to Agnes Humbert, is similar to the sculptures of the Maoris; its abstract tendencies enchanted Paul Klee. In 1905 he executed three bas-reliefs *Damned Women*, which were inspired by the poem by Baudelaire.

GEORGES LACOMBE *The chestnut gatherers*. 1892

Nabis. Sérusier decorated the studio of Lacombe in Versailles with compositions which unhappily have been lost. For his part Lacombe painted some large panels for the drawing-room of Gabrielle Wengner, representing the allegory of the four seasons. Those concerning Spring and

LE SIDANER Henri (Port-Louis, Mauritius 1862 – Versailles 1939). He was ten when his parents went back to France to live in Dunkirk. He obtained a scholarship from the town of Dunkirk and went to Paris in 1880; there he became a pupil of Cabanel at the School of Fine Arts where he

HENRI LE SIDANER *Sunday.* 1898

MARIE DUHEM *Portrait of Henri le Sidaner*

was admitted in 1884. But he rapidly moved away from classic teaching, attracted by Manet and the Impressionists. In 1882 he installed himself in the Pas-de-Calais at Etaples, and for five years worked alone in the little fishing port which had become a watering place. He took part for the first time in 1887 in the Salon of French Artists and then, in 1894, in the Salon of the National Society of Fine Arts. He became friendly with Henri Martin and Ernest Laurent, and after 1896 his works showed a more literary inspiration. In 1898 and 1899 he left Etaples for Bruges, which Rodenbach had sung about. This town cast a magic spell on him, its transparent light fascinating him, and he felt its influence as had many writers and Symbolist painters. But 1900 was the year of his return to France. He stayed at Beauvais to start with, and then went nearby to the charming little town of Gerberoy before finally settling down in Versailles. His art of nuances is faithful to Symbolist aestheticism: he was not content merely to interpret nature, he also wanted to impregnate it with the spirituality, the sweet melancholy which was characteristic of the Symbolists. It is an essentially intellectual type of painting where memory transposes observation and reclothes it in mystery. He is 'a painter of the soul' when he makes white-robed young girls gradually appear from an 'atmosphere of bells'. As Gabriel Mourey wrote: 'they are a white choir of undefined dreams, snowy figures with unsuspecting eyes who...contemplate life.'

In his later paintings he shows landscapes where all human presence is lacking, which leaves us an impression of calm and composure.

LUCIEN LEVY-DHURMER *Appassionata*

LEVY-DHURMER Lucien Alger 1865 — Le Vesi-
net 1953). From 1879 he attended the courses at
the High School of Design and Sculpture in the
Rue Bregnet in Paris, where he was a pupil of
Vion and Wallet. Around 1886 he met Raphael
Collin, who helped him with advice. From 1887 to
1895 he worked as an ornamentalist in the faience
factory directed by Clement Massier at Golfe-Juan,
where he became artistic director and rediscovered the technique of metallic lustre. His
ceramics, in very sober forms, always had a vegetal
decoration.

When he was about thirty he left for a journey
of study in Italy. There he made the acquaintance
of classic Italian art which corresponded to his
aspirations as much as to those of other Symbolist

LUCIEN LEVY-DHURMER *Beethoven*

LUCIEN LEVY-DHURMER *Salome*. 1896

painters, and of the Pre-Raphaelites before them.

His first exhibition was held at the George Petit
Gallery in 1896. There he showed under the name
Lévy-Dhurmer (thus adding part of his mother'
name, Goldhurmer, to his patronym Lévy). His
first paintings and his pastels reveal an artist who
can reconcile a technique of academic precision
with an Impressionist vision of the world, and
can thus treat his Symbolist subjects loaded with
mystery. This exhibition stirred up the enthusiasm
of those critics sensitive to Symbolist art, such
as Camille Mauclair, Gustave Soulier, George
Maurey, Léon Thévenin and Francis de Miomandre who devoted important articles to him.
Georges Rodenbach, whose portrait he painted
honoured him with his friendship and his support. His success was as great also in ordinar'
circles as it was among the artists. From this tim
on, he executed works of varying inspiration
idealized subjects where the Pre-Raphaelite in
fluence can be seen, *femmes lianes* similar to thos
of Khnopff, portraits, landscapes still faithful t
Impressionism, strange figures that he met in th
course of his frequent journeys to France o

ᴸUCIEN Lᴇᴠʏ-Dʜᴜʀᴍᴇʀ *Hymn to Joy*

Wɪʟʜᴇʟᴍ Lɪsᴛ *The Offering*. 1900

r abroad, dream silhouettes inspired by music or terary subjects.

He exhibited regularly at the Salon of French rtists from its beginning, and then in 1897 at that f the National Society of Fine Arts and, after 930, in the Autumn Salon. Several private exibitions of his works were held, notably in 1937 t the Charpentier gallery, in 1952 at the Museum f Decorative Art and, in recent times, in 1973 at he Grand Palais where, under the title 'Autour de .évy-Dhurmer, visionnaires et intimistes en 1900' n important presentation of paintings by the rtist permitted an unjustly forgotten work to be einstated in honour.

Lévy-Dhurmer represented Symbolism in its nost diverse aspects, at times expressive with all comprises of mannerisms and affectation, at ther times hardly indicated, full of sobriety and estraint.

.IST Wilhelm (Vienna 1864 — Vienna 1919). He equented the Academy in Vienna, where he was pupil of Griepenkerl, and then attended the lasses of Bouguereau in Paris. In March 1897 he xhibited at the first Viennese Secession. Comarable to Osbert and Klimt, he revealed himself s a remarkable portraitist, as shown in *The Woman black and white*, where his technique of divided olours and fine long brush strokes, with a ominance of blue, evokes the works of Amanean during the same period. But List is best nown for his engravings, where he used wood nd lithography in turn. He collaborated on the eview *Ver Sacrum* from 1898 to 1903, and he was ne of the twelve illustrators of the 1902 catalogue

for the Viennese Secession which was dedicated to Beethoven.

MAILLOL Aristide (Banyuls-ser-Mer 1861 — Perpignan 1944). Before becoming the great sculptor we admire, Maillol worked successfully in pictorial art and tapestry, and it is under that heading that he figures in this encyclopedia of Symbolism.

Son of a modest merchant in Banyuls, a small fishing port near the Spanish frontier, the second

MAURICE DENIS *Portrait of Aristide Maillol*. 1902

of four children, he was brought up by his aunt Lucie. He remained attached to the country of his birth during his whole life, and to that Mediterranean light which left a deep impression on him. At thirteen, when he was at college, he painted his first picture, a seascape, and felt he had a

ARISTIDE MAILLOL *The Sea*. 1895

ARISTIDE MAILLOL *Night*. 1902

a vocation as an artist. He arrived in Paris when he was twenty, failed his entrance examination for the School of Fine Arts, but was accepted by Cabanel into his studio. He remained for five years at the Fine Arts, spending the summers at Banyuls where he painted sunny landscapes. Daniel de Monfried introduced him to Gauguin, a meeting which was decisive for his later work. He abandoned academicism for a decorative style which was less ornate, and Gauguin encouraged him in this. Having discovered the tapestry in the museum at Cluny, he decided to take up this art,

in line with his new studies, and set up a modest studio in the house of his aunt at Banyuls. His first patterns shown at the Salon of the National Society of Fine Arts and the Libre Esthétique received a certain amount of success. In 1893, sponsored by the painter Rippl-Ronai, he joined

ARISTIDE MAILLOL *The Wave*. 1898

the Nabis, and was profoundly influenced by Maurice Denis. But a serious eye illness altered his plans. He had to abandon painting and devoted himself henceforth completely to sculpture. In 1902 he exhibited at Vollard and met Rodin. To be nearer to the Nabis he settled in Marly-le-Roi in 1903, and the following year showed for the first time in the Autumn Salon. In 1905 he made the acquaintance of Count Kessler who became his admirer, his friend and his patron. His bronze, *The Mediterranean*, shown in 1905, established him, as Gide says, as the great sculptor of his age. 'From this *Mediterranean* modern art must be born.'

MALCZEWSKI Jacek (Radomin 1854 — Cracow 1929). Having been the pupil of Lonozkievisch and Mateiko at the School of Fine Arts in Cracow, and then having studied at the School of Fine Arts in Paris from 1876 to 1878, he worked in Munich and made numerous trips to Greece, Asia Minor and Italy. On returning to Cracow he was appointed rector of the Academy of Fine Arts. The realist pictures of his early period, inspired by the struggle against Russian imperialism, were soon abandoned in favour of studies directed towards Symbolism. His colours became brighter

JACEK MALCZEWSKI *Vicious circle*

JACEK MALCZEWSKI *Self-portrait*. 1914

and more airy, but he kept his nostalgic and patriotic spirit of revolt. He took environments which were familiar to him, peopled them with real characters, his own friends, who could be seen side by side with mythological beings — fauns, sirens, angels and, in *Thanatos*, death who assumes

the characteristics of an adolescent and who, from behind a flowering tree, contemplates the artist's father asleep forever against the support of the window in his house. Again, in the same way in *Whirlwind*, death, represented by a female silhouette, drags the enchained children away in a whirlwind of dust to the middle of a vast sunny plain. In the work of Malczewski, this theme of death and human destiny alternates with that of the independence of Poland, as the two above-mentioned pictures show.

MAREES Hans von (Elberfeld 1837 — Rome 1887). The son of a father belonging to an old noble family and a Jewish mother, he began his artistic studies in Berlin in 1854 and 1855, with the animal painter Carl Steffeck. In 1857, he settled in Munich where he continued his artistic development and had as friends Adolf Lier and Franz von Lenbach, of whom he painted a portrait with himself in 1863. He also attracted the attention of a German patron, Count Schäck, who commissioned him to paint copies of Italian Renaissance works. In 1864, therefore, he left for Rome with Lenbach. The knowledge of the ancient world transformed his pictural conceptions, and inspired in him a sombre manner lightened with reddish-brown and golden glints. Marcel Brion wrote on this subject: 'The gods who people the pictures of

Hans von Marées are like those of Böcklin, the genies of the earth and forest, stripped of their conventional attributes and become the forces which close up on one the more rapidly when one does not see them.

Count Schäck hardly appreciated his new compositions, and did not pay him. But in Italy he met the writer Conrad Fiedler who enabled him to pursue his studies. They travelled together to Spain, Holland France, where he familiarized

especially in his pictures of antiquity such as *Arcady* and *The Golden Age*.

A great retrospective exhibition in Munich in 1891 was the start of his influence on German painting, an influence recognized as much by Franz Marc as by Paul Klee.

MARTINI Alberto (Treviso 1876 — Milan 1954). Fascinated by German graphic art of the sixteenth century, that of Dürer and Cranach, he went to Munich where he first came into contact with the Jugendstil. From 1895, he devoted himself to engraving and illustrating books. He discovered Edgar Allan Poe, and between 1905 and 1909 he illustrated his stories; this work established him as the greatest Italian engraver in the Symbolist stream. His love of the fantastic shows fully in his interpretations of the works of Dante, Boccaccio, Rimbaud, Verlaine and Mallarmé. When he started to paint he appealed to the dream and psychological introspection. He stayed in Paris from 1928 to 1931, and there met the Surrealists, but he refused to follow their doctrine. He went to Milan in 1934 where he remained until his death.

ALBERTO MARTINI *The double murder of the Rue Morgue.* 1905-7

HANS VON MAREES *The Ages of Man.* 1873-74

himself with the work of Delacroix whom he saw as a descendant of Rembrandt. After a period in Berlin and Dresden, in 1873 he went back to Italy and settled in Naples. There he met Böcklin, and completed some large decorations with the sculptor Adolf von Hildebrand. After a short stay in Florence, he settled in Rome where he undertook the composition *The Garden of the Hesperides* in which the characters immersed in shadow have the solemnity of statues in a mysterious garden.

His work was similar to that of Böcklin, and had harmony between man and nature as its principal theme. It equally resembles that of Puvis de Chavannes to whom he is often compared,

His most important work is the cycle *The Struggle for Love*, a series of eighty-six drawings in Indian ink, executed between 1903 and 1905 with a pathetic bitterness and an anguish similar to that of Munch, while his illustrations for Edgar Allan Poe plunge us into the world of fantasy and of a hallucinatory Symbolism.

MASEK Vitezlav Karel (Komarau 1865 — Prague 1927). An artist who was particularly representative of Art Nouveau in Czechoslovakia, Masek started his artistic studies in Prague and continued them in Munich and Paris. He became a disciple

KAREL MASEK *The Prophetess Libuse*. 1893

of Seurat, and practised his style of pointillism in the manner of certain French Symbolists such as Osbert and Henri Martin. In 1894 he exhibited in Munich and Dresden, and in 1898 became professor at the School of Decorative Art in Prague. *The Prophetess Libuse*, 1903, preserved in the Louvre, is characteristic of the Symbolism of Masek which in this case was adapting a nationalist theme, Libuse being a queen of Bohemia, to an art glittering with colours which Klimt adopted after him.

MAURIN Charles (Le Puy-en-Velay 1856 — Grasse 1914). Winner in 1875 of the Crozatier competition in le Puy, he was granted a scholarship. Having been a pupil of Julian, he was admitted two years later to the School of Fine Arts. He showed in different Salons including

CHARLES MAURIN *Maternity*. 1893

those of the Rose + Croix in 1892, 1895 and 1897, and the Libre Esthétique in Brussels in 1895 and 1897. He had many private exhibitions in Paris: with Toulouse-Lautrec at Valadon's gallery in 1893, at Vollard in 1895 and Sagot in 1901.

He collaborated on *La Revue Blanche*, and was a friend of Vallotton. His art was diverse, for he was as good at pastel, painting and tapestry as at engraving. He had a style which was classic for nudes and portraits, open to the innovations of the synthetists with their use of uniform colours, and progressing to compositions of exaggerated Symbolism.

MAXENCE Edgar (Nantes 1871 — Le Bernerie-en-Retz, Loire-Atlantique 1954). A pupil of Elie Delaunay and Gustave Moreau, he exhibited in the Salon of French artists from 1894, and in the Rose + Croix Salons from 1895 to 1897. Mainly a portraitist, he also painted landscapes, but he is numbered among the Symbolists for those of his compositions which were inspired by medieval legends, painted under the influence of the Pre-Raphaelites, such as *The Soul of the Forest* (1898) and *Serenity* (1912).

Focillon wrote in 1913 in his review of the Salon: 'The art of Maxence is deliberately empty.

EDGAR MAXENCE *Profile with peacock.* Before 1896

illustrations were very like those of van Gogh during his period in Nuenen. After journeys to Germany, Switzerland and Austria, he devoted himself to decorative art and, in his large compositions against a golden background, he

XAVIER MELLERY *Towards the Ideal*

expressed himself by symbols and allegories. He was first of all an intimist painter whose vividly contrasted interior scenes evoke a silent life full of mystery and poetry. He was a friend of Oscar Maus and exhibited at the Libre Esthétique. He had Khnopff as his pupil.

From the romantic defrocking — which interpreted coldly still hinders so many artists' studios – he has retained some medieval ornaments with which he reclothes every year, with an impassiveness and a stiffness far removed from the style, one or two characterless and expressionless models. Nevertheless he is a good painter whose beautiful and supple reliefs one can still remember. He has been spoilt by success and sale.'

MELLERY Xavier (Brussels 1845 — Brussels 1921). From 1860 to 1867 Mellery attended the classes at the Academy of Brussels, where he won the Grand Prix for painting in 1867. Having won the Grand Prix de Rome in 1870, he went to Italy where he was enraptured by Carpaccio and the Sistine Chapel. In 1897 he went to the isle of Marken to illustrate a book by Charles de Coster which had this landscape as its background. The

MENARD Emile-René (Paris 1861 — Paris 1930). Pupil of Baudry and Bouguereau, he also went to classes at the Julian academy. He was influenced by Millet and Théodore Rousseau, whom he had met as a child at Barbizon. But stronger still was the hold which his father and his uncle, a philosopher, exercised over him. They passed on to him their love of antiquity and from 1897 Mênard travelled the Mediterranean countries visiting Greece, Sicily, Palestine and Italy in turn. From his travels he collected hundreds of studies which he used in his great compositions for the decoration of the Faculty of Law in Paris and the School of Advanced Studies at the Sorbonne. His first works were inspired by episodes from the Bible or ancient legends, and then he moved on to mythological subjects such as the *Judgement of Paris* which he treated several times. But his favourite themes were pastoral, with more or less unclothed nymphs moving in a rustic landscape. Mênard tried to bring together the idealism of Puvis de Chavannes with the Impressionists' conception of

EMILE-RENE MENARD *Bathers.* 1916

W. HUNT *Portrait of John Everett Millais.* 1860

light, and was one of the first to fall in love with the intimism for which the fashion kept growing right up to the First World War, and which produced artists such as Le Sidaner and Lévy Dhurmer.

MILLAIS Sir John Everett (Southampton 1829 — London 1896). His family originally came from Jersey where he lived until, at the age of nine, he went to the School of Design in Sass. In 1840 he was accepted at the Royal Academy where he spent six years. A child prodigy, he was so precocious that Ruskin wrote that even when he was seven his drawing was as precise as that of an adult. He met Rossetti and Hunt, and together they established the Pre-Raphaelite Brotherhood. His first Pre-Raphaelite work, *Isabella*, illustrates a passage from Keats' poem, *Isabella and the pot of basil.* Shown at the Royal Academy in 1849, this canvas did not receive the success anticipated for it, certain critics being disconcerted by the realist, almost photographic aspect of the idealized

figures. Millais kept to this style until about 1855, the date of his marriage; then, in order to please the public, he changed his way of painting, and created a number of Impressionist portraits and popular subjects.

Elevated to the rank of baronet and having become President of the Royal Academy, at the height of his success, he was making something in the region of thirty thousand pounds a year. His paintings overcame the Pre-Raphaeilite reveries, as is shown by the comparison between the two versions of *The Bridesmaid*, one painted in 1851 as if in a dream, the other in 1897, a conventional portrait of his daughter Marie. In 1866, a great exhibition brought together one hundred and fifty-nine of his canvases at the Grosvenor Gallery.

JOHN EVERETT MILLAIS *Ophelia.* 1852

William Hunt noted that Millais had confided to his friends: 'I am not ashamed of admitting that my maturity has not fulfilled the hopes and ambitions of my youth.'

Pre-Raphaelism was for him only a transitional period, which permitted him to experiment with new techniques that revived the academic style. He knew how to give proof of his sensitivity and imagination with a remarkable feeling for the setting, coupled with extraordinary gifts of execution.

MINNE George (Gand 1866 — Laethem-Saint-Martin 1941). George Minne and Constantin Meunier were the two great Belgian sculptors at the end of the nineteenth century, but while the latter remained faithful to the Naturalist concept, Minne turned towards an essentially human art which could be called Symbolist or spiritualist.

GEORGE MINNE
Disconsolate Mother
1890

GEORGE MINNE
Mother mourning her child. 1886

Son of an architect who did not believe in his vocation, he had a difficult start. Admitted to the Academy in Gand from 1882 to 1884, he worked alone up till 1889. His tormented spirit, his leaning towards mysticism, brought him closer

to the Symbolist poets who became his friends: Maeterlinck, Gregoire Le Roy, van Lerberghe, Verhaeren. He joined them in their studies and their meetings, and illustrated their poems. Thus his designs for *Les Serres Chaudes* of Maeterlinck, although hieratic and sometimes affected, always have a spellbinding beauty.

His first sculptures, *Christ on the Cross* (1885), *Mother mourning her child* (1886) and *Mother mourning her two children* (1886) show the influence of both Rodin and the sculptors of the Middle Ages in their pathetic and tense style.

Around 1899 he retired to Laethem-Saint-Martin where he led a life of silence and contemplation close to several intimate friends who were equally keen to create an art of faith and fervour. The exhibition of the German primitives in Bruges in 1902 confirmed his desire to do this, and their lessons inspired him to work for more purity and strictness of style. He spent the years 1914 to 1918 in Wales where he was content to draw. On his return to Belgium he carved new sculptures in marble and granite, the theme of mother and child still remaining dominant.

André Ridder, in a work devoted to Minne, wrote: 'This thoughtful artist, turned in on himself, has constantly run away from exuberance, from verbosity, from overloading the movement which would displace the line. His art is one of contemplation and of silence, of a profound, lyrical resonance, quite interior...What Minne captures is much more than the expressiveness of a face, of a gesture or of an attitude, by which the soul expresses itself in a way which is all the more communicative because it is more confidential.'

MOORE Albert Joseph (York 1841 — London 1893). Taught at first by his father, he later attended William Etty's classes at the Royal Academy in London. He travelled in the north of France and then stayed in Rome in 1862 and 1863 before returning to England where he showed his painting *The Four Seasons* at the Royal Academy. He met representatives of romantic classicism such as Alma Tadema, Poynter and Leighton, and became friends with Whistler. He was inspired by the aesthetic conceptions of the latter, adopted a motif of palmettes as his signature, and in 1860 became deeply involved in decorative art, where he created friezes, tapestry and stained glass.

In 1877 he showed at the Grosvenor Gallery and in 1884 at the Royal Watercolour Society of which he was an associate member. Around 1890 his health deteriorated and there was a noticeable change in his technique which, from being classic, became stamped with a symbolic and emotional character.

MOREAU Gustave (Paris 1826 — Paris 1908). Son of a Paris architect, Gustave Moreau revealed at a very early age his gifts for drawing and painting. He was encouraged by his parents and went to the School of Fine Arts in 1846; there he joined the studio of François Picot who taught him the basics of the craft. However, he failed in the Prix de Rome and left Picot's studio. He admired Delacroix whose style is visible in his early paintings such as *La Pietà*, shown in the Salon of 1852. He became friendly with Chassériau and worked according to his suggestions: an influence that lasted until the death of the latter in 1856. Together with Puvis de Chavannes, he was Chassériau's spiritual heir. Like Delacroix he loved the female body and had a taste for rich ornaments and accessories. On October 10, 1856, Delacroix noted in his diary: 'Funeral procession of poor Chassériau. Met

GEORGE ROUAULT *Portrait of Gustave Moreau*

Dauzats, Diaz and Moreau, the young painter there. I rather like him.'

Moreau, who was then about thirty, went to Italy for two years. He brought back several hundred copies of the Renaissance old masters. He also did pastels and watercolours which were reminiscent of Corot. During this period he met Bonnat, Elie Delaunay and the young Degas whom he helped with his early studies. The romantically inspired style which he adopted, and which was to be his from then on, became congealed and hieratic, excluding all movement and action.

1864 marked a decisive turn in the career of Gustave Moreau. He showed *Oedipus and the Sphinx* at the Salon; the painting aroused numerous reactions, and in any case no critic could have remained indifferent to it. It was symbolic and allegoric, and it was the true start of Moreau's

GUSTAVE MOREAU *The Voice*

art. Henceforth he took the subjects of his paintings from mythology or the Bible, giving preference to female characters and lending them the attitudes and spiritual outlook that went with his idea of Eternal Woman; she was a mythical woman, unreal, beautiful with a graceful figure,

GUSTAVE MOREAU *Fairy with griffins*

He devoted himself to watercolour as well: these sketches, inspired principally by the fables of la Fontaine, had a great freedom of expression, a great spontaneity, and charm us by their fluidity and an ingenuous grace which is not found in his overworked paintings.

Gustave Moreau lived alone and remained apart from the general public, communicating only with a refined elite who were capable of appreciating his mythological or medieval Symbolism, where the heroines were Salomes and Galateas in provocative attitudes, or ambiguous young girls caressing unicorns. These legendary characters had been sung about by the Parnassian and Symbolist poets, from Théodore de Banville and Jose-Maria de Heredia to Jean Lorrain and Albert Samain, from Henri de Regnier and Huysmans to Jules Laforgue and Milosz. He was the favourite of the drawing-rooms of the Faubourg Saint-Germain, where Robert de Montesquiou and Oscar Wilde sang his praises, while Marcel Proust called him to mind when he included the painter Elstir in his work *A la recherche du temps perdu*.

Something of a misanthropist, he refused to exhibit his pictures or even allow them to be reproduced, and only sold them with reluctance;

GUSTAVE MOREAU *The Angels of Sodom*

and laden with jewels. She was named Salome, Helen of Troy, Leda, Pasiphae, Galatea, Cleopatra or Dalida, incarnating in turn the *femme fatale* who had decided the destiny of a man, or the animal woman who had seduced him. She appeared as a phantom, clothed in sumptuous apparel enriched with precious stones. Moreau remained unmarried and his mother, who lived until 1894, was the idol of his thoughts and his only confidante. This could perhaps explain the immense place which woman holds in his work.

In 1869, *Prometheus* and *Europa*, which he had sent to the Salon, were strongly criticized, and he gave up exhibiting until 1876. He then showed again at the Salon with *Salome* and *The Apparition*. 1880 marked his last exhibition with *Helen under the walls of Troy* where the woman appears as an object of depravity, seduced by war and death, and *Galatea* where, as an object of lust, she is contemplated in vain by the triple eye of the Cyclops.

Although he withdrew from the Salon, Moreau worked with no less ardour; cloistered in his studio he went back to enormous allegorical compositions like *The Suitors* and *The daughters of Thespis*, which he enriched with magnificent details.

GUSTAVE MOREAU *The Unicorns.*

'I love my art so much' he said, 'that I am only happy when I do it for myself.' He was elected to the Academy of Fine Arts in 1888, and accepted in 1892, at the entreaty of his friend Elie Delaunay, to succeed him as professor and director of the studio at the School of Fine Arts. His teaching was exemplary if one judges it by the memories of Rouault, his favourite pupil, and the letters of Evenepoel.

In the first half of the twentieth century, the work of Gustave Moreau fell into oblivion; it took André Breton and the Surrealists to rediscover it. He was only recognized for one good quality — that of having formed some of the masters of the younger generations: Rouault, Matisse, Marquet, Manguin and Camoin. It is true that he knew how to develop their characters, and, without influencing them by his own work, to guide them towards the great painters of the past. 'The great quality of Moreau' wrote Matisse, 'was that he thought of the spirit of a young pupil as having to undergo continual development during his whole life, and did not push him to fulfil the different scholastic tests which, even when the artist has succeeded in the biggest competitions, leave him at around thirty with a warped mind...' Let it not be forgotten that it was by discovering *Oedipus and the Sphinx* that Odilon Redon became conscious of his vocation and that his first paintings were inspired by those of Moreau.

On his death he left to the state his large house with his studio, which comprised nearly twelve hundred paintings and watercolours and more than ten thousand drawings. As he sold very little in his lifetime, it is possible for us to admire his almost complete work in this museum and to appreciate it in all the excess of an art which never ceased to aspire to the greatest spiritual heights.

Gustave Moreau can be thought of as the Symbolist painter par excellence. But, what attracts us to him more than the precious gloss of his materials, more than his refinements as a colourist and his esoteric intentions, is the technical studies which gave birth to the abstract sketches which foreshadow Abstract Art.

MORRIS William (Walthamstow 1834 — Kelmscott Manor 1896). William Morris was a painter and designer, a writer and a poet. He was convinced that a Golden Age would soon come, in which the directors of industry would be replaced by artists who would bring happiness and a love of beauty to all the workers. He lived according to his theories and tried, by his diverse activities, to promote and apply them.

Born into a well-to-do family, as a young man he led the life of a dilettante. Very soon he proclaimed that industrial civilization brought ugliness. He was the first to react to safeguard the

quality of the environment, and to ameliorate the boundaries of the daily life of the workers, crowded into their dismal and unhealthy lodgings, which Taine compared to penitentiaries worthy of the depths of Hell.

He thought of the machine and industrial production as a calamity, and he left London to live in the country. Excited by the paintings of Burne-Jones, his friend at Oxford, he left his architectural studies for painting. Attracted by the legend of Isolde, he painted her and married the model who had brought her to life in his eyes. With Philip Webb he built his house on the outskirts of London, The Red House. It was a red brick house, built according to the conception of organic unity, the plan being conditioned by the practical disposition of the rooms which determined the structure of the façade. Morris designed the furniture and the usual objects, but he entrusted the interior decoration to painter friends of his.

It was the first stepping-stone on the road to Art Nouveau. The second was marked by the

.G.F. WATTS *Portrait of William Morris*

creation in London in 1861 of the firm Morris Marshall, Faulkner and Co. In this shop it was possible to find furniture and ceramics as well as stained glass windows, furnishing fabrics and wallpaper. The purpose of the exercise was to put the public in contact with utilitarian works of art. Rossetti and Burne-Jones were involved in this enterprise, and other artists, inspired by the

WILLIAM MORRIS *Queen Guinevere*. 1864

his patron, Count Khuen Belassi. In 1887 he went to the Académie Julian and contributed illustrations to *Le Figaro illustré* and other journals.

1894 marked the turning-point in his career with the commission from Sarah Bernhardt for the poster for the play *Vismonda* by Victorien

ALFONS MARIA MUCHA *Slavia*. 1908

ommunity spirit, joined them, including Walter Crane, Mackmurdo and Charles Annesley Voysey. They established in this way the prestige of craftsmanship and accepted that the artist should participate in the framework of social life.

Morris was not content with the minor arts connected with the interior furnishing of a house; he also revived the graphic arts. He designed new printing characters, the Golden Type, and produced more attractive books with flowered margins full of interlaced arabesques and creepers which were similar to the illuminated manuscripts of the Middle Ages. He set down his principles in one of his works, *The Decorative Arts and their Relationship with Modern Life*. By word and by pen he never stopped preaching his subversive ideas, going as far as saying that 'it was necessary to make a bonfire with what circulates between the hands of the wealthy.'

MUCHA Alfons Maria (Ivancice, Moravia 1860 — Prague 1939). The original ambition of this Czech artist was to be an actor or a musician. In order to get into the world of the theatre, at twenty-seven he painted the decorations for the Theater am Ring in Vienna. He completed his artistic studies at the Academy of Art in Munich with the help of

Sardou, in which she had the leading part. For the first time the typically Art Nouveau style of Mucha established itself and was very successful. The actress, from then onward, charged him with the execution of the posters for all the plays in which she acted, until *L'Aiglon*. He also designed to order plans for stained glass windows, decorative panels, jewellery and clothes.

111

He was very interested in spiritual phenomena and transformed his studio into a veritable 'profane chapel' where he received the experts of esoteric Symbolism, currently fashionable. Maeterlinck and Huysmans were numbered among his friends. He also visited a hypnotist, Albert de Rochas, who explained the phenomena of parapsychology to him.

He became the most fashionable poster painter in the whole world, without achieving the success to which he had aspired as a painter. He went to the United States in 1904, where, after a difficult start, he received commissions for decorative projects. In 1911 he went back to his own country where he celebrated, in a series of tableaux, the epic Slav poems. But although he was a painter of esteem, Mucha is principally known for the particular impetus which he gave to Symbolist graphic art.

MUNCH Edvard (Loîten, Norway 1863 — Ekely, near Oslo 1944). Munch, whose father was a doctor, was born into a bourgeois Norwegian family which included pastors, officers and professors. Illness and death darkened his childhood and his adolescence. He was only five when his mother died of tuberculosis, and fourteen when his sister Sophie, who was a year older than he, was carried off in her turn by the same illness

His father, attentive to the education of his fiv children, was troubled by financial difficultie which were not designed to brighten up the famil life. Edvard wrote later: '...illness, madness an death are the black angels who watched over m cradle and who have accompanied me throughou my life.' The madness to which he referred wa

EDVARD MUNCH *Self-portrait*. 1895

EDVARD MUNCH *Eros and Psyche*. 1907

the mystic crises through which his father passed when he spent entire days in prayer in his room.

After a year of studies at the technical colleg in Oslo — his father had planned a career i engineering for him — he was passionatel determined to paint, and abandoned his classes i order to enrol at the School of Arts and Crafts. I 1885 the artist Thaulow, one of the first to hav recognized his talent, gave him the means t spend three weeks in Paris. There he had th wonderful experience of seeing the Impres sionists' pictures which altered the evolution of hi studies and lightened his palette. On his return he painted *The sick child*, which was a poetic an concise evocation of his sister Sophie in a chro matic atmosphere which was entirely Impres sionist. In 1889, he showed at Oslo for the firs time, bringing together one hundred and te works where his austere nature showed in th gravity of the countenances, and in the uneas atmosphere which surrounded them. After thi exhibition the government awarded him a trave scholarship and he spent three years in Paris. H stayed for four months in Bonnat's studio, an discovered Manet, Gauguin, Seurat and the Nabis He was influenced by pointillism and some of hi

OVARD MUNCH *Madonna.* 1894

EDVARD MUNCH *Separation*. 1893.

pictures were painted using this technique. However, he soon gave it up because how to paint was not as important as what to paint: 'It must be living beings, who breathe, who feel, suffer and love. I will paint a series of such pictures; men will understand their sacred nature and in looking at them will discover themselves, as in church.' He wandered across Europe: Italy, and Berlin where he met poets and writers. He associated with Strindberg, whose portrait he painted, and with Ducha, a Norwegian girl who was the inspiration for many of his pictures including *Jealousy*. In 1892 he held an exhibition in Berlin which provoked such a scandal that it had to be closed, but it was probably the origin of the Berlin Secession. He became a member of that movement, and completed his famous *Frieze of life*, the principal theme of which was love and death.

He remained in Germany until 1908, which did not prevent him from visiting Paris or spending the summer in Norway. His 1896 visit to Paris was very important, since he met Gauguin, Emile Bernard and Maurice Denis there, as well as some of the Symbolist poets such as Mallarmé. He then learned to etch and to engrave on wood and stone

In full command of his style, an expressionist Symbolism, using forms simplified in the extreme with his bloodless faces and their hallucinated expressions, he painted and then engraved *The Cry*, which is the face of a phantom rising out of a landscape of sinuous lines and a sky broken by a tempest of colours. The following year, in 1896, his typically Art Nouveau style reappeared in *Anguish*, with its pallid faces reflecting their fear of death.

This fear of death went hand in hand with the mistrust of Woman: she is in turn harpy, vampire or immodest madonna with her equivocal puberty which is not offered to covetous desires. Speaking of *The Kiss* Strindberg wrote in *La Revue Blanche*: '...the fusion of two beings where the smaller seems to be on the point of devouring the larger, following the custom of vermin, microbes, vampires and women.' In 1908 Munch fell prey to nervous depression, provoked by his emotional conflicts, the obsessions of which were reflected in his art, and his abuse of alcohol. He was cared for in a neurological clinic in Copenhagen where he remained for seven or eight months; while he was there he worked on his portraits and a story, *Alpha and Omega* which he illustrated with lithographs.

Although he came out cured, it seemed that a new spirit animated his artistic creations. It showed in his work as an increase in violence and discordance, while appeasement and serenity, which he had found as a man, were completely lacking in it.

He bought a property on the Oslo fjord so that he could do more work there at leisure. In 1910 he was commissioned to decorate the banqueting hall at Oslo University. His compositions made a new *Frieze of life*, with the sun, the human mountain, the seekers etc. To search in it for the Munch of 1892 would be in vain.

He became the pride of his country, was invested with honours, and Norway devoted large exhibitions to his work.

The influence of Munch on the Germanic countries is considerable, more by the actual essence of his work than by his realization of it, for he was Symbolist in spirit but a precursor of Expressionism in style. The feeling of despair, anguish and impotence to 'change life' which characterized his work was not experienced by the painters of the Brücke nor by those of the Blaue Reiter, but his way of expressing it and of making it appear in his canvases belonged to the Expressionists.

On the other hand, it is logical to think of him as a Symbolist painter, because it is truly to this movement that he belongs, by virtue of the influences he sustained in France before going to Germany, and the very essence of his inspiration. Everything in the art of Munch is symbolic or allegorical — love and the obsession with death were his two favourite themes, and Michael Hoog said very justly in his preface to the catalogue for the 1974 exhibition: 'For him, as for many of his contemporaries, painting could and must express something more than the carefree sunshine of the Impressionists, the bourgeois detachment of Manet and Stevens, the Maori escapism of Gauguin, the historic dream of Gustave Moreau or of Böcklin.' Moreau said: 'I do not believe in what I touch, nor in what I see. I only believe in that which I do not see, and only that which I feel.' Whilst agreeing with him in rejecting everything which might have the musty smell of trivial realism, Munch diverged from him in order to refuse to paint 'the gods with watch chains.' Munch was impervious to what might be called the wave of Wagnerian and troubadour Symbolism which was so powerful at that time. 'I do not paint what I see, but what I have seen' he said to Moreau. It is rather in Mallarmé, whom he knew and painted, in Verlaine whom he does not seem to have approached, and in Redon that one could find an analogous step. Moreau and Maeterlinck escaped. Munch did not escape — he drove himself mad in painting his hell, behind closed doors from whence he did not emerge.

ALPHONSE OSBERT *Self-portrait*

ALPHONSE OSBERT *Hymn to the sea.* 1893

ALPHONSE OSBERT *Classical evening*. 1908

OSBERT, Alphonse (Paris 1857 — Paris 1939).

He attended classes at the School of Fine Arts where he was a pupil of Lehmann, Cormon and Bonnat. He was originally influenced by Spanish art, and especially by Ribera. After 1887 his meeting with Puvis de Chavannes, Seon and Seurat altered his technique. He abandoned dark colours and was attracted by idealist subjects or female silhouettes, generally clothed in long white robes and standing still and silent in idyllic landscapes. They were sisters to the women sung about by the Symbolist poets, notably Stuart Merrill. 'Always the same glades, always the same sky, the same trees, the same colours, and always the same woman, endlessly started over again,' said Fagus à propos of the exhibition of this artist's work held in 1899.

He showed regularly at the Rose + Croix Salons, as well as abroad, in Germany and Belgium. He often visited the Nabis, and met Maurice Denis. At the time of his one man exhibition at Georges Petit Gallery, the critic Degron stated, speaking of *The Vision of St. Geneviève*, that it was a figuration of Faith: 'The white lambs group themselves around her, like a halo of innocence, like a veil of intrinsic chastity.'

PELLIZZA DA VOLPEDO Guiseppe (Volpedo

1869 — Volpedo 1907). Having commenced his studies at Bergamo and the Brera gallery in Milan in 1883, he continued them in Rome and then Florence, where he attended classes in literature

and history of art. He very soon abandoned the verist style of his first works for Divisionism. Influenced by Tolstoy, he took an interest in social problems while his paintings reflected mystic and religious resonances. At the Universal Exhibition of 1900 he showed his *Mirror of life*, which gave him an opportunity to go for a second time to France where he admired the paintings of the Impressionists and of Seurat. On returning to Italy he took up an allegorical Symbolism, harmonizing delicate tints which recalled those of Previati. The triptych, *Love of life*, is characteristic of this period. In a series of paintings he took the sun as his principal theme, and reclothed it in an emotional power which was leading towards abstraction. His later works are reminiscent of those by Balla and Boccioni.

Pellizza da Volpedo is considered as the greatest of the Italian Divisionists, but rather than developing his style to the extreme limits of Pointillism he preferred to come back to a new form of Impressionism.

PETROV-VODKIN Kosma Sergeyevitch (Chwalynsk-on-Volga 1878 — Leningrad 1939). He studied design and painting at the Stieglitz School in St. Petersburg, and then at the School of

KOSMA SERGEYEVICH PETROV-VODKIN *Self-portrait*. 1918

Painting, Sculpture and Architecture in Moscow from 1897 to 1905. He then went to Munich and London, and travelled in Italy. From 1906 to 1908 he worked in Paris and then went to North Africa, followed by a return to St. Petersburg where he taught at the Academy of Fine Arts from 1918 until 1933. He achieved real fame during his

second stay in France in 1924-25. Around 1920 he elaborated a *Theory of colour and volume* which dealt with the spherical perspective which he applied in his works. he was also the author of plays, novels and two autobiographical accounts: *Chlynowsk*, 1930 and *Euclid's space*, 1932.

In the early years of his artistic career he was influenced by some of the French Symbolists, in particular Puvis de Chavannes and Maurice Denis, and by Hodler. He then tried to express, according to the ideal of Puvis de Chavannes, the beauty of the human body, love, and the happiness of the serenity of the soul by painting, in his dream landscapes, pensive and reflective feminine figures. But his art moved gradually away from Symbolism and became Realist.

PREVIATI Gaetano (Ferrara 1852 — Lavagna 1920). He began his studies at Ferrara and

GAETANO PREVIATI *Paolo e Francesca.* c.1901

Florence, where he was a pupil of the Romantic painters. He then settled in Milan, where he was a regular visitor to the Brera gallery from 1877 to 1880. His illustrations for the tales of Edgar Allan Poe brought him into contact with European Symbolism, particularly that of Rops and Redon. He was open to new techniques and under the impulsion of Grubicy he took up Divisionism. In 1891, at the triennial exhibition of the Brera gallery, on the occasion of the first public manifestation of the Italian Divisionists, Previati showed his great Symbolist work, *Maternity*, which unleashed a violent controversy: enthusiasm from some, strong criticism from others. This brought him, however, an invitation to the Rose + Croix Salon of 1892 in Paris. The contacts which he had with the Parisian artistic milieu strengthened his mystico-Symbolist and decadent tendencies. But more than his compositions of a grandiloquent, allegorical and decorative Symbolism, such as those of the *salle onirique* painted for the Biennial Viennese exhibition of 1907, his less ambitious works express better his aspirations to subtleties of colour and light in a golden brightness which was his alone. Balla admired him, and those who subscribed to the Futurist manifestos recognized him as the champion of anti-naturalism and of the avant-garde.

PUVIS DE CHAVANNES Pierre (Lyons 1824 — Paris 1898). More than any other artist connected with Symbolist aestheticism, Puvis de Chavannes shows us by just how much this movement was more literary than pictorial. He refrained from becoming a Symbolist and yet he is more Symbolist than anyone else, since his great pictures are all inspired by symbols or by allegories. When he painted young girls by the sea, they were not the young girls of his era, they were of all time with their busts naked and the rest of their bodies draped in white material.

Puvis was an anti-Manet, a classic by temperament, who wanted to be the heir to the fresco painters who had decorated the walls of palaces and temples. With his clear colours, his stiff characters and his love of simplification, his painting was classical and timeless, as he wished it to be. If one compares his work to that of Gustave Moreau, one finds in the work of the latter the same stiff concept, and the same hieratic quality of the characters, but his crowded colours and the exuberance of his decor and accessories come from a completely different personality.

Puvis was in essence a painter decorator, he had a feeling for the monumental and his compositions are always of a noble and majestic arrangement which has no equal in the whole of French painting.

This concern with grandeur is present even in his pictures of small format, such as the one

RODIN *Pierre Puvis de Chavannes*. 1910

pictures and then attacked big compositions. He had already decorated the dining-room of his brother's house at le Brouchy in Sâone-et-Loire. In 1863 he painted allegories of Peace and War, of Work and Rest, of the foster-mother Picardy, which contributed to the ornamentation of the museum at Amiens. In 1866 he decorated the vestibule of the town house of Claude Vignon at Passy, and the palace of Longchamp at Marseilles. Then, after *Girls and Death*, *The Woodcutters* and *Summer*, he did two large paintings for the staircase of the town hall at Poitiers. They depicted *Charles Martel conqueror of the Saracens* and *Radegonde in the Convent of the Holy Cross*. 1874 to 1878 saw the first phase of the mural paintings of the Panthéon, which were devoted to *The Life of St. Geneviève*. In 1882 he painted the town house of the artist Bonnat, in 1884 the staircase at the Sorbonne, in 1887 the Lyons museum and in 1888 the museum at Rouen and the salon du Zodiaque at the Hôtel de Ville in Paris. In 1892 he decorated the

PIERRE PUVIS DE CHAVANNES *The sacred wood of the Arts and the Muses*. 1884-89

entitled *The Poor Fisherman* which makes us think of the Italian fresco painters of the Renaissance. Masaccio or Ghirlandaio come to mind on seeing the great composite decorations in the Sorbonne or the Panthéon.

The influence of Chassériau and a voyage to Italy in 1847 had more effect on the direction of his development than the teaching of the studios which he had visited, first that of Henri Scheffer and then those of Delacroix and Thomas Couture. In the Salon of 1850 he showed a *Pietà*, but he had to wait until 1859 to exhibit there again. He painted portraits, religious or biblical

staircase of the same building following the deco of the library of Boston, and completed th second phase of the mural paintings for th Panthéon which, like the first, were devoted to th life of St. Geneviève. All these large 'constructions did not prevent him from working on pictures c smaller size, of which the most famous is still *Th Poor Fisherman* which he showed in the Salon c 1881 and which, from the outset, scandalized an divided the critics. Albert Wolff, who had liked th compositions at the Panthéon, found the subjec banal and 'unworthy' of the artist; Huysmans wa 'irritated by this buffoonery of Biblical grandeur

RE PUVIS DE CHAVANNES *Girls by the sea shore*. 1879

PIERRE PUVIS DE CHAVANNES *The Dream.* 1883

Few paintings have ever been attacked with so much vehemence, while Camille Mauclair declared: 'It is the poem of the man of sorrows, the man of earliest time or of today. Never has the effective power of resolutely synthetic art been seen better than in this unusual picture, which has a sure pictorial charm but in face of which one entirely forgets the painting.'

In his easel paintings, as in his mural paintings, Puvis de Chavannes infringes the laws of perspective and sets ethereal figures in broad daylight. In his decorative paintings he has the problem of marrying colour to stone, and it is thus that the sky has an aspect of ivory or of the timeless golds which come from the style called 'Byzantine' (gold backgrounds, hieratic figures) adopted by Flandrin in the *Christian Panatheneans* and by Puvis in the Pantheon friezes.

He gradually gave up all chiaroscuro effects. His figures became ethereal and the opaqueness of his colours contributed to their dream-like quality. This warranted the reproach of having 'unhappily adopted a system of abridged execution and arbitrary colouring which removes all reality from the figures.' He did not try to show tactile values nor depth of volume, and he has been blamed for his disregard for detail.

He found historic scenes repulsive and his preference was for sacred themes which illustrated the value of faith, purity and solitude.

The painting of Puvis de Chavannes is, taken in its entirety, only a poetic dream which he followed during the whole of his career. And Gauguin said of him: 'Puvis will entitle a picture *Purity* and then to explain it he will paint a young virgin with a lily in her hand. A symbol like that can be understood. Gauguin under the title *Purity* will paint a landscape with clear water.' This was because Puvis de Chavannes very frequently used the allegory rather than the symbol as Gauguin saw it. But he used it with a dignity and a spiritual elevation which inspired respect and yet were not without a certain coldness in spite of the charm of the figures. Gauguin, whatever he might have said, was not insensitive to this, since he decorated his cabin in Tahiti with a reproduction of *Hope* of which Puvis had made two versions. In one, the young girl is clothed in a long white robe, and in the other she is naked. Painted in 1872, it is an allegory, because Puvis was alluding to the war of 1870. It was not particularly well received by the critics and Bertall wrote in *Le Grelot*: 'Hope by M. Puvis de Chavannes: She is so thin!...The fact is that she is a little lacking in patriotism.' And Castagnary: 'This puny little girl, holding a blade of grass in her hand, facing some childish little hills; what possible lift of the heart could this inspire in us? For a Hope she is certainly very lacking.'

Puvis was snarlingly criticized during the whole of his life, and indeed after his death. The great retrospective exhibition which was quite recently devoted to him at the Grand Palais before going to Ottawa, did nothing to resolve the dilemma: was he a lingerer, or was he an innovator? However, it is incontestable that insofar as his mural painting is concerned, he is the only one of our epoch who could possibly be compared to the great Italian fresco painters of the Gothic and pre-Renaissance periods. Inspired originally by Chassériau, and by Ingres, he equally followed the teachings of Delacroix and Couture, and despite the contradiction, he fulfilled himself in a quite distinctive way according to his own personal aesthetics.

RANSON Paul (Limoges 1861 — Paris 1909). At the time of his birth his father, Gabriel Ranson, was mayor of Limoges. A few days after his birth, his mother succumbed to an embolism, and his father, who was inconsolable, appealed to his in-laws to help him bring up this puny, sickly and capricious child. As he showed his talent for drawing at a very early age, he was able to get into the School of Fine Arts in Limoges, which he later left to go to the one in Paris. In 1888 he went to the Académie Julian where he met Sérusier. He was one of the first Nabis. Before he came of age he married a young girl of seventeen, who, like him, came from the bourgeoisie. She was quick-witted and cultivated, and she welcomed his friends gracefully. His studio, at 25 Boulevard du Montparnasse, became the 'temple' of the Nabis. It was the old town house in which Madame de Maintenon had brought up the children of Madame de Montespan. Ranson, who had neur-

PAUL RANSON *Pastoral scene*

PAUL SERUSIER *Portrait of Paul Ranson*. 1890

asthenic crises, was otherwise a joyous companion, and the 'temple' welcomed a noisy company. They set up a marionette theatre there, where they

PAUL RANSON *Two women beneath a flowering tree*, tapestry

acted farces written by Ranson devoted to the Abbé Prout. They drank, they laughed, they celebrated the betrothal of Maurice Denis, 'the Nabi of the beautiful icons' to Marthe Meurier, 'the pale young girl', and Paul Sérusier there painted the portrait of Maurice Denis in Nabi clothing. France Ranson, the 'light of the temple' was not admitted to the monthly dinners. It was with his friends that Paul Ranson exhibited at Le Barc in Boutteville (1892-1896) and then at Vollard (1897), the Salon des Indépendants in 1892 and from 1900 to 1903, the National Society of Fine Arts in 1895 and 1898. In 1906, a private exhibition at the Drouet gallery was prefaced by Charles Morice.

Following Aristide Maillol and Rippl-Ronai, the Nabis tried their hand at tapestry. Ranson composed a great number of patterns of which some were executed by his wife who did not use a tapestry frame, but a canvas which she embroidered with stitches in very thick wool. These compositions, of which the sinuous lines were taken up by Matisse at a later date, are full of boldness and subtlety, and very much in the Art Nouveau style which inspired, during the same period, Guimard's decorations for the entrances to the Métro. In 1908, Ranson founded the Academy which bears his name, which his wife directed after his death, and where his friends Denis, Bonnard, Maillol, Sérusier, Vallotton and van Rysselberghe all taught.

Ranson's Symbolism, nourished by reading Schuré and by a profound knowledge of oriental cultures and esoteric doctrines, was swept along by a lively imagination and the cult of the Arabian. He was still more 'Japanese Nabi' than his friend Bonnard.

REDON Odilon (Bordeaux 1840 — Paris 1916). A pupil of the watercolourist Stanislas Gorin in Bordeaux, then of Gérome in Paris, he returned to his native town where he followed the counsels of the botanist Clavaud and the engraver Bresdin. After 1870 he settled in Paris, used mainly charcoal, and then, following the advice of Fantin Latour, he used his 'blacks' for lithography. His first album *In the Dream* appeared in 1879 and was followed by isolated plates and other albums: *The Origins* (1883), *Night* (1886) and *Dreams* (1891). He also illustrated books such as *Les Fleurs du Mal* in 1890. His two exhibitions of 1881 and 1882 brought him to the notice of Mallarmé, Huysmans and Hennequin. He showed in the Salon des Indépendants of which he was a founder member in 1889, and at the eighth exhibition of the Impressionists and the Groupe des XX in Brussels. His success became unshakable and he showed at Durand-Ruel and Vollard next to artists such as Emile Bernard and the Nabis. He was invited to the Libre Esthétique in 1894, 1895 and 1897, to

ODILON REDON *Red thorns*

ODILON REDON *Astral head*

The Hague in 1894 and the Viennese Secesson in 1903.

Towards the end of his life the pessimism which had troubled him for a long time gave place to a great confidence in life and in joy. Colour took the place of his blacks, which for a long time had restricted his artistic world, especially in his pastels and his flower paintings.

Odilon Redon incarnated the dream in a pure state; the mystery was there behind the most reassuring appearances, the fantastic was always ready to give birth to the most normal reality. It was quite natural for him to transform reality into the imaginary: the plant becomes a face and the balloon an eye. The fantastic is not a theme, and not a myth; it establishes itself in its own right, and Redon declared: 'No one can take from me the merit of having given the illusion of life to my most unreal creations.' But the unreal in his work allies the fascination of the imaginary to the reassuring contact with life. His originality consists of giving human life to improbable beings according to the laws of probability. While Gustave Moreau remained prisoner of his mythological and Biblical heroes, Redon drew from his own inner life the images which translated the anxieties and the phantasms of his unconscious. The unusual, as far as he is concerned, always assumes an exceptional solemnity, and this is why it intrigues and unsettles us. A spider with a human face smiles at us in an ambiguous way, a severed head with closed eyes rests in a cup, a flower supports on its stalk the head of a child with melancholy eyes, there is another one right inside an eye which looks at us with intensity, while a marsh flower joins a Pierrot's head to the little bells of the lily of the valley. For Redon flowers lived, flowers had a soul, flowers suffered: have not certain botanists affirmed the same thing in their turn? It is as if nature is always watching us: Redon saw eyes everywhere — in the forest, in all the rooms of his memory, eyes which are wide open in spite of the poppy of sleep on the eyebrow.

The fantastic became for him the very expression of the inner life, and in the preface to the catalogue of the exhibition in July 1910, at the end of his life, the artist summarized his aesthetic doctrine in the following words: 'I speak to those who yield, quietly and without the assistance of sterile explanations, to the secret and mysterious laws of the sensibility of the heart.'

124

ɴ REDON *The silent Christ*

Redon never obeyed the call of his intellect: the image was born spontaneously from his unconscious, it was the materialization of a dream, of an inner vision. Bresdin, the master of his youth, put it into black and white as 'the reproduction of imaginary things.' Redon wrote about Bresdin in *A Soi-même*: 'Suggestive art can provide nothing without recourse to the mysterious game of the shadows.' It was in charcoal that Redon first found his way. He played with chiaroscuro, and he darkened the shadows to make the lighting effects stand out better. His first collection of engravings had a revealing title: *In the Dream*. It was in the dream, in the unconscious, that he continued to direct himself; even when he was content to represent a shell, the ambiguity of the colouring made it into an unusual object. Redon, by the homage he paid to Goya and to Edgar Allan Poe showed just how much he was still haunted by the fantastic. The cyclops which fixes us with its sad eye, the wall which opens on to a death's head, the crow which clutches at the window, the eye which, like a bizarre balloon, gazes into infinity, the mask which tolls the funeral bell, the actor with a domino over his shoulders, are questions loaded with meanings which reflect the oppressive anguish of his youth. If the later vision of Redon appears more serene and more luminous, it is no less constantly equivocal and enigmatic. A figure with its

ODILON REDON *Parsifal*. 1892

finger to its lips asking for silence, a Buddha meditating in a flowering garden, a red boat on an unusual sea, a Roger freeing Angelica in explosions of colour, all remind us that the world of Redon will never be the world of every day. Even his portraits, even his bunches of flowers hide

something unreal and uncertain.

To the end of his life he remained the painter of the fantastic and the imaginary. 'For that which is of me' he wrote, 'I believe I have made an expressive, suggestive, indeterminate art. Suggestive art is the radiation of various plastic elements which are combined and brought together with a view to stimulating reveries which will illuminate and exalt it, whilst encouraging thought.' He knew how to be this artist: 'The continual and always flexible centre of feeling, hypnotized by the wonders of a Nature he loves, which he studies,' and submitting 'the day to the day, the fatal rhythm of the pulses of the universal world which surrounds him', 'without renouncing his own adventure, his own unique, happy or magic case wherein destiny has placed him.'

In giving himself to the exploration of the unconscious, he prepared and predicted Surrealism, and he opened very wide the door to the monsters of the subconscious which Freud endeavoured to tame.

But, as René Huyghe said in *La Relève du réel*, the lesson of Redon was only very partially understood, as was that of Cézanne. And modern art, preferring to flee the real and to take refuge in the subsoil of the subjective, or in purely abstract combinations, is only the evidence of the disorder of a period swept adrift by the calamities it had produced. Redon wanted to return to the infinite riches of man in harmony with Nature, but passing it and pulling it towards an adventure which Man alone can conceive and pursue — perhaps for ever.'

Redon in fact has never really been understood. His world of silence and mystery, with its anxieties and hallucinations, its wonders and its ecstasies, opens to us doors of a parallel world — that of the unconscious.

He had to choose between Symbolism and Impressionism, and it must be remembered, in conclusion, that it was he who had been the strongest critic of the movement: 'I have refused to embark in the Impressionist boat because I found its ceiling too low.' He also said that in 'the palace of truth' the Impressionists had only seen 'the flue of the chimney.' He continued: 'Everything which passes, illumines or amplifies the object in the world of mystery, in the confusion of the irresolute and its delicious anxiety, is completely closed to them. They shield themselves against, and are frightened of everything which belongs to the symbol, all that our art allows of the unexpected the imprecise, the indefinable, and which gives it the aspect which remains enigma. True parasites of the object, they have cultivated art on the purely visual field, and have closed it, in some degree, to what might pass beyond it and be capable of putting light and spirituality into even humble efforts, even into black. I can feel a radiance which possesses the soul and which escapes all analysis.'

RIPPL-RONAI Jozsef (Kaposvar 1861 — Kaposvar 1927). After his pharmacological studies in Budapest, this son of a school teacher went to Munich in 1884 and was admitted to the Academy of Fine Arts where he worked until 1887. Having obtained a grant from the Hungarian government, he went to Paris. To start with he frequented the studio of the Hungarian painter Munkacsy, and the following year he met Lazarine Bourdrion, whom he married. He became a friend of Aristide Maillol and made the acquaintance of Vuillard and other Nabi painters. He took part in the Symbolist movement, and collaborated on *La Revue Blanche*. In 1889 he painted his first painting, *Woman with white-spotted dress*, in a style which was truly personal and very like that of Vuillard. His paintings, his pastels and his lithographs from this period clearly reflect the aes-

JOZSEF RIPPL-RONAI *Self-portrait*

JOZSEF RIPPL-RONAI *Girl with roses*, tapestry. 1898

thetics typical of Art Nouveau, with its cult of curved lines, delicate colour harmonies and its love of decoration. His coloured lithographs, collected by Bing, were accompanied by a text by the Belgian poet Rodenbach. In contrast to these stylized forms he devoted himself, during his 'black period', to very different studies, and then, when he returned to Hungary, he played a bigger part in realism, with his portraits as much as his landscapes, without abandoning the technique which was his own.

The Hungarian critics, who had been reticent at first about his Symbolist works, recognized his talent and he died loaded with honours.

RODIN Auguste (Paris 1840 — Meudon 1917). He was born into a modest family, and as soon as he could hold a pencil, his only desire was to draw. At sixteen he went to the School of Design in Paris where he had as his master an exceptional teacher, Lecocq de Boisbaudran, who was able to discern in him the gifts which were going to blossom. At the same time he joined Barye's class at the Museum, but he failed in the competition for the School of Fine Arts. To earn his living he worked as a decorator, and then went to the Sèvres factory where he met Carrier-Belleuse whose assistant he became. He went with him to Brussels where they worked together on the decorations for the Bourse. He also carved busts of his friends and exhibited the *Man with the broken nose*. 1875 saw him leave for Rome and Florence, where he discovered Donatello and Michelangelo. Later he told the sculptor Bourdelle: 'I was liberated from academicism by Michelangelo who, in teaching me (by observation) the rules which are diametrically opposed to those which I had been taught (Ingres school), has liberated me.'

In 1881, at the house of Madame Adam, who

127

F. Flameng *Portrait of Auguste Rodin.* 1881

held a political salon, he made the acquaintance of Léon Gambetta and other personalities who helped him to gain recognition for his talent. He received from the State a commission for a monumental door destined for the future Museum of Decorative Arts. He was inspired by what he remembered from reading Dante's *Inferno*, and he took from it the theme for the bas-reliefs for this 'Porte de l'Enfer', the great work of his life where his visionary power was let loose. The door absorbed his creative mind for twenty years, but it was only with difficulty that he integrated his sculptures with the architectural framework imposed on him, and he abandoned it unfinished.

This door interprets his love of life in all its forms; there he mixed the sensuality of the flesh with the most frantic idealism; it symbolized all his dreams and all his hopes and marked clearly the new spirit of which he was going to be one of the

Auguste Rodin *The Kiss.* 1886

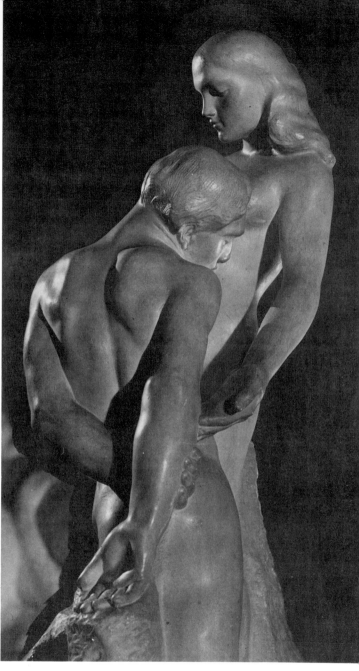

AUGUSTE RODIN *Thoughtfulness.* 1886
AUGUSTE RODIN *I am beautiful.* 1882

AUGUSTE RODIN *The eternal Idol.* 1889

ew spirit of which he was going to be one of the
ophets. 'Rodin has given free rein to his imagin-
ion: he mixes the God of the Bible with the gods
Greece; the heroes of Dante with the damned

women of Baudelaire. In truth, art alone is his
morality, his religion and his conception of
salvation' wrote Bernard Champigneulle in his
study of Rodin.

A series of sculptures carved in marble, all shown on a rock, are the symbols of the human being, as if torn from the earth, who tries in vain to escape from it: *Fugit amor, The eternal Idol, The Bacchantes, The Kiss,* and *I am beautiful.* Sometimes the head alone emerges from the unworked stone: *Thoughtfulness* is the best example of this. A face with a look lost in infinity, heavy with reflection and solitude, is very close to the *Silence* of Fernand Khnopff, where the figure seems to rise up from

Auguste Rodin in his studio in 1905

the table it rests on, nonchalantly leaning on its two hands. It is essentially Rodin's work more closely related to Symbolism which we are interested in. But let us not forget that he, too, was moved by the touching expression of Romanticism, by the concern for truth of Naturalism, by the fluidity and arabesques of Art Nouveau. In 1902 he met Rainer Maria Rilke who became his secretary in 1905. Having been subjected to the most severe criticisms during the length of his career, at the end of his life he knew success; he received important personalities in his studio, and at the height of his fame saved the Biron hotel, the future Rodin Museum, and installed his studio there. In his artistic testament he wrote: 'The artist sets a great example. he adores his métier: his most precious recompense is the joy of doing

something well...The world will only be happy when all men have the souls of artists, that is to say when all take pleasure in their work.'

Felicien Rops *Self-portrait*

ROPS Félicien (Namur 1833 — Essonnes 1898). At first a pupil at the Academy of Namur, Rops studied law at the University of Brussels, and at the same time frequented the studio of Saint-Luke where he met Artan, Charles De Groux and

Felicien Rops *Dancing death.* 1865-75

Dubois. He created, in 1856, *Uylenspiegel*, a satirical weekly paper where his gifts as a sketcher became apparent. It is possible to distinguish three periods in his artistic life. The first, which stretched from 1855 to 1860, was romantic. During these five years Rops engraved more than a hundred and ninety lithographs, which either appeared in *Uylenspiegel* or separately. These were his studies of bourgeois or peasant customs from the Walloon and Flemish countries, portraits of writers, artists or actresses.

Then from 1860 to 1870, he expressed himself in a Symbolist style which was influenced by his meetings with Baudelaire, Glatigny and Poulet-Malassis. Having completely abandoned lithography, he went to Paris in 1862 to perfect his etching. His first plates were still romantic, but his style changed rapidly and became Symbolist,

especially in his illustrations for *Le Vice suprême* by Péladan, and *Les Diaboliques* by Barbey d'Aurevilly. But it must not be forgotten that he was also a painter, influenced first by Daumier and then by Courbet. His figures are generally treated with a thick paste with warm tonalities. He also executed landscapes and seascapes.

ROSSETTI Dante Gabriel (London 1828 — Birchington-on-Sea 1882). Coming from a family of Italian origin — his father was a political refugee — Rossetti was, from his childhood, familiar with Italian literature and lulled to sleep by verses from *The Divine Comedy*, the importance of which was visible during the whole of his life. He was put down for King's College, London, when he was nine, and at nineteen he went to the Royal Academy. He became friends with Hunt and Millais, and in 1848 they founded the Pre-Raphaelite

ELICIEN ROPS *Pornocrats*. 1896

DANTE GABRIEL ROSSETTI *Self-portrait*. 1847

specially in those published by Poulet-Malassis. He illustrated the Symbolist poets, Baudelaire, Péladan and Barbey d'Aurevilly.

In 1872 he gave up Symbolism and turned towards Naturalism. He was still producing etchings, but soon became interested in soft varnish and aquatints.

Known principally for his engravings, his tinted drawings and his gouaches, Rops was above all the painter of the 'depraved', 'Satanic' woman, a representation which his contemporaries enjoyed,

Brotherhood. From 1845 to 1848 he only did two oil paintings, in a Pre-Raphaelite style which was like that of Hunt and Millais. However, he devoted most of his time to water-colours, which were more spontaneous and more in line with his instinct and his temperament both far removed from realistic representation, and to drawing where he gave free rein to his imagination, without the constraints of the period, to illustrate Dante, Shakespeare, Browning and the epic of King Arthur by Sir Thomas Malory.

In 1850 he met his muse, Elizabeth Siddal, and she became his wife in 1860. He then went back to oil painting and began the gallery of touching

DANTE GABRIEL ROSSETTI *Astarte Syriaca*. 18

feminine figures who were ardent and passionate, or dreamy and nostalgic, in which Elizabeth could always be seen. In 1862 she committed suicide. *Beata Beatrix* (1864) was homage to his beloved spouse, an idealized dream figure, whose memory dwelt in him until his death. His physical and mental health was affected by her disappearance.

DANTE GABRIEL ROSSETTI *Beata Beatrix*. 1863

He became paranoic and his work reflected his psychic state. He painted less and devoted himself to a literary activity (poems and translations) which lasted until his death.

SCHWABE Carlos (Hamburg-Altona 1866 — Avon, Seine-et-Marne 1929). Born in Germany, raised in Switzerland, he became a Swiss national in 1888. Having attended courses at the School of Industrial Art in Geneva, he went to France, where he settled first in Paris and then at Barbizon. In 1891 he showed at the Salons of the National Society of Fine Arts, and also at the Rose + Croix Salons. He designed the poster for the first of these Salons which took place at Durand-Ruel's in 1892. He was the strangest of the Symbolist engravers, and rivalled Mucha as far

Art Nouveau illustrations were concerned. At the beginning he designed wallpapers using stylized motifs of flowers with sinuous lines. From this period he retained a particular facility for depicting plants, in his own Symbolist style, in both his oil paintings and watercolours as well as his book illustrations.

His watercolours for *L'Evangile de l'enfance* by Catulle Mendès were shown at the first Rose +

CARLOS SCHWABE *Spleen and Ideal*. 1896

Croix Salon, and those for *Le Rêve* by Zola at the National Society of Fine Arts. Those for *Les Fleurs du Mal* by Baudelaire went to the National Society in 1897, and the Universal Exhibition in 1900. He also illustrated poems by Albert Samain and Maeterlinck. His drawing was of a delicate and painstaking precision, and has often been compared

compared to that of Dürer, Mantegna or Botticelli, although the influence of the Pre-Raphaelites cannot be overlooked. 'His decorative work' wrote Philippe Jullian 'was like a piece of embroidery; he hemmed it with an appropriate motif and here and there covered the whole page with a random design.

SEGANTINI Giovanni (Arco, Trentino 1858 — Schafberg 1899). The years of Segantini's youth were difficult, full of misery and suffering. He went to the Brera Academy in Milan. A powerful realism marked his first works which were inspired by scenes of peasants and mountain people. In 1866 he left his original style in order to adopt the neo-Impressionist technique which, coupled with a Symbolist inspiration, gave birth to pictures full of sensitivity and emotion in which he tried to mix 'the ideal of nature with the symbols of the spirit which our hearts teach us.' He tried to realize a synthesis between nature and the ideal, as is hown by his Symbolist canvases *The Angel of Life* (1894) and *Amor of the Fountain of Life* (1896). Speaking of the latter composition in a letter to a friend, Segantini wrote: 'This represents the joyous and

GIOVANNI SEGANTINI *Self-portrait*. 1895

carefree love of woman and the thoughtful love of man drawn together by the natural elan of youth and Spring. The path they are walking

GIOVANNI SEGANTINI *Amor at the Fountain of Life*. 1896

along is narrow and flanked by rhododendrons in flower and they are clothed in white (pictorial representation of lilies).' After 1894 he met painters from other European countries; these contacts enriched his inspiration. He retired to Switzerland with his family where he read and studied a great deal, especially Tolstoy, D'Annunzio, Maeterlinck, Goethe and Nietzsche who were his favourite authors. In 1898 he published an article in the review *Ver Sacrum* in which he explained how art betrayed the ideal of the Pre-Raphaelites, the social ideas of William Morris, and the Wagnerian aesthetics. His last large work, *Triptych of nature*, evidence of his great mystic pantheism, is the testament he left us.

SEON Alexandre (Chazelles-sur-Lyon 1888 — Paris 1917). He began his artistic studies at the School of Fine Arts in Lyons and finished them in Paris in Lehmann's studio. In 1881 he became a pupil of Puvis de Chavannes, who took him on as a collaborator for about ten years. He was notable for his share in the decoration of the Panthéon. He showed in the Salon of the National Society of Fine Arts and at that of the French artists. He also

GIOVANNI SEGANTINI *The wicked mother.* 1894

figured in group exhibitions with the Impression-
sts and the Symbolists at Le Barc de Boutteville,
and at different Salons of the Rose + Croix of
which he was a founder together with Péladan and
Count de la Rochefoucauld. A friend of Osbert
and of Seurat, he explained his theories on Symbolist art, which were commented on by Alphonse
Germain in *La Plume*: 'Séon is the first to expound
theoretically on the reaction against the neo-realist
tendendies towards the cult of the Beautiful...He
works towards an idealist renaissance: to embody
in lines a symbol in an amplified form, and to
homogenize this symbol by means of colour.' Séon
illustrated books by Péladan, Mazel, and Haurau-
court. Preoccupied with social questions, he was
often labelled as an 'idealist-ideaist' painter. He
remained faithful to the aestheticism of Puvis de
Chavannes and, although his drawing was always

ALEXANDRE SEON *The lament of Orpheus*. 1896

of great purity and absolute exactitude, he used soft colour tones where mauve, grey and blue harmonized.

SERUSIER Paul (Paris 1864 — Morlaix 1927). Coming from a family from the French Flanders, Paul Sérusier, whilst following his secondary studies, showed a pronounced liking for the arts, philosophy and oriental languages. His father, director of the Houbigant perfumery, had planned a commercial career for him, and placed him in the Marion papermill in the Rue Joubert. He ended, thanks to the entreaties of his mother and the intervention of his family doctor, by obtaining permission to follow his vacation. He went to the Academie Julian and in 1888 he was put in charge of the student fund by the little studios which were frequented by Maurice Denis, Ranson and Bonnard. In the Salon of 1888 he showed a canvas *The workshop of a Breton weaver* which achieved an honourable mention, without doubt because it was conventional. His family was reassured. He then went to Pont-Aven and met Gauguin who initiated him into his new technique. He brought back the decorated lid of a cigar-box, a 'talisman' which he showed to his dearest friends who were Ranson, Ibels, Maurice Denis, Bonnard, René Piot, Roussel and Vuillard. Sérusier had the idea of founding a

brotherhood, that of the Nabis, the prophets of a pictorial evangelism (in Hebrew prophets are *nebiim*), which would meet every month for a ritual dinner in a little café in the Passage Brady where Ambroise Vollard was an invited guest, and of which he speaks in his *Souvenirs*. Sérusier thought

ODILON REDON *Portrait of Paul Sérusier*. 1903

of Gauguin as his master. He went to rejoin him at Le Pouldu during the summer of 1889, and there discovered other painters including Charles Filiger and the Dutch Meyer de Haan.

In 1890, besides their monthly dinners, the Nabis gathered every Saturday in 'the temple' which was none other than Paul Ranson's studio at 25 Boulevard du Montparnasse. On the walls could be seen decorations by Maurice Denis, Bonnard, Roussel and Vuillard. Georges Lacombe and the musicians Pierre Hermant and Claude Terrasse joined the original Nabis. Through Paul Fort and Lugné-Poe they expanded into the world

where he stayed more and more often, and established himself completely in 1912. He made many journeys from there outside France; he went to Italy in 1895 and with Denis to Germany in 1904, where he discovered the art of the primitive Germans.

He went to Prague and to the Benedictine monastery of Beuron where Verkade had retired to devote himself to various works of sacred art. It is known that the school of sacred art at Beuron, inspired by P. Desiderius and Didier Lenz, had a close relationship with a real influence on the art of the Nabis, and particularly on that of Sérusier.

PAUL SERUSIER *The vision by the stream.* 1897

of the theatre, and held their meetings in the Libre Théâtre. Sérusier painted the canvas background for *Ubu Roi* by Alfred Jarry, as well as the decorations for Lugné-Poe whom he also helped with the staging. He remained faithful to Brittany and returned to Pont-Aven, where in 1891 he met the Dutchman Verkade and the Dane, Ballin. He then went to Huelgoat and Chateauneuf-du-Faou

Charles Chasse wrote: 'The sequel to Sérusier's career has shown that his main artistic inspiration was to realize a balance between his soul and the universe, and thus to give a mathematical base to his ideal. In the same way he wanted to give a human and religious base to mathematics itself.

'The synthesis' explained Sérusier, 'consists of gathering all forms back into the little number of forms that we are capable of envisaging: straight lines, some angles, arcs of circles and of ellipses; if we depart from these we lose ourselves in the ocean of varieties.'

near another who talks; ferny grottoes; mosses and waterfalls in rocks...'

SPILLIAERT Léon (Ostend 1881 — Brussels 1946). He taught himself to draw when still young and in an independent and uneasy way devoted himself to his art in solitude. 'I have always been frightened, I have never dared' he confided to a friend. 'My life has passed alone and sadly, with a great coldness all around me.' His work, which was very diverse, remained unknown for a long time, and yet Francine Legrand wrote: 'Spilliaert was, with Ensor, one of the essential hinges between Symbolism and Expressionism. He was also one of the precursors of Surrealism in Belgium.

PAUL SERUSIER *The talisman*. 1888

LEON SPILLIAERT *Self-portrait in the mirror*. 1908

Sérusier, who in his early days had been a disciple of Swedenborg and of Schuré, became an adept at the aesthetics of the 'sacred numbers' which inspired his own theory of relationships and harmony between form and colour. He taught it at the Ranson Academy from 1908 to 1912 and summarized it in the *ABC of Painting* (1921). M.A. Leblond, at the time of the exhibition devoted to the works of Sérusier at Druet's gallery in 1919 said of him: 'Sérusier seems to me like the water-diviner of Breton mystery; his soul of a pilgrim in the wilderness quivers wherever the humid and penetrating mist of the Celtic legend gushes forth; undergrowth which conceals all colours, and the smell of mushrooms; tops of trees rising above the "deep valley"; autumn on the foliage in the hollow of the grasslands; the haze; a woman who spins

Very much influenced by his friend Verhaeren he found himself mixing quite naturally with the literary and pictorial movement of the period. He met Stefan Zweig and Franz Hellens. In Paris he made the acquaintance of the works of Van Gogh Gauguin and Picasso, and then, after a period in Brussels from 1917 to 1921, he returned to Ostend, and then settled permanently in Brussels in 1935. He was a member of numerous artistic circles, and did not really adhere to any particular group. His work is dominated by two themes: the sea and solitude. He used mostly watercolour pastel, gouache and coloured crayons, and mixed the various techniques in his small compositions.

TRATHMANN Carl (Düsseldorf 1866 — Munich 1939). Having studied at the Academy of Fine Arts in Düsseldorf from 1882 to 1886 and the School of Fine Arts in Weimar until 1889, Trathmann went to Munich where he collaborated as illustrator on *Fliegende Blätter* and *Jugend*, and then partly turned to the decorative arts. He took the Symbolists' favourite themes for his compositions: the *femme fatale*, sin, lust and erotic subjects in general. He was influenced by the Byzantine mosaics and by the affected painters of the Low Countries, and used a precise technique, iridescent colours enriched with embroidery, with precious stones, pearls and gold leaf, and an abundance of decoration characteristic of his style.

STUCK Franz von (Tettenweiss, Bavaria 1863 — Munich 1928). Having studied at the School of Plastic Arts in Munich between 1881 and 1884, Stuck frequented the Academy of Lidenschmidt and of Bruno Piglheim. He familiarized himself with the work of the Pre-Raphaelites and of Fernand Khnopff, who was already recognized as a Symbolist artist.

He showed himself at first to be a very good illustrator by his work for reviews such as *Fliegende Blätter* and *Allegorien und Embleme*. He then concentrated on painting, and approached Symbolist themes. Under the influence of Dietz, Thoma, Böcklin and Lenbach he painted a number of male and female fauns. After that it was his memories of the technique of von Marées and Hildebrandt which guided his inspiration in paintings which were pure Jugendstil.

In 1892 he founded with Uhde and Trübner the Munich Secession which was a manifestation of the breach with official academic societies. At the beginning it was a purely pictorial phenomenon, but later on the decorative and graphic arts allied themselves to it, as did architecture. The movement reached its peak in 1896 with the creation of the review *Jugend*, and acquired its true personality and its complete independence.

In Munich, the formation of this new group had important consequences. It did not only

FRANZ VON STUCK *The Sphinx*. 1895

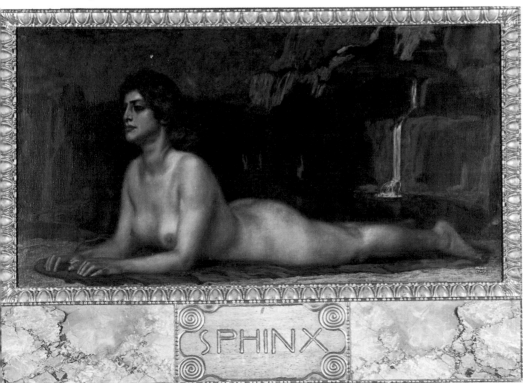

inspire artists, but it also reached a large public who was interested in the review and who brought its support to the International Exhibition in 1897. While the Viennese Secession was directed towards a decorative Symbolism, the one in Munich was more intense and was divided between two tendencies which were sometimes complementary and sometimes contradictory: Symbolism and Expressionism. Symbolism prevailed with Stuck, still influenced by Böcklin and Lenbach in his canvases such as *Fight between fauns.* 1889, *Fight between Amazons*, 1897, *War*, 1894, where a rider crushes dead bodies, or *The Sphinx*, 1895. He took

delight in a certain eroticism which is noticeable i his pictures where a woman abandons herself to snake; he took up this theme many times betwee 1889 and 1912, giving it different titles: *Sin, Vic Sensuality*. The woman, who is sensual, attractiv and deadly, offers herself to the seducer wh envelops her in his coils. Sometimes also, as i *Innocence*, 1889, Stuck took his inspiration fror Burne-Jones and Whistler to represent a youn girl holding a lily. But one can see the awakenin sensuality in her eyes and Bierbaum wrote: 'I shu my eyes, and my soul saw the same picture, th same pure look, so lovely and so full of love, bu

FRANZ VON STUCK *Sin.* 1890-91

instead of a spray of lilies a sleeping child lay in her arms. Maternal innocence!...That day the world seemed beautiful to me.'

Although he played a major role in the spreading of Jugendstil, Franz von Stuck had an even greater influence on the younger generation of painters since he was the master of Kandinsky, of Albers and of Paul Klee at the Academy of Munich where he taught from 1895. In 1898 the Villa Stuck was completed; there he showed himself as painter, sculptor, decorator and architect at the same time. This house was the model of a *cadre de vie*, which made him the equal of the Renaissance artists and the sacred 'prince of painters'. This famous Greek villa heralded the approach of rectilinear Art Nouveau which was dear to the Viennese, and of which the masterpiece was the Stoclet palace in Brussels which was decorated by Klimt.

Franz von Stuck was given a title in 1906.

THOMA Hans (Bernau, Bade 1839 — Karlsruhe 1920). Having started as a lithographer, Hans Thoma went back to Bernau where he painted landscapes inspired by the surrounding countryside. He met Johann Wilhelm Schirmer, director of the School of Fine Arts in Karlsruhe, who encouraged him to continue in this course, and became his pupil. In 1868, he arrived in Paris together with Scholderer who came from Frankfurt, and persevered with his technique which brought him closer to the French realists and above all, to Courbet. He returned to Germany where, in 1870, he met Böcklin in Munich; it was a meeting which gradually influenced the evolution of his studies. Imaginary subjects appeared henceforth in his art, but he was opposed to Böcklin who was tormented by Death, and interpreted nature in its most peaceful aspects. He had the soul of a dreamer and of a contemplator who took pleasure in limited horizons.

This aptitude for the contemplative life came from his early years spent in the forests which surrounded the village where he was born. He was the son of a miller, and he learned the rudiments of painting from a painter of clocks, the famous cuckoo-clocks of the Black Forest. From his earliest youth he showed an aptitude for art, and as he came from a modest family, he received an allowance from the Grand Duke of Baden which permitted him to pursue his studies.

Paris was not his only journey abroad. He also travelled in Italy, where he stayed for the first time in 1874. He returned there in 1880, 1886, 1892 and 1897, attracted by the Italian landscape and the art of a country which brought him new sources of inspiration. He then introduced the nude into his paintings as well as mythological scenes, which entitled him to figure among the Symbolist painters. In 1889 a large exhibition in Munich showed an important collection of his work. Having been almost unknown as an artist until then, his talent was finally recognized, and he took the place which was rightfully his: that of one of the most interesting masters of the German school of the second half of the nineteenth century.

THORN PRIKKER Johan (The Hague 1868 — Cologne 1932). Having studied at the Academy of Fine Arts in The Hague from 1883 to 1887, Thorn Prikker was attracted by Impressionism, and then by neo-Impressionism. He gradually moved away from this in order to devote himself to the study of the primitive Flemish painters which influenced him strongly. On the other hand, his acquaintance with the works of Gauguin together with his admiration for Maurice Denis and for his compatriot Jan Toorop, guided him from 1892 onwards towards Symbolism. The scenes he composed, usually religious in feeling, were inspired by a mystic sensibility of great purity. He collaborated on the review *Van Nu en Straks*, was in touch with the Groupe des XX, and became the friend of Henry van de Velde. In *The Bride*, his most famous picture, 'the first function of the schematism of the arabesque and its astonishing dynamism' wrote José Pierre, 'is to materialize the mystic union between the nun

JOHANN THORN PRIKKER *The Bride*. 1892

taking her vows and Christ crucified, by welding humanity on to both of them. The blossoming of the flowers, like flaming candles, is there to underline the tension of the feelings of "the bride of Christ" on an erotic scale, which should not astonish if one thinks, for example, of St. Theresa of Avila. And one cannot but admire the poetic expedient which transforms the nun's crown of orange blossom into a crown of thorns.'

This art, with its subtle arabesques, where outward appearances withdraw in order to give priority to the actual essence of things, was not very well received in the Low Countries where Thorn Prikker remained isolated and on the outside of his group of friends (which included H.P. Bremmer who bought many of his canvases for the collection of Madame Kröller-Müller). He stated precisely, in his correspondence with Henri Borel, the only literary man among his friends, the vision which he was pursuing in order to pin down, not the visual impression of the phenomena, but their essence, such as love, hate and faith.

In 1895 he decided to abandon Symbolist painting in order to put his art exclusively into the service of life. In 1904 he became professor of the Kunstgewerbeschule at Krefeld. Like Maurice Denis he turned more and more towards sacred art, and henceforth concentrated on mural compositions, stained glass windows and tapestries destined for church ornamentation.

TOOROP Jan (Poerworedjo 1858 — The Hague 1928). Originally from Java, Toorop was Dutch; he was affected by many diverse influences, but

G. LEMMEN *Portrait of Jan Toorop*. 1886

never lost his loyalty to the Indonesian art which had marked his youth, and which can be seen especially in the bas-reliefs of the Temple of Borobudur. He arrived in the Low Countries in

AN TOOROP *Trio with flowers*. 1885-86

872, and studied design in Delft and Amsterdam. Having obtained a grant to go to Brussels, he made contact with the Groupe des XX which in 894 became the Libre Esthétique. He became a member of it and met artists of the Symbolist trend which was then in vogue in Belgium: de Groux, Khnopff, Ensor, van Rysselberghe and Finch. In 1884, accompanied by the poet Emile Verhaeren, he made a journey to London. On his returned to France he met the Sâr Péladan and Redon both of whom had an influence on his work. He visited and admired the Parisian

JAN TOOROP *Aggressivity of Sleep*. 1898

museums with Ensor, and then discovered Italy. In 1886, in London, he met Whistler; he was charmed by the Pre-Raphaelites and the theories of William Morris on 'art and socialism'. He discovered Seurat and painted for a time in the pointillist manner. His painting, inspired by theosophic, social and religious ideas in turn (he became a Catholic in 1905) was prolific and varied. His Symbolism from 1890 onwards became more personal, and of an astonishing virtuosity which he put to the service of Mannerism and literary reminiscences such as those of Maeterlinck, Péladan and the Rose + Croix. His mystic feelings were expressed through unreal characters laden with magic, sacred or profane symbols which arose from a world of arabesques taken from Art Nouveau, a world of phantoms where fantasy reigned.

TRACHSEL Albert (Nidiau, Switzerland 1863 — Geneva 1929). A faithful fellow-student of Hodler, he began his architectural studies in Geneva, followed by Zurich and Paris. In 1897 he published, in issues of the *Mercure de France*, a collection of drawings entitled *Les Fêtes réelees* which he showed the same year at the Rose + Croix

Salon. He was a pupil of Menn at the Fine Arts School in Geneva, and became friendly with Hodler and the sculptor Vibert. He concentrated on painting landscapes of his native country which he represented in a dreamlike atmosphere that entitled him to be counted among the Symbolist artists. At the same time he was purusing his architectural studies and wrote poems and articles on art criticism.

VALLOTTON Félix (Lausanne 1865 — Paris 1925). The Vallottons came from an old and well known family in Vallorbe, in the canton of Vaud. Félix went to the cantonal college in Lausanne in 1875. He showed a talent for drawing while still young, went to evening classes under the direction of the Vaudois painter Guignard and, in 1882 went to Paris and was accepted into the Academie Julian. He preferred to visit the Louvre, where he copied Antonello da Messina, Vinci and Dürer to the classical teaching of Lefebvre, Boulanger and Bouguereau. In order to earn a living he did fashion designs and collaborated on such journals and reviews as *Le Rire*, *L'Assiette au Beurre* and *La Revue Blanche*. In 1899 he married Gabrielle Rodriques-Henriques who came from the Bernheim family, the picture dealers. His material wealth was assured. He lived in Paris until his death, and made numerous journeys abroad as well as in France and Switzerland.

Vallotton, who wrote three novels, of which *La Vie meurtrière*, which was autobiographical in character was one, as well as plays for the theatre, also left a *Livre de raison* which gives us information on his work. Whilst exhibiting paintings regularly in Geneva, Lausanne and Berne, he also, from the time of his arrival in Paris, learned the techniques of etching and woodcuts. He showed in 1891 at the Salon des Indépendants and the first Rose + Croix Salon, and with the Nabis from 1893 onwards. He was a friend of Bonnard and Vuillard. He engraved plates for numerous books, including those by Jules Renard, Remy de Gourmont and Tristan Bernard. In 1899 he went back to painting more intensively, and produced pictures of the inside of bourgeois homes, of nudes, and of landscapes, in which he tried to reconcile his wish to be realist with his Symbolist leanings. His purely Symbolist paintings, which are fairly rare, are in total disaccord with the aspirations of his friends. He never tried to paint 'prettily' — on the contrary, his compositions, which are often brutal, have something of the caricature about them. In the little book which José Pierre wrote about Symbolism, he quite rightly said: 'In the tisane of the Nabis, Vallotton has the effect of a large tot of brandy...In his work the placid scenes of lower middle class digestion by lamplight, which are the delight of the Bonnards and the Vuillards, assume an outrageous ferocity. it is because Vallotton is inhabited by a violence which gives him no respite and which in his portraits, for example, leads him to behave like a psychiatric case.'

And Dunoyer le Segouzac said of him: 'Vallotton has revealed and asserted himself from the beginning. His art, which is scrupulously sincere, is linked unconsciously to that of the primitive Swiss and Germans; but he is not inspired by

FELIX VALLOTTON *The football.* 1899

Felix Vallotton *Ideleness*. 1896

them. Although he profoundly admired Holbein, he has never tried to emulate his work, nor has he ever been an offshoot of any teacher. He has rediscovered the precise art of the sixteenth-century masters in a way which is instinctively spontaneous.'

VOGELER Heinrich (Bremen 1872 — Kazakhstan 1942). Having been a pupil of Jaussen and of Kampf at the Academy in Düsseldorf, he then went to Worpswede where he joined the artists of the Worpswede group. In line with their ideas, he pursued the ideal of a return to nature, animated by a spirit of pantheism. In Florence, where he went in 1898, he met Rainer Maria Rilke, and fell in love with the works of Botticelli. He shared this admiration for the Florentine master with the Pre-Raphaelites whose influence on his work was undeniable. He went to Munich where he illustrated books such as *Die Insel*, and then returned to Worpswede where he became one of the most representative artists of the group which numbered among its members Otto Modersohn, Paula Modersohn-Becker, Fritz Mackensen, Rainer Maria Rilke and his wife, the sculptor Clara Westhoff, as well as Carl and Gerhart Hauptmann. At this time Vogeler was painting works in the Symbolist style. During the First World War he was mobilized on the eastern front, an experience which had a determining influence on the evolution of his art and his ideas. The Russian revolution and the works of Tolstoy, Bakunin and Kropotkin converted him to Communism, and in 1919 he founded the Barkenhoff cell. The paintings which he did then were primarily inspired by Expressionism and then by socialist realism. From 1931 onwards, he settled in Russia,

in Moscow and Odessa. In 1941 he was deported on the approach of the German armies to Kazakhstan, where he died.

VROUBEL Michael Alexandrovich (Omsk, Siberia 1856 — Saint Petersburg 1910). This artist, whose ambition was to 'uplift the soul by means of grandiose images which surpassed the meanness of everyday life', showed his gifts for drawing and music when he was a child. An heir to the romantics, he was the most authentic of the Russian Symbolists. He started his law studies at St. Petersburg, but interrupted them to attend the Academy in the same town. He was influenced by Répine and Christajakov, and in 1884 he collaborated on the restoration of the church of St. Cyril in Kiev; he painted some icons for the iconostasis. He made a journey to Italy and then settled in Moscow where he worked for the theatre. He drew his inspiration from the poetry of Pushkin and Lermontov, from which he took certain

Michael Alexandrovich Vroubel *Self-portrait*. 1904

characters such as the *Swan princess*, that confused creature of legend, and *The Demon* which showed Man tormented by contradictory aspirations. The professional female singer Nadezda Zabela, whom he married, was the model for his female figures. Her fame went beyond the frontiers of Russia, thanks to his participation in international exhibitions. In 1902, he was admitted to a psychiatric hospital, but he continued to paint, during his lucid moments, compositions full of anguish and visionary forebodings.

Michael Alexandrovitch Vroubel *The Swan-Princess*

MICHAEL ALEXANDROVICH VROUBEL *The conquered demon*

WATTS George Frederick (London 1817 — London 1904). Although Watts played a very important role in English Symbolist painting, his personality remained on the edge of the properly called Pre-Raphaelite movement. When he was very young, he showed surprising gifts for design and in 1835 went to the Royal Academy School where he won first prize in a competition for the decoration of Westminster Hall. In 1843 he went to Italy where he stayed for four years. On his return to England, he undertook a series of monumental compositions, and at the same time

France his success was equal to that of Burne Jones, and in 1887 his exhibition at the George Petit Gallery contributed to his renown.

His *Hope* and his melancholic ladies had a great influence on Khnopff. 'Watts' philosophi thought' wrote Philippe Jullian, 'his palette o moonlit tints, his filmy drawing, made his work far preferable to that of the Pre-Raphaelite whose moral preoccupations, bright colours and

GEORGE FREDERICK WATTS *Hope*. 1885

GEORGE FREDERICK WATTS *Self-portrait*. 1864

he executed works of smaller size devoted to subjects dealing with social problems. He was appreciated in intellectual spheres and was elected a member of the Royal Academy in 1867. In

meticulous realism simply could not please those painters who had turned away from realism. The whole generation which has adopted the taste of Huysmans' hero sees Watts through the eyes of Des Esseintes.' Watts only enjoyed the allegory — an allegory far removed from the outward appearances of daily life or of history, which distinguishes him from the Pre-Raphaelites who have not given up the historic past.

VELTI Albert (Zurich 1862 — Berne 1912). When he was very young, he left Switzerland and went to Munich where he attended the Academy of Fine Arts; there he had Gysis and Lofftz as masters. On his return to Zurich, Böcklin took him into his studio as his assistant, to help him with the preparation of his colours; he remained there for two years. After a period in Venice and in Paris, he went back to Munich where, thanks to a patron, he was able to devote himself entirely to his art. His best known pictures date from this period. He also did numerous series of etchings. In 1908 he left Munich and went to live in Berne, where he was commissioned to do part of the decorations in the Federal Palace, but he died suddenly before he had finished the fresco in the Privy Council chamber.

WHISTLER James Abbott McNeill (Lowell, Massachusetts 1834 — London 1903). He was the son of a military engineer, and on the death of his father he went to the Military Academy at West Point. His undisciplined character led him into giving up his military career, and he became the hydrographic designer for the department in Washington. During his visit to Russia where his father was supervising the laying of the St. Petersburg to Moscow railway, he went to drawing classes at the Imperial Academy of St. Petersburg, where he did his first etchings. He went back to America in 1849, and several years later moved to Paris. There he went to Gleyre's studio where he had Degas, Legros, Bracquemond and Fantin-Latour as fellow-students. The series of etchings from this period shows the influence of Courbet and of realism. Together with Fantin-Latour and Legros he started the 'Society of Three' which established close connections between the literary and artistic circles in Paris and those in Great Britain. He went to London and decided to stay here. In 1859 he published a series of etchings showing the banks of the Thames, but started to concentrate more on portraits, an art in which he came to excel. He was influenced by Velasquez and Rossetti, and also by Japanese painting which taught him the art of understatement, whilst

taking his place as a forerunner of Impressionism. Talking about this school he stated: 'Nature contains the elements, the colour and form of all pictures in the same way as the keyboard contains the notes of all music. But the artist is born to use his knowledge to take these elements and group

JAMES ABBOTT MCNEILL WHISTLER *Girl in white*. 1864

them together, just as the musician collects the notes and forms them into harmonies of glorious sound.' In reality, Whistler turned away from the Impressionists in his creation of a world of equivalences which suggests more than it describes in its use of musical terms associated with colour: *Harmony in blue and gold, Nocturne in blue and grey, Symphony in white*. In this he came closer to realism.

Around 1883 he exhibited in Paris, became one of the regular attendants at Mallarmé's Tuesdays, and went back to the milieu which had look favourably on his Parisian debut. His meetings with the French Symbolist painters encouraged

P. Hellen *Portrait of James Abbot McNeill Whistler.* 1897

Nouveau a considerable impetus in Denmark. Together with most of the Scandinavian and German artists who had been involved with Symbolism, he was on the side of Naturalism and ended as an Expressionist having passed through Symbolism first. He made two trips to France

Jens Ferdinand Willumsen *Self-portrait.* 1916

him in his search for a world where the figures of reality seemed 'suspended in the air as if in a fairy world' as he expressed it in a lecture on his art entitled *Ten o'clock lecture.* He repeated this talk in Oxford and Cambridge after London, and the honour of translating it into French fell to Mallarmé.

Following the example of William Morris, he became an interior decorator. He did some Japanese interiors and arranged, for a client, a room which was designed after one of his pictures, which was then hung in it: the Peacock Room. In the same manner as some of Morris' studies, he suggested some stylistic arrangements which ended in the world of Art Nouveau. These studies showed a consideration of a very high order, and an aristocratic feeling which Baudelaire had already aroused and for which Oscar Wilde became the mouthpiece.

Whistler remained a precursor of Impressionism as much as of Symbolism. He knew how to impose discipline on both of them, as well as how to reconcile pure sensation with the organization of a world which had been recreated by the imagination.

WILLUMSEN Jens Ferdinand (Copenhagen 1863 — Cannes 1958). Painter, sculptor, architect and ceramist, Willumsen played an important role in the Nordic countries because his art remained faithful to the aesthetics of the Pont-Aven school; he was a member of this school and gave Art

from November 1888 to June 1889, and from March 1890 to July 1894; these had a great influence on his future style. He was connected with the Nabis, and exhibited at the Salon des Indépendants and at Le Barc de Boutteville. In Pont-Aven and at Le Pouldu he met Gauguin, Sérusier and Meyer de Haan, and, like them, was influenced by Carlyle's theories. During the winter of 1890-91, he saw Gauguin again in Paris, where he was present at the sale of February 23 and the farewell banquet which his friends gave him on March 23. Théo van Gogh introduced him to the works of Odilon Redon, whose fantasy he found very stimulating. He also frequented Mallarmé's Tuesdays. In 1892 he stayed in Norway where the mountainous nature of the country fascinated him, and inspired him to paint numerous landscapes.

Between 1897 and 1900 he was artistic director of the Bing and Gröendahl studios, and he then showed himself to be as good at painting and sculpture as in architecture and decor for the theatre. He was thrilled by the old techniques, and tried to renew them and adapt them to modern art. Germain Bazin has placed him beside Odilon Redon in a stream which started with Gustav Moreau, and which ended with Surrealism.

JENS FERDINAND WILLUMSEN
Two Breton women. 1890

WOESTYNE Gustave van de (Gand 1881 — Louvain 1947). He was a pupil at the Academy of Fine Arts in Gand, but his health was far from robust, and from his childhood he had to spend long periods in the country. In 1899, he went to live in Laethem-Saint-Martin, a little village in the valley of the Lys; there, with his brother, the Expressionist poet Karel van de Woestyne, he discovered George Minne and other artists. They formed together the first group of the Laethem-Saint-Martin artists, the second being composed of Smet, Permeke and van den Bergh. They all admired the primitive Flemish artists, who showed them how to rediscover concrete realities.

Woestyne started by painting small portraits, using the meticulous technique inspired by the primitives. These portraits were close to those of the Pre-Raphaelite works in the dreamy attitudes of the models; the crowded drawing of the landscapes is sometimes reminiscent of Bruegel.

In his second period he concentrated on religious compositions in the style of Maurice Denis, while his landscapes were stylized according to the symbolist conception. Like his friends at the two schools of Laethem-Saint-Martin, he exhibited at the Sélection gallery in Brussels; certain of his works remained faithful to Symbolism, others were moving towards Expressionism. In 1920, his drawing became harder and more geometric while his colours had greater impact and the expression of his faces became more dramatic. He abandoned his elegiac scenes then in order to interpret physical suffering and the feeling of solitude.

GUSTAVE VAN DE WOESTYNE *The Last Supper*

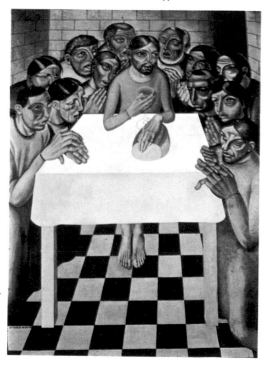

WITOLD WOJTKIEWICZ *Spring*

WOJTKIEWICZ Witold (Warsaw 1879 — Warsaw 1909). He started his artistic studies at the Gerson School in Warsaw, and continued them in Cracow, from 1903 to 1906, in the School of Fine Arts. He exhibited in Warsaw, Berlin and Paris. André Gide was personally interested in his work, and helped him to organise an exhibition in the Druet Gallery in Paris in 1907 for which he edited the introduction to the catalogue. Wojtkiewicz is the principal representative of the last generation of Polish Symbolists.

Animated by an imaginative spirit, he knew how to draw the viewer into a fantastic world. He painted scenes of childhood inspired by tales of fantasy. Under the influence of Toulouse-Lautrec he portrayed scenes of burlesque which were imprinted with lyricism. His Symbolism was already mingling with Expressionism, and indeed sometimes tainted with Surrealism.

Literature

The importance of a name

Symbolism is the group of people who have believed that the word *symbol* had a meaning.' This quip by Paul Valéry in his *Cahiers* (X,81) was not just a joke. It stood somewhere between a naive faith and an unavoidable disillusionment, which was probably the most difficult to grasp of all the literary movements — it was, rather, a 'passage'. It stated the importance of a name which, today, is somewhat devalued, but which was perhaps, at a certain moment in history, a very meaningful term.

Certainly one is seized with vertigo when one reads the definitions of the word *Symbolism* as listed by Remy de Gourmont in 1896 in *Le Livre des masques*: 'individualism in art; freedom of art; a tendency towards what is new, strange or bizarre; idealism; disdain for the social anecdote; anti-naturalism; and finally, *vers libre*.' One is tempted to say 'everything and nothing.'

But perhaps it would be better to query the word *Symbolism* less than the word *symbol*. It originally designated the sign by which a guest makes himself known, the part of the stick which he presents. But here is how the stick becomes a forest — in a sonnet by Baudelaire, a 'forest of symbols'. And this metamorphosis is decisive in its proliferation. If symbolic poetry had already been content for some time with the reference to one object, (a rose, for example), Symbolist poetry played with a multitude of signs which constituted the whole of the sensible. The signs could be those of familiarity: a soul recognizes itself in a landscape, or makes itself known, from the Verlainian moonlight to the great cry of acceptance from Rilke in the *Elegies of Duino*. Equally, the signs could be those of a transcendence which, as in Platonic philosophy, returns to ideas and to prototypes. Milosz, a Symbolist at the last moment, expounds this again in *Cantique de la Connaissance*.

> Only the spirit of thing has a name. Their substance is indefinable. The ability to name some sensitive objects which are absolutely impenetrable to the spiritual being stems fromthe knowledge of archetypes which, being of the nature of our spirit, are like it situated in the conscience of the solar system.

In this other forest, therefore, the forest of definitions, two directions revealed themselves. One was that of subjectivism, and the other that of philosophic idealism. Interference was inevitable. In the definition of Charles Morice, for example: 'The symbol is the fusion of our soul with those things which have awakened our feelings, a fiction which carries us beyond time and space.' (*Du sens réligieux de la poesie*, 1893).

SYMBOLISM AND DECADENCE

If Symbolism is a 'subjectivism pushed very far' it appeared as an incarnation of romanticism. It would be easy to show, as Henri Peyre did, the importance of the Lamartine model in poetry during the years 1885-90, and it would not be altogether unjust to present Samain, in the manner of Paul Morand, as 'a Lamartine for the top of an omnibus.' But this continuity seemed above all to be assured by decadence and made possible by the confusion between decadence and Symbolism.

Decadence, the word which Verlaine saw at some stage 'all glistening with purple and gold' was a new evil of the century. Baudelaire described its symptoms before Paul Bourget wrote the theory of it in 1881: 'Is it not the fatal lot of the exquisite and the rare to be wrong in the face of brutality?' The eccentricities of the Bohemians, the refinements of the dandies, were the illustration of this, but as a defence against the 'Barbarians'. The languors of Verlaine, the sarcasm of Tristan Corbière, the fevered élan of Germain Nouveau, were all the expression of it, infinitely diverse even when passing through the clichés of the period. Marcel Schwob described this term and this *fin de siècle* feeling well in *Coeur Double*: 'We had reached extra-ordinary times, when the novelists had shown us every aspect of human life and all that lay beneath thought. One was quite weary of feelings before one had experienced them: many people allowed themselves to be drawn towards a gulf of strange and unknown shadows; others were possessed by a passion for the strange, for the quintessential search for new sensations; still others relied on a great compassion which spread over everything. Huysmans' Des Eisseintes (*A Rebours*, 1884), Gabriele D'Annunzio's Andrea Sperelli (*The Child of Voluptuous-ness*, 1889) and Oscar Wilde's Dorian Gray (*Portrait of Dorian Gray*, 1891) make up the type of "decadent" so elegantly brought to life by Count Robert de Montesquiou. Because they had enjoyed, without counting, the pleasures which had brought them riches, because they had exhausted even the rarest sensations, these characters sought refuge in an imaginary period of Latin decadence, and in modern literature which was "irreparably affected in its arrangement and forced into explaining everything at its decline".' But the refuge showed itself to be a mirror.

It only needed the flick of a finger to substitute Symbolism for decadence. Jean Moréas did it. Stating firmly that the word 'decadent' was worn out, that it had become 'silly', as Verlaine said, or that it was dead, as Verhaeren proclaimed, he made the changeover in a shattering declaration which was published in the *Figaro* on September 18, 1886 under the title *A Literary Manifesto*. The competition was open: Anatole Baju and René Ghil took up cudgels on behalf of decadence. The rivalry was there to stay, as much in France as abroad. In England, the last number of *Savoy* announced, under the title *The Decadent Movement in Literature*, a book by Arthur Symons which was going to appear under the title *The Symbolist Movement in Literature*. In Russia, Zinada Vengerova introduced Verlaine, Mallarmé, Rimbaud and Moréas in an article publish-ed in 1892 in the *European messenger* (Vestnik Evropy) which was entitled 'the Symbolist poets in France'. One year later and this time in the *Northern Messenger*, Oussov devoted 'A Few Words on the Decadents' to the same Verlaine, Mallarmé and Rimbaud, and to Baudelaire.

THE SYMBOLIST START

Were they decadents or Symbolists, those 'Russian Symbolists' of 1895 with Briussov as their ringleader? They were, rather, united in one feeling of nausea in the presence of which they saw one revolt against the teaching of their elders, one attentiveness to the Western poets. It was necessary to wait until the beginning of the century for that which produced the start, described by Biely in *Between two centuries*: 'Those who yesterday were called *decadents* replied by proving that it was the decadents who had produced the *decadents*. And it was then that the winged word *Symbolism* appeared; the product of the decadence of the period 1901 to 1910 had marked perseverance, firmness and the will to live; instead of decomposing, it concen-trated on gathering its forces, and on struggling against the "fathers" who surpassed them in number and in authority.' These Symbolists adopted the thinking of the masters: Soloviev, but also Kant and Nietzsche.

Western Symbolism was already supported by a widespread philosophy. Robert de Souza, endeavouring to make a point in *Où nous en sommes* when launching *La Revue Blanche* in March 1905, recognized that every poet 'had chosen the moral or philosophical armour which suited him.' Villiers de l'Isle-Adam, for example, was an adept and a convert of Hegel, professing that 'the spirit constitutes the end and the bottom of the Universe.' Yeats became impregnated with Hindu thought. D'Annunzio knew of it through Schopenhauer. *Le Monde comme volonté et comme représentation*, of which two French translations appeared at the end of the century, exercised a major influence. In *Si le grain ne meurt*, Gide recounted how it was then in good taste to believe only in the ideality of the world, and only to see the world here below as a representation of it. Gourmont made a Schopenhauerian profession of faith: 'In relation to man, a thinking subject, the world, that is everything which is exterior to me, only exists according to the idea which one conceives about it! Moreover, Schopenhauer, in distinguishing the world as willpower, source of sadness, from the world as representation by art, enhances the prestige of pure art, the inevitable recourse of the thinking man, since it is the only reality.

At the end of *A Rebours*, Des Esseintes, pursued by his neurosis and forced to leave his gilded

THEO VAN RYSSELBERGHE *A Reading*. 1903 (from left to right: F. le Dantec, E. Verhaeren, F. Vielé-Griffin, H.E. Cross, F. Fénéon, A. Gide, H. Gheon, M. Maeterlinck.)

cenobitical existence, implores the God of the Christians: 'his tendencies towards artifice, his eccentric needs', were perhaps nothing other, at the bottom, than 'transports, leaps towards an ideal, towards an unknown universe, towards a distant blessedness.' He launched a new appeal to 'the azure eternal' which haunted Mallarmé in 1864, and which Ruben Darío was praising in 1888. The ideal, one of the subjects for Baudelaire's minute examination, is as difficult to define as the symbol, but it is also one of the passwords of the movement. The idealism of the Symbolists, as Etiemble noted, is derived as much from the *idea* in the philosophical meaning of the term, as from the *ideal* with its moral sense. The first conception is unfolded in the Manifesto of Moréas: 'Symbolist poetry tries to clothe the idea in a perceptible form which, nevertheless, is not an end in itself, but which, while serving to express the Idea, remains the subject.' But when Louis le Cardonnel denounces 'unlucky love, the ravisher of sleep', the 'jealous frenzy' of the body and attacks the 'victorious sabbath' into which Ludwig II of Bavaria was dragged, he is contributing to the most conventional moralism.

René Ghil already thought that 'the same, almost unconscious appetite for idealism' gave an 'appearance of cohesion' to 'the rising poetic generation'; 'idealism which, being revealed to itself, progresses on the one hand, by short and particular diversion, through Baudelaire, haunted by the magnetizing fear of the sin to which Beauty condemns him, and through *Sagesse* to a vague and depressing mysticism — and, on the other hand, through the Baudelaire of the *Correspondances* and Mallarmé, who inherited the Baudelairian negation of science to which imagination is in opposition: idealism which evolves in the manner of spiritualist art, it could be said, rather than in a precisely determined concept of philosophy. Supreme games, if one likes, of the creative idea of vain appearances under which, by going from analogies to analogies, it is found to be eternal — by an *a priori* of intuition of the Self participating in it.'

AN INCOMPLETE TRANSLATION

From that time it seemed satisfactory to define the symbol, in the manner of Henri de Régnier, as 'the most perfect and the most complete figuration of the Idea', 'the expressive figuration of the Idea'. But such a formula appeared in 1900, at a Symbolist meeting where the Symbolist doctrine was being established. The excesses of poetic Platonism, such as in *Le Traité du Narcisse* by Gide and the *Cantique de la Connaissance* by Milosz were yet to come.

In his Manifesto of 1886, Moréas took care to state precisely that 'the Idea in its turn must never let itself be seen to be deprived of its sumptuous long gown of exterior analogies; for the essential character of Symbolist art consists in never going as far as the conception of the Idea in itself.' This was 'to reserve the translation', as Rimbaud had asked, to refuse 'the too precise meaning' as Mallarmé had commanded. Pierre Louÿs in this respect fixed a rule which could well be decisive: 'One must never explain symbols. One must never penetrate them. Have confidence — oh! do not doubt. He who has drawn the symbol has hidden a truth inside it, but he must not show it — or else why symbolize it in the first place?'

The mystery, therefore, is not only that of the unknown, it is in the actual indecision of the search, and in the expression of the Ideal or the Idea. Mallarmé, who frequently used the term (even in its medieval sense) declared to Jules Huret, for the *Enquête sur l'évolution littéraire* of 1891 that 'it is the perfect usage of this mystery which constitutes the symbol.' In this the symbol differs from the simple allegory. The allegory, as Hegel had already stated, is only a 'chilled symbol', the bringer of a single meaning. The symbol, on the other hand, is heavy with multiple meanings. It is in the order of what Goethe called the *schankenden Gestalten*, the 'vague, confused, indeterminate images'. In a book which appeared in 1893, and which made a great impression, *The Causes of decadence and the new currents of contemporary Russian literature* Merejowski stated that 'symbols must flow naturally and involuntarily from the depths of reality. If the author invents them artifically to explain some idea or other, he transforms them into dead allegories, which can awaken only disgust as does everything which is dead.' And he took the example of the theatre of Ibsen, through which a profound current passed, without spreading out too clearly the thought which it uttered.

The major action at that time could well have been the 'hyperbole' invoked by Mallarmé at the beginning of *La Prose pour Des Esseintes*. By a return to its etymological meaning, the word shows the audacious leap of one who passes from the world of feeling to the world of intellect, and submits to 'Ideas', the 'glory of long desire'. But, in the rhetorical sense this time, it is also a way of expressing what passes expression, the magic formula from a conjuring-book. Thus was founded the esotericism of the Symbolists.

A new poetic art

Descended from the anti-intellectual currents which could go as far as mysticism, Symbolism was however looked on as a suspect of intellectualism. 'Everything in the Symbolist work carries the mark of a too conscious creation' wrote Jacques Rivière, thinking without doubt of Mallarmé, and of the one who tried harder and better than anyone to clarify poetic action — Valéry. André Breton, who was even more austere, accused the Symbolists of 'making the public stupid with their more or less rhythmic lucubrations.' This meant giving, without doubt, too much importance to the lucubrations, which were often forgettable, and to neglect the elements of a new poetic art.

A mythological creation

Mythological figures occupy an important place in Symbolist imagery. It suffices to reflect on the *Hérodiade* (that is to say Salome) of Mallarmé, or on *L'Après midi d'un faune* which strove to perpetuate the nymphs on whom Pierre Louÿs, however, in *Les Chansons de Bilitis*, pronounced the death sentence; or on the figure of the Sappho of Viélé-Griffin, and in the *New Poems* of Rilke; or, again, on the importance of the myth of Leda in Jean Lorrain's and Yeats' work. They wanted to revive the national myths (Yeats' and Maeterlinck's Celtic myths; the American Indian myths of Rubén Darío) or to escape into the mysterious world of distant myths (like Schuré in *The Soul of New Times* with the 'Trilogy of Destiny: Karma, Nirvana, Immortality'). They also wanted to establish the personal myths, born from the imagination of the poet, like the Maximin of George or the Belle Dame of Blok.

No catalogue here, no collection as with the Parnassians. For it is the chosen gods, as it is the 'chosen landscapes'. Besides, they were founded in daringly syncretic figures: for D'Annunzio, 'the royal Hérodiade' was at the same time

Gorgone antica ne la grande chioma...	Like an ancient Gorgon in her thick long hair...
Ella era Circe ed Elena ed Onfale,	She was Circe and Helen and Omphale,
Dalila meretrice de le risa	the meretricious Dalila with her
terribili, Erodiade regale...	terrible laughter, regal Herodias...
(Prelude to the *Intermezzo*)	

The *correspondances* were established to suggest the 'dark and deep unity' of the myth, that 'tree', said Baudelaire, 'which grows everywhere, in all climates, under all suns, spontaneously without cuttings.' Myths are universal, but also seem as ancient as the world, and it is possible to understand why Yeats relied on 'imaginary beings....created by the deepest instincts of man' as being 'the best approach to truth which he could possibly attain.

An instrument of knowledge, the myth thus maintains a privileged relationship with the symbol. The poet can make a simply allegorical use of it, charging it with a totally different meaning, and only one. This is what Henri de Régnier expressed in 1900 in his lecture on *The Poets of Today:* 'A myth is the sonorous conch shell of *one* idea.' For Yeats, Helen presented the fatal power of all beauty. For George, Algabal was 'the symbol of a despotic and inhuman soul which, in its omnipotence, finds only solitude and sterility'.

The myth, properly so called, is only Symbolist if it is the bearer of several possible meanings, and the setting for mystery. It draws towards an unknown which it never permits to reach. That is why the Symbolist poets were attracted by ambiguous figures: fauns, chimeras, hermaphrodites. One and the same figure appears and disappears in the halo of multiple meanings: Salome, a victim of artificiality according to Laforgue; in love with suffering, according to Constantin Cavafy; incarnated by Huysmans as Hysteria or the Goddess of Syphilis. A cold Artemis in Mallarmé and Laforgue, she becomes again the 'Salome of instincts' with Milosz and, as a Bacchante, she enters into delirium with Oscar Wilde (*Salome*, 1896), with Kasprovics (*The Banquet of Hérodiade*, 1905) and with Herman Suderman (*Johannes*, 1898).

The Symbolists believed that, as in Dionysiac religion, mythological characters were possessed by the forces of nature; from this came more correspondences, which became clear in the light of the 'naturalist' conception dear to the great mythologists of the end of the century, and which Mallarmé echoed in the preface to *Dieux antiques*: 'What pleasure mingles with our surprise at seeing familiar myths slowly evaporate, by the same magic which the analysis of the ancient work implies, into water, light and the elementary wind.' It was a chance to rediscover life and the things of the earth.

MUSIC BEFORE ANYTHING ELSE

The Symbolist period was that of an 'exquisite crisis, fundamental,' for literature. Mallarmé, who recorded it, distinguished two languages: 'a double state of a word, rough and immediate here, essential there'. This separation was the actual sign of the crisis. To choose the essential word was, quite obviously, to choose poetry, in which the Symbolists understood the affinities with music. As Mallarmé wrote again, 'Music joins with Verse to form Poetry.'

He was thinking here, it is true, of the collaboration between music and poetry, such as existed in Wagnerian drama which, in this aspect as well, was a model. But he did not ignore the efforts made in order that poetry might become music. He said this variation was 'underneath and in advance, unexpectedly prepared by Verlaine, so fluid, come back again to the primitive spellings.'

The celebrated *Art Poétique* of *Jadis et Naguère* stated in effect the laws of the 'chanson grise', and spoke the word of command:

De la musique avant toute chose   Music before anything else

By that the poet meant a language adapted to the fleeting states of the soul, and mobile like them, made appropriate by their improprieties. Huysmans, thinking of Verlaine, defined poetry in this way: 'Something vague, like a music which allows one to dream of a beyond, far from the American prison in which Paris makes us live.'

There again, it is necessary to guard against a misunderstanding. When Mallarmé spoke of 'putting what is its own backbone into music', or of 'putting everything back into music', he was not thinking of any imitation of music whatsoever on the part of poetry, or of a 'verbal instrumentation orchestrating a poem', as René Ghil wanted. In a letter addressed to the latter he took care to state: 'I will blame you for one thing alone: it is that, in this act of just restitution, which must be ours, of putting everything back into music, its rhythms, which are only those of reason, and its actual colours, which are those of our passions evoked by dreaming, you were allowing the old dogma of the Verse to fade a little. You phrase like a composer rather than a writer.'

It is in this way, with its own processes and in the conceptual usage that it makes of language, that poetry is musical: 'It is not from the elementary sonorities of the brass, the strings or the woodwinds, but undeniably from the intellectual word at its highest, together with fullness and clearness as well as the ensemble of rapports that exist in everything, that Music must result.' It is possible to come closer to this statement in, for example, this declaration by Rubén Darío: 'Every word has a soul; there is in every verse, apart from the verbal harmony, an ideal melody. Music often comes only from the idea.'

In fact, the *modernismo* which, in Latin America and then in Spain, took the place of Symbolism without becoming in any way confused with it, did not allow itself to be defined by a new thematic alone (a denial of life, of America, to the benefit of 'princesses, kings, imperial things, visions of distant or fabulous countries', preface to *Profane Prose*, 1895) but also by musical scenery:

> It was a sweet refrain of a measured beat,
> The Harmony Fairy marked the rhythm of its rise and fall,
> And floated its elusive phrases and gentle sighs
> Among the sobs ofthe 'cellos.

Like Darío, Valle Inclán wrote *Sonatas*. Manuel Machado, in the manner of Verlaine, preferred, to the long and sonorous verse pecular to the Spanish lyric, the short verse, undulant, musical and in 'a minor key.' Antonio Machado, on the other hand, still near to modernism in his *Solitudes* of 1903, kept his distance realising that the study of musicality at any price could lead to futile chatter.

Another problem: more than ever, this poetry was untranslatable, and yet, perhaps, people had never tried harder to translate it, if only to make new works known (one thinks, for example, of the role of Ueda Bin in Japan, and of his translations of the French Symbolists). Here is a sample of a successful effort, and yet inevitable deviations from the original are still noticeable. Arpad Tóth translates thus the beginning of Verlaine's *Chanson d'Automne*:

Text	Translation	Translation of the translation
Les sanglots longs	Osz hurja zsong	La corde de l'automne vibre
Des violons	jajong, busong	Pleure et s'afflige
De l'automne	a tajon	Dans le paysage
Bercent mon coeur	s ont monoton	Et verse une langueur
D'une langueur	but konokon	Obstinée et monotone
Monotone	és fajon	Douloureusement

Tóth tried hard to respect the rhythm and a certain melodic colour, but the homophony which he created in the rhyme is excessive, and really too 'monotonous'; the liquid alliterations, the diaereses have disappeared, certain details of the text are omitted (les violons, le coeur blessé), and the translation turns to paraphrase — which is the price paid for the conciseness of the Hungarian.

VERS LIBRE

Verlaine had a tendency to disjoint verse inside itself, in order to make rhythm predominate in the framework of syllabic verse. The *vers-libristes* went even further: they did not count the syllables. The only things that mattered to them were the rhythmic measurements, affirmed and confirmed by the measurements which corresponded to them. They hoped thus to be able to replace 'mathematical rhythm' with 'psychological rhythm', more suited to reproduce the interior movement of the soul. Rimbaud, instinctively, found the formula in two poems which were situated between the proses in his *Illuminations: Marine* and *Mouvement*. These texts, published in *La Vogue* in 1886, were, according to the evidence of Dujardin, 'the trigger thanks to which some of the young people, who were searching for their formula, found it, and were more or less able to perfect it.'

The role played by Gustave Kahn in the publication of Rimbaud's poems is well known. When, the following year, he published the collection of which he was the author, *Les Palais nomades*, he claimed paternity for the invention of *vers libre*, 'the elastic formula', as he said later, 'which, by liberating the ear from the always-binary purr of old verse, and by suppressing the empirical cadence which seems ceaselessly to remind poetry of its mnemonic origins, allows everyone to hear the song which is inside himself and to translate it as accurately as possible.' A certain rivalry ensued: Moréas claimed that Kahn had stolen the invention from him, and a poetess from Montmartre, Marie Krysinska, recalled texts which she had published in *Le Chat noir* in 1882. It seems no one thought of Laforgue, who had been a long way in this field, or more particularly of Walt Whitman (whose *Dedications* had previously been translated by Laforgue). Here is, for example, the beginning of *Drumbeats* (1865), one of the entries in the great collection *Leaves of Grass*, over which he had ruminated deeply:

> First O songs for a prelude,
> Lightly strike on the stretch'd tympanum pride and joy in my city,
> How she led the rest to arms, how she gave the cue,
> How at once with lithe limbs unwaiting a moment she sprang,
> (O superb! O Manhattan, my own, my peerless!
> O strongest you in the hour of danger, in crisis! O truer than steel!)

Mallarmé approved of this 'delicious liberation' and, taking care to distinguish *vers libre* from a versification of varying metres, such as is found for example in *Psyche*, in *Amphitryon* or in the *Fables* of La Fontaine he paid homage to the young poets: 'All the novelty concerning *vers libre* is now becoming established; not such as the seventeenth century attributed to the fable or the opera — this was only an arrangement, without strophe, of various well-known metres — but, as we call it "polymorphous", which suits it: and let us now envisage the dissolution of official metre into what one wants, for ever, provided that pleasure is still to be found in it. A little while ago, there was euphony, fragmented according to the assent of the intuitive reader, with an artless and valuable accuracy — Monsieur Moréas but lately; or a gesture, languid from dreaming, or starting with passion, which scans — Monsieur Viélé-Griffin; or, recently Monsieur Kahn with his very knowledgeable notation on the tonal value of words. There are other names I could mention; those of Messieurs Charles Morice, Verhaeren, Dujardin, Mockel and so on, as proof of what I have said; one can go back to publications for reference.

Audaciousness was not always so great. Sometimes with Verhaeren, and most of the time with Henri de Régnier, one is nearer to the assorted versification of earlier times than to *vers libre*, the 'verse with neither rhyme nor metre' which the poet Coeuvre praised in *La Ville* by Claudel.

Symbolism in time and space

There were 'some' Symbolisms rather than 'one' Symbolism or 'the' Symbolism. Without doubt it was France who launched them. When thinking of foreign Symbolisms it is at once evident that they were most of the time either amalgams or deviations, and this was even more so when they took place late by comparison with the French.

THE PRECURSORS

Symbolism was born from encounters: encounters of literary men and of artists, but also of more or less diffuse currents. It would be difficult to untangle the skein of this genesis. At least some precursors of the movement can be evoked.

It would be possible, with Huysmans, to go as far as the authors of the Latin decadence, to the *Metamorphoses* of Apulius, which are so impregnated with mysterious cults. Or even to the esotericism of Jacob Boehme or Swedenborg. In any case, Romanticism had some mystic aspects which predicted Symbolism. For Coleridge, poetry was 'the faculty to evoke the mystery of things'...Novalis praised the night, which is the setting for revelations', and for him the whole of nature was only a vast symbol.

The Baudelairian doctrine of correspondences looked for a guarantee in German Romanticism, especially in the works of E.T.A. Hoffmann. But it was in Edgar Allan Poe particularly that Baudelaire found his chosen brother. The translations which had done so much to make the work of the American author accepted in France were well known. It was Edgar Allan Poe again who led Baudelaire to state precisely his conception of understanding, 'queen of the faculties'. 'The imagination is not fantasy; nor is it sensitivity, even though it would be difficult to envisage an imaginative man who was not sensitive. The imagination is a faculty which is almost divine, which first perceives, in a way apart from philosophic methods, the intimate and secret relations of things, their correspondences and their analogies.' Poe came to exercise a major influence on Villiers de l'Isle-Adam, Mallarmé, Valéry and even on Claudel who sang the praises of *Eureka* during the time he was preparing to compose the *Cinq Grandes Odes* and *L'Art poétique*.

In France, Nerval together with Baudelaire, went the furthest in the direction of Symbolism. As Gaétan Picon wrote: 'Nerval is the only romantic poet who has exclusively and rigorously lived that which the whole epoch has felt in diffuse and disordered fashion...Breaking with the abundance of romantic discourse, he decisively made poetry lean towards the slope which led to Baudelaire and Mallarmé.' His writings graduated from the world of the reverie to that of reality, and he presented *Aurélia* like 'the outpouring of the dream into real life'. The twelve sonnets, regrouped at the end of *Filles du Feu* under the title *Les Chimeres*, concentrate the whole of Nerval's poetic experience; they open with the agonized prelude of *El Desdichado* and end with an eternal hymn to Pythagorean wisdom, *Vers dorés*. The intellectual climate of Symbolism could not be recreated without alluding to the idealism of Carlyle, of which the characteristic was, as Taine said 'to see a double meaning in everything'; to the pessimism of Schopenhauer, which only showed the hidden force of willpower in order to invite us to liberate ourselves from it; to Hartmann's philosophy of the unconscious, which left a particular imprint on Laforgue; above all, to the 'world of unknown possibilities' opened by Richard Wagner: for him the object of art was to grasp the reality which sleeps in the depths of nature and human soul.

A LOOK AT SYMBOLISM IN FRANCE

Verlaine, Rimbaud, Cros, Corbière and Nouveau are still the precursors of Symbolism; but it would be wrong to establish watertight compartments; Mallarmé published first in *Le Parnasse contemporaine*, Rimbaud sent verses to Banville, Verlaine visited the 'artistic' poets, and there were the Symbolist Parnassians such as Henri de Régnier. It is essential to understand that, at the time of the Symbolists, a young writer who had never dreamed of becoming one could find himself associated with the movement, even, sometimes, against his will. If Mallarmé and Verlaine allowed themselves some time to come round to it, what can be said about Rimbaud, who was in North Africa at the time, and did not know the fate which the literary Parisian world was reserving for his work?

1886 was assuredly a beginning. That year *Les Illuminations* and *Une saison en enfer* were published in *La Vogue*. That year Moréas, who had already, in an article the preceding year, demanded the appellation 'Symbolist' for the 'so-called decadents', published his literary Manifesto. In fact, that year there was no school, and no feeling of a school. The groups were too diverse, with the elders (Samain, Moréas, Le Cardonnel, Régnier), the Verlainians (Du Plessys, Tailhade, Ernest Raynaud), the Wagnerians (Wyzewa, Edouard Dujardin) the 'Condorcet group' (René Ghil, Stuart Merrill, Quillard, Mikhaël). The pass-word was 'the old-fashioned must be dropped', but it was possible to read in a journal entitled *Le Décadent* that a 'future' was promised for 'decadentism'. The first collective realization was the suite of eight sonnets which appeared in the January 1888 number of *La Revue Wagnérienne*, among which figured prominently Verlaine's *Parsifal* and Mallarmé's *Homage*.

1887 was, rather, the year of the advent of consciousness. Although Wyzewa swore he had not very clearly understood the notion of the symbol in his article on *The Symbolism of Monsieur Mallarmé*, one of the 'Belgians of Gand', who contributed in a very sensible way to the illustration of the doctrine, Maeterlinck, explained in an article in *L'Art moderne* on April 24, 1887, that the actual symbol is the inverse of the classical symbol: instead of going from the abstract to the concrete (Venus incarnated as a statue represents love), it goes from the concrete to the abstract, 'from the thing which is seen, heard, smelt, touched and tasted, to make its image born of the idea', and he recognized in Mallarmé 'the true master of Symbolism in France'.

But Mallarmé, although he invited the young writers to a 'spiritual task', was too concerned with following his solitary quest to play this role; and this is the source of the misunderstandings borne out of his relations with the most active of the Symbolists. They first appeared with René Ghil, that last minute Mallarmist, for whom he had written a foreword to *Le Traité du Verbe*, but who in 1888 confused Ideas with the Darwinian idea of evolution. And with Jean Moréas who, perhaps vexed by not having collected all the éclat from the banquet which he had organized on the occasion of the publication in 1891 of his *Pélerin passionné*, announced that his ideal had obliged him to break with Mallarmé, and to be a Symbolist no longer.

Meanwhile, the role of spokesman of Symbolism fell to Téodor de Wyzewa and to Dujardin. But the 'Wagnerians' understood the doctrine of the master of Bayreuth better than that of the master of the Rue de Rome. There was also Gustave Kahn, who fought for *vers libre* more than for Symbolism. It was possible in 1889 to believe that the school had found its 'brain' with Charles Morice who, enlightened by the sudden fashion for occultism in France (it was the year when Edouard Schuré published his *Les Grands Initiés*) had had the merit of trying, in *La Littérature de tout à l'heure*, to integrate the new literary doctrine into the larger framework of esoteric traditions. But Morice had never seen himself as the director of the school — a school in whose reality he did not believe. When, in 1891, Jules Huret wrote his famous *Enquête sur l'évolution littéraire*, he replied: 'The Symbolist school? First of all, there must be one. I, for my part, do not know of one.'

The disparity, in fact, was too great. Around Mallarmé and in his shadow could be found decadents who never stopped singing, in languid verse, about the evils of their existence (Mikhaël, Samain and even Maeterlinck in *Serres Chaudes*), the *vers libre* experts, the mystics who sometimes tried to go back to religious sources, and, above all, too many 'literary men' who were desirous of being spoken about, or of profiting from a fashion to make it benefit their own work and their own theories.

After 1891, the disciples consolidated the doctrine and reduced it to simple formulas which made it insipid: Remy de Gourmont, Henri de Régnier. The time of the vulgarizers had arrived for a doctrine which had been founded on disdain for the vulgar. And, curiously, those who exposed it with the most clarity were those who had least put it into practice: Verhaeren, for example, and Gide, when, in his *Traité du Narcisse*, he gave the 'theory of the symbol' its true Platonic colour. It was also the time of the reaction against Symbolism, which was reproached for its deliquescences, and people were talking of a return to life — naturalism by Saint-Georges de Bouhélier, Nietzscheism by Gide in *Les Nourritures terrestres*, and Jammism; but a conversion to life was effected by the Symbolists themselves, whether they were praising joy after sorrow (Stuart Merrill, Viélé-Griffin), or evoking by the hundreds the images of an exuberant life (Saint-Pol Roux, Claudel), or praising the modern world (Verhaeren in *Campagnes hallucinées*, *Villes tentaculaires* and *Villages illusoires*). Symbolism was blamed for the imagery which neither Valéry nor Apollinaire found easy to renounce; it was blamed for its doctrine without realizing that, stripped of the idealism of a school, there was still a durable Symbolist message which Claudel in his *Cinq Grandes Odes* and Milosz in the Cantique de Connaissance extended while changing it.

Symbolism was not dead. At the same time that Georges le Cardonnel and Charles Vellay were conducting their inquest on contemporary literature, and when each one was ready to declare it defunct, in 1905 there was an attempt to contradict these reports and to restore the defunct claimant. Tancrède de Visan strove to associate Bergson's philosophy with Symbolist doctrine. Jean Rogère tried to reunite those who, after his death, remained faithful to Mallarmé, and revived the 'dream of grasping the Essence', although from then on it was less the Platonic essences than the essence of poetry, the pure poetry of which Valéry, after his silence, became the champion.

A LOOK AT SYMBOLISM IN ENGLAND

It was hardly usual to speak of Symbolism in England. The term reserved for the literature of the 'Nineties was rather 'decadence'. But it is not certain whether that term translates completely the multiple aspirations which were met with at that time.

The period was still Victorian. But under the thrust of subversive forces, the Victorian edifice split and started to crack all over. In literature it was necessary to make allowance for the part played by foreign influences, and in particular that of Baudelaire. Perhaps no one was more sensitive to it than Swinburne (1837-1909). From the first series of *Poems and Ballads* (1866) he showed a vein of complacent morbidity which recalled, although more frenetic and in a more artifical form, that of *Fleurs du Mal*. And the premature funereal homage paid by' Swinburne to Baudelaire *Ave atque vale* had the value of confirmation.

The neo-romanticism of Swinburne is indissociable from aestheticism. He frequented the Pre-Raphaelites' group, who were in their way precursors of Symbolism (if one thinks of *The chosen Maiden* of Dante Gabriel Rossetti and of the use which Claude Debussy made of it in his early days). It could appear curious that Walter Pater, that scrupulous humanist, that educator who was so conscious of his mission, was able to exercise an influence which went in the same direction. That is how, in spite of himself, he was the starting-point of English decadentism with his *Studies on the Renaissance* (1873) and his novel *Marius the Epicurean*, which was, it is true, an evocation of literary decadence.

It fell to Oscar Wilde to express Pater's ideas in the form of a paradox. Like him, and like Baudelaire, Wilde was of the opinion that 'a certain strangeness, something like the blossoming of the aloe, is an element of all true works of art.' But what does one retain from a work such as *The Portrait of Dorian Gray*? The cynical immorality for which Wilde was so much reproached, especially once he had been cast down? A tragedy of sin and of growing old? The reception given to influences, whether distant (the Italian Renaissance) or near (Gautier, Baudelaire and Huysmans)? George Moore shared with Wilde the taste for recent French literature: his *Flowers of Passion* (1878) obviously was an extension of *Les Fleurs du Mal*. Tempted at one time by the naturalism of Zola, Moore was pulled into the Symbolist stream; he was involved with Dujardin, he contributed to *La Revue indépendante*, he practised 'correspondences' and, obviously, the author of *A Mere Accident* knew *A Rebours*. The *Confessions of a Young Man* (1888) which appeared simultaneously in England and France, contained a homage to Mallarmé, praising to the skies the *Fêtes galantes* by Verlaine, and formulating this lapidary definition of Symbolism: 'Symbolism consists of saying the opposite of what you want to say.'

Moore afterwards borrowed from other fields. After 1890, however, the password was more than ever 'new'. At the time when the traditionalist party was straining to discredit 'decadence', the young people were openly advertising the term, in which they found a certain charm. This was the case with the members of the Rhymers' Club, a society which had been thought of by W.B. Yeats, and which lasted from 1891 to 1894. Ernest Rhys, Richard Le Gallienne, Arthur

Symons and Dowson could all be found there, and they profited from the support of the editor John Lane who, in March 1892, published the first *Book of the Rhymers' Club*. A second book, in 1894, brought together the rhymers who were near to leaving the club, and their continuity was assured by a review, *The Yellow Book*, a defence of modern intransigence. The editor was Lane again, the literary editor Henry Harland, and the artistic director Aubrey Beardsley. The exquisite forms which the latter designed, bearers of unwholesome notions, could have been the emblem for what has sometimes been called the 'Beardsley period'. The review did not last long, by reason of its subversive character and the fatal blow which Oscar Wilde's condemnation dealt it.

In 1896 a new review, *The Savoy*, tried to resume the programme of *The Yellow Book*. It lasted an even shorter time. Symons played a front line role in it. 'We are neither romantics, realists nor decadents', he affirmed. It was concerned with defending art and poetry as expressions of truth. Yeats and Dowson appeared among the contributors, as did Beardsley.

It fell to Symons to draw up the balance sheet in the *Symbolist Movement in Literature*: he wrote 'Art' comes back to the one and only road that leads, through lovely things, to eternal beauty.' Although the 'Nineties had been above all a period of agitation, the restive young people were going to leave room for more certain talents. The ground was prepared for the blossoming of a Yeats, and later, of a T.S. Eliot.

A LOOK AT SYMBOLISM IN GERMANY

Germany discovered naturalism at the time when, after the *Manifesto of Five* (1887), it was already in decline in France. In 1890 it still knew practically nothing of the revival awakened by the poetry of Baudelaire, Verlaine or Rimbaud. It was up to Stefan George to dissipate this ignorance, and to establish a loftier conception of poetry: revived by contact with French Symbolism, German lyricism would rediscover, he thought, the forgotten art of the great old masters, Jean-Paul, Novalis and Hölderlin.

It was in 1889 that George had discovered Symbolism in Paris. *The Hymns* which he published in 1890 were in part the fruit of his Parisian experience: the titles of his poems — *Love Forests, In a Park, On the Terrace, Hymn of Night* — which recall the themes so often chosen by the Symbolists, showed this quite well. But, beyond this superficial plagiarism, George went straight to the sanctuary of Mallarmian thought: the only subject of his *Hymns* was the power of the poet, the priest of art, who alone can discover the hidden significance of the world, thanks to the ineffable charm of a sacred and strict language; and the title of this collection expressed only the religious attitude of this poet.

In 1892 George established his review *Leaves for Art*, which published the works of numerous young writers, in particular the *Death of Titian* by Hofmannsthal, and translations from French authors such as Mallarmé and Baudelaire. While denouncing the materialism of German society, George insisted that art should be limited to its unique function: the search for beauty. This was clearly taking up a position against all the social preoccupations of the naturalism which reigned at that time.

George even became the guide of a literary group. Among the disciples that he cherished no particularly original talent appeared: Wolfskehl (1869-1948) and Derleth (1870-1948), who were especially responsible for developing the master's prophecies without in any way inheriting his artistic gifts, were the most noteworthy. Max Dauthendey (1867-1918), one of George's first companions, pushed Symbolism as far as fantasy in his collection, *Ultra-Violet* (1893). In Germany, as in France, the tomorrows of Symbolism were confused and disappointing. A conventional Middle Ages gave pleasure to the neo-romantic writers around 1900: sad and mysterious souls, living in diaphanous bodies, expressed their feelings in a bizarre and studied language. Among these second generation Symbolists could be found authors such as Ernst Hardt (1876-1947) and Vollmüller (1878-1948). Among the others, Symbolism degenerated into even stranger forms: occultism, 'decadent' eroticism, a taste for cosmic grandeur. But these tendencies were already getting close to Expressionism.

In Austria, Symbolism developed under different conditions. There was no reaction against naturalism here: the Viennese intellectual life, thanks to its cosmopolitan character, was quickly impregnated with the decadent spirit which in France marked the years when the various Symbolist groups were forming themselves. To pin down the unutterable, to describe the indescribable in refined language, that seems to have been the ambition of Hofmannsthal and Rilke from their very first works. During the time of D'Annunzio and Maeterlinck, this conception of literature delayed nothing: Austria as well repudiated, but without the German violence, the age of the imitators.

Two curious and cultured spirits played an important role in this opening of Austria to outside influences. The journalist, Hermann Bahr (1863-1934) who lived in Paris, and who introduced Vienna to the poetry of Baudelaire and Verlaine, the novels of the Goncourts and Huysmans; and the doctor Arthur Schnitzler (1862-1931), a refined connoisseur of French and English literature, a typical representative of the *fin de siècle* feeling, amoral and sceptical, the analyst of innumerable drawing-room comedies about the illusions and the lies of love.

Hofmannsthal attained perfection right from the start in his poems written when he was seventeen and in his play *Hier*. His very rigorous forms served to translate impressions and states of soul, which were both simple and mysterious, into a musical language. His encounter with George, their collaboration on *Leaves for Art*, did more than just establish a hyphen between Austrian Symbolism and German Symbolism. It was a fertile experience, even if afterwards relations between the two men were a little strained. Then Hofmannsthal questioned George's aestheticism; his symbolism often covered Baroque forms and could even turn towards neo-Romanticism or go back to Classicism. Nevertheless, he followed his thinking on the meaning of life. And his *Woman without Shadow* (1919) marked a return to the subtleties of Symbolism, while the unfinished novel, *Andreas or the United Ones* retraced the spiritual itinerary of a young man who leads us from Venetian gracefulness at the beginning, to mysterious initiations. Certainly Hofmannsthal was not a man of a single idea or a single style. A spirit cultured by an eclectic admiration, sensitive to the tendencies of the time and to voices from the past, he escapes classification: the multiple currents of Symbolism came together in his work, which recalls in turn the musical and misty manner of Maeterlinck, the aesthetic idealism of Mallarmé, the light and suggestive fantasy of Verlaine in *Fêtes Galantes*, and the allegorical myths of German romanticism.

A LOOK AT RUSSIAN SYMBOLISM

If it was necessary to establish a classification, it could be said that Russian Symbolism was the most important after French Symbolism. It is particularly difficult to study it because, in Russia, the great currents of modern poetry mixed with and succeeded each other without exact division, so that it is hard to say which is decadentism and which Symbolism, or to state precisely when Symbolism, acmeism and Futurism started or finished.

One certain thing is that modern poetry started in Russia with Symbolism; acmeism and Futurism are defined by their relationship to it. It introduced a 'new spirit' which remained alive for a long time, even if it was contested. This aestheticism, then frequently qualified by 'revolutionary', was at first borrowed from French Symbolism, which made its entrance into Russian literature in 1892 under the pen of Zinada Vengerova: in an article published by the *European Messenger*, she dealt with Verlaine, Mallarmé, Rimbaud, Laforgue and Moréas without making the least distinction between Symbolism and decadence. Baudelaire must be added here: his poetic of correspondences was taken up again by Briussov and Balmont, the founders of the Russian Symbolist school. This first Symbolism was, between 1895 and 1900, a clandestine existence, or, if one prefers it, a marginal one. Merejkowski, whose wife was the poetess Zinaide Hippius, Briussov, Balmont, Dobroliubov and Konieski wished to liberate the imagination from the yoke of a tradition which was felt to be too constraining. Biely wrote in his *Mémoires*: 'That which unites the young Symbolists is not a common programme, a "yes" to the future, but a same resolution in the negation and denial of the past, a "no" thrown in the face of the "fathers".'

It was usual to distinguish two groups, two waves and even two periods in Russian Symbolism. It would require a lot of words to shade this division, (Biely, for example, began by writing in *The Balance* by Briussov, and it would be very hard indeed to find deep affinities between the *mal de vivre* of Sologoub, the urbanist poetry of Briussov, and the Dionysiac hymns of Balmont). Nevertheless, it is certain that from 1900 onwards, the western pattern exercised a less great fascination, and that there was, on the other hand, with Blok, Biely and Ivanov, a return to populism and a desire to continue the great tradition of national poetry.

It is essential to take into account, for this second Russian Symbolism, the influence of Vladimir Soloviev (1853-1900): poet and philosopher, he was the theoretician of this catastrophism of Christian Orthodox inspiration which saw in Russia, in its sorrows and its grandeur, the country of salvation, the 'third Rome' where a theocracy would come to be established, a centre for the reconciliation of humanity. Towards the end of his life, when he was losing faith in his ideal, Soloviev predicted the next coming of the anti-Christ who would submerge Europe. At the centre of these idealist systems which inspired him could be found Sophia, the eternal Wisdom, a marvellous feminine personage who suggested to Blok some of his most beautiful verses. The second Russian Symbolism differed from the French by an apocalyptic meaning of the history which prepared the religious welcome given to the revolution by a part of the *intelligentsia*.

It is possible to see where the dividing line really lay: it was less concerned with the distance which separated two generations, or with the variation between two poetics (for every poet has his poetic), than with the rebirth of an old, an eternal discussion between the Slavophiles and the admirers of Europe.

The year 1910 is considered as marking the end of Russian Symbolism as a movement, with the two articles published by Ivanov and by Blok in the art review *Apollon*. That of Ivanov, the *Precepts of Symbolism*, affirmed the religious mission of Russian Symbolism. Blok's article, *Of the actual State of Russian Symbolism*, went in the same direction. That started a whole polemic, with Briussov replying that Symbolism had never been and had never wanted to be other than an art.

However, the masterpieces of these two great Russian Symbolists, Biely and Briussov, were after that date. Biely published *Petersbury* in 1913, and Blok *Italian Verses*, the *Rose and the Cross* in 1914, the *Verses on Russia* in 1915, *The Twelve* and *The Scytheans* in 1918. But it was then Futurism, the 'slap to the public taste' which was acquiring renown. Khlebnikov dreamed of 'finding the miraculous stone which would transform all Slav words into each other', creating 'the intrinsic Word outside life and living utility': the old dream, after all, of an 'alchemy of the word'. More discreet were the voices of Anna Akhmatova, Goumiliev and Mandelstam, who did not accept the renunciation of earthly things to which Symbolism seemed to constrain the poet: from 1912 onwards, these 'acmeists' proposed to elaborate 'in a greater equilibrium of forms a more exact knowledge of the relations between object and subject.' For this they relied on the word in itself, the only poetic reality, an emphatic and conceptual entity which hovers above the object like the soul above an abandoned corpse.

A CASE IN POINT - HUNGARIAN SYMBOLISM

It is the countries which, at the beginning of the century, knew an intellectual, spiritual or literary revolution whose effervescence recalls that of the Reformation era. This was the case with Hungary. Around 1906-1908, a pleiad of young writers decided to battle against a retrograde mentality and to open Hungarian culture to modern horizons without betraying the national traditions. In 1908, a poetic anthology appeared in Nagyvarad, a kind of manifesto of the young poets, and in Budapest was published the first number of the review *Nyugat* (Occident), the title of which recalls curiously a Spanish publication of the same era. Many names appeared in it, such as Nietzsche and Bergson, French Symbolists, Poe and Swinburne, Yeats and Walter Pater, Rilke and D'Annunzio.

The flag-bearer was a thirty-two year old poet, Endre Ady, whom the reactionary factor blamed for his anti-patriotism, his 'French immorality' and his 'aesthetic anarchy'. From his *New Poems* of 1906 to his *On Elijah's Chariot*, he expressed existential anguish, solitude, physical decay, waiting for death, the struggle with the angel, cursed love, the battle of the poetic prophet against the 'Magyar morass'. Whilst creating a network of original symbols and using a very personal system of versification, he was able to reconcile the conquests of the French

Symbolists with the tendencies of Biblical poetry, Nietzschian and socialist eloquence with the tone of the Calvinist psalmists and *kouroutz* chants.

Behind him came Babits who, after the war, gave a more liberated direction to *Nyugat*; Kosztolanyi, whose *Lamentations of a Poor Little Child* had a considerable success; Juhasz, the tortured poet; Arpad Tóth, the excellent translator; Balazs who was Bartok's librettist; and Milan Füst, poet of 'objective sadness' and father of *vers libre* in Hungary.

One would like to provide a complete list, for Symbolism was a world-wide literary phenomenon. At least the most genuine cases and those with most impact have been covered.

In Italy 'decadentism' was used much more than 'Symbolism'. It enriched Italian culture which, however, grasped badly and often superficially the basic European ideas. Pascoli, in the best of his poetry, played cleverly with the correspondences. D'Annunzio, a superbly gifted artist, was a Symbolist of eclipses, and the Symbolism of *Paradisiac Poem* is not that of *Laudes*. The 'crepuscular' poets (Gozzano, Corazzini) sensitive to the influence of Verlainian *grisaille*, and to Laforgue's irony, were, rather neo-romantics. The same remark could be made about Spanish modernism or the generation of 1880 in Holland.

The Symbolist theatre

The observations which have already been made about Symbolism in literature deserve to be repeated when talking of the Symbolist theatre, a reality so difficult to pin down that it is arguable whether it really existed. Perhaps it is sufficient to describe some of its aspects or some of its temptations.

THE TEMPTATION OF WAGNERIAN DRAMA

Wagnerian drama fascinated the Symbolists, and persuaded them to extend their experiments to the theatre. The founders of *La Revue Wagnérienne*, Téodor de Wyzewa (1863-1917) and Edouard Dujardin, set the tone of it, and Dujardin illustrated it with his *Légende d'Antonia*, a vast trilogy where the heroine, tearing the Maia's veil, 'awakes from the sleep of the pallid life' and expresses

...l'envol	...the flight
De l'âme au-delà de l'apparence par le symbole	Of the soul beyond the appearance by the symbol

Another Wagnerian fanatic, the Sâr Péladan, enlighted by Parsifal, conceived at that time 'the foundation of the three orders of the Rose + Croix, the Temple and the Grail, and the resolve to be the literary pupil of Wagner in the theatre.' His 'Wagneries', *Babylon, Oedipus and the Sphinx, Semiramis*, and the *Promethiade*, were evidence of the sincerity of his intentions rather than of his talent.

A complete performance, Wagnerian drama realized a true union of the arts: poetry, music, dance and scenery. However, if Camille Mauclair, a listener at the 'Tuesdays' is to be believed, 'in the work as Mallarmé dreamed of it...the fusion of words, gestures, decoration, ballet and musical expression was indispensable.' This ambitious realization was, in fact, almost impossible, because it involved expenses which were too high. Also, the Symbolists were praising a simplified aestheticism. Again, the direction of the performance must, according to Mallarmé, come back to the poet who, taking his contribution away from the music, turns drama into a temple for the word. Edouard Schuré (1841-1929) declared that he preferred 'a spoken play with intermittent music' to a musical play. Claudel finally declined the offer of Florent Schmitt who wanted to put *Tête d'Or* to music. And Maeterlinck ended by disowning the admirable *Pelléas* of Debussy.

Like Wagnerian drama, the Symbolist theatre had frequent recourse to the myth. Baudelaire had already rendered homage to Wagner for having understood 'the sacred and divine nature of the myth', and for having searched 'the universal heart of man...for universally intelligible pictures' (*Richard Wagner and 'Tannhäuser' in Paris*). Schuré, in his turn, stated that the 'idealist theatre', the 'theatre of the dream...recounts the Great Work of the Soul in the legend of humanity.' Mallarmé, who used finer distinctions, claimed that 'the French spirit, firmly imaginative and abstract and therefore poetic...is reluctant to reconcile Art in its integrity, which is inventive, with the Legend.' Which does not mean that he excluded myths. On the contrary, according to him: 'the theatre demands them: nothing fixed, secular or notorious, but an entity, freed from the personality, because it composes our multiple facets: which, corresponding to national functioning, evoke the Art of illusion in order to reflect it in us.' A kind of abstract myth, with *Igitur* missing. In its absence we are left with the work of mythological inspiration, resuming either Greek myths (this is the case with the mythological tragedies of Annenski who wished to fill the gap left by the lost dramas of Euripides, or by certain plays of Hofmannsthal) or national legends (Yeats depicts the mythical heroes of Ireland, such as Cuchulain, Emer and Conchubar). A dramatist like Wyspianski can pass easily from one register to another.

THE TEMPTATION OF HISTORICAL DRAMA

The dramatists of this time passed with the same ease from history to myth, or from myth to history. The romantic model of historical drama still preserved its prestige, but had nevertheless been overtaken. Jean-Louis Backès, (in *Aspects du drama poétique dans les symbolisme européen*) showed very well how, for example, since *La Rose et la Croix* is one of the Symbolist dramas in which historic reality is most inconsiderately presented (he studied characteristics of various customs capable of evoking a picture of life in the Middle Ages), Alexandre Blok refused to give it the name of historical drama. Furthermore he did not propose to stage a historic fact, and the plot is pure fiction even if the action is set at the beginning of the thirteenth century. There is no indication at all of this type of theatre in the early works of Claudel: it was later, in *L'Annonce faite à Marie*, although not in *La jeune fille Violaine*, that the history of the martyr of Combernon is set in the Middle Ages. And yet it is always a Middle Ages of convention, just as *Soulier de Satin* is about conventional Spain.

In the theatre of Yeats can be found plays where the action is fairly precisely dated: 1798 in *Cathleen in Houlihan*, which makes allusion to an actual historic event — the disembarkation of the French expedition of General Humbert in the Bay of Killala and the revolt against the English occupation which followed; the start of the nineteenth century for the *Unicorn of the Stars* on a similar subject. But the work of reconstitution stops at practically nothing, and the playwright wished to incarnate a reality which goes further than history: the image of patriarchal Ireland takes a back seat for the benefit of a different picture of Ireland, that of the old woman who is suddenly rejuvenated.

It is this process of accession to another truth and another reality which is essential. The adventure of *Tête d'Or* led the conqueror, whose heroic deed recalls the epic of Napoleon, towards the discovery of 'the colossal church of the blaze' and his passion like that of Christ which in many ways, served him as a model, taking him away from things temporal. In *La Rose et la Croix* Gaétan does not stick to history; at the end of the play nothing remains but wretchedness, and there is an impression of not going anywhere at all. As Jean-Louis Backès, again, wrote: 'The survival, among the Symbolists, of figures borrowed from historical romantic drama, does not in any way signify a return to realism on the part of the poets. On the contrary, reality is only intended in order that it may be confronted by an extra-historic reality which denies it.'

In spite of his links with romanticism, Ibsen soon left the iron collar, and when, at the end of the century, Jarry in *Ubu roi* went back to the format of historical drama (and in particular to that of Shakespearian historical drama, including *Richard III*) it was to parody it, therefore to deny it again. The return of Ubu to Paris like a 'maître des phynances', the multiple anachronisms, are as many ways of breaking the ranks, and the long flowing gowns of the ever-renascent hero show that the cyclical form outweighs the linearity of the time. As Blok wrote: 'There are, it seems, two levels of time and space: one is historic, linked to the calendar; the other is immeasurable, musical. It is only the first level of time and space which are present in civilized consciousness; we only live in the second when we are aware of our proximity to nature, when we abandon ourselves to the musical wave which comes from the cosmic orchestra.'

THE TEMPTATION OF THE IDEALIST THEATRE

In fact, the Symbolist theatre was in search of another totality. In *Crayonne au theatre* Mallarmé said that the new drama would be the representation 'of the play written in the folio of the sky and mimed, with the gesture of his passions, by Man.' According to Schuré, he tried to 'link the human to the divine, to show in earthly man a reflection and a sanction of this transcendent world, this beyond', in which he must believe. Undoubtedly, the strict application of the doctrine is not possible: one must be content to suggest 'the tenebrous side of existence', as Ibsen did in *Ghosts* , or even to realize it 'by the scenic means of the author addressing himself to the imagination of the reader' like Villiers de l'Isle-Adam in *Axël*.

Villiers' hero, Axël d'Auërsperg, had, in spite of the efforts of his tutor Master Janus, begun by choosing reality over the ideal. The desire for gold and for life had invaded his soul. But the most absolute idealism, revealed by the message in 'the passionate world' triumphs in the end. It is towards this escape to the ideal, rather than to words, appearances and ideas (its own task, assigned to it by the ideo-realism of Saint-Pol Roux) that the Symbolist theatre invites us.

The seeker after the absolute appears many a time in the theatre of this period: Ibsen; Brand, who broke with the social conventions to concentrate exclusively on sincere works of truth; Solness, who built a tower and wished to crown the top of it. But the presentation does not allow ambiguity: the failure of the hero (Solness) and his mockery (Jean-Gabriel Borkman) dealt a fatal blow to idealism. Besides, if realism is excluded and impractical, is absolute idealism any more admissible? It is at most a goal. Should the hero lose his spirit, the play be reduced to a philosophic thesis, or the performance turn into a draught, the theatre would die.

Camille Mauclair claimed that Symbolism was incapable 'by its very principles to manifest itself in the theatre'. That is why without doubt it found itself in an uncomfortable position. Mallarmé pronounced the actor undesirable, Maeterlinck considered that 'the representation of a masterpiece with the help of accidental and human elements is antinomic' because 'the symbol never supports the active presence of man', and yet it happened that this theatre, which ought to have remained shut away inside its book, was played. The theatre was public, and people dreamed of secret mysteries. Then it was necessary to use cunning, to imagine, for example, the hierarchy proposed by Schuré of a popular theatre which, 'descending towards the people would awake their sleeping soul with its best instincts and its most poetic traditions'; a theatre of the City (that of Ibsen and Tolstoy) which would 'study contemporary reality with the penetrating look of acute observation and profound sympathy'; and a theatre of the dream or the soul, reserved for an élite, which would 'evoke a superior humanity in the mirror of history, of legend and of the symbol': *Axël*, the dramas of Péladan or of D'Annunzio.

Experience proves that this theatre would only have been possible if it stayed within bounds. In this respect Maeterlinck's work remains exemplary: it wants to make us aware of our 'tragique quotidien', yet for all that, can be content with so little: silences, expectations and signs.

Conclusion

There are two ways of approaching and presenting European Symbolism. To hold to a strict definition, that of Symbolism as idealism in literature, one would obtain a straight list of authors and one would still be obliged to agree that each one of them (Mallarmé, for example) became at certain times unorthodox. To adopt a wide definition, that of Symbolism as the *fin de siècle*, would be to lose the actual notion of the literary current, because Symbolism was a diffuse movement which had to be manoeuvred between these two methods of approach.

Was Symbolism, after all, a myth, as Valéry tried to suggest? And has the term no merit other than its elasticity? It seems much more likely that it corresponds to certain aspirations which were themselves very precise: to rival music, renew the poetic, to see through poetry to its essence, to discover the world of Essences, and in any case to give the feeling of the mystery of the 'beyond' of phenomena and the depths of the self. As Gaëtan Picon accurately wrote: 'Language privileged within language or experience privileged within experience, it is in the privilege that the diverse forms of Symbolism come together.'

ADY Endre (Erdmindszent 1877 — Budapest
1919). A Hungarian in whose soul flickered the
fire of a frisky colt: that is how he described himself in his poetry. In fact he was a forceful personality; he knew how to stress interior conflicts as
well as those of his country which were almost
congenital to him.

> In my soul the Hungarian tree
> and its foliage yield, fall;
> in the same way I must
> sink into foliage, foliage.

That, without doubt, is the basic analogy in the
work of this master of Hungarian Symbolism.

He was born in Transylvania, studied at the
University of Debrecen, and went into journalism.

Portrait of Endre Ady

In 1899 he settled in Nagyvarad where, in 1903,
he met a married woman, Adel, with whom he fell
passionately in love. By an anagram of her name,
she became the Leda of his poetry. At her instigation he went to Paris in 1904, and again from
1906 to 1908. There he was astonished to discover
western society, and he led a dissolute life. On
returning to his own country he denounced both
the semi-feudal system which existed there, and
the way of life to which his exacerbated personality objected. In 1906 his collection *New Poems* ('Uj
versek') represented a revolution in Hungarian
poetry, and broke completely with the manner of
his first two collections. Proclaiming himself a
child of the people, the poet claimed to have
brought with him from the west the songs of new
times. The book aroused controversy which
doubled when *Blood and Gold* ('Vér és Arany') was
published in 1907. The world is influenced by
two great forces, sensuality and cupidity, and the
two images in the title of the book are their symbols. Man wages a desperate struggle against the

'ancestral Devil', demon of drunkenness and lust.
As for Woman, she is idolized and hated at the
same time in his cycle of poems *Leda in the Garden*.

In 1908 Ady became the patron of the revue
Nyugat (Occident), a central point for the rallying
of the young Hungarian writers who wished to
abolish what was out of date, and to make new
voices heard. He then published many collections:
On Elijah's Chariot ('Az Illés szereken', 1908), *I wish
someone loved me* ('Szeretném ha szeretnének', 1909),
Poems of all Secrets ('Minden titkok versei', 1910),
where he gradually abandoned the pleasures of
the Symbolist style in order to adopt the accents of
the Biblical prophets, and to develop visions of
the apocalypse. Time, Death, and Nothingness
made up a kind of terrifying Trinity. 'I have not
come to be a virtuoso' declared Ady: 'I have
wanted All, I can thus accept Nothing.' Having
broken with Leda, Ady married in 1915 a young
girl of noble birth, Csinska. The verses which he
dedicated to her exalted the beauty and purity of
love, the ultimate refuge in a world ravaged by the
war. Ady, who had seen the catastrophe coming,
had no expression violent enough to condemn it.
In a last vision he saw the whole Magyar people
rushing headlong, at the same time as himself,
into death (*The Army of the Dead*, 'A halottak élén',
1918).

Ady read the French poets; in his work can be
found the passionate accents of Baudelaire and
the peaceable cadences of Verlaine. But his
Symbolism was powerfully original. He took his
metaphors from the reality of Hungarian daily life
or from great Biblical stories. Above all he made a
voice heard, a voice which has often been compared to that of Nietzsche, a man surrounded by
inhumanity.

> To the proud Hungarian no more happiness
> will ever be given by a hundred skies, a hundred
>   hells:
> I am a man amongst inhumanity,
> I am a Hungarian in the Hungarian downfall;
> revived, I refuse to die.

ANNENSKI Innokenti Fedorovitch (Omsk 1856 –
St Petersburg 1909). A Russian poet who was
orphaned at an early age, he was brought up by
his elder brother, Nicolas, in St Petersburg. He
studied literature and became director of the
Lycée in 1896. Dismissed from office for pro-
tecting pupils involved in the revolutionary
disturbances, and then appointed superintendent,
he died prematurely of a heart attack. He was
forty-eight years old when, in 1904, he published
under his pseudonym Nikto (No one) his first
verses, the *Calm Songs* to which were added the
translations of Baudelaire, Rimbaud, Verlaine and
Mallarmé. Blok and Briussov received the volume
favourably. Annenski also published plays during
his lifetime (*Melanippus the Philosopher*, *The Tsar Ixion*
and *Laodamia*), two books of critical essays (*The*

Book of Reflections, 1906, 1909), and other translations. His second collection of verse, *The Cypress Casket*, appeared one year after his death and was acclaimed a masterpiece.

Annenski had no concern for a transcendental absolute; his quest was that of the unity of self with the world. 'I am', he wrote, 'the child of a sick generation, and I shall not go in search of the Rose of the Alps; neither the whisper of the world, nor the roar of the first storms give me feelings of joy. But figures in tear-drop diamonds on a rose-coloured glass, the patterns of frost, a mass of roses appearing on the table, and the embroidery of the evening fire — these are the things which are dear to me.'

BABITS Mihály (Szekszárd 1883 — Budapest 1941) A Hungarian writer. He studied literature, soon became a teacher, and made his debut at the same time as the review *Nyugat*. He was more of a literary man than Ady and he carefully looked for unpublished ideas and themes. His culture was very wide (his numerous translations constitute additional proof of this) and he was alert to the great voices of European poetry (Browning, Poe, Baudelaire, Verlaine, Carducci, Liliencron) to

RIPPL-RONAI *Portrait of Mihály Babits*

enrich that of his own country. *Leaves from the Crown of Iris* (1908), *Prince, the Winter may come* (1911), *Recitative* (1916), are all brilliant works which show

a poet who, nevertheless, had difficulty in leaving his 'magic circle':

> I am my only hero, from poem to poem,
> over me my song shuts itself up even as it opened.
> I would like to enclose the world in my verses.
> But I cannot succeed in leaving my theme.

Major events such as the First World War and the rise of Nazism brought him out of himself. To relate all his achievements (which were never those of a militant), the manifestations of his Catholic faith, the considerable role he played as director of *Nyugat*, his success in the world of the novel and the essay, would go beyond the boundaries of a work on Symbolism. The last image which he left of himself, in *The Book of Jonas* (1940), must not be forgotten, however: it was that of a prophet whom God ordered to denounce sin, and who, lacking the necessary strength, abandoned his task.

BALMONT Konstantin Dmitriev (Ivanovo-Voznesensk 1867 — Paris 1943). A Russian poet. René Ghil considered him his Russian disciple, the only one who could have unreservedly accepted his system of verbal instrumentation. But Balmont's name is principally linked with that of Verlaine, for whom he translated, with a very happy result, the *Romances without words*.

There was a certain similarity, to start with, between the destinies of Verlaine and Balmont. His slightly unbalanced temperament and his morbid nature became apparent at a very early stage; he knew the temptation of suicide. In 1886 he enrolled at the university of Moscow, but he was sent down for holding subversive opinions and for having taken part in a student demonstration. His first verses, published in 1890, told of the torment of a youth spent 'in the trough of the waves'. But *Under the Northern Sky* testified to his desire to grasp life and to open his mind to it. In the preface to the second volume of his complete works, Balmont explained that he had wanted to show in them what a poet who loved music could do with Russian verse. *Silence*, his third collection, was perhaps even more remarkable in this respect. Ellis wrote: 'It is really only in the works of van Lerberghe and the best of Verlaine's stanzas that one can hear an equally angelic music, coming from one knows not where.'

Balmont announced, however 'something different.' His next collections *In the Unlimited* (1895), *Ardent Edifices* (1900), *Let us be like the Sun* (1903), *Only Love* (1904) and *Liturgy of Beauty* (1905) showed a provocative and cynical tone where traces of Nietzscheism could still be found. Speaking about them he said: 'I want to be the first to be insolent. Involved by Gorki in the revolution of 1905, and yielding to the temptation of political poetry in *Songs of the Avenger*, published in 1906 in Paris where he had taken refuge, Balmont had gone beyond Symbolism. His theoretic essay of 1915, *Poetry like Magic*, proposed a new formula for a reconsidered and extended Symbolism. For him poetry only rediscovered an ancestral and immemorial use of language, such as was found in ancient civilizations where the poet was the mage. Music, of course, is the art of magic par excellence. The musician, like the poet, interprets the world, establishes a liaison between man and nature, recreates the world in naming it, and creates harmonies out of chaos. Balmont insisted on power of letters:

> 'Each letter wants to speak separately...In M there is the dead cold of winter, in A the sovereign spring. M is like the stone, A like the vermilion ruby, but sometimes the opal of lunar charm — more often the diamond which plays in the sunshine, the whole range of colours.'

He recognizes thus one of the obsessions of Symbolism: to transform the word into pure musical incantation. And if Balmont is in debt to Nietzsche, it is probably less the vindication of the superman than a Dionysiac predilection for music.

Having returned to Russia in 1913, Balmont gave vent to his patriotism in 1914. In 1917 he returned to the Revolution for a while, but quite soon chose liberty. He took refuge in France, taking advantage of an official mission. Perhaps, as mandelstam said of him, he had been 'a foreigner in Russian poetry'.

BAUDELAIRE Charles (Paris 1821 — Paris 1867). This French poet could not be considered as a representative of any Symbolist school whatsoever. However, all works on Symbolism, or practically all, devote a first chapter to him. Mallarmé had already raised a 'Tombeau' to him, and Valéry underlined, in an article in *Variété* ('Situation de Baudelaire'), his influence on the major *fin de siècle* poets, as much in France (Verlaine, Rimbaud, Mallarmé) as abroad (Swinburne, D'Annunzio, George).

A POET'S DESTINY

Perhaps the word 'quest' has never been more appropriate. Baudelaire was always in search of an 'elsewhere'. Paradoxically this man who travelled little (in 1841 his family put him aboard the 'Paquebot-des-mers-du-Sud' on its way to Calcutta, but he did not get further than the islands of Mauritius and Bourbon; at the end of his life he went to Belgium in 1864 and came back physically weakened, with a packet of vindictive notes against so much 'menacing stupidity') was the poet of travel: the poet of the departure desired by all those who had 'the wish to travel and to get rich' (*Le Port*, in the *Spleen de Paris*), of the looking-glass countries where all the most secret wishes are

fulfilled (*Invitation au Voyage*), of the endless odysseys which wish to lead 'to the bottom of the Unknown to find the new' (*Le Voyage*).

Guy Michaud, who saw in Baudelaire 'the eternal traveller in search of an impossible elsewhere' said again of him that he 'had realized his destiny, he had not vanquished it.' It was a weighty destiny in truth, marked, if one is to believe the poet, by the curses of his mother, and one which

COURBET *Portrait of Baudelaire*. 1848

constantly fell back on to the Sisyphus who tried to lift it. The remarriage of the widow Baudelaire-Dufaÿs to the future general Aupick, the dismissal from the Louis-le-Grand college, the intervention of the family council which endowed him with legal advice in the person of Maître Ancelle, a lawyer from Neuilly — there were so many events and incidents which placed him very early on in an uncomfortable position.

To escape the turmoil of his life, the 'misery' which he never stopped lamenting, and the illness of which he felt the first serious attack in 1850, Baudelaire looked for some refuge. By another paradox, this poet of profundity belonged to the cult of the appearance, dandyism, that elegance which was both haughty and flippant at the same time, which in 1845 Barbey d'Aurevilly was eulogizing. Samuel Cramer, the hero of a novel entitled *La Fanfarlo*, could have passed for a self-portrait of Baudelaire the dandy, ultra-fashionable with his black coat and his ox-blood cravat. The rivalry must not mislead us. For Baudelaire, dandyism had the value of a truly modern stoicism, it was the smile of Lacedaemon under the biting of the fox.

Excluded from the 'green paradise of childish loves', Baudelaire went in search of other paradises, natural or artificial. The latter are well known from his essay *Du Vin et du Haschisch* (1851), from the *Poème du Haschisch* (1860) and from the study of Thomas de Quincey, *Un Mangeur d'Opium*: there he analyzed the 'mysterious effects' and the 'morbid pleasures which drugs can engender', the 'inevitable punishments which result from their prolonged use', and finally 'immorality itself involved in this pursuit of a false ideal.' It is significant, and Baudelaire lays stress on it, that the collection *Paradis artificiels* should be dedicated to a woman, the woman 'who projects the greatest shade or the greatest light in our dreams', and who 'lives spiritually in the imaginations which she haunts and fertilizes'. A poem from *Fleurs du mal* 'The Poison', puts on to the same plane the four parts of the series which he develops: wine, opium, the poison which flows from the green eyes of a loved woman, her 'saliva which bites'.

BAUDELAIRE *Portrait of Jeanne Duval*

Jeanne Duval, the mulatto for pleasure and distaste, Madame Sabatier, the false madonna, Marie Daubrun, the actress, and others, have their place less in the anecdotal recital of Baudelaire's loves than in a subtle eroticism, which is still the creation of a paradise. And, at the end of the journey across the sea of darkness of which Poe spoke, what does Baudelaire ask of death if not to be another poison?

Refuge of refuges: work. To live, in every sense of the word, Baudelaire had to write. Literary creation, born of an inner necessity, corresponds also to an economic necessity. The first publications of the writer were not very nourishing: articles on art criticism (*Salon de 1845, Salon de 1846*) and some translations of the *Tales of Fantasy and Imagination* of Edgar Allan Poe — a 'great affair' in which he was swindled by the publisher. As for his actual muse, Baudelaire stated that it was 'venal'. Another disillusionment: the collection of *Les Fleurs du Mal*, put together and published in 1857, was seized by Parquet, attacked, condemned, and submitted to a mutilation that successive editions (the one of 1861, the posthumous one of 1868 on which the poet had worked) never quite succeeded in making him forget altogether. Baudelaire did not dream of becoming rich; he only wanted to pay his debts. Also, more than ever, he had to write. He carried in his head 'about twenty novels and two plays', and a quantity of plans. There remained rough drafts, fragments (the astonishing intimate notes regrouped under the title of *Fusées* and *Mon coeur mis à nu* and his 'poèmes nocturnes', of which there should be a hundred, and only fifty have been found and published under the title *Spleen de Paris* or *Petits Poèmes en Prose*. Just like his quest, the work of Baudelaire must remain unfinished: this was truly his fate.

THE SYMBOLISM OF BAUDELAIRE

The burden of pathos in Baudelaire's poetry is such that at first one remembers the theme. When Valéry discovered in him 'the powerful and confused mixture of mystic emotion and sensual passion which developed in Verlaine' and 'the frenzy of departure, the movement of impatience excited by the universe...which render the brief and violent work of Rimbaud so energetic and so active', he was yielding to this temptation. The decadent literature reassembled the themes of Baudelairian *morbidezza* and pushed them into paroxysm. Bu the important thing is perhaps not there. And decadence only being, after all, a neo-Romanticism, or an aggravation of Romanticism. Baudelaire is in this only a Romantic.

In the manner of Romantic poetry, his poetry is symbolic before being Symbolist. A celebrated piece such as *L'Albatros* provides a good example of this. A comparison is developed here between the 'vast birds of the seas' who, 'kings of the azure look so woeful when the sailors set them down on the planks of the deck, and the poet, made for the Ideal and captive of the spleen, who is 'exiled on the ground' and whose 'giant wings prevent him from walking'. The albatross is a symbolic image of the poet, it is another way of speaking of him and an allegory in the proper meaning of the

. GERVEX and A. STEVENS *Portrait of Charles Baudelaire.* 1889
rom left to right: V. Massé, Sainte-Beuve, Barbey
Aureville, Manger and Baudelaire)

ord. The poet multiplies allegories in a similar
ay: to speak of his exile, he summons in turn
ndromache in Epirus, a swan escaped from its
age, Ovid in Tomes, the negress who, in Paris,
reams of her superb Africa — and he is so
onscious of the process that he admits '...every-
ing for me becomes an allegory' (*Le Cygne*).

This feeling of exile introduces us, however,
 the Symbolism of Baudelaire. This land of
e Ideal, from which he has been chased but
 which he is conscious of belonging, has some-
ing of the Platonic world of Ideas. For the poet,
nsible forms are only representations, symbols
 an ideal reality, and more true. The 'secret
ouloureux' of which the sonnet *La Vie antérieure*
eaks, is the hidden desire to arrive at this
preme state of elevation, suggested in another
em, which permits to 'soar above life' and 'to
nderstand without effort':

'the language of flowers and speechless things'.

Elevation would be a privileged method of
cess to completeness, but remains a method of

dreams. Baudelaire knew the pangs, which can
become delightful, of patient deciphering. He
wrote: 'The whole world is only a store of images
and signs to which imagination gives a place and a
relative value.' It is in this that the imagination is
'queen of the faculties'. The sonnet *Corresondances*
could, from that time, appear as a key text:

> La Nature est un temple où de vivants piliers
> Laissent parfois sortir de confuses paroles;
> L'homme y passe à travers des forêts de symboles
> Qui l'observent avec des regards familiers.
>
> Comme de longs échos qui de loin se confondent
> Dans une ténébreuse et profonde unité,
> Vaste comme la nuit et comme la clarté,
> Les parfums, les couleurs et les sons se répondent.
>
> Il est des parfums frais commes des chairs
>   d'enfants,
> Doux commes les hautbois, verts comme les
>   prairies,
> Et d'autres, corrompus, riches et triomphants,
>
> Ayant l'expansion des choses infinies,
> Comme l'ambre, le musc, le benjoin et l'encens
> Qui chantent les transports de l'esprit et des sens.
>
> Nature is a temple where living pillars
> Sometimes allow confused words to escape;
> Man passes there through forests of symbols
> That watch him with familiar glances.
>
> Like long-drawn-out echoes mingled far away
> Into a deep and shadowy unity,
> Vast as darkness and light,
> Scents, colours and sounds answer one another.
>
> There are some scents cool as the flesh of
>   children,
> Sweet as oboes and green as meadows –
> And others corrupt, rich and triumphant
>
> Having the expansion of things infinite,
> Like amber, musk, benzoin and incense,
> Singing the raptures of the mind and senses.
> (Translated by Anthony Hartley, Penguin Book
> of French Verse, No.3. 1957)

The religious vocabulary of the first quatrain
suggests a mystic experience, the presence of the
sacred in a world where everything is only symbolic of a higher reality ('vertical' correspondences). But correspondences, 'horizontal' this
time, also exist between the feelings in the 'tenebrous and profound unity' of the sensible. Baudelaire was confirming an intuition which he had
noticed in the works of the German romantics,
especially Hoffmann, and Edgar Allan Poe, and
which the experience of artifical paradises had
confirmed. The consequence of this revelation
was a double one; on one hand poetry must be in
correspondence with the other arts, architecture,
engraving, sculpture, painting and music. On the
other hand, poetry must translate the correspondences between the sensations, whether it remains
content to describe them or whether it invents
alliances of bold words and a poetic of the
transfer ('green perfumes', 'blue hair', 'resonant
jewels'). Valéry claimed that we owe to Baudelaire

the 'return of our poetry towards its essence'. It is in any case a poetry which looks for the essence, and which finds the essential.

Portrait of Andrei Biely. 1899

BIELY Andrei (Moscow 1880 — Moscow 1934). His real name was Boris Nicolaevitch Bougaev, and he was the son of Bougaev the mathematician. He himself attended advanced studies at the faculty of sciences, and always dreamed of bringing together the exact sciences and music.

He assumed a pseudonym in order not to shock his father by the publication of decadent verse. Biely, which means 'candid' was a mystic and an idealist and he came under the influence of Soloviev. From the time of his first collection of poems, *Gold on Azure* (1903), his morbid obsessions were apparent. *The Symphonies* (1902-1908), constructed on leitmotivs, inaugurated modernism. Although the symbol was for him a method of access to the mystery of life, he did not exclude the hope of 'changing life'. His subsequent works reflected his own fate in the fate of Russia: *Cinder* (1909) united their miseries. At about the same time, he wrote the novels which perhaps constituted the best of his work: *Petersburg* (1909) and *The Silver Pigeon* (1910).

In 1911, he met Assia Tourguenev, who was to become his wife. The following year he went with her to Switzerland, and they participated with Rudolf Steiner in the erection of the Goetheanum, a temple of anthroposophy. The war led him back to Russia, where he became the theorist of Symbolism. His investigations into the structure of verse constituted the origin of formal criticism. His links with reality became more and more slack,

as *Notebooks of a Crazy Man* (1922) show. Biely, furthermore, abandoned poetry in order t compose a trilogy of souvenirs: *At the Turn of th Century* (1930), *The beginning of the Century* (1933) and *Between Two Revolutions* (1934).

For the historian of Russian Symbolism, th evidence of Biely is irreplaceable. As for his work it shines with apocalyptic brilliance in a languag of radiant power which, in spite of its excesses remains incomparable.

BLOK Alexander (St Petersburg 1880 — Petro grad 1921). A Russian writer, grandson of Andre Betekov, who was a botanist and rector of th University of St Peterburg, he was brought u by his mother and two aunts, and his early lif had two centres: the apartment in St Petersbur and the little white house in Chakmatovo, nea Moscow, where he spent his holidays. In 1898 h commenced his law studies, but the discover of Soloviev and of modern poetry turned hir towards literature. He made his own the religiou and philosophic myths of the 1900s, by recreatin them according to the development of his ow universe. The eternal feminine, which is the Hol Mother of God, the angel woman, was also th prostitute of the town to whom, by an ironi change of direction, Blok attributed the burden the souls of the world. In poems such as *The Litt Fair Booth* he came to parody his own mysticism.

Portrait of Alexander Blok

In 1903 Blok married Liubova Mendéléeva (the daughter of the illustrious chemist): he made three trips to Italy and France, and every six years he stayed in Bad-Nauheim to which he attributed a mystic significance. And thus his life went by, without notable incident, until the October Revolution which inspired him to write *The Twelve*: supreme hope, but also bitter disillusion which only added to his later sufferings.

The lyrical work of Blok is divided into three parts. The first (1898-1904) was marked by the influence of Soloviev and dominated by the mystic symbol of the Belle Dame.

The second (*The Mask and the Snow*, 1907), was dominated by the face of the Unknown, the Gipsy; his versification was freer, his vocabulary less formal, and his inspiration became more down to earth the more his scepticism grew. The third was devoted to Russia; because, however personal the vision of Blok, it went beyond the egocentricity which was characteristic of the first Russian Symbolism, and of which Briussov's title *Me eum esse*, was the motto. The nationalism of Blok, evidently, was a rapport between persons: the poet invoked Russia as his wife in the *Field of Woodcock* (the name of the battle which freed Russia from the Tatar yoke) and, in another poem in 1908, he declared: 'Russia, unhappy Russia, the grey of thy isbas, thy songs in the wind are like the first tears of love.' But such identification of the nation with woman can only be understood in the function of the myth of the eternal Sophia.

Blok soon became interested in the theatre. In his youth he had taken part in amateur performances in the house of his future wife. Later his liaison with an actress, Nathalie Volokova, gave the theatre a larger place in his life. His first *Lyric Dramas* (1906), which included *The Little Fair Booth*, *The King on the Spot* and *The Unknown Woman*, expressed the modern soul 'necessarily solitary', 'full of chaotic and inextricable notions', resolved to remain apart from life. There were no more 'characters'; the personages were only 'the masks of their creator'. *The Song of Destiny* (1908) was directly autobiographical. And it was Blok again who was the troubadour in *The Rose and the Cross* (1913). Scenery of a legendary Brittany permitted Blok in this play to portray the tragedy of the lyric poet, one of the elect, but misunderstood and alone.

Like the Nietzsche of *The Birth of Tragedy* (a work which exercised a great influence on him) Blok thought that music was the essence of the world. The poet should listen to it, and if he can be called 'symbolist', it is because he is a 'magician, possessed of a secret knowledge, behind which a secret action takes place.'

BRIUSSOV Valéry Iakovlévich (Moscow 1873 — Moscow 1924). A Russian poet, considered as the most important of the first Russian Symbolists. He was still a student at the University of Moscow when he published at his own expense the three little volumes of *Russian Symbolists* (1894-95), which made him instantly famous, or rather, if one is to believe it, made him into 'the sad hero of the cheap papers and the shrewd newspaper serialists who were not scrupulous over their choice of subject'. In reality, the influence of Heine mixed with that of the French poets; the Parnassian precision exercised its influence on the same grounds as *vers libre*, the verbal instrumentation of René Ghil, the hermetism of Mallarmé and the cult of rare words in the manner of Laurent Tailhade. Briussov was asked to become the director of a Symbolist school; this he did, but he soon found himself in the position of a leader without an army.

Portrait of Valéry Iakovlévich Briussov

A tireless worker, organizer of editions of the *Scorpion* in 1899, chief editor of *La Balance*, travelling often to western Europe (where he knew Verhaeren in particular), Briussov translated a great number of French and Belgian Symbolist poems in his anthology *Lyric French Poets of the Nineteenth Century* (1909).

From 1894 onwards, he translated the *Romances without Words* of Verlaine, and it was under the influence of this poet that he put his first collections together. In the preface of *Masterpieces* he stated that 'the extreme individualism of poetry' should henceforth be 'centred on the personality of the artist.'

His relationship with Baudelaire revealed another ambiguity: Briussov had made an orthodox Symbolist credo understood, founded on metaphysical dualism; there, where there is no mystery, there is no art. But Briussov was lacking in vision, and it could be said that he had 'substituted that which he invented for that which he could not see'. He frequently changed his model, and it was soon Verhaeren who became his favourite. At a stroke he abandoned the contemplate Symbolism of his first period to sing the praises of the modern town and the powers of which it was the bringer (*Urbi et orbi*, 1903). The theme of modernity predominated again in *Stefanos* (1906) which was an appeal for action. Briussov also believed in the 'scientific poetry' predicted by René Ghil.

His fame became immense. His novels (*The Angel of Fire*, *The Altar of Victory*), his critical essays (*The Far and the Near*), all contributed to it. But academicism was lying in wait for him. Were his activities as correspondent for several newspapers during the war, his loyalty to the Bolshevik party after the 1917 revolution, going to tear him away from it? No — because at heart he had only disdain for politics. 'I have other things to do' he said; 'I am more inclined to teach advanced poetic mathematics than political arithmetic...Art must be free from all fetters; it is only then that it can grow.' From then on, if he referred to Symbolism, it was because it had taught him the processes of creation, nothing more, because it had been a movement of 'liberation of artistic creation in general.' But Symbolism from then on became established in the wider current of modern art.

CASTRO Eugenio de (Coimbra 1869 — Coimbr[a] 1944). A Portuguese poet who was responsible fo[r] introducing Symbolism to Portugal. A trip to Pari[s] in 1889 gave him the chance to discover this ne[w] literature. He remembered principally the feeling[s] and the unusual expressions, a gratuitous refine[-] ment of form noticeable in his anthology *Oarist*[os] (1890). The preface to this work and the audacit[y] of *Hours* gave rise to a scandal. Afterwards Eugenio de Castro expressed his philosophi[c] restlessness by means of myths: *Sagramor* (1895) wa[s] a reincarnation of Faust; *King Galaor* shut hi[s] daughter away to remove from her the temptatio[n] to live. He came back later, little by little, to simpl[e] and tender poetry which was more in accord wit[h] the traditional Portuguese lyricism.

FELIX VALLOTTON *Portrait of Paul Claudel*

FELIX VALLOTTON *Portrait of Eugenio de Castro*

CLAUDEL Paul (Villeneuve-sur-Fere 1868 – Paris 1955). A French writer. Should we think [of] him as a 'delayed Symbolist', or, on the contrar[y] state, as Jacques Madaule did, that he was onl[y] 'superficially the disciple of the Symbolists'? H[is] literary debut, in any case, coincided with th[e] period when Symbolism was at its height. In 188[?] he did not only have the revelation of the joy [of] Christianity in the vaults under Notre Dame i[n] Paris; he also discovered in *La Vogue* the genius [of] Rimbaud, which exercised, as he himself put it, [a] 'seminal influence' on him. It must not be thoug[ht] that he would retain from this a vague imagery, [

fashionable ways of writing; the encounter with Rimbaud was very much a spiritual adventure, which prepared the way for his conversion. Claudel had hardly visited the literary milieux, but he had been to Mallarmé's house. When he published, without signature, his first important play *Tête d'Or* in 1890, he took good care to send it to Albert Mockel, and his production of it was certainly that of a symbolic drama. 'Cébès is ancient man in relation to modern man, and also pitiable weakness, situated beyond the help of his brother who, not knowing anything either, can only give him blood and tears. The Princess, besides her theatrical role, represents all the concepts of sweetness and gentleness; the soul, womanhood, Goodness and Piety.' It is Symbolist also if one thinks that it is first a book which is frequently esoteric, that it makes use of *vers libre*, or rather that which has been called — in a manner which he did not much like — Claudelian verse. The first version of *La Ville*, written in 1890, published like *Tête d'Or* anonymously and at the bookshop of Independent Art, was more difficult and more swarming with ideas, and carried the mark of the visits of the young writers who were his friends — Marcel Schwob, Camille Mauclair, Jules Renard — who formed at that time a sort of literary circle at the café Harcourt.

La Jeune Fille Violaine, the drama of Tardenois, *L'Echange*, an American play, *Le Repos du Septième Jour*, a Chinese drama, were added to two new versions of *Tête d'Or* and *La Ville* to make, in 1901, the collection of *L'Arbre*, which has the right to be considered the finest work of theatrical Symbolism. At the same time Claudel, a diplomat in China, wrote prose on the *Connaissance de l'Est* where he applied Mallarmé's rule: 'learn to see'. It is a book of exercises' he explained later to Frédéric Lefèvre: 'I compare it to a diplomatic grill, artful lace made of fullnesses and voids which give a meaning to a collection of ordinary words.'

At the beginning of the century, Claudel composed one after another, a poetic collection, the *Cinq Grandes Odes*, a treaty, *L'Art poétique*, and a new play *Partage de Midi*. These three works were imprinted with the seal of the burning passion he had just experienced. But they also illustrated an actual effort to reply to the questions which press on us, and to search in 'all moving or living things which surround us...the sparse explanation of the interior thrust which makes our own life.' When Claudel wrote that 'the image is not a part of the whole; it is the symbol of it', he was going in the same direction as the Symbolist doctrine: man, being both the image of God, and carrying in himself the image of the universe at the same time, is capable of bringing the image of the world back in to a divine plane, and of finding again in each image the symbol of invisible reality.

Guy Michaud considered the whole of the later work of Claudel was 'a long and magnificent development of the premises contained in *L'Art poétique*.' It is impossible to give here even an idea of the great dramas of his maturity (*L'Annonce faite à Marie* the trilogy of the Coûfontaine, *Le Soulier de satin*), numerous poetic collections of which *La Cantate à trois voix* is the most outstanding, and a work in marvellously varied prose which goes from the circumstantial article to free literary interpretations of the Bible. All this without doubt goes beyond Symbolism (if by Symbolism one means a movement limited in duration), but it all comes under the sign of religious Symbolism: because, according to Claudel, it is 'by the symbol that one goes truly and substantially towards God.'

CORBIERE Tristan (Morlaix 1845 — Morlaix 1875). A French poet. Verlaine called him 'a Breton, a sailor and disdainful par excellence.' He was born near Morlaix, suffered the 'caged life' of the school at Saint-Brieuc, which he had to leave when he contracted acute rheumatism. On the advice of the doctor he went in 1863 to live in Roscoff, 'the Nice of the north', where he frequented the haunts of the sailors and listened to their tales. He was so emaciated that they called him 'ankou', the spectre of death. In 1871 he followed two friends to Paris, Count Rodolphe de Battine and his mistress, an actress nicknamed 'Herminie'. Later on he decided to become a true Parisian, trimmed his beard, curled his moustache and dressed like a dandy at a good tailor. He gathered together his poems, and published them at the expense of his father in August 1873; this collection was called *Les Amours Jaunes*. Emile Henriot asked him if he meant by that title that there was a way of 'jaune' (yellow) loving, as there was a way of 'jaune' (forced) laughing. It was also the colour of Judas, of treachery, of putrefaction and death, as well as — and this time without a sense of disparagement — the colour of Brittany, 'the yellow lands of Armorica'. After a prologue, there were seven sections: *Ça*, *Les Amours Jaunes*, *Sérénade des Sérénades* (a parody of pseudo-Spanish love poetry), *Raccrocs* (poems of love and Parisian impressions), *Armor*, *Gens de mer*, and *Rondels pour après*. He was questioned about the distortion which the logical order of the book placed on the chronological; in fact, it concerned a symbolic order: Corbière wanted to make his readers aware of the nostalgia for Brittany which engulfed him when he went to live in Paris.

Gens de Mer then took on the value of an imaginary autobiography of Corbière, and the ship appeared as a masculine world from which woman was excluded. It can be seen that this poetry was symbolic rather than Symbolist. In fact the term here would have been an anachronism. But Corbière taught prosodic freedom, and musicality founded on discord, for example in *Les Litanies du Sommeil* which were justly praised by

Huysmans. Here the poet tries to seduce sleep by song, because it is the only means remaining to him to escape solitude. In December 1874, a friend found Corbière unconscious on the floor of his Parisian apartment, and had him moved to the Dubois hospital. This incorrigible humorist wrote to his parents from there: 'I am in the Dubois (in the wood) of which they make coffins.' Death was waiting for him a few months later.

CROS Charles (Fabrezan 1842 — Paris 1888). A French writer who was also an erudite man (he had learned Hebrew and Sanskrit), a scholar (he studied chemistry and medicine), an inventor (he discovered the phonograph at the same time as Edison, and found the principle of colour photography), a musician and friend of the Impressionists. Perhaps he embraced too much to be able to clasp anything fully:

> J'ai tout rêvé, tout dit, dans mon pays
> J'ai joué du feu, de l'air, de la lyre.
> On a pu m'entendre, on a pu me lire.
> Et les gens s'en vont dormir, ébahis.

> I have dreamed everything, said everything, in my
>   country
> I have played with fire, with air, with the lyre.
> People could understand me, people could read
>   me;
> and they went away, dumbfounded, to sleep.

He was with Verlaine when the latter went to the Gare de l'Est to await Rimbaud, in September 1871, he took part in the reunions of the Vilains Bonshommes and later in those of the Hydropaths. He read poems at the Tout Paris soirées, and was the first to talk at the Chat Noir. In other words, the world of Charles Cros was that of the bohemians, where, as for instance in the salon of his mistress Nina de Villard, he was a burlesque and tireless source of vitality.

Nevertheless, the exuberant and eccentric southerner was a poet of solitude. 'When all the world is at home, egotistically and heavily asleep', then, at the 'cold hour', the 'horror' creeps in, the horror described in one of his prose fantasies in the collection *Le Coffret de santal* (first edition 1873; second edition 1879): the terror of being engulfed in the downward spiral of an artificial life, in the flood of absinthe, in the giddiness of perpetually uncertain thought.

The collection of poems passed unnoticed except for one funny monologue, *Le Hareng saur*. Verlaine, however, was not wrong when he said: 'You will find there the setting for feelings which are in turn wonderfully fresh and almost too refined, jewels which are in turn delicate, barbarian, bizarre, rich or simple like the heart of a child, which are verses; neither classic verse, nor romantic nor decadent, but with a leaning towards decadence if it is essential to put an outward label on such independent and spontaneous literature.

D'ANNUNZIO Gabriele (Pescara, Abruzzi 1863 – Carcagno 1938). An Italian writer whose lively existence gave rise to scandal: to enumerate his liaisons, the names of the ladies who inspired him, to linger over his deeds in the war, his political involvement, to describe his feasting at Le Victorial, would hardly throw light on the link which existed between D'Annunzio and Symbolism. It is doubtless fairer to him to speak, as Guy Tosi did, of the 'Symbolist temptation' which attracted him.

D'Annunzio was not Symbolist at the beginning.

Portrait of Gabriele D'Annunzio

His first collection, *Spring* ('Primo Vere'), owed a great deal to the *Barbarian Odes* of Carducci together with an insolent, rather than an unusual talent for a young man of seventeen. All the same the *New Song* ('Canto Novo', 1882), which introduced him to the public, is like a great hymn to the sun and the sea. His daily life, his tumultuous passions, of which the first of his *Novels of the Rose, Child of Sensuality*, gave an excellent transposition became visible in his next collections, *The Intermezzo, Isotta Guttadauro* and *The Chimera*. This last deserves a moment's attention. It is inseparable from the hero of *Child of Sensuality* who was, also, 'the too of a monstrous aesthetico-aphrodisiac chimera'. There is also in it a long poem addressed to Andrea Sperelli. These verses were a breath of fresh air, and introduced the Symbolist years of D'Annunzio (1890-93). He read many different authors and came under various influences; he pilfered French literature, Gautier, Huysmans, Péladan, Baudelaire and Verlaine, and his reminiscences sometimes showed that he had done so.

Could it be said that D'Annunzio had access to the mysterious secrets of the Symbolist doctrine

Verbal decorum with him was always a little misleading. Up till then the poetic word had been, for him, 'divine' because he felt it as if drunk with it. When, in his *Paradisiac Poem*, he addressed himself to the word as to a 'mystic and profound thing', when he spoke of its 'mystery', its 'terrible force', was he not yielding to a way of poetic narcissicism? Nevertheless, as Guy Tosi observed, the word is no longer only in the service of pure beauty, but in a redeeming art which is capable of revealing the depths of life:

> Could you be for me the greatest
> among the great rivers, and, limpid,
> carry my thought to the centre of Life.

D'Annunzio's sense of mystery was purified by reading Maeterlinck's *Hothouses. The Novel of the Rose* proves this. Sperelli saw in the landscape 'a symbol, an emblem, a sign, an escort to guide us through the labyrinth of the interior.' Georges Aurispa, protagonist of *Triumph of Death*, possessed a religious soul with a leaning towards mystery, suitable to live in a forest of symbols'. Without doubt he was concerned most of the time with an accord between place and self, the 'secret affinities between the outward life of things, and the intimate life of desires and souvenirs'. Nevertheless, he became inspired with the idea of an analogy of the universe:

> Look. The earth surrenders all
> its thoughts to you. Read. Never will she explain
> more profound thoughts through her forms.
> (I know well how to read them now
> since you no longer hide the sun from me
> in broad daylight). Look how she sleeps
> in her thoughts. — And we? What shall we do?

However, D'Annunzio never joined the quest of Mallarmé. He very soon found himself drawn towards Nietzsche; this influence is apparent already in *The Triumph of Death* (Trionfo della Morte'), and from 1894 onwards it ruled his work. The heroes of the new novels illustrated various aspects of the superman (*The Virgins of the Rocks, Fire, Perhaps yes, perhaps no*). The theatre into which he had been attracted by Eleonora Duse, permitted the performance of the efforts of those who had broken the rules of common morality in their search for the discovery of truth. As for the ambitious poetry of *Praises* ('Laudi') it wished to be 'superhuman'. After the *Paradisiac Poem*, his prose became bolder. D'Annunzio discovered in particular the resources of *vers libre*, which was more suited to the exuberance of his rejoicing. Should it be said that the five books of his collection (which should number seven), *Maia* (1903), *Electra* (1904), *Alcyone* (1905), *Merope* (1912), and *Asterope* could be put to the credit of a second Symbolism? More than ever, he seemed to have abandoned, if he had ever dreamed of it, the search for the pure essence of things. As Guy Tosi, again, wrote: 'While Mallarmé died at his task, D'Annunzio,

abandoning the philosophic notion of the symbol, went on with the conquest of his superb halcyon myths without ceasing to come back to the allegoric and symbolic themes of the end of the century. In doing this, he obeyed his sensual artistic nature, which was sometimes intuitive and anxious, but never abstract.'

DARIO Rubén (Metapa 1867 — Leon 1916). Félix Rubén Garcia y Sarmiento was the real name of this Nicaraguan poet who was the best representative of Symbolism, or to abide by the Spanish idiom, Modernism in Latin America. A Creole, he doubtless had the complex of his race, but he also had what Salinas has called the 'Paris complex': nourished by French literature, he seemed to be dreaming of this intellectual Eldorado even while he was wandering across Latin America pursuing his journalistic activities. He had to wait until 1893 to make the journey which he had so long desired, to visit Remy de Gourmont, Moréas, and above all Verlaine. He celebrated this visit in 1896 in a poem entitled *Response* ('Responso').

R. MARTINEZ *Portrait of Rubén Darío*

Father and magical master, celestial lyrophore
who to the Olympic instrument and the rustic Pan-
pipes
hast given thine enchanting accent,
O Panidus! Pan thyself who led the chorus
to the sacred propylaeum which thy sad soul loved,
to the sound of the sistrum and drum!

For four years he exercised his duties of consul in Buenos Aires before going back to Spain in 1898, and France in 1900. He then toured Europe as he had done America. In 1906 he was in Spain, this time as Nicaraguan minister, and in 1910 in Paris again, following his dismissal. By the time he returned to America in 1914 his health was failing and two years later he died in his own country, but he had published his autobiography entitled *The Life of Rubén Darío written by Himself* ('La Vida de Rubén Darío escrita por el mismo', 1916).

He had already published three collections when *Azure* ('Azul') made him famous in 1888. Until then he had appeared as the poet of 'mental gallicism'. Reacting against the excesses of a languid and dreamy romanticism, Darío in effect joined the school of the poets of art for art's sake, and the Parnassians. He was thus nearer to Catulle Mendès than the Symbolists in this collection, where his short, simple phrases, strongly rhythmic, come in a sparkling assortment of images to express the rapture of the desires and feelings of a young man of twenty-one. The *Profane Proses* ('Prosas profanas') of 1896 were dedicated to modernism. Aspiring to develop an 'infinite melody', he obeyed the musical suggestion of Verlaine's *Fêtes Galantes* as well as Théophile Gautier's *Symphonie en Blanc majeur*, which here became *Symphony in Grey Major* ('Sinfonia en gris mayor'). Darío's originality remains in his refined epicurism and his eroticism. His thematic became richer in the *Songs of Life and Hope* ('Cantos de vida y esperanza', 1905). These poems which, as he said himself 'enclose the essences the vitality of autumn' still yielded sometimes to Symbolist mythology — the evocation of Leda in *The Swans*, for instance — but equally show a Darío who was unhappy with the lot of Latin America. Proof of this comes with the striking *Salutation of the Optimist* ('Salutacion del optimista'), the hymn to *Christopher Columbus* ('A Colon') and the warning *To Roosevelt*:

...America
who shakes with hurricanes and only lives by love,
men with a Saxon look and a barbarian soul —
America lives. And dreams. Loves and vibrates; she is
the daughter
of the sun. Take care. Spanish America lives,
a thousand lion cubs straying from the Spanish Lion.
It is necessary, Roosevelt, to be, through God himself,
the terrible sharpshooter and the powerful hunter,
to be able to hold us in your iron claws.

In the last collections of Darío, the *Wandering Song* (1907), *Poem of Autumn* (1910), the tone is more disenchanted, but a decisive step had been accomplished. Not only had Spanish poetry been freed from its constraints, but Modernism had escaped the stumbling-block of European imitation in order to strike the right note for the place and the period. As Pierre Darmangeat wrote: 'Thanks to the universality of his good breeding, Dario brought to the Spaniards in Spain this priceless message from a Spaniard of America: a poetry which knew the themes and techniques of European poetry, but which remained American and Spanish. It sealed the solidarity of the two Spanish worlds, after which the younger one was freed from the brutal clasp of constraint.'

DOWSON Ernest Christopher (Lee, Kent 1867 — Catford 1900). An English writer who spent a large part of his childhood and adolescence abroad with his consumptive parents. In 1886 he went to Queen's College in Oxford, where he led a dissipated life which rapidly wore him out. Two years later it became necessary for him to work, and he settled in London where he published poems and stories. He made some appearances at the Rhymers' Club, but abandoned himself more and more to vagrancy and to alcohol. The death of his father, the suicide of his mother, the marriage of someone he loved, Adelaide Foltinowicz, to someone else in 1897, and his own illness all precipitated the catastrophe to which his life seemed doomed.

Dowson had felt the influence of Poe, of Baudelaire, of Swinburne and of Verlaine. The first note he struck was that of a very pure idealism which he had preserved in a sordid world. He wrote novels, in collaboration with Arthur Moore, *The Comedy of Masks* (1893), *Adrian Rome* (1899) a book of short stories, *Dilemmas* (1895) and above all he left collections of verse: *Verses* (1896), *Decorations* (1899). Most of Dowson's poems are written for a young girl whom he loved desperately, and they unfold in an atmosphere of tenderness and melancholy. The long day was only bearable with patience and resignation.

His poetry recalls that of Rodenbach or Mikhaël. It tried, above all, to be like that of Verlaine, from whom came the actual inspiration in an explicit manner, for the scenic fantasy of *The Pierrot of the Minute* (1897). A piece such as *Amo Profanus* gives an idea of this relationship:

Beyond the pale of memory,
In some mysterious dusky grove;
...I dreamed we met when day was done
And marvelled at our ancient love.

Met there by chance, long kept apart,
We wandered, through the darkling glades;
And that old language of the heart
We sought to speak: alas! poor shades!

DUJARDIN Edouard (Saint-Gervaise, Loir-et-Cher 1861 — Paris 1949). A French writer. He was a pioneer of Symbolism who, as Jean Thorel said, always went 'all the way'. All the way with Wagnerism — he inspired, with Téodor Wyzewa, *La Revue wagnérienne*. All the way with a project for a Symbolist theatre with *La Légende d'Antonia*, a vast idealist trilogy in which he tried to embody the exaltation of a spiritual life and 'the eternal tragedy of humanity'. All the way with the Christian truths of which poetry had allowed him to glimpse a little, and to which he had devoted himself. There is, curiously, among the works of Dujardin, a book which was, for him, a starting-point: it is the little novel entitled *Les Lauriers sont coupés* (1887) where, for the first time he used the interior monologue.

FELIX VALLOTTON *Portrait of Edouard Dujardin*

GEORGE Stefan (Büdesheim, Rhenania 1868 — Minusio, near Locarno 1933). He was a German poet who was born into a Catholic family. He studied at the college of Darmstadt, and went abroad very soon. He arrived in Paris in 1889, where he was introduced into the Symbolist milieux, especially that of Mallarmé. At that time he had only written one collection of poetry,

which was fairly conventional in its inspiration and its form, *The Spelling-Book* ('Die Fibel'). Without entering into the quarrels between opposing factions, George took from French poetry the virtue of evocation without rhetoric, and the strength of esotericism. Verlaine taught him that

Portrait of Stefan George

'a simple flute is all that is necessary to reveal to men that which is most profound, Mallarmé that 'every true artist arranges his words in such a way that the initiate alone can recognize their majestic destination'. Baudelaire, above all, left a deep imprint in his spirit, and he became the unforgettable translator of *Les Fleurs du Mal*.

The *Hymns* of 1890 ('Hymnen') revealed the essential characteristics in George's art: these 'fugitive poems' made the accents of a prophet heard, and the poet was writing in a sacred mood. Already his predilection for evoking works of art ('An Angelico') was making itself felt, as was his desire to make many pilgrimages — as yet he did not know where to. *Pilgrimages* ('Wallfahrten') was the title of a new collection published in 1891, where he expressed his need for a peaceful existence, but also the desire to reign over beings and things in a world which would be of crystal. The hook was a symbol both of these bonds and of this hardness:

I wanted it made of cool iron
Like a smooth, strong band;
Yet in the mine, on all the rails
There was no such metal ready for casting.

But now it must be shaped
Like a large, strange flower cluster
Formed of flame-red gold
And of rich, sparkling precious stones.
(*The Buckle*)

Heliogabalus, the Syrian who became emperor of Rome, was one of the major figures of decadence. George chose this character in 1892 (Algabal) as a symbol of the arrogant and solitary soul, of the domineering and sterile will under this 'tunnel of precious stones' which Baudelaire had already evoked, the subterranean palace with its gardens which have never seen the meaning of spring.

1892 marked a turning point in the life and the career of the poet. In October he started a review, *The Pages for Art* ('Blätter für die Kunst') in which the double requirements of beauty and spirituality were affirmed, and round which a kind of literary group was to form. For George it was also the year of a grave physical and moral crisis. His discouragement can be felt in his poems, which were regrouped in the *Book of Eclogues and Praises, of Legends and Songs and Hanging Gardens* ('Die Bücher der Hirten- und Preigedichte, der Sagen und Sänge, und der Hängenden Gärten' 1895) and in *The Year of the Soul* ('Der Jahr der Seele', 1897).

Soon George was becoming receptive to the great national paragons: Holbein, Goethe, Jean-Paul, Nietzsche, and surmounted his pessimism in the very scholarly composition *The Carpet of Life* ('Der Teppich des Lebens', 1899). In a long prologue, the Angel brings a message of reconciliation and of action, the announcement of a new beginning to other people. Or to The Other: the adolescent maximin and his inconceivable fate which leads him towards an unknown end. He was celebrated in *The Seventh Year* ('Der Siebente Ring', 1907) and *The Star of Alliance* ('Der Stern des Bundes', 1913) as a new Messiah.

This disciple is a master, this supernatural being is a man, but he brings the vision of the divine into the world. This surely is, in spite of the change of tone, the old quest which continues. George wrote in the *Preface to Maximin* ('Vorrede zu Maximin'): 'We need someone who could be deeply moved by the simple side of things, and who would show us things as the gods see them.'

Thenceforth, George lived almost exclusively among his disciples and devoted himself to them. During the torment of the war, and the dark years which followed, he wanted to hasten the coming of 'the true Man' who would rupture the chain and re-establish order among the ruins. In *The New Reign* ('Das neue Reich') he expressed an exacting patriotism which some people tried abusively to confuse with national socialism. But far rather than the Third Reich, George dreamed of a mystic community, a kind of invisible Church, a reunion of the élite which, under the guidance of the poet, would be employed to save the world from future catastrophe. It was necessary to serve in silence, but to know that:

> Only through magic does life stay awake.
> (*Man and the Sorcerer*)

He was in truth an odd figure, this poet who died in 1938 near Locarno. His work produced at the same time a vigorous trajectory and an alternation which proved that the links with Symbolism were not so easy to break. From the time of his poem to Nietzsche published in the *Pages for Art* in 1900-1901, and which he came back to in *The Seventh Ring*, George launched appeals which recall Zarathustra. But the wilted element was still present; roses and gold served as scenery for the 'breathless kisses' and for a feast of the senses.

Perhaps Maximin was he who, preceding the breath of spring, could 'dispense roses which were not faded', and make a Symbolist landscape which was too pale pass into a more real Symbolism which was in search of the essential truth. Because as Maurice Boucher wrote: 'The poetry of Stefan George is turned towards the unchanging, the motionless and eternal mirror of all movements' and 'in all the images of the world and the dream of the spirit', the Master 'wanted to grasp and pin down the eternal realities of which we only see the shadows and reflections on the walls of the cave.'

GHIL René (Tourcoing 1862 — Niort 1925). A French poet whose real name was René Guilbert. He called himself, and wanted to be, the faithful disciple of Mallarmé when, in 1885, he published a series of articles in the Belgian review *La Basoche* entitled *Sous mon cachet*. In these he united for the first time the notion of the symbol and that of

FELIX VALLOTTON *Portrait of René Ghil*. 1896-1898

uggestive poetry-music. The same year, his *Légende* *âmes et de sang* unfolded in a Mallarmian atmos-here. The master wrote a preface to *Le Traité du erbe*, which was very well received. Several major rinciples were expressed in a harsh and learned rm: the use of words in their full value of eaning and sound at the same time; the creation f a poetry which could symbolically reproduce e order of the universe. In the wake of *Voyelles* y Rimbaud, René Ghil proposed a theory of oloured audition and of verbal instrumentation. hen, discovering the concept of evolution and a tional God, and finding in the physiology of elmholtz a confirmation of his intuitive feelings, hil threw himself into new speculations, as own in the second edition of the *Traité* (1888), hich caused Mallarmé to break with him. Foun-er of the review *Les Ecrits pour l'art*, Ghil isolated imself more and more in his 'philosophico-strumentalist' school, and was unable to get his eatise *De la poésie scientifique* (1909) accepted. As to e applications of the theory, they were very rigid nd very deceptive: *Le Geste ingénu*, 'twenty-eight oems preceded and followed by an Overture nd a Finale' which would 'give wings to all the strumental and harmonic powers', rarely went eyond simple imitative harmony and the mere lay of images.

In 1923, in the preface to his recollections (*Les ates et les oeuvres*), Ghil distinguished between, and ompared, the two movements which, according him, divided French Symbolism: 'where, for ome, the idealist Self intends, by going from nalogy to analogy where appearances are imma-rial, to free the pure, constructive Idea of a sym-olic union; or where, for others, the materialist elf demands from Science the relationships f phenomena which allow it the impersonal notion of a synthesis.' But the second movement perhaps confirmed to him alone.

IDE André (Paris 1869 — Paris 1951). A French riter, who was applauded by the Dadaists for his tirical farces (of which the most important was *s Caves du Vatican*) and by Sartre for having 'lived is ideas' (on homosexuality, on colonization); he ad been at first a follower of Mallarmé and a ymbolist of stricty obedience. It is this Gide, the ide of *Traité du Narcisse*, who must be evoked here.

'Born in Paris of a father from Uzès and a other from Normandy', enclosed on both sides y Protestantism, Gide pursued his studies on the enches of the Alsation school, where his literary ocation was decided. He was a friend of Pierre ouis (the future Pierre Louÿs) and soon met aléry, with whom he exchanged an important orrespondence. His adolescence was troubled: he as divided between mystic effusions which he

shared with his cousin Madeleine, and the dis-covery that he was not 'the same as others'. His struggle was that of one of his characters, who was his double, André Walter: after each defeat, he would cry out 'I am pure, I am pure, I am pure.' In the Symbolist milieu, the novel was not very popular; on the other hand it was fashionable to make oneself known by a collection of verse; and that is why the confession of Gide, *Les Cahiers d'André Walter* (1891) was followed by the *Poésies d'André Walter*.

Le Traité du Narcisse was dedicated to Paul Valéry and sub-titled 'Theory of the Symbol'. The idea

H. BATAILLE *Portrait of André Gide*

for it came to Gide at Montpellier, in the botanical gardens where he was with Valéry, near a tomb which local legend attributed to Narcissa, the daughter of the English poet Young. He worked on it more than anything else in 1891. His Narcissus dreamed of Paradise, of a 'garden of Ideas, where forms, rhythmic and sure, effort-lessly revealed their numbers; where all things were what they appeared to be; where proof was unnecessary.' Adam made the mistake of grasping a branch of the logarithmic tree: when a woman was born from his ribs, time was established, and the pages of the sacred book which lay at the foot of the tree scattered: it belongs to the poets to gather piously 'the torn pages of the immemorial Book where can be read the truth which must be known.'

Narcissus was wrong not to turn round; he was absorbed in the contemplation of the water which passed like fleeting forms. The poet is he who looks, and who sees Paradise: 'The poet, who knows that he creates, who perceives through each thing — and a single thing suffices to reveal to him the archetype of his symbol; he knows that appearance is only the ostensible reason for it, a garment which screens it, and which halts the profane eye, but which shows us that it is there.' The work of art, the poem, is a crystal where the anterior Idea blossoms again. Louÿs recognized his *Credo* in this treatise. And in fact this profession of Platonic faith seemed to crystallize the Symbolist doctrine in all its purity. When Gide wrote: 'We live to reveal' he meant the term in its Symbolist sense: that of 'revealing' the truths which lie behind forms. It remained perhaps for him to reveal himself, and to reveal himself to himself.

therefore on the Symbolists, are irreplaceable (*L Livre des Masques*, 1896). If he only showed on gallery of portraits, it was because, for him ther had not been a Symbolist school, but 'a very varie orchard, very rich, — too rich'. He defined Sym bolism as 'the expression of individualism in art 'the renunciation of taught formulas', 'the trend towards what is new, strange or even bizarre'. I was 'liberty and anarchy, children of idealism' an signified 'the free and complete development c individual aesthetics.' This precept seemed likel to lead to a new affectation.

GOURMONT Remy de (Bazoches-en-Houlme, Orne 1858 — Paris 1915). A French writer, and one of the best critics of the Symbolist period. He began quietly in 1886 with a novel, *Merlette*. A curious and original spirit, who had a liking for erudition, he contributed to the *Mercure de France*. In his novel *Sixtine* he gave a glimpse of the complex sensibility and the multiple currents of thought of his time. He wrote other novels (*Le Pèlerin du Silence*, 1896; *Une Nuit aux Luxembourg*, 1906; *Un Coeur virginal*, 1907), plays for the theatre (*Lilith*, 1892; *Théodat*, 1893) and some poems (*Hiéroglyphes*, 1894; *Oraisons mauvaises*, 1900; *Divertissements*, 1913). But the essay was the favourite means of expression of this voluntary recluse. His wide culture

Raoul Dufy *Portrait of Remy de Gourmont*

Charles Filiger, illustration for *L'Idéalisme* by Remy de Gourmont

could be deployed there (*Promenades Litteraires*, 1904-1913; *Le Latin mystique*, 1892); here could be felt the strangeness of a spirit which was both dry and sensual (*Physique de l'Amour*, 1903); *Lettres d'un Satyr*, 1913; *Lettres à l'Amazone*, 1914). As a critic, he was in the opposing camps of Tainian dogmatism and Impressionism; he was dedicated above all to defining what made up the quality of a style of writing. His essays on the writers of the time, and

HOFMANNSTHAL Hugo von (Vienna 1874 – Rodau 1929). An Austrian writer. He suffere from his reputation of being Viennese and fron having been made official poet. Nevertheless, h was not just the librettist for *Der Rosenkavalier*, and is not just that aspect of him which interests u here. He was also heir to and a representative o Symbolism.

His debut was precocious and easy: his famil was well off and his studies were brilliant; his fir verses, his first writings, were all favourabl acclaimed in the reviews, and his reputatio went rapidly beyond the boundaries of the caf Griensteidl, where the young writers of the da used to meet. Stefan George even travelled i order to see him, and was hopeful of making hir join his literary group. His first drama in vers *Yesterday* ('Gestern'), expressed the sad immoralit of his hero, Andreas, for whom 'sin alone was infinite richness'. This was followed by *The Death Titian* ('Der Tod des Tizian', 1892), a kind of hym to Beauty written in the form of an elegy wit ialogue, and *Death and Death* (1893). Hofmannsthal's first poems expressed voluptuous abandon ɔ the moment, the only way of escaping the cycle f life, death and putrefaction. The poet was ware of this link which bound him to all other

ortrait of Hugo von Hofmannsthal

eings and to the world, to those correspondences *h*ich are revealed by mirrors and by pools.

> While the treetops move as they breathe
> And the fragrance descends and night and dread
> And along the path — our path — the darkening
>   path
> In the evening light the silent pools shimmer
> And, as the mirrors of our yearning, dreamlike
>   sparkle
> And with all hushed words, with all soaring to the
> evening air and the first twinkling of the stars
> The souls, as sisters, profoundly tremble...
> (*Tercet IV*)

ike George, Hofmannsthal went through a blank eriod and for four years he practically stopped *r*iting. *The Letter to Lord Chandos* (1901) later bore *r*itness to this crisis, which was very much, as it *r*as for Mallarmé a crise de vers. This text, which reserved all the flavour of strangeness, expressed ᴉe discouragement which the poet felt in the face f any effort of expression: 'The language in *r*hich it has perhaps been given me not just to *r*rite, but also to think, is neither Latin, nor nglish, nor Italian, nor Spanish, but language of *r*hich not a word is known to me, a language in *r*hich mute things speak to me.' The Symbolist niverse and the problems of the metaphor, the ᶃlistening colours flowing into one another', ɔccupied him all the less when his whole work was meditation on the real and the unreal. The *Tale f the Six Hundred and Seventy-Second Night*, an *x*tension of the *Thousand and One Nights*, mixed

dream and reality so strangely that the reader ends by not knowing in which world he is moving. And it is known that Hofmannsthal was obsessed with the predicament of Sigismund, the hero of Calderón in *La Vida es sueño*: the adaptation which he made of this play in 1901 only preceded the creation of a new play, *The Tower*, which it inspired in 1925.

If the theatre occupied so much space in the output of Hofmannsthal, it was because it brought a solution to the problem of language. Faithful to Mallarmé's reflections in *Crayonné au Théâtre* ('Sketched in the Theatre'), he departed from outward reality in favour of a reality where language was the Creator. Such historic evocation permitted him to turn reality into a sort of moving

Illustration for *Jedermann* by Hugo von Hofmannsthal

and coloured shadow where Destiny took on a different dimension; it shows the personal anxieties of the author who, Hermann Broch observed: 'likened himself, when all was said and done, to the Void', and 'could not have done otherwise'. The brutal death of Hofmannsthal after his son's suicide proved sufficiently that he had lived an existence torn between worldly successes and the interior abyss.

When Hofmannsthal, having lived through his four-year crisis, went back to writing, he remained faithful to the formula of the little play in verse. He came closer to the style of Maeterlinck in *The White Fan* (1897). In *The Little Theatre of the World* he returned to a theme which was baroque par excellence, and evoked semi-allegorical characters, of whom the last is the madman, walking past on a bridge above the river of time. The author went then in search of rare decors, the Persia of *The Wedding of Zobeida* the Venice of *The Adventurer and the Singer, or the Presents of Life* ('Der Abenturer und die Sängerin', 1899). He also turned towards the great models: the Greeks (*King Oedipus, Oedipus and the Sphinx* and *Electra*, from which Richard Strauss made a powerful musical drama); the English (he adapted *Venice Saved*, by Otway). To these he added his own frenzy, which especially animated his *Electra*, a fury who dissolves into joy when she learns that her revenge is accomplished.

His collaboration with Richard Strauss was especially happy. It was eclectic in that it passed from *Electra* to the unrestrained life of *Der Rosen-kavalier* (1911), to the fantasy of *Ariadne in Naxos* ('Ariadne auf Naxos', 1911), and then to the secret Symbolism of *Woman without a Shadow* ('Die Frau ohne Schatte', 1919). But it was perhaps *Jedermann* (1911) for which he deserved the widest audience, and this time without competition from his chosen composer. Recreated from two ancient works, one English and the other German (*The Comedy of the Death of the Rich Man* by Hans Sachs), this 'morality play' is given every year at the Salzburg Festival; it shows a rich man who is called by Death, and who looks for a companion on his last journey. Abandoned by his parents, his friends, his mistress, and by his gold, he can be comforted only by his Good Works and by his Faith. For the Salzburg Festival, Hofmannsthal also wrote *The Great Theatre of the World* ('Das grosse Salzburger Welttheater', 1922) an *autosacral* piece where the principal character is the beggar who will enter into the Kingdom of Heaven while the rich man will be sent down to outer darkness.

Hofmannsthal thus progressed from a Symbolist art to an art which it would be more correct to call allegorical. Without a doubt a theory of the symbol can be found in his work; Hermann Broch condensed it well: 'The symbol is formed from the encounter with the dream and with life, and it is by the symbol that all poetic knowledge on the subject of the reality of the world is set alight, and by the symbol that the problem of this reality is kept alight.' But it was above all to the theatre that he trusted his concern to show how life and the dream join together and separate, by projecting on to the stage great silhouettes which monopolize the attention, and make the Symbolist landscape and the sisterly souls of the first poems forgotten.

IBSEN Henrik (Skien 1828 — Oslo 1906). A Norwegian writer. Regis Boyer wrote: 'He was neither naturalist, nor Symbolist, nor anarchist.' Nevertheless, after a performance of *Ghosts* in

France, a critic of the period wrote: 'After the spiritual pessimism of Schopenhauer, after the still tolerable mysticism of Tolstoy, the hospital-like Symbolism of which *Ghosts* is, on the face of it, the most accomplished expression, seems superfluous to me, and leaves me bored and cold.' Ibsen was certainly claimed by the supporters of the Symbolist theatre, but Catulle Mendès, who did not like him, was for once more clear-sighted when he wrote, having seen *Little Eyolf*: 'The symbols which people wish to find in his work are perhaps there, if one puts them there; but he hardly thought of them when he was totally himself, that is to say before the prostrations of enthusiasm had revealed the height of his brow to him.'

Symbolist or not, Ibsen was a pilgrim of the Absolute. In one of his most beautiful poems, he

J. MARTIN *Portrait of Henrik Ibsen*. 1895

confides: 'The noise of the crowd dismays me. do not want to let my coat be spattered with th mud from the roads. I want to await the day c the coming in spotless feast clothes.' He was bor in a little southern town of Norway, and studied i Oslo. Committed to pharmacy, he undertook th study of medicine, but soon gave it up. He read great deal, particularly the romantic Norwegian and in 1850 he published a play *Catilina*, unde a pseudonym. In a somewhat clumsy form h presented some of his great themes for the futur that of vocation and that of the combat which th antagonist forces conduct in the human sou Then, in *The Hill of the Warrior* (1854), he drew h inspiration from the old Nordic themes. Th decisive event in his life was his engagement a instructor and as author in the Norwegian theatr of Bergen: here he gained a complete experience of the theatre, and he was obliged to produce. In 1858, the year of his marriage to Susannah Thoresen, he was appointed director of the new theatre in Oslo, and he carried off a resounding success with *The Warriors of Helgeland* ('Hoermoen-dene pa Helgeland'), a play based on Icelandic sagas. But the theatre went bankrupt: Ibsen then went through a dark period (this pessimism shows in *The Comedy of Love*, 1862) and he only regained the favour of the public with a historical play, *The Pretenders to the Crown* (1863). A travel grant allowed him to leave the country, which he did for twenty-seven years. He lived in Rome, in Dresden, in Munich and again in Rome. This was the period of his great works, starting with *Brand* (1866), the tragedy of the sacrifice of a little Lutheran pastor of the mountains, who abandons everything to attain his ideal, and is called by Gerd, the mad woman of the glaciers, who invites him to take refuge in the great church of ice, where only his mind finally finds rest. The central character of *Peer Gynt* (1867), a good-for-nothing who dodges reality, is an anti-Brand. His weakness is due to the crazed imagination of his old mother Ase, whose fantastic notions were the lullaby of his childhood and whose mad fantasies he was forever fleeing. It is only on the threshold of death that he finds the ideal in the heart of Solveig, the sweetheart of his twentieth year, who has waited for him for thirty years.

In 1867 Ibsen was famous; he had triumphed over hatred, over the jealousies which surrounded him, and he was in control of his talent. He gave up writing romantic dramas and poetic plays full of symbols in order to attack society directly through modern comedies. The first was *The Union of the Young* (1869): the leader of this association is Stensgaard, a barrister who has started from a low level and is eaten up with ambition. In *Pillars of Society* Ibsen is trying to combat lies and hypocrisy 1877). In *Doll's House* he defended woman, but exacted from her that she should live true to herself, not just as an adorable doll, as Nora is to start with. *Ghosts* (1881) is the continuation of the preceding work: Madame Alving is another Nora whose life has sustained a complete development with every possible type of unhappiness in similar circumstances. Here Ibsen approached subjects which were considered taboo at that time, and the work was at first refused.

In *An Enemy of the People* (1882) he launched a kind of challenge to his compatriots: he established that the minds of the people are shut to the great truths, and that they consider as the worst of their adversaries he who opens their eyes to their own sores, and wants to cauterize them. But in *The Wild Duck* he turns against himself, and in any case against the dreamer who, in his imperious need of an ideal, brings about the ruin of all: Werle ends by killing himself after having destroyed the home of Hjarlmar Ekdal and induced the charming

Hedvig to commit suicide. *Rosmersholm* (1886) shows the misery of noble souls in despair, the intelligence of the select few who have lost their way. Poetry is here triumphant, in this gracious and solemn countryside, the seat of Rosmersholm, the peaceful estate where the eye looks down long avenues of venerable trees with a stream at the bottom. It is still the same in *The Lady of the Sea* (1888).

Hedda Gabler (1890) spends her whole life mocking others, stealing their happiness without scruples: she is a 'bird of prey' as Ibsen himself nicknamed her, and at her death, she mocks herself.

In 1891 Ibsen, at the height of his glory, returned to his own country. He was not happy. Nietzsche's literature did not appease him. *The Master Builder* (1892), who fell from the tower which he had built for his beloved, could only be himself: 'This is the play into which I have put most of myself,' he confessed. *Little Eyolf* (1894) was a more tender and moving play, in which the misery caused by the death of a child (a little cripple whom the 'Woman of the rats' dragged into a fiord) managed to reunite two beings who were tearing each other to bits. *John Gabriel Borkmann* (1896) is the drama of the genius who believes that he must sacrifice everything and break every bond for his work: on the day he wishes to resume contact with life, he dies. *When we Dead awaken* was another tragedy of genius, and it was the last play to be published by Ibsen during his lifetime; here the sculptor, Rubeck, is buried in the middle of the mountains with his favourite model, Maya.

'Here the situation dominates the beings', wrote Laurent Tailhade on the subject of Ibsen's theatre: 'necessity overcomes them. It throws a phantom light on them, an unhealthy atmosphere which envelops them like a winding-sheet and excludes them for ever from the world.' In fact, these characters possess an aura of burning truth about them, and it is certainly from reality that the dramatist starts to defend his ideas. For this theatre is assuredly a theatre of ideas, one which defends idealism even when it knows and shows the dangers in it. His characters also live by the supreme idea which they make of themselves and of their vital mission. But is it possible, is it desirable to live thus on the heights? This work is gnawed by doubt. To realize himself is perhaps the mission of the individual and, as Ibsen wrote to Bjornson, 'the highest ideal to which man could ever attain.' In any case, the essential is to shun the lie and to renounce it, to be born again and to partipate in the rebirth. In *Brand*, Agnes cries:

'But I see a great earth, its outline
Sharp against the air.
I see oceans and the mouths of rivers.
A gleam of sunshine pierces through the mist.
I see a fiery red light playing about the mountain
    peaks.

I see a boundless waste of desert.
Great palm trees stand, swaying in the sharp
    winds.
There is no sign of life;
It is like a new world at its birth.
And I hear voices ring:
Now shalt thou be lost or saved.
Thy task awaits thee; take up thy burden.
Thou shalt people this new earth.'

With replies like this, and whispers like this, how could Ibsen have failed to impress the Symbolist generation? Performed for the first time in Paris in May 1890 (with *Ghosts* in the Théâtre Libre) he passed from Antoine (therefore a more 'naturalist' staging) to Lugné-Poe (therefore a more 'Symbolist' staging). Impersonated by Georgette Camée, Ellida, the lady of the sea, became a mysterious white phantom, which caused Henri de Régnier to write that Ibsen's characters were 'like their own ghosts'. The critics made of this theatre a theatre of allegories, searching for the symbolic significance of the wild duck, and trying to see behind each character an idea of moral or philosophic order. August Ehrard, the author of a book on *Ibsen and the Contemporary Theatre* published in 1892, defined thus the Ibsenian Symbolism: 'Symbolism is the art form which satisfies both our desire to see reality represented, and our need to go beyond it. It is the foundation for the concrete and the abstract together. Reality has an underside, facts have a hidden meaning: they are the material representation of ideas; the idea appears in the fact. Reality is the sensible image, the symbol of the invisible world. Symbolism thus understood differs greatly from the refined type which was inaugurated several years ago in France, which rests on an excellent principle, on the necessity to *suggest the whole man*, to guess at a vague immensity behind actual things, but which, until now has hardly existed except as a pure work of form and which is discredited by several charlatans and many bunglers. True Symbolism is the idealization of the material, the transfiguration of the real; it is the suggestion of the unfinished by the finished.' If there really is an Ibsenian Symbolism, it may well be that it is not the same as the Symbolism of the Ibsen of the Symbolists.

IVANOV Viatcheslav Ivanovitch (Moscow 1866 – Rome 1950). A Russian poet. In June 1910 his article entitled *The precepts of Symbolism* appeared in the review *Apollon*; in it he affirmed the religious mission of Russian Symbolism. This turning-point — which allowed certain people to speak of a second Russian Symbolism — was to be decisive. While Balmont, Briussov and Sologub were looking towards the west, Ivanov, like Blok and Biely, wanted to continue the great tradition of national poetry. He had been so obsessed by the

philosophy of Nietzsche that he had himself studied the origins of tragedy and the cult of Dionysus (he wrote a thesis on Dionysus and the primitive Dionysiac cult). But his aim was to bring Dionysus and Christ together, Nietzschian individualism and the Christian community according to Soloviev. The eschatological myth was essential to his work. He was an erudite poet (Biely called him 'the Faust of our century'); he played with the doctrines of etymology and neology.

Between 1905 and 1907 he gathered together in his famous 'tower' in St Petersburg, poets, philosophers and artists. He was also very involved with the 'Religious and Philosophic Society' of Petersburg, and contributed to various reviews: *The Golden Fleece, The Balance, Apollon,* and *New Way*. His principal collections of verse were *Transparency* (1904), *Eros* (1907), *Cor Ardens* (1911) and very much later, the *Roman Sonnets* (1936). By that time he had emigrated to Italy, and had become a Catholic priest and a lecturer at the University of Padua.

JARRY Alfred (Laval 1873 — Paris 1907). A French writer. He was born in Laval, and led 'a literary life pushed to the point of absurdity'. He

F.A. CAZALS *Portrait of Alfred Jarry.* 1897

had a taste for scandal, and left an abundant work inspired by pataphysics, 'the science of imaginary solutions', which knocked the dreams of the metaphysicists and the speculations of the so-called serious philosophers into nothing.

Jarry made his debut in an atmosphere of waning Symbolism, under the auspices of Marcel Schwob: hermetism and excess marked the poems and the prose of *Minutes de sable memorial* (1894). Novels, or rather stories, followed which, while cultivating the unusual, posed major problems: the quest of the double (*Les Jours et les nuits*, 1897), of the mother (*L'Amour absolu*, 1899), and of the battle of the sexes (*Messaline*, 1901; *Le Surmâle*, 1902). *Les Gestes et opinions du docteur Faustroll* (1911) was a ridiculous chronicle in the style of Lucian, which showed the vanity of the only recourse of man — systems and their keys.

But Jarry was, first and foremost, the creator of Ubu. Taking a schoolboy situation, elaborated by the pupils of the Lycée at Rennes, of a physics master who, in their eyes, embodied 'everything that was grotesque in life', he realized successive versions, and was soon dreaming of a series which would always be imperfectly constituted. The 'hénaurme' character very soon attracted the attention of the literary men, and in particular that of the director of the *Mercure de France*, Alfred Valette, with whom Jarry published for the first time *Ubu roi* in its definitive form in 1894. The work was performed in 1896 by Lugné-Poe at the Théâtre de l'Oeuvre, where it created quite a stir.

Ubu roi appeared at the beginning to be a parody of the historic dramas of Shakespeare: it is the story of a usurpation, and of the fall of the usurper; and Ubu's wife, at the side of the new king of Poland, makes one think of Lady Macbeth. This play was very soon seen as a political farce, 'a bald-faced philosophico-political satirical work', said the reporter of the *Echo de Paris*, Henry Bauer. But it could be seen that the political interpretations of *Ubu roi* were too divergent to follow, and in any case, Jarry had taken care to specify that he had not had the intention of writing a historical play, but a play about Utopia — Poland is Nowhere. The Surrealists were leaning more towards a psychoanalytic meaning of what was to them a poem rather than a dramatic work: Breton saw in it 'the triumph of the instinct and of the instinctive impulse' and, to his way of thinking, 'the *self* claims for itself...the right to correct which only truly belongs to the *ego*, the ultimate psychic entreaty.' The drama is sufficiently rich to be able to support these different interpretations, and it can be thought of, with Michel Arrivé, as a work containing 'many seeds'. Is it a Symbolist work? Jacques Robichez replies 'Yes, because the cumbersome hero gets all the limelight, and the other characters have to take a back seat.' (See Mallarmé: 'It needs dumb actors!'). Yes, also, because Ubu evokes a multiple reality where the imagination of the spectators has room to choose. 'But, because of the triviality in the work it could equally pass as a parody of a Symbolist drama.

During the following years, Jarry was not happy just to defend his play and to have it performed on occasion. He worked to complete the cycle with a new version of *Ubu cocu ou l'archéoptéryx* (1897), *Ubu enchaîné* (1899); *L'Almanach du père Ubu* presents an Ubuian look at *political, colonial, literary and artistic* events of interest. Finally, the marionettes of the théâtre Guignol des Gueules de Bois performed, at the 4 Z'Arts in Montmartre, *Ubu sur la butte*, a short time before the premature death of Jarry. In reducing the beauty of the 'théâtre à phynances' to the 'good operation of the trap-doors' was it not perhaps the theatre itself that Jarry was pulling through the trap-doors? At least he recalled the essential principals, in particular that of the participation of the public on the occasion of a true 'civic feast' (*Douze arguments sur le théâtre.*) He also suggested that — to take a previous formula of Artaud — the theatre is the twin of life. 'I wanted to show' he said 'that, once the curtain has been raised, there is in front of the public as in front of this mirror the scene of the tales of Madame Leprince of Beaumont, where anything nasty would be seen with the horns of a bull or the body of a dragon according to the exaggeration of its vices; and it is not surprising that the public was stupefied at the sight of its ignoble double which had never before been completely shown to it.'

KAHN Gustave (Metz 1859 — Paris 1936). A French writer, who played an important part in the inauguration of the Symbolist movement.

Portrait of Gustave Kahn

Having completed his literary studies at the Sorbonne and at the Ecole des Chartes, he went to Tunisia to do military service; from this he derived his liking for the East. In 1886 he founded with Moréas an ephemeral review, *Le Symboliste*. Had he not in fact been one of the first followers of Mallarmé? Convinced that the 'poem in verse was insufficient' and that it was necessary to modify the verse and the strophe, he was very aware of the work of Rimbaud, who, as he said himself, played for him 'the role of a trigger'. In *La Vogue*, the new review of which the first number appeared on April 11, 1886, he disclosed *Les Illuminations* and reissued *Une saison en enfer*. He also published in it some verses which he had written, and some *vers libre*. Rumour had it that he and Moréas had fallen out over it. According to information produced by Dujardin: 'Moréas and Kahn used to watch each other, and in the café, each would have his poem in *vers libre* in his pocket, ready to bring it out like a weapon to put under the nose of the other.' In 1887, Kahn published a collection, *Les Palais nomades*, with a preface in which he praised *vers libre* which allowed writing to have 'its own individual rhythm in place of putting on a uniform made in the past, and which... diminishes one to the status of a pupil of such a glorious predecessor.' The collection itself was decadent in inspiration: poems of the past, of 'the implacable and slow hour', of 'the minor chord', with certain elements of Symbolist scenery, 'the nuptial march of pale lilies', 'the netting adorned with pearls of ideals of Ophir'. Kahn, who went on to manage *La Revue indépendante*, then *La Vogue* again, left other collections: *Chanson d'amant* (1891), *La Pluie et le beau temps* (1895), *Limbes de lumière* (1895), *Le Livre d'images* (1897). There are also Jewish tales, novels (*L'Adultère sentimental*, *Les Petites Ames pressées*), works of art criticism (*Boucher, Rodin, Fragonard*). His information on the Symbolist era is precious (*Symbolistes et decadents*, 1902; *Silhouettes littéraires* 1925; *Les Origines du symbolisme*, 1939) but must be used with caution.

KOSTOLANYI Deszö (Szabadka 1885 — Budapest 1936). A Hungarian poet, the 'Ariel of Hungarian literature', to use the expression of André Karatson. He studied at the University of Budapest, and then at the University of Vienna; like his companions, the future contributors to the review *Nyugat*, he was open to the ideas of Schopenhauer, of Nietzsche, of Freud, and to the voice of Parnassian and Symbolist poetry. The translations collected by Kostolányi in 1913, in *The Modern Poets*, must have created a new awareness, and he himself felt it, as his first book, *Between Four walls* ('Négy fal között', 1907) showed. His sensibility was directed above all towards an intimist style like that of Verlaine or Rilke, as can be seen in his *Lamentations of a Poor Little Child* ('A szegény kisgyermek panaszai', 1910). The vers refrain, 'Sadness is betrothed to my sister' is characteristic of a dismalness which tried to hide itself in the verbal virtuosity of his next collections, (*Game of Cards, Magic, Pavot*) but increased during the war and the immediate post-war distress of his

country (*Bread and Wine, To the Naked.*) Apart from this, Kostolányi was not spared atrocious physical suffering in his later years. Nevertheless, he was the defender of the poet's ivory tower to the end.

LAFORGUE Jules (Montevideo 1860 — Paris 1887). A French poet. Admired by foreigners (for example T.S. Eliot) Laforgue remains little known in his own country. After his premature death some friends took on the task of publishing his unpublished poems (posthumous edition of *Derniers Vers* published by Félix Fénéon in 1890); some young people liked his dandyism, and his strange manner of mis-shaping his verse. Today he is still underestimated.

He was born in Uruguay, and at a very early age his parents entrusted him to an austere boarding school at Tarbes. He felt abandoned, as he did again on his arrival in Paris. He visited the decadents, became secretary to a rich collector, and then, in 1881, he went to Germany as French tutor

F.Skarbina *Portrait of Jules Laforgue*. 1885

to Augusta of Prussia. In December 1886, he married an English girl whom he had met in Berlin, Miss Leah Lee, and he died of consumption several months later. The distressing life of 'this poor human body' was accompanied by a 'desperate hope' which he drew from Hartmann's *La Philosophie de l'inconscient*.

Le sanglot de la terre (1880-1882) was not published until after his death. Laforgue had himself described this first collection as 'history, the diary of a Parisian of 1880 who suffered, doubted and arrived at nothingness, and this in the Parisian scenery, the sleepers by the Seine, the sudden downpours, the greasy paving-stones, the Jablochkoffs, and this in the language of an artist researched and modern, without concern for the rules of taste, without fear of the crude, of the frantic, of the licentious or of the grotesque'. The influence of Baudelaire is noticeable here, less that of his Symbolism than that of his poetic naturalism.

Les Complaints appeared in 1885. The poet had had the idea for this work since 1880, when he was listening to the wretched singers of the fairs at the feasts which marked the inauguration of the 'place d'Enfer' in Paris. Put together between November 1882 and November 1883, the collection was really composed only in Coblenz, after a decisive night which revealed to Laforgue the 'metaphysical principles' of the new aesthetics. Arranging his language 'in a painstaking fashion, almost "clownesque" he wrote 'little poems of fantasy having only one object: to be original at any price.' But he became doubtful, and at the start of *La Complainte sur certains ennuis*, he was asking himself if he had not fallen back into the banal:

> A sunset of Cosmogenies!
> Ah! this life is so everyday...
> And for the best of memories,
> Those paltry talents we display.

In 1885, at the same time as the prose works *Moralités légendaires*, where he embroidered old canvases with fashionable feelings, Laforgue was writing, very quickly, *L'Imitation de Notre-Dame la Lune*. Under the pale light of the barren star, dressed for sacrifice and symbol of death, the clowns 'dandies of the moon' palavered among the overwrought 'fêtes galantes'.

The shadow of Hamlet floats over the collection *Des fleurs de bonne volonté*, in which the preface is dated 'Elsinore 1 January 1886'. Here the poet can be seen 'clowning', more multiple 'defrockings' in order to translate his hesitant feelings.

It is in the posthumous poems that can be found most of the examples of liberated prosody. *L'hiver qui vient* is the most celebrated example:

> Sentimental blockade! Levantine shipping
> companies!...
> Oh, the falling of the rain! Oh! the falling of the
> night!
> Oh! the wind!...
> All Saints' Day, Christmas and the New Year,
> Oh, all my chimneys, factory chimeys —
> in the drizzle.

(Translated by Anthony Hartley, Penguin Book of French Verse No.3, 1957)

Laforgue was without doubt sensitive to the influence of Whitman, whose work he partly translated in collaboration with his future wife. To tell the truth, his poetic language tended towards liberation: claiming to belong not to the concious, but to the unconscious, it 'constituted a necessary aggression', dislocating the phrase,

running on to the next line, eliminating the superfluous words, mixing the words ('l'eternullité', 'les violuptés'), introducing what could well be called modernity.

LILIENCRON Detlev von (Kiel 1844 — Alt Rahlstadt, near Hamburg 1909). A German poet, born into a family of soldiers, he himself became an

Portrait of Detlev von Liliencron

officer and took part in the wars of 1866 and 1870. He was then to be found in the United States, where he exercised various professions, before establishing himself in a little Friesian island, where he became inspector of dykes. In time, an income from the emperor William II assured him the tranquillity he needed in order to write.
„His first collection of poems, *Cavalcades of an aide camp and other poems* ('Adjutantenritte und andere Gedichte', 1883) treated classic themes: the war, patriotism, death, the love of nature, common settings of lyricism.

Only his style was new: short and well finished stanzas each made an impression. The poet told nothing and explained nothing; he let the meaning disengage itself from the feeling. *News of war* ('Kriegsnovellen', 1894) recounted in a discreet key, and in moderate language, brief episodes of the 1870 war. *Poggfred* (1896-1908) is, on the contrary, a humorous and ridiculous epic: in twenty-nine songs, the poet analyses himself, taking instances from his sensitive and picturesque life. His last poems, *Late collection* ('Späte Ernte') contain his masterpiece, *Hans*, where the correspondence between the waves which menace the island and the *femme fatale* who menaces the happiness of the inhabitants, is very much in the Symbolist style. Lyric Symbolism has been spoken of in conjunction with Liliencron; perhaps he was preponderantly an Impressionist, one of the rare representatives of this diffuse style which often accompanied Symbolism and which can be found again in the works of Verlaine, Maeterlinck, D'Annunzio, Dehmel and Max Dauthendey.

LOUŸS Pierre, Pierre Louis called (Gand 1870 — Paris 1925). A French writer. He was impressed to start with by his meeting with the masters of the Parnasse, Leconte de Lisle and Hérédia, whose youngest daughter, Louise, he married. That was perhaps the reason he kept his distance with regard to the literary Bohemia, writing for example to Gide (who had been his fellow-student at the Alsation school): 'Today the Bohemian life no longer exists. No one is more a man of the world than Hérédia, no one more serious than Leconte de Lisle, unless it is Mallarmé. Therefore I believe that we should forget our large hats and

H. BATAILLE *Portrait of Pierre Louÿs*

our long cravats...it is a question of fashion.' He was introduced into Mallarmé's salon. In 1891 he founded the review *La Conque*, where he published his first poems, collected together in 1893 under the title *Astarté*. The inspiration in them is varied, a little according to the dedication of each one,

but a Mediterranean inspiration dominates in the descriptions (*Un port*, for example); mythology abounds, and the goddess Astarte, called upon in one of the first poems, holding in her hand a fabulous lotus flower, is invoked again on the final page entitled *Le Symbol*. Louÿs thus indicates in a devious way what he intends to praise; he says it more clearly still in the introductory poem, addressed to Valéry:

> I will take your hand in the silence, deacon,
> and we will walk together through the narrow paths.
> I will have the brilliant sunflower in my fingers
> and you will carry a lily like a mother of pearl vase.
>
> We will go, I towards Cyprus and you towards Saint-
>   Jean-d'Acre,
> to touch the great Symbol and to see the Holy Cross.
> Knights not knowing how to conquer for their kings,
> but subjects of the blue dream and the empty
>   simulacrum.
>
> You will let me flee to the isle of irises
> to adore and to kiss, in spite of the bacchanalia,
> the tracks of the bare feet where Kypris wandered.
>
> But in the mystic and sanctosepulchral night
> you will see the Three Nails on the altar, and our eyes
> will unite, better than our fragile fingers do, on the
>   gods.

It is therefore not surprising when, after such a declaration of intention, Pierre Louÿs gives proof of a sensual and refined paganism in the famous *Chansons de Bilitis* (1894): affected descriptions interspersed with erotic scenes and an audacious chastity. He had other successes in the world of the novel with *Aphrodite* (1896), *La Femme et le pantin* (1898) — from which Buñel took the scenario of his film *Cet obscur objet du desir*, *les Aventures du roiPausol* (1901). *Psyche* remained unfinished.

For Pierre Louÿs, 'poetry is an Oriental flower which does not live in our hothouses. Greece herself had received it from Ionia, and it was also from there that André Chénier and Keats transplanted it among us, in the poetic desert of their time; but it dies with each poet who brings it to us from Asia. One must always look for it at the source of the sun.'

MACHADO Antonio (Seville 1875 — Collioure 1939). This Spanish poet was the principal representative of the 'generation of '98', or thought of as such because, although originating from Seville, he was far more conscious of Castile than most of its native poets.

It would be wrong to place the whole career of Machado under the sign of Symbolism. He started there; indeed, in 1899, a journey to Paris gave him the opportunity to meet the French writers, as well as Oscar Wilde and, more especially, Darío with whom he became friends. The collection *Solitudes* (Soledades) in 1902, was characteristic of this first style. Machado started from a reality, the

arth, and from an analogy, the correspondence
etween the earth and ourselves:

> There is some kind of earth in our veins
> and it feels
> the humidity of the garden.

Portrait of Antonio Machado

'A profound palpitation of the spirit' is felt 'in
nimated reply to the contact of the world', and
eads to the discovery of God in oneself. In 1907,
Machado produced an augmented edition of his
collection, *Solitudes*, ('Soledades, galerias otros
poemes'), where other symbols appeared. From
907 to 1912 he lived in Soria, where he taught
French. There he married Leonor Izquierdo
Cuevas, whose premature death inspired him to
write some heart-rending verse, entitled *Chemins*:

> It was a summer's night
> The window was open
> And so was the door.
> Death came into my house
> And drew near to her bed —
> Without even a glance towards me —
> With his thin fingers broke
> Something frail:
> Speechless, without a look,
> Death went by again
> In front of me — What have you done?
> But Death did not reply.
> My child is in peace
> And my heart is in grief.
> That which Death broke
> Was only a thread between the two of us

In 1912 Machado published a new collection of
verse entitled *Countryside of Castile* ('Campos de
Castilla'). He was more than ever master of the art
of description (*By the banks of the Duero, The Oaks*),
but one also feels that he had entered into communion with this earth, and he was able to find
epic accents with which to praise it (*The country of
Alvar Gonzales*). The self is relegated to the background, or rather it allows itself to be invaded by
nature or by the past which pervades these places.
Castile becomes a place of the soul.

In *Countryside of Castile*, Machado made the
experiment of dividing everything in half. 'I
thought', he wrote on this subject, 'that the mission of the poet was to invent new poems of the
human eternal, animated stories which, although
personal, could nevertheless stand alone.' He put
between parentheses his own personality and his
own past to allow other voices to be heard, of
which the most lasting are those of Abel Martin
and Juan de Mairena. This 'apochryphal song' is
not without resemblance to the analogous temptation of the Portuguese poet Fernando Pessoa.

In a parallel way to the search for a poetry of
'thou', Machado was studying forms and symbols.
The results of this are given in *New Songs* ('Nuevas
Canciones', 1924): through his models as diverse
as the sonnet, the *haiku*, and the national forms
such as the *cante hondo* from Andalusia or the *coplas*,
Machado tried to attain the absolute of the poetic
word.

Philosophy and, at the end of his life, politics,
called increasingly upon Machado. His poetry
became richer with each new edition of his *Complete
Poems*. Having left Symbolism, Machado had formed a personal conception of poetry. 'I think',
he said 'that the poetic element is not in the
word in so far as its phonetic value is concerned,
nor in colour, nor in line, nor in the complex of
feelings — but it is certainly a profound spiritual
palpitation.' He dreamed of an 'extemporal
poetry' and of a book which would be like 'the
shadow of ourselves'.

MAETERLINCK Maurice (Gand 1862 — Nice
1949). A Belgian writer. 'I have no biography'
he said. Therefore it would be to betray him to
persist with details of his place of birth, his studies
in law which took him into the profession of
barrister, his meeting with Georgette Leblanc, his
Nobel Prize (1911), his ennobling (1932) and his
death in that Orlamonde where he retired and the
name of which recalls so much the atmosphere of
his dramatic work.

He was a Symbolist of the first rank, or very
nearly. Indeed he went to Paris in 1886, where he
frequented the literary circles and met in particular Villiers de l'Isle-Adam. In a modest review,
La Pléïde, his signature ('Mooris Maeterlinck')
appeared for the first time in March of that year.

F.MASEREEL *Portrait of Maurice Maeterlinck*

This play was not destined for performance. Nevertheless, Maeterlinck, harassed by demands, finally entrusted his text to the Théâtre Libre. In May and December 1891, two shorter plays, *L'Intruse* and *Les Aveugles*, were performed; Lugné-Poe figured among the cast. On May 13, 1893, he would play Golaud in *Pelléas et Mélisande*, a short time before the foundation of the Théâtre de l'Oeuvre.

Pelléas was (at least as far as the conflict is concerned) the *Hernani* of the Symbolist theatre. Camille Mauclair had, in 1891, described thus the characteristics of Maeterlinck the dramatist: 'While

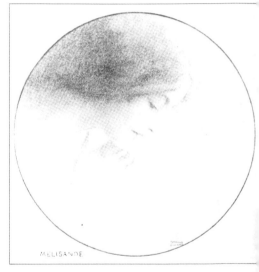

FERNAND KHNOPFF *Mélisande. c.*1902

But it was the publication in 1889 of *Serres Chaudes* which provided the essential evidence of a very end-of-the-century feeling of *mal d'être*. His 'torpid soul' was wasting away in modern society, his monotonous sadness spoke and sang about itself in almost motionless complaints:

> I await a little awakening,
> I await the passing of sleep,
> I await a little sunshine
> On my hands frozen by the moon.

This modest collection ws rich in all the aspirations and innovations of Symbolism (misty scenery, strange escapes, 'desires abandoned under harvests of sadness', the charm of silence, a mixture of modern vision and outdated vision) but it passed unnoticed.

On the other hand, in the same year 1889, a dramatic work, *La Princesse Maleine*, revealed his talent to the public and scored a decisive success for his reputation and for the direction of his work. Octave Mirbeau, in an article which appeared in *Le Figaro* on August 24, 1890, of which he himself exaggerated the importance, greeted this drama as 'the most wonderfully clever work of the time, as well as the most extraordinary and the most naive, comparable and...superior in beauty to whatever is most beautiful in Shakespeare'. It is indeed of Shakespeare that his sensual and murderous queen, who sinks into her dementia, and this young princess, the innocent victim, make one think.

remaining a dramatist in the true sense of the word', he wrote, 'he shows himself to be highly nourished by idealist philosophy, and from that he draws the soul and the secret meaning of his works. He realizes the ideal of the theatre: to rise to the most noble metaphysical concepts and to incarnate them in fictitious beings, to offer them for the meditation of artists and thinkers, while keeping back for the crowd the passionate and perfectly intelligible drama of simple beings where they can divine and discover themselves. To move to tenderness the people invited to the spectacle of their sadnesses and miseries, and to draw from this same spectacle a very great philosophy.' These ambitions were lost, however, in *Pelléas* to the benefit of feelings of humanity and emotion: the jealous passion of a man, whose hair begins to go grey at the temples, for an unknown girl he met in the forest; the love which awakes in

eart of the young wife of Pelléas, the young
rother Golaud, the confrontation of the two
nen, the death of Mélisande at the very moment
he becomes a mother, renew the old myth of
Tristan (and it is no bad thing if the superb musi-
al score of Debussy owes something to Wagner).

The poet in Maeterlinck was quiet after *Les
Douze Chansons*. *Pelléas* was followed by other
dramas in which the style was less happy — as if,
n the theatre also, Symbolism was shutting itself
.way in a new academicism: *La Mort de Tintagile*,
ntérieur (1894), *Aglavaine et Sélysette* (1896), *Monna
'anna* (1902). The best, *L'Oiseau bleu* (1909) had a
great international success, especially in the Anglo-
Saxon countries.

At the same time, Maeterlinck was pursuing
iigher speculations. Translator of Ruysbroeck the
admirable (*L'Ornement des noces spirituelles*, 1891), of
Novalis (1894), of Emerson (1895), tempted by
different ways of mysticism, he wanted to extract
rom silence the tiny bits of unknown truth. *Le
Trésor des humbles* (1896), the fruit of different
readings, was an invitation to penetrate the depths
f self and to accept life, at the same time as the
promise, always renewed and never kept, of total
ruth. He developed sometimes the effort of the
ndividual conscience (*La Sagesse et la destinée*, 1898;

Le Temple enseveli, 1902), sometimes the intermediary of things more humble than man (from
whence come his famous lives of animals such as
La Vie des abeilles, 1901 and *La Vie des fourmis*, 1930).
With *La Mort* (1913), he becomes metaphysicist and
professes a kind of pantheism, based on poetry
rather than reality (*Le Grand Secret*, 1921). It is
fashionable today to disregard these ambitious
works, and to find them laughable with regard to
science. They gave Maeterlinck's work a particular
unity, nevertheless, and it is extremely enlight-
ening to start with them in order to go back to his
theatre. He did it himself when he was writing a
similar preface to the edition of his dramas. If he
discovered then, in *La Princesse Maleine*, 'many
dangerous naivetés, some useless scenes, and most
of the repeated surprises which give the characters
the appearance of slightly deaf sleep-walkers who
have been woken from a painful dream', he
approved of the idea which inspired the drama,
the meaning of these confused calamities, the
somewhat haggard vision of the world, the obsession with the presence of death: 'In painting
this immense and useless weakness, one comes
closest to the radical and ultimate truth of one's
being, and, if from the characters thus handed
over to hostile nothingness one can draw some
deeds of grace and tenderness, some words of
sweetness, of fragile hope, of pity and of love, one
has done all one can humanely do when trans-
porting existence into the confines of that great
motionless truth which freezes the energy and the
wish to live.'

CARLOS SCHWABE, illustration for *Pelléas et Mélisande*
by Maurice Maeterlinck

MALLARME Stéphane (Paris 1842 — Valvins
1898). A French poet. If he was, as suggested
by Guy Michaud, 'the last Romantic', 'the first
decadent', he was above all more qualified than
anyone else, when in 1868 he 'came down again
from the absolute' to formulate the highest
ambitions for literature and to define the use of
the symbol in poetry: 'The contemplation of
objects, the image which takes wing from the
dreams they stir up, these are the song: those
Parnassians take the objects in their entirety and
show them: in that way they lack any mystery; they
take back from the spirits which they create the
delightful joy of belief. To *name* an object is to
suppress three quarters of the pleasure of the
poem which is made to be understood little by
little; to *suggest* it — that is the dream. It is the
perfect usage of this mystery which constitutes the
symbol: to evoke an object by degrees to show a
state of soul, or, inversely, to take an object and
separate a state of soul from it by a series of
deciphering.' This, however, did not mean that
Mallarmé was the leader of the Symbolist school
('I abominate schools' he said,) and contrary to
what Wyzewa wrote, he never claimed to be a

Symbolist. He was too independent and too solitary for that. He was born in Paris, and his childhood was saddened by the death of his mother in 1847, and that of his sister, Maria, in 1857. The poems he wrote during his studies at the Lycée in Sens expressed the obsession with death and the search for a refuge. In 1860, he discovered *Les Fleurs du mal*, and this reading left a profound impression on him. Knowing that in his time it was not possible to live by the pen, he chose to teach English, which he had learnt in England when he was twenty. He married Marie Gerhard, and was able to assure her daily bread. In 1863 he was appointed lecturer at the Lycée of Tournon. His daughter was born there in 1864, the same year that he started the composition of *Hérodiade*.

This work plunged him into pangs of anguish. 'I have spent a terrifying year', he wrote to his friend Cazalis, 'my Thought has thought itself and has arrived at a pure Conception. All that my nature has suffered as a result of this, is indescribable, but happily I am perfectly dead...I am now impersonal.' Psychological crisis, metaphysical crisis, poetic crisis: in July 1865, Mallarmé decided to interrupt *Hérodiade*, leaving it 'for the cruel winters.' *Le Monologue du faune*, the first version (a project suggested by Banville and destined...for the Comédie Française) of the future *Après-midi d'un faune*, filled the time of the interlude. *Hérodiade*, the tragedy turned poem, was not slow to grasp him again, together with the pangs of creation of which *Don du poème* and the poem in prose entitled *Le Démon de l'analogue* are the evidence.

In 1869, he sent a fragment of *Hérodiade* — a sketch for the dressing-room scene — to the *Parnasse contemporain* which was preparing its second collection. In the first collection, in 1866, ten of Mallarmé's poems had appeared: *Les Fenêtres, Le Sonneur, A celle qui est tranquille, Vere novo, L'Azur, Les Fleurs, Soupir, Brise marine, A un pauvre, Epilogue.*

In 1868, Mallarmé was appointed to the Lycée at Avignon. Was this change of place enough to produce 'the Tournon crisis'? One could not doubt it when one reads the prose tale, Igitur, which he wrote at that time, and by which he hoped to vanquish 'the old monster of Impotence'. It is a strange work which recounts the spiritual death of the poet, who describes the obsessional fixation with the Absolute, the *'maladie d'idéalité', the ordeal of the mirror, the haunting memory of the white page. Igitur* is the spirit itself, which tries to recapture itself in such as himself: descending the staircases of the human mind it goes to the bottom of things; it tries to become pure concept again, desiring to rejoin that moment where the past touches the extremity of the future, to paralyze the beating of life itself, and finally to abolish the danger. Mallarmé read *Igitur* in front of Catulle Mendès, who disapproved of the work, and Villiers de l'Isle-Adam, who was enthusiastic about it.

In 1871, Mallarmé established himself in Paris, after 'a winter of supreme anxieties and struggles'. He then published several poems in prose, and a

translation of the poetry of Edgar Allan Poe. After several years of poetic silence, he wrote in Brittany, during the summer of 1873, an excellent poem to the memory of Théophile Gautier, *Toas Funèbre*. In 1874, he was living in the Rue de Rome in the apartment which the celebrated 'Tuesdays' were soon to make famous, and he rented a little house in Valvins, by the Seine. Henceforward those were to be the two poles of his peaceful

EDVARD MUNCH *Portrait of Stéphane Mallarmé*. 1896

existence, saddened in 1879 by the death of his young son, Anatole. The theme of death never ceased to haunt him, as his *tombeaux* show. Of these, the *Tombeau d'Edgar Poe* (1876) was commissioned for the Poe Memorial in Baltimore. He spent part of his time on works which were unexpected, to say the least: a feminine review *La Dernière mode*, the adaptation of a manual of mythology, *Les Dieux antiques*, another manual or *Les Mots anglais.*

Mallarmé was not concerned with what has come to be called literary fame. Nevertheless, this fame came to him gradually: a study of him by Verlaine in the series *Poètes maudits* (1883), the pages which Huysmans devoted to him in *A Rebours* (1884), the poem entitled *Prose pour Des Esseintes* all had a great deal to do with it. René Ghil was soon to show him speaking, 'like a supremely initiated priest, of the Symbol'. The celebrated sonnet, *Le Vierge, le vivace et le bel aujourd'hui*, which

vas published in *La Revue indépendante* in March
1885, was in fact entirely representative of that
which, several months later, would carry the quasi-
official name of Symbolist poetry: the imagery
(the swan), the thematic (the nostalgia of an elsewhere), the music:

> The virginal, living and beautiful day,
> Will it tear for us with a blow of its drunken wing,
> this hard, forgotten lake, haunted beneath the frost
> by the transparent glacier of the flights that have not
>   flown.
> A swan of long ago remembers that it is he,
> magnificent but freeing himself without hope,
> for not having sung the country to live in
> when the tedium of sterile winter shone.
> His whole neck will shake off this white agony
> inflicted by space on the bird that denies it,
> but not the horror of the earth where his feathers are
>   caught.
> A phantom condemned to this place by his pure
>   brilliance,
> he stays motionless in the cold dream of scorn
> worn in his useless exile by the Swan.

(Translated by Anthony Hartley, The Penguin Book
of French Verse No.3, 1957)

Mallarmé is not content here to develop the
romantic theme, now banal, of the poet who is
prisoner of the contingencies of life, exiled from
his natal purity; he is expressing his major obsession, the attempt, perhaps impossible, to bring
together purity and equivocacy, desire and regret,
the same and the other.

When, several months earlier, he defined poetry
thus: 'Poetry is the expression, by means of the
human language brought back to an essential
rhythm, of the mysterious meaning of the aspects
of existence. It thus endows our stay here with
authenticity and constitutes the only spiritual task',
was he defining Symbolist poetry, or simply
poetry itself? Mallarmé's disciples let themselves be
caught by this ambiguity, but not he. He was without doubt lavish with his prefaces, his speeches at
literary banquets, his letters of encouragement,
and even his words ('No one has ever spoken like
him', said Valéry) at the Tuesday receptions,
which he inaugurated in 1880. But he knew how
to keep his distance, and to maintain the reserve
which was necessary to break with Ghil, and in
1891 he declared to Jules Huret for his *Enquête sur
l'évolution littéraire*: 'For myself, the position of a
poet in this society which does not allow one to
live, is the position of a man who isolates himself
in order to carve his own tombstone. What has
given me the attitude of leader of a school is, first,
that I always interest myself in the ideas of the
young people; secondly and without doubt, my
sincerity in recognizing what is original in the
material of the newcomers. Because I am at heart
a solitary person, I believe that poetry is made for
the celebration and pomp of a set society with
room for the glory of which people seem to have
lost the idea.'

While he was working, he 'applied himself to
getting old'. The relationship which he maintained
with a former actress, Méry Laurent, whom he
had met at Manet's house, permitted him to
dream with complete freedom of questions about
the theatre, dancing, and the sacred: as many
Divagations appeared in *La Revue Indépendante* in 1897.
She also gave him the courage to launch himself
into the supreme effort of *Un coup dés jamais n'abolira
le hasard*, 'an act of madness'. Taking after *vers libre*
and a poem in prose at the same time, the text,
thanks to an unpublished typographical arrangement, mimed the trajectory of a thought to establish an exact 'spiritual setting'. Pensioned in 1894,
Mallarmé spent longer and longer periods in
Valvins, where he died from choking in 1898.
Thus his life came to an end, a life which he
himself had shown, in a brief *Autobiographie* addressed to Verlaine, as inextricably mixed with the
plan of what had to be his work: '...I have always
dreamed and tried other things, with the patience
of an alchemist, ready to sacrifice all vanity and
all satisfaction, just as in olden times one used
to burn one's furniture and the beams of one's
house, to feed the furnace of the Great Work.
What is it? It is difficult to say: a book, quite
frankly, a book in many volumes, which would be
a book, architectural and premeditated, and not a
collection of random inspirations however marvellous they might be...I will go further; I will say the
Book, for I am convinced at heart that there will
only be one, I am tempted unknowingly by anyone who has ever written, even the Geniuses. The
Orphic explanation of the Earth is the only duty
of the poet and the literary game par excellence:
for the actual rhythm of the book, while impersonal and living as far as its pagination is concerned, puts itself next to the equations of this
dream, or Ode.'

Portrait of Stuart Merrill

MERRILL Stuart (Hempstead, New York 1863 — Versailles 1915). A French-speaking American poet. The son of an American diplomat, he was born in the State of New York, but he spent his childhood in Paris and, having completed his studies at Columbia College, he settled there finally in 1890. He only went back to English in order to translate Baudelaire, Mallarmé and Aloysius Bertrand. But he borrowed the alliteration of Anglo-Saxon poetry and turned it to a use which can be somewhat tedious. Was he Symbolist at the beginning, at the time of his *Gammes* which appeared in 1887? It is not certain, even if he tried to interpret music in his own way. His Symbolism was no more than decorative in *Les Fastes* (1891) and *Les petits poèmes d'automne* (1895). Then a change occurred: convinced, to start with, that the mission of the poet was to create from the transitory forms of an imperfect life, Stuart Merrill came to celebrate the absolutely simple life such as revealed itself to him in Ile-de-France. The symbol is there, in *Les Quatre saisons* (1900), in the measure where 'each flower is the image of the world', a world where 'everything lives'. *Une voix dans la foule*, where the democratic emphasis makes one think of Whitman, makes this fervent cry still understood:

> No, spring sunshine! No, heart of my ancestors!
> I laugh at all the skies, I am turning towards all beings!
> I wish to clasp the world in my arms
> and die from the perfume of the earth and the seas...

Portrait of Ephraïm Mikhaël

MIKHAEL Ephraim (Toulouse 1866 — Toulouse 1890). A French poet whose premature death made his hopelessness even more sad. As Gour-

mont wrote in the *Deuxième livre des masques*, one can feel in his poems 'the wearisomeness of the chosen who feel obscurely, like the frozen water in a swollen river, the waves of death flowing up the length of their limbs'. In 1886 he published the fourteen poems of *L'Automne*, where he evoked the 'grey Sundays' of Paris, and where boredom master of landscape, grabbed hold of him: this was a significant inversion of his style, which distinguished this poetry from Romanticism. He was an assiduous reader of Spinoza, and convinced of the 'emptiness of joy and sorrow', he wrote poems in prose which appeared after his death.

MILOSZ Oscar-Venceslas de Lubicz-Milosz (Czereïa, Bielorussia 1877 — Fontainebleau 1939). A French-speaking writer of Lithuanian origin. Jacques Bellemin-Noël, who devoted an important thesis to him, thought of this foreign poet as 'a Romantic lost between the end of Symbolism and

Portrait of Oscar-Venceslas Milosz

the beginnings of Surrealism'. Nevertheless, it was certainly as a Symbolist that Milosz started. Born on the enormous estate of his ancestors, he went to live in Paris in 1889 . Ten years later he published *Le Poème des décadences* where, among 'women and phantoms', appeared a 'Salome of instinct and of our shames, who had nothing about her of a princess from afar. The parks, the swans, the calm waters recall the most conventional Symbolist scenery; *La Dernière orgie* and *Le Coup de grâce* are the

ltimate evocations of Latin decadence. Perhaps it
is in a poem such as *Brumes* that one should look
or the true style of Milosz, and the expression of
is uneasiness:

Ah! for pity's sake be quiet, nasal music
Which skips over there, in the cold, in the dark.
No one listens to you and no one looks at me!
Be quiet, wine-sodden melody which is the death-
    rattle of my hope!

I am dreaming of the song of breezes and wasps,
And of the azure streaked with the great flights of
    white birds.
How far away it is! The sounds are stifled in the
    crêpes
Of my distress, and I can only hear

You, forgotten waltz, panting and lame,
In tatters in the wind of the deserted crossroads,
Requiem of the forsaken, old lullaby,
Whose poor emaciated fingers relently work on my
    nerves.

Les Sept Solitudes (1906) still shows a belated Sym-
olism. But Milosz soon found a more original
yle in his novel *L'Amoureuse initiation* (1910), in
hich he draws a spiritual itinerary, and in the
ieratic plays *Miguel Manara* (1912), *Mephiboseth*
914) and *Saul de Tarse* (posthumous publication).
his avid reader of the Bible — he learned
ebrew for this — was as passionately interested
. occultist literature. On December 14, 1914, he
iought he saw the 'spiritual sun', and this illumi-
ation directed his work towards the revelation of
 message, the gospel of a Nothing: that is to say
 'outside-God' in the breast of God: *Ars Magna*
924) and *Arcanes* (1926).
It must be seen that these works were placed in
ie actual continuity of a Symbolism which was
iunted by the knowledge of the Absolute. The
irprising *Confession de Lemuel* (1922), a man who
id known the torments of Hell, 'that separate
ace, different, hideous, that immense delirious
ain of Lucifer', culminates in *Le Cantique de la
nnaissance* where the poet hears the voice 'from
e realm of the other sun'. From the graceful
mbolism of his youth, Milosz attained, through
e voice of asceticism, the world of the
rchetype.

OCKEL Albert (Ougrée-lez-Liège 1886 —
elles 1945). A Belgian poet. He founded a
ietic review, *La Wallonie*, in Liège, to which most
 the Symbolist poets sent texts: he thus played
 important role in the history of the movement.
 1889, he went to Paris, attended the 'Tuesdays'
Mallarmé to whom he devoted a book (*Stéphane
allarmé, un héros*, 1899) and a cult. His theories
ere most frequently those of Mallarmé, for
ample when, for the theatre, he dreamed of

Portrait of Albert Mockel

actors who would be the officiating priests of Art,
and of simple 'forms' given to 'ideas'. In poetry,
he was one of the promoters of *vers libre*. His first
collection of poetry, *Chantefable un peu naïve* (1891),
was in a discreetly archaic style, and of a slightly
too studied ingenuity. In *Les Clartés* (1902) he came
back to the national tradition of chiaroscuro.
Later, *La Flamme immortelle* (1924) was more intense
in its lyricism.

MORÉAS Jean (Athens 1856 — Paris 1910). He
was a French-speaking writer of Greek origin,
whose real name was Ionnis Papadiamantopoulos.
He went to live in France around 1880, and published in *Lutèce* and *Le Chat noir* before producing a
somewhat Verlainian collection, *Les Syrtes*, 1884:

Listen no more to the plaintive bow which laments
Like a wood-pigeon expiring along the bowling greens;
Attempt no more the soaring of wandering dreams
Which drag their golden wings in the degrading clay.

The diverse imagery in *Les Cantilènes* is an imagery of the period as well. The epithet 'decadent'
would frequently be applied to these two collections if Moréas had not protested against it and
laid claim to that of 'Symbolist'. He insisted on
the esoteric quality of the poetry which was
called decadent, and observed that the term was
ambiguous and that 'the critic, since his mania for
labelling things is incurable, could more fairly call
them *symbolist*'. From this proposition to the

Manifeste littéraire, published in the literary supplement of *Le Figaro* on September 18, 1886, was only a step. For him, 'Symbolist poetry tries to cover the idea in a sensible form, which is not an end in itself, but which, while serving to express the idea, remains the subject of it'; this ambition necessitates 'an archetypal and complex style: unpolluted vocables, significant pleonasms, mysterious ellipses, the suspended anacoluthon, everything very bold and multiform'. His actual realizations were less audacious. Moréas had no success at all when he tried with Paul Adam to write a great Symbolist novel, *Les Demoiselles Goubert* (1886). The banquet organised on the occasion of the publication of *Le Pèlerin passionné* in 1891 glorified Symbolism very much more than the author of the collection, and Mallarmé, who was presiding, laid stress on the 'dawning youth' which surrounded him. Moréas soon broke with Symbolism and founded the romanesque school: to the Symbolist mists he opposed the Graeco-Latin light, to hermetism the clear lines and stripped language of his *Stances* (1899-1901), in which can be felt the sadness of a lonely man growing old.

MORGENSTERN Christian (Munich 1871 — Merano, Italy 1914). A German writer. He was a precocious poet who invented, like Stefan George, a language: the 'laloula'. At the age of twenty he was inspired by socialism, but later changed to mysticism and to the theosophy of Rudolf Steiner. He died of tuberculosis at forty-three: his life was spent with a sanatorium as his daily background. Morgenstern dedicated his first work 'to the spirit of Nietzsche': it was a sign of his opposition to a materialist and philistine society, of the deep dissatisfaction which projected him into the study of God. Having found His truth, he expressed his mystic joy in his poems, *Melancholy* (1906) and *We have found a way* ('Wir fanden einen Pfad', 1914). But his true originality lay in the celebrated *Songs of the Gallows* ('Galgenlieder', 1905) and in the collections of like inspiration which followed. Manipulating humour and irony with discrimination, Morgenstern seemed, in his poems of great formal perfection, to aspire only to mockery and parody. But this play of words and ideas revealed a more profound intention: seen through the naive eyes of a 'big child', reality becomes demythified, and a renewed language discovers unusual and smiling symbols in it. In these interesting works, Symbolism takes the form of an amusing and ingenuous lyricism: this makes up perhaps for the grandiloquences and prophetic trifles which it has so often had to put up with in the works of so many mediocre writers.

NOALLES Anna de Brancovan, Comtesse de (Paris 1876 — Paris 1933). She was a French poetess of Rumanian origin, who wrote poetry while she was still at school. Her first collection, *Le Cœur innombrable*, did not appear, however, until

Portrait of Anna de Noailles

1901. Rather than recalling the Symbolist affectations it inaugurates a kind of Neo-Romanticism. Its originality comes from a pagan mysticism, a wish to embrace life:

> I shall apply myself so well and so hard to life,
> with such a strong clasp and such squeezing,
> That before the sweetness of the day is taken away
> from me it will warm itself in my embrace.

L'Ombre des jours (1902) is inspired by a pantheist confidence in the universe. However, touches of anxiety gradually become apparent. Marked by illness, haunted by the idea of nothingness, Anna de Noailles developed her preferred theme, death (*Les Vivants et les morts*, 1913; *L'Honneur de souffrir*, 1927). Her versification remains classic, and this poetry does not strangle the grave, often sad eloquence which enables the work of Anna de Noailles to survive.

PASCOLI Giovanni (San Mauro, Romagna 1855
— Bologna 1912). An Italian poet. His childhood
was saddened by mourning — his father was
assassinated, his mother and three of his brothers
died within a few years — and by poverty. He

Portrait of Giovanni Pascoli

studied at Bologna, where he became a socialist,
and was even imprisoned in 1879. He then entered upon a university career, and succeeded
Carducci in Bologna, in 1907. His personality
always remained gloomy and closed, and his
ideology marked by the obsession with a superior
force which crushes the oppressors as much as the
oppressed. He left an important poetic production in Latin, which earned him numerous prizes.
The collection of poems which he published in
1891, *Myricae*, introduced a new tone into Italian
poetry: here the landscapes and the reminiscences
were spontaneously expressed, without cultural
intrusions, in an anti-literary mood, and were
the best illustration of what has been called the
'poetics of a small child': a delicate surprise in face
of the most simple realities, a pleasing break with
academic tradition. But Pascoli sometimes poured
out his poetry in a plaintive sentimentalism, full of
grim affectedness and capricious puerilities.

In his subsequent collections, *First Poems* (1897),
Songs of Castelvecchio (1903), *New Poems* (1909), the
themes tend to develop superficially, the tone
becomes inflated, and the inspiration becomes

entangled with philanthropic intentions. Nevertheless, in *Songs of Castelvecchio* Pascoli reaches the
height of his art, and the musical transcription of
sensations and the play of correspondences are
truly Symbolist.

Afterwards he forced the style, and composed
works where rhetoric stifled the slender vein
of a delicate and shy inspiration, which could
only support a whisper, and which seemed to be
emitted in the same way as damp grass in the
spring emits a perfume of freshness, of verdure
and of youth ('odor di fresco e verde e gioventù').

POE Edgar Allan (Boston 1809 — Baltimore
1849). An American writer, who was by the dates
of his life and by his inspiration, a romantic. But,
as the fraternal double of Baudelaire, honoured
by Mallarmé, followed by Valéry, and admired by

Portrait of Edgar Allan Poe

all the writers of the Symbolist generation, he
deserves at least a brief mention in this work.

Raised in Virginia, he fled to Boston following
quarrels with his adoptive father, John Allan.
There he published *Tamburlaine and other Poems*.
After a period in the army and a second edition of

his poems (1831) he went to stay with his aunt, Maria Clemm, in Baltimore. He then started to write his tales, of which *Manuscript found in a Bottle* was rewarded with a prize in a competition. In 1836 he married his cousin, Virginia Clemm, aged fourteen years, and settled in Richmond. He became a critic and was overwhelmed with work. He profited from this by publishing his tales in various reviews. In 1840 he put them together,

ALFRED KUBIN, illustration for *The Raven*

and published them under the title *Tales of the Grotesque and the Arabesque*. However, it was the publication of a poem, *The Raven*, which ensured his fame in 1845.

During the same year, he published a selection of his *Tales* and a collection of poetry, *The Raven and other Poems*. In 1846 he commented on the composition of *The Raven* in the *Philosophy of Composition*. Virginia died in 1847. Poe then published *Eureka*, a poem in prose which dealt with the structure and the evolution of the Universe, his critical testimony *The Poetic Principle*, tales, poems, including the enigmatic *Ulalume*. He died in the street, in Baltimore, in circumstances which have remained

mysterious but from which the abuse of laudanum is probably not far removed.

This is not the place to evoke the Symbolism of Poe in his *Tales*. On the other hand, his quest for Truth in *Eureka*, the discovery of a 'spiritual soul' in *The Universe*, are certainly those of a precursor of Symbolism. Mallarmé, who thought of him as his teacher, translated his poems. Above all one retains from the work of Poe a theory of poetic effect obtained by a scholarly and contrived arrangement which one can nevertheless forget. As Mallarmé said, speaking on the subject of Poe, 'To avoid the reality of the scaffolding around this spontaneous and major architecture, does not imply a lack of powerful and subtle calculations, but one ignores them — they purposely make themselves mysterious'.

PRZYBYSZEWSKI Stanislav (Lojewo, near Inowroclaw 1868 — Jaronty 1927). A Polish writer who wrote in German to start with, and then in Polish. He made his debut as a critic, and published studies on Chopin, Nietzsche and Ola Hansson; he was then attracted to Huysmans, Barbey d'Aurevilly, and strongly felt the influence

EDVARD MUNCH *Portrait of Stanislav Przybyszewski.* 1895

of Strindberg (the Popoffsky of his novel *The Abbey*). He soon gained the reputation of being a cheerful poet with a bubbling imagination and the manner of a satanic magus. He had a taste for the xciting and a morbid eroticism. Convinced that the Absolute is the soul, and what art alone xpresses', he nevertheless belonged more to ymbolism than to decadence. Symbols as well layed an important role in his exploration of the ubsoil of the 'naked soul'.

In 1897, he became the chief editor of the eview *Life* (Zycie) in Cracow. He published in it, mid uproar, his understanding of the new art, berated from all moral and social constraints: it ad to be the expression of absolute and pro->und individuality, the 'reflection of the Absolute 1 all its manifestations, beyond good and evil, eyond the beautiful and the ugly' (*Confiteor*).

Bathed in a dazzling but ephemeral glory, uthor of a work which soon showed itself to be ransitory, Przybyszewski exercised a considerable nfluence, on Dehmel and Wyspianski among thers. He imparted a decisive momentum to ne tendencies which restored poetry to some of s living sources: the anxieties of the soul, the xploration of the inner world, the mysteries of ne unconscious, the symbolic meaning of things, ne questions of the spirit in the grip of meta-hysical anguish.

EGNIER Henri de (Honfleur 1864 — Paris 936). A French writer, born in Honfleur of an ld aristocratic family. He spent his childhood and is adolescence in dwellings where, as he wrote, ired lives finished their powers, and gently xhausted their decline'. He studied law in Paris, ontributed to various reviews under the pseudo-ym of Hugues Vitrix, and published in 1885 *Les endemains*, a picture of disappointed love amid cenery of sea and forest. His images tended to ettle into symbols in *Sites* and *Episodes*, his two ollections of 1887 — 'dreams of gold', 'lies', and hade', — but only to record another failure. Vith his friend Viélé-Griffin, Régnier visited the ymbolist milieux and was one of Mallarmé's steners. *Les Poèmes anciens et romanesque* (1890), with neir mixture of languor and affectation, their berated versification, inaugurated an approach-ble Symbolism, of which the masterpiece was *Les ux rustique et divins* (1897).

In 1896, Régnier married the second daughter f José Maria de Hérédia. His style was becoming ss and less Symbolist, and more and more close > that of ancient Parnassus. If the symbol was still ere, it was nearer to the allegory, the representa-on of a feeling rather than of an idea. He con-nued thus in *Les Médailles d'argile* (1900), *La Cité des ux* (1902) — where he takes his dream for a walk own the empty garden paths of Versailles — *La andale ailée* (1905), *Le Miroir des heures* (1910). At the me time, Régnier became an elegant and courtly ovelist of an aristocratic and free-thinking re-nement, in the delicate style of the eighteenth

century which he loved (*La Double Maîtresse*, 1900; *Le Bon Plaisir*, 1902; *La Pécheresse*, 1920).

RILKE Rainer Maria (Prague 1875 — Val-Mont, Switzerland 1926). This writer was born in Prague, and spoke German. Between the tender Neo-Romanticism of his debuts (the collection *Life and Songs*, 1891, and the famous *Song of the Life and the Death of the Cavalry Officer Christopher Rilke*) and the Expressionism to which he was linked on account of the realist images of the *New Poems* (1903-1907) or the pathetic cries of the *Elegies of Duino* (1911-1922), is there a place for Symbolism? It could be passionately argued. Rilke knew he had links with family, national, artistic and literary traditions; but

P. MODERSOHN-BECKER *Portrait of Rainer Maria Rilke.* 1904

he knew as well that his taste for writing had come from 'early sufferings and bitter experience', and that his poetic art would always remain separate from his life. Whence came the advice which he expounded in the first of his *Letters to a Young Poet*, and which he doubtless never needed himself: 'You are looking outwards; this, above all, is what you must never do. No one else can give you advice or help — no one. It is a lonely road. Go into yourself, and search out your need to write: see if it is pushing its roots into the depths of your heart'. The encounter between Rilke and Symbol-ism took place under the auspices of Maeterlinck;

he discovered the Belgian poet at the time when he was preparing to leave Prague for Munich, in 1895. He developed Maeterlinck's theme of pity, and that of evanescence, that flight from oneself, that dispersion into the sensations of the moment of which the *Books of Hours* (1899-1903) give the poetic proof. It is also necessary to realize the influence of the Danish writer Jens Peter Jacobsen (1847-1885), who gave him 'the inner certainty that there are, in Nature, the sensible equivalents of the lightest and most elusive things in ourselves'. As to Mallarmé, whom he admired as much as Stefan George did when he met him in Munich, he was perhaps for him the poet of *Les Fenêtres* rather than the poet of *Azur*.

The Rilke of the *Book of Hours* assuredly was Symbolist in as much as he tried to perceive wonders in their outward appearances as much as in their spiritual nature, and that he had the feeling of the mystery within Nature:

> You believed to have recognized the strength
> By grasping the fruit,
> Here again is the enigma.

This enigma was for him, as it was for others, the starting-point of a quest which took him to Russia where he travelled with Lou Andreas-Salomé in 1899 and 1900, and to Italy where he wished to be like Fra Angelico looking for God in his work as a painter; he also went to Worpswede, the village near Bremen, where there was a colony of painters, friends in silence. To listen, to vibrate in receiving the form of the day, that was the attitude of the poet in prayer, the pilgrim, and the birth of his song mingles with 'this ascent of God outside the living heart, with which the sky covers itself, and its descent again in rain' (letter to Ilse Jahr 22.2.1923). In Worpswede, Rilke met Clara Westhoff, the girl who was to become his wife and give him a daughter.

She had to rejoin him in Paris, where he felt called to go partly by the occasion (a monograph on Rodin which a publisher had commissioned) but above all by an irresistible appeal, by his own need to 'recapture an infinity of things to which solitude had made him a stranger' (*Journal*). 'I am a lonely Hope' he wrote to Clara when he finally arrived in the capital on August 28, 1902. Hope of friendship in a town where — as *The Notebooks of Malte Laurids Brigge* testify — 'faces are hostile, and where the smallest thing, even a gesture, is enough to plunge the regard beyond known and friendly things' and for 'the contour, later the comforter, to show itself as the brink of terror'.

But what friendship could be hoped for from a solitary man such as Rodin, who, besides, told him of the necessity for an artist to be alone? It was much more the lesson of a look which, in a hostile world, makes friends of things. Thanks to Rodin alone the menaces of the unknown town, of which he was henceforth to be the centre, disappeared.

From the sculptor, Rilke learned to see thing[s] instead of allowing himself to be carried away b[y] the spirit emanating from them. To see is to gras[p] the unique — and to describe is to restore th[e] unique. Rodin clung to singularity, showing fo[r] instance in his *Les Bourgeois de Calais*, that each on[e] of them had lived that moment in his own person[al] fashion, as the death of the chamberlain Brigg[e] in the *Notebooks* had been personal to him. The *Ne[w] Poems* of Rilke were also a series of isolated image[s] fragments of the 'poetry of things': the panthe[r] in the Garden of plants, the gazelle, the blue h[y] drangea, the garden of la Chartreuse de Champ[?] molle, the balcony in Naples, the orchard o[f] Borgeby-Goard. That way the poet escaped th[e] temptation of transience, but also that of th[e] ready-made beauty which he denounced in hi[s] lecture on Rodin in 1907. Paying homage t[o] the sculptor after their disagreement, Rilke sai[d] in 1912: 'It is thanks to him, and thanks to hi[s] animated work...that I became accustomed to th[e] incommensurable being which he had confronte[d] so differently; he led it, half tamed, right up t[o] me; and, while it allowed me to stroke the mane o[f] its Paris, the presentiment gradually began t[o] form in me of the type of ferocity, of danger an[d] of bound which I could expect of my own'. (Lette[r] to Norbert von Hellingrath, 13.2.1912).

This bound, once again, was the leap int[o] enigma. In the *New Poems*, it is 'the Angel' wh[o] reveals that moment when the influence of Rodi[n] tightens, and Rilke starts to stifle. One moment h[e] is able to take pleasure in the immovability of a[ll] things, and then, suddenly he takes fright in thi[s] petrified world. The Angel is a supernatural bein[g] who, by the slightest movement of his counten[an]ance, can chase in front of him everything whic[h] obliges and everything which limits, the creator [of] space — but the creator of emptiness, the creato[r] of absence:

> Bowing his head a little, he absolves
> himself from things that limit and direct,
> for through his heart moves, mightily erect,
> the eternal future, that revolves.
>
> Before him full of shapes deep heaven stands,
> and each can call to him with pleading claim.
> Put nothing into his unburdened hands,
> from your encumbrancy. Unless they came
> by night for wrestlinger investigating,
> and crossed like raging furies your threshold
> and seized on you as though they were creating
> and breaking you from your retaining mould.

The appeal which opens the series of the *Elegi[es] of Duino* is directed towards the angels. It is a ma[n] of a continuity, the desire to find a meaning in th[is] life, of saving, in an extemporal space, the perish able things of which man is the preserver. Betwee[n] the first elegies written in 1912 by the Adriatic, o[n] the cliff where the castle of the princess of Tou[r] and Taxis was built, and the last, ten years passe[d] as well as the war and the wandering life whic[h] nly ceased with his installation in Muzot, in witzerland. But the quest lived on — the overowing quest. Hence came the cry of the lover in he seventh elegy:

No further quest, no quest...

Hence came, in the few days between 7 and 11 'ebruary, 1922, the completion of the interrupted ollection. Hence equally, and in almost as short a pace of time, the double blossoming of the *Sonnets* ∍ *Orpheus*, dedicated to the dead young girl, Vera Duckama Knoop.

It would be impossible to overestimate the mportance of the meeting with Valéry. The eading of *Architecture*, the working out of the ranslations which Rilke presented to the French oet as a 'sum of his assent, of obedience', marked he end of a waiting period. Not that Rilke borowed from Valéry elements which were foreign o him. What he discovered there was above all vhat he had expected to discover. One has the eeling, when reading the last great works of Rilke, and also his French poems, that they ɔo were written in the wake of Valéry, that he solated themes and motifs, and that from them he ɔrmulated the replies to the questions which he ad been asking himself for a long time. He saw Valéry's world not as it was, but in the image f what he desired: an enchanted world, an enhanted existence. Thus it was that while Valéry's ee came, in time, to sting him and make him take ote ('the Bee' in *Charmes*), the Rilkian bee coninued to gather the honey from the visible in rder to transform it into the invisible. In *Eupalinos* nd *L'Ame et la danse* the metamorphosis comes rom the discovery of a rapport between the thing nd ourselves, from the link which we have woven vith it during our existence (ninth elegy). To save he object means, for Valéry, to take it away from he misshapen, from the mediocre, from nothing-ess; for Rilke it means to pull it into the visible, nto the exterior world that we have not changed nside ourselves. To state a thing is to say more han itself. In his sonnets, on flowers, on fruit, on nirrors, on the dancer, Rilke gives a name to the bject of the poem and then unfolds the series of ariations which the name by itself suggests. Thus ɪ can 'climb from a more confident song' and clamber up the steps of praise to reascend into ɪure Rapport'.

RIMBAUD Arthur (Charleville 1854 — Marseilles 891). A French poet. Both his name and his work re mingled, in spite of him, with the history of

Symbolism. In fact, although he became a merchant in Africa and was, as Mallarmé said, 'a living patient of poetry', the publication of *Illuminations* and *Une Saison en Enfer* in the review *Vogue* in 1886, following the introduction on him by Verlaine in the series *Poètes maudits*, transformed him into a legendary character, a master of both writing and thought. A little group used to meet in Paris with the idea of founding a literary system on the sonnet *Voyelles*. On July 17, 1890, Laurent de Gavoty, director of *La France moderne*, wrote to him in these terms: 'Monsieur and dear Poet, I have read your beautiful verse: it is up to you to say if I shall be happy and proud to see the head of the decadent and Symbolist school contribute to *La France moderne*,...'

Is it necessary to state precisely that he had never sought to play this role of director? Nevertheless, he had known the temptation of literary glory, and even felt the need to be enrolled into a school. But this was the Parnassian school, and he was still a college boy at Charleville when he wrote to Théodore de Banville to tell him about his 'hopes', his impossible notions, and to send him three poems (*Sensation, Ophélie, Credo in unam*) in the hope that he would give to his verse 'a little place among the Parnassians'. He did not know the decadents; but since his arrival in Paris he had been a visitor to the 'Vilains Bonshommes', he had contributed to the *Album Zutique*, he had been, under diverse titles, the companion of Verlaine, Germain Nouveau and Charles Cros. None of this meant that he followed them in a literary way; he had very quickly 'found the celebrities...of modern poetry laughable', and he had searched alone for his own way.

In the blue summer evenings, I will go along the paths
And walk over the short grass, as I am pricked by the wheat,
Daydreaming I will feel the coolness on my feet
I will let the wind bathe my bare head.
I will not speak, I will have no thoughts
But infinite love will mount in my soul
And I will go far, far off like a gipsy
Through the countryside, — joyous as if I were a woman.

(Rimbaud, *Complete works and selected letters*. Wallace Fowlie, University of Chicago Press, 1966)

This verse, dated March 1870, formed part of the *Recueil Demeny*, two notebooks of poetry of which Rimbaud made a fair copy in the autumn of the same year, and gave to a young poet of Douai. They already showed the native independence of the poet who wanted, in literature as elsewhere, to live 'free liberty'. Of these notebooks, the first, more composite, makes the different notes of lyric poetry heard: summer poems, long tirades, humorous sketches and sometimes those of vengeance, occasionally tender poems of political verse full of bitterness and spite. On the other hand, the second notebook was of a surprising unity, and had an even rarer quality: it allowed the reader to live again the adventure of the Bohemian Orpheus who, 'like lyres...plucked the elastics of (his) wounded shoes'. (*Ma Bohème*)

1871, the 'terrible year', was for Rimbaud the year of the declaration of war on 'objective poetry...horribly dull', and on those who did nothing else 'but go back to the spirit of dead things' (Gautier, Leconte de Lisle, Banville). This was much more important than the extremely dubious participation of Rimbaud in the Commune. The two letters from 'le Voyant' (one addressed to Isambard, his old teacher, on May 13, and the other to Demeny on May 15 were letters of rupture, and of rupture with himself. Rimbaud intended to substitute a new literature for former literature, and for the poetry of the past a new poetry – the poetry of another – of which he produced the first samples: *Le Coeur supplicié, Chants de guerre parisien, Mes petites amoureuses, Accroupissements, Les Poètes de sept ans, Les Pauvres à l'église, Ce qu'on dit au poète à propos de fleurs*. The frightful work which the poet imposed on himself spared neither his body ('the disturbance of all the senses'), nor his soul ('all the forms of love, of suffering, of madness'), nor his language. Rimbaud waxed violent on the subject of vocabulary, syntax and metre; he dreamed of a 'universal language', which would be 'of the soul for the soul, summarizing everything, perfumes, sounds, colours, hanging one thought upon another and pulling'. These obscure formulas recall the correspondences of Baudelaire (who is hailed as 'the first prophet, king of the poets, *a true God*'), and they seem to predict the Symbolist doctrine: 'The poet will determine the quantity of the unknown which awakes in the universal soul during his time'.

But it would be wrong to make Rimbaud a Symbolist before the letter. These formulas remained formulas, and their application only appeared here and there. To come back to the two most celebrated poems of the year 1871, *Le Bateau ivre* is a superb piece for effect, and the coloured spelling-book, *Voyelles*, reveals an alchemical project. *Alchimie du verbe*, the central section of Une saison en Enfer (1873), presents a strangely negative account of this project. In the meantime, the poetic of Rimbaud was still developing, less under the influence of Verlaine, and life *à deux*, than following the process of incessant quest. The best title for the verse of the spring and summer of 1872 would be *Etudes néantes* perhaps, as Verlaine showed us. The free play of associations drove the images to flight, even panic (Michel et Christine), which left an impression of emptiness, of a continual evanescence of the being.

The voluntary madness was set off in *Alchimie du verbe*, during a moment of crisis; but it was also clarified there, all the more because Rimbaud illustrated his 'histoire atroce' by new or voluntarily distorted versions of his poems from the year 1872. Not only did he give himself up to this fever

to this fire, and to 'General Sun', in order to be no more than 'a golden spark of *natural* light', but he still wished, like the alchemists, to effect transmutations, to discover origins, to reduce poetic language to powdered rubies, and to extract from the world the dazzling substance far more than the essence or the Idea. Where should one place his prose collected later under the title *Illuminations*? Neither the historians, nor the graphologists, nor the fortune-tellers have been able to establish the true chronological order. Sometimes they are thought of as other illustrations of his prophetic powers, even when they foretold failure; sometimes one can read in them a new project, such as Yves Bonnefoy called 'the harmonic attempt'. Indeed, Rimbaud often spoke of himself as a kind of musician, and put forward as his model the simplicity of the 'musical phrase' (*Guerre*). But this 'work' which consists of arousing 'all the possible harmonic and architectural combinations' had high ambitions. The poet tried to capture the harmonics of the world in order to transform them: 'Your memory and your senses are only the nourishment of your creative impulse. As for the world, when you leave it, what will it have become? Anyway, nothing like it appears now' (*Jeunesse*). The process clearly remained that of 'simple hallucination', that is to say substitution. Just as, for a tranquil landscape of the Oise valley an exotic landscape can substitute itself, virgin soil for the gold-digger (*Larme*), just as for the dream of royal lovers can be substituted the evocation of workers painting artificial skies (*Bonne Pensée d' matin*), so can bridges be built of desired agreements, of complex scenes, of gigantic and proliferating towns which are not just suburbs linked by streets, but sections of nature, sometimes mountainous, sometimes wooded, brought together in one prodigious, but fragile symphony.

For over *Les Illuminations*, as over the attempt at the alchemy of the word, hovered the threat of failure. *L'Adieu* in *Une Saison en Enfer*, and *Solde* in the collection of poetic prose, are acts of liquidation or, to quote Yves Bonnefoy again, 'of the underselling of all Rimbaud's hopes'. What followed is known and so is his silence. Everything happened as if the artist had made an experiment of the limits of the poetic word, extracting from his failure a paradoxical success, which was that of a tightrope walker.

> I strung cords from steeple to steeple; garlands from window to window; golden chains from star to star and I am dancing.

RODENBACH Georges (Tournai 1855 — Paris 1898). A Belgian writer. A native of Tournai and pupil at the Sainte-Barbe college in Gand, he went o Paris in 1877 where he stayed after a brief time t the bar in Brussels. And he decidedly appeared ar more Parisian than a poet of Bruges. Lévy-Dhurmer left an excellent portrait of him, making he the most of his fine profile, his light, fair hair, his blue eyes and his thoroughbred air of elegance.

His literary career spanned only twenty years, rom the booklet *Les Foyers et les champs* (1877) and *Le Coffret* (1879) which expressed his filial feelings,

L. LEVY-DHURMER *Portrait of Georges Rodenbach*

o *Miroir du ciel natal* (1898). His poetic activity was especially intense between 1881 and 1889, when he made himself the spokesman of *La Jeune Belgique*. It was then that he published *La Mer légante* (1881), *L'Hiver mondain* (1884) and *La Jeunesse blanche* (1886) in which he attained full mastery of his art. Already he was evoking the 'Town of the Past' where 'a bundle of assorted souvenirs' was gathered together. After *Le Livre de Jésus* (1888), his last collections, *Le Règne du silence* (1891), *Les Vies encloses* (1896) and *Le Miroir du ciel natal* established a Symbolist style based on the poetic of correspondences: from an object, from a landscape, from a town, impressions of a theme are released and a mystic reverie where the world and the self are mingled spreads out:

A dream lasts there, a wish leaps;
A hope lives, although disappointed;
A reflection is betrothed to the water;
And this moves my unawareness
In the chiaroscuro of myself:
A whole badly conceived Universe,
And all those unbaptized dreams.

Rodenbach also wrote stories, of which the best known is *Bruges-la-morte* (1892). There he conjures up Flanders with its belfries, its old, silent dwellings, its beguinages, its quiet waters. Rilke was very aware of it; but, before him, Verhaeren, a

friend and compatriot of Rodenbach, had classed him 'among the poets of the dream, among those of fine phrases, in the sphere of his two friends and masters who love him as much as he loves them: Edmond de Goncourt and Stéphane Mallarmé'.

SAINT-POL ROUX Pierre-Paul Roux called (Saint-Henry, near Marseilles 1861 — Brest 1940). A French poet. The solitary life which he led slowly at the extreme point of Brittany, his assassination by a German soldier in the same district, make one forget his southern origins, his birth at Marseilles and his upbringing in Lyons. In Paris he took part in the demonstrations which prepared for or accompanied the birth of Symbolism. He left there in 1884. His name figures in the summary of the first number of *Mercure de France*. Péladan counted him among the seven who made up the 'Rose + Croix esthétique', and Mallarmé called him 'my son'. In 1884 he published *Golgotha*, followed by *Seul* and *La Flamme* (1885) and, above all, the *Reposoirs de la procession* (1893-1906). A procession of images passes by, which made Gourmont write in *Livre des masques* that the poet was 'one of most fertile and most surprising inventors of images and metaphors'. His work was supported by a theory, 'ideorealism', which inspired the most interesting studies into Symbolism. According to Saint-Pol Roux the task of the poet is to restore the brightness of beauty which is

Portrait of Saint-Pol Roux

hidden under outward appearances: 'Man seems to me only to inhabit a fairyland of indeterminate signs, of light pretexts, of timid provocations, of distant affinities and of enigmas...The world is a peaceful catastrophe; the poet extricates and looks for the things which are hardly breathing under the rubble and brings them up to the surface of life'. To the Baudelairian 'forest of symbols' he meant to substitute a 'forest of opposites', and the task of the poet was to try to unite them. That is why he bestowed an important order of *Reposoirs*, which made up a cycle, or rather cycles, in the strongest sense of the word: for 'each volume starts with the dawn, follows the course of the sun, and ends with the stars'.

Saint-Pol Roux also wrote fabulous dramas, *L'Ame noire du prieur blanc* (1893), *L'Epilogue des saisons humaines* and especially *La Dame à la faulx* (1899), which was the first part of a trilogy of which the two others, *Le Tragique dans l'homme* and *Sa Majesté la Vie* were destroyed by the Germans when they plundered his manor at Camaret. In the preface to *La Dame à la faulx* he foretold a new direction in which he proposed to restore art to life and 'produce healthy work'. In this he approached the thinking of Francis Jammes and Paul Fort. From 1907 onwards he refused to publish his work, and made no exceptions other than certain circumstantial and minor texts. In his haughty solitude, 'Saint-Pol Roux the Magnificent' entered the infinitude of language, not finishing his books, and progressing amid what he himself called trash (his one established work, *La Synthèse legendaire*, executed in 1926 by means of two hundred and fifty narrators, was oral). Nevertheless, he dreamed of a 'great book', the fragments of which have been recently assembled: the *Répoétique* (that is to say *res poetica* as one speaks of the Republic, *res publica*). The project was born between 1914 and 1918: the 'formidable poem of the new world', a 'monstrous drama, made up of forms which are ideas turned into matter'. From the beginning he promises man to his cosmic future and hails the Word, the unknown god. But, if 'worlds are poems finally made corporeal', of what is the poem of words made? 'A poem', replies Saint-Pol Roux, 'is a supplementary life, a contribution, the third person born to two spirits...born to start with under the form of the Word, ringed by numbers, from the substance gradually granulating around these rings which will become united by the breath of rhythm, this will become Flesh, this third will augment the Life hitherto limited to it, and this is why, through this miracle, poetry is creation'. The influence of the creative god of *Illuminations* will have been recognized here, and it is certainly of Rimbaud that this new alchemy of the Word makes one think.

SAMAIN Albert (Lille 1858 — Magny-les-Hameaux 1900). A French poet. Ernest Raynaud, in *La Mêlée symbolist* shows him 'fleeing the Bacchic

tumult and the wine-soaked crowd to isolate himself in his dreams as in a walled garden where he seemed only to be nourished by pure ambrosia'. Truth to tell, life had not been kind to him:

Portrait of Albert Samain

orphaned at fourteen, he had been obliged to accept unflattering jobs, and had vegetated in office employment. His health was bad as well. From all this came his introspection and his poetry which was conceived a little in the style of the Romantics whom he admired. But, in spite of himself, he was very much attracted to the Baudelairian conception of 'a supreme art, rarified and crystallized in its faultless form'. He was especially conscious of Verlaine's art, whose 'chosen landscapes' he extended. *Au jardin d l'Infante* (1893) brought him instant fame: but from Symbolism he kept almost nothing but the imagery, unless only to define it, together with one of his commentators, as 'the affirmation of an essential analogy between a moment of the duration of myself and a moment of the duration of things'. His style changed in his second collection, *Aux flancs du vase* (1898): he turned towards a happier simplicity with the help of a return to the ancient, or more exactly, as he himself specified, to visions of former times which pleased his soul. The death of his mother plunged him again into confusion as is shown in the poem *Ténèbres* which was published in the posthumous collection *Le Chariot d'or*. Samain was also author of stories and of a two-act play *Polyphème*. From this minor Symbolist — and this minor Symbolism — has remained the picture of 'a child in his best clothes' and the memory of delicate sensibility which expressed itself in slightly prim form.

SOLOGUB Fedor Kouzmith Teternikov called (Saint Petersburg 1863 — Leningrad 1927). A Russian poet of whom it has been said that he was more decadent than Symbolist. But in Russia this implied above all that he had been more conscious of western sources than desirous of creating a national poetry. This does not meant that the poetry he has left us is not strong, sincere and original. Born into a modest family (his father was a tailor and his mother a laundress) he studied at the teaching Institute and became a mathematics teacher. His first novel, *Weighty Dreams*, described a college professor, who struggled against a vice-ridden and limited society. The second novel, *The Pitiful Demon*, (1905), on which is based the renown

Portrait of Fedor Sologub

of the author, described the paranoia of another professor.

However, Sologub had already published some verse. His major theme was, as it was for Baudelaire and in every sense of the word, the theme of evil. He explained: 'In poetic creation, I distinguish two aspirations; one is positive, ironic which says "yes" to the world and, by so doing, throws light on the contradiction of life, and the other is negative, lyrical, which says "no" to the known world, and creates in so doing another world, desired, indispensable and impossible without the transformation necessary to the world'. Irony allows the veil to be lifted and truth discovered. Here no gleam of hope can be found:

We are imprisoned beasts,
We give voice when we can.
The doors are double locked
And we dare not open them. (*Imprisoned Beasts*, 1905)

Without doubt there are in existence 'magic circles inside which impure forces cannot pene-

trate' and 'the poet — just like a magician traces these circles; but he leaves chinks in them, and during the terrible moments of poetic creation, the demon insinuates itself into the centre of the improperly closed circle'. In *Les Poésies* (1896 and 1904), in *Le Cercle de feu* ('Plamennyj krug', 1908), the 'subjective visions of the world and of life' can be found, which, as Briussov stated, constitute the limits of Sologub's work.

SYMONS Arthur (Wales 1865 — Wittersham, Kent 1945). An English writer who deserved better than the reputation of 'commercial traveller in the literary Bohemia' that people wished to give him. Albert J. Farmer recognized in him 'one of the most interesting and most audacious figures in this daring and fertile period of the Nineties'. He was a Celt, son of a Cornish pastor. He knew Walter Pater at Oxford, and was influenced by him, wishing 'to maintain that ecstasy which is the real success in life'. In 1889, he went to Paris in company with Havelock Ellis, returning again the year after, and visiting the Tuesday salons of

R.H. SAUTER *Portrait of Arthur Symons*. 1935

Mallarmé. He had already published one collection of verse, *Days and Nights* (1889). In 1891 he joined the 'Rhymers Club', founded by Yeats, and contributed to the first collection of the group with a poem praising dancers, as he was accustomed to do. Another book of poetry, *Sil-houettes*, bore witness to his development: he did not strike the familiar human note in the manner of Browning, nor the Baudelairian echo, as much as the fleeting and beautiful image, the impression. He showed himself to be an admirable poet of the town by night, with its quays gleaming in the rain, its lights which fell on curtains and paving-stones, its 'eyes which blaze in the street', its depraved passions in discreet alcoves. Should he be reproached with being a decadent? He defended the 'decadent movement in literature' in an article which appeared in *Harper's* magazine (November 1893) where he praised French poetry and 'the representative literature of today' which was 'an illness'. In 1895 he contributed to the *Yellow Book* and then, at the time when the decadent movement was exposed to general reprobation, he made two audacious moves: he agreed to take on the direction of a new publication, the *Savoy*, which was going to 'show the meaning of what is most beautiful in living reality', and he produced another collection, *London Nights*, in which he particularly evoked the music hall and how he used to wait outside the artists' entrance:

Under the archway sheer
Sudden and black as a hole in the placarded wall
Faces flicker and veer
Wavering out of the darkness into the light
Wavering back into night
Under the archway, suddenly seen, the curls
And thin, bright faces of the girls.
(Arthur Symons' *London Nights*, second edition, Leonard Smithers 1897)

Apart from this, Symons was already known as a critic. In 1899, he dedicated to Yeats an important work, *The Symbolist Movement in Literature*, which passed from 'decadence', a transitory deviation from the main road to literature, to Symbolism, 'by which art comes back to the one and only path which leads, through lovely things, to eternal beauty'. The book contained eight chapters, dedicated successively to Nerval, Villiers, Rimbaud, Verlaine, Laforgue, Mallarmé, Huysmans and Maeterlinck, which did not allow of precise analyses of text, but tried to rediscover a road. The definition which he gave to the symbol perhaps recalled that of Carlyle, but the vindication continued of French poetry which said that the invisible world had ceased to be a dream, and which 'became a kind of religion, with all the duties and all the responsibilities of the sacred ritual'. This spiritual quest unfolded in the same way in another collection, *Images of Good and Evil*, (1899), where, while dreams disappeared, the poet asked himself if death was not perhaps the only reality. This obsession with universal mystery, like that of Maeterlinck, reappeared in the *Spiritual Adventures* (1905), where Symons showed himself to be a prose writer of equal talent.

TAILHADE Laurent (Tarbes 1854 — Combs-la Ville 1919). A French writer. Ernest Raynaud, who had recounted in *La Mêlée symboliste* a visit which h had made to him in hospital ('a tender and warm hearted man', and finally 'this terrible Tailhade...'

C. LEANDRE *Portrait of Laurent Tailhade*. 1891

expressed the opinion that he had remained faith ful to the Parnassian formula, but that he wa impregnated with the new spirit of Symbolism. I fact, after his elegiac debut, Tailhade had devise a ferocious Symbolism. His satiric poems (*A pays du mufle*, 1891; *A travers les groins*, 1899) wer assembled in 1904 under the general title *Poème Aristophanesques*. But can Symbolism be Aristo phanic? As Guy Michaud remarked, perhap Tailhade's irony prevented him from graspin what was noble and big, behind so much basenes and mediocrity, in the aspirations of his time.

VALERY Paul (Sète 1871 — Paris 1945). A French writer, who studied at the college in Sète and then at the lycée in Montpelier. He wa attracted to both poetry and painting, and by th time he entered the faculty of law in 1888 he ha already written several poems. The reading o Mallarmé and Verlaine, the friendship of Pierr Louÿs and Gide, the visits to the Symbolist milieu (he was introduced to the Rue de Rome in 1891 decided his vocation. He only agreed in 1920 t the publication of his *Album de vers* , in which h poems from his Symbolist period were collected At any rate they were lost in various magazines, i particular *La Conque*, Pierre Louÿs' review. Hi mythological imagery (Venus, Orpheus, Hele

Narcissus) and has evocation of historical characters (Caesar, Semiramis) are found there beside
genre scenes (*La Fileuse, Au bois dormant*), descriptions
Valvins, Eté), and moving reminiscences:

THE FRIENDLY WOOD
We thought of pure things,
side by side, along the paths;
we held each other by the hand
without speaking...among the hidden flowers;
we walked as if betrothed
alone in the green night of the meadows;
we shared this fruit of fairyland,
the moon kind to the insane;
and then we died on the moss,
very distant, quite alone in the gentle shadows,
and up there in the immense light,
we found each other in tears,
O my dear companion of silence.

. RIGAL *Portrait of Paul Valéry*

L'Album was accompanied by a piece in prose,
'Amateur de Poèmes, which was dated 1906, in which
Valéry looked at 'his true thought', questioned
himself on his language, and meditated on the
writing of poetry. This main turning-point came
at the end of a crisis. It was in 1892, in Genoa, that
he departed from the path which seemed to have
been laid down for him. Deeply disturbed following an emotional crisis, and privately disappointed
by a literary activity which fell short of his ambitions and the example achieved by Mallarmé,
he had given up writing poetry. Henceforth he
resisted the confusion of his love life and his
literary world, to which he opposed his rigorous
intelligence. 'My intellectual life', he explained
later 'had been developing since 1892 down an
axis of study of my true mental functioning'. His
Cahiers prove this, regularly written up as they
were every morning. Official in the Ministry of
War, and then private secretary to a director of
the Havas office, Valéry gave himself to his new
preoccupations in works of prose, *L'Introduction à la
méthode de Léonard de Vinci* (1895), *La Soirée avec M.
Teste* (1806); he was concerned all the time to give
'a view of the detail of an intellectual life'. However, he continued to visit the poets, painters and
musicians. At the suggestion of Gide and Gaston
Gallimard, he agreed in 1912 to go back to the
poems of his youth. In the wake of this work of
revision, he composed from 1913 to 1917 a long
poem, *La Jeune Parque*, in which appeared the
complex symbol of the conscious perception of
the struggle against the contradictory tendencies
of suppression of self and awareness of the
sensible world. *Charmes* (1922) were, once more,
strict exercises, 'children of their own form',
having a rhythm (*Le Cimetière marin*), or an image
(*La Pythie*) in which he applied his mind 'to the
simultaneous command of syntax, harmony and
ideas'.

According to Charles du Bos, Valéry disliked
above all to be thought of as a poet. Were not
Charmes and *La Jeune Parque* a new method of
exploring the potential of the spirit? Their life,
therefore, could only be extended in a compre-
hensive critical work (*Variété*, 1924, the first volume
in a series of five) which covered the most diverse
subjects, of which Symbolism was one. The essay
entitled *Existence du symbolisme* began, in the manner
of Valéry, by a genesis: 'We are in process of
constructing Symbolism, as one has done with a
crowd of previous intellectual existences where,
if the presence of reality has been lacking, definitions never have; everyone has offered his
own, and has been free to do so'. There was
certainly something here, not a school, not a
doctrine, but a common negation: the Symbolists'
agreed in their common resolve to renounce the
vote'. Thus liberated, they were able to give
themselves to their experiences. The heros of
poetry and of the poetic: this could well have
been a self-portrait of Valéry. In the steps of his
masters, Edgar Allan Poe and Mallarmé (to whom
he delicately paid homage in his Socratic dialogue
Eupalinos, ou l'architecte, in 1923), Valéry tried to
overcome 'the central attitude from which the
enterprises of knowledge and the operations of
art are equally possible'. The end of *La Jeune Parque*
and of *Cimetière marin* are there, nevertheless, to
recall his hesitation between pure speculation and
adherence to the tumultuous forces of life:

The wind is rising — I must try to live!
The vast air tosses the leaves of my book,

The wave leaps high in powder on the rock!
Scatter in flight, white bedazzled pages!
Break waves! Break with rejoicing waters
This quiet roof where pecked the sailing doves.
(*William Alwyn, An Anthology of Twentieth Century French Poetry*. Chatto & Windus, 1969)

Celebrated, elected to the Academie Française in 1925, appointed lecturer in poetry at the Collège de France in 1937, Valéry kept more and more at arm's length from his poetic work. As he wrote in 1943, on the eve of his death, his one constant had been 'to represent more and more accurately the workings of his mind, and to keep or resume, as often as possible, his freedom regarding illusions and the "parasites" which the unavoidable use of language inflicts on us'.

VERHAEREN Emile (Saint-Amand, near Antwerp 1855 — Rouen 1916). A Belgian poet, born on the banks of the Scheldt, who studied at the college of Sainte-Barbe de Gand, and the universities of Brussels and Louvain. He enrolled as a probationer barrister, but soon left the bar for literature. He joined the Decadent group, *Le Jeune Belgique*, and published a collection, *Les Flamandes*, which created a scandal: in it he evoked 'the outrageous scenery of the greasy kermesse':

RASSENFOSSE *Portrait of Emile Verhaeren*. 1916

...an unleashing of instincts and appetites,
Of frenzies of the stomach, of the guts, and of debauchery.

One thinks, in face of so much vitality and impudence, of Naturalism rather than future Symbolism. But, in *Les Moines* (1886), the result of a retreat to the monastery of Forges, near Chimay, he expressed a mysticism which is totally different from this aggressiveness. Dogged by illness, and haunted by the fear of madness and by a feeling within himself of an insurmountable duality, Verhaeren tried to live 'a kind of heroic exaltation of thought'. His journey deeper into pessimism corresponded to the three stages which marked his three collections, *Les Soirs* (1887), *Le Débâcles* (1888), and *Les Flambeaux noirs* (1890), in which he appeared to be, as Albert Mockel put it 'a poet of spasm'.

Then Verhaeren opened his mind to the world, he became a socialist, he founded with Emile Vandervelde the art section in the Maison du Peuple; henceforth he wanted to 'understand the sadness of the world', but also 'to participate in the joy of everything that lives', and from then onwards, that was the 'double condition of his poetry'. That was the period of *Campagnes hallucinée* (1893), of *Villages illusoires* (1894), and of *Ville tentaculaires* (1895).

By his consciousness of the mysterious force which animate and transform the world, thos 'unanimous forces' which he mastered and praised in *Les Forces tumultueuses* (1902), *La Multiple Splendeu* (1906), *Les Rhythmes souverains* (1910), he was indeed a Symbolist. 'The poet' he proclaimed, 'has at this time only to let himself be invaded by what he sees, hears, imagines or guesses in order for young, new vibrating works to come out of his heart and his brain'. Verhaeren met with a brutal death at the Rouen railway station.

VERLAINE Paul (Metz 1844 — Paris 1896). A French poet, who is the most universally admired as well as the most discredited among the great figures of the Symbolist period. But — was he Symbolist? Valéry rightly remarked that 'his work did not aspire to define another world which was harder and more indestructible than our own, an complete in itself, but it recognized in poetry an the diversity of the soul, such as it is'. Verlaine was the poet of intimacy, of the 'paysage choisi', which is an interior landscape, of the 'chanson grise' where 'the Uncertain joins the Precise' ('Art poétique' in *Jadis et naguere*).

To his contemporaries, Verlaine was at first a character, with his short beard, his fixed gaze, his uncertain steps, someone 'who had given himself up to the interior forces of his being'. Born in Metz to a lonely old couple, he had a childhood which he himself called 'joyous'. On the retirement of his father, the family settled in Paris: this was for Paul the time of undistinguished secondary studies, of a boarding-school with 'childish sensualities', of the introversion from which his poetry was born. Verlaine contributed to the first *Parnasse contemporain*, and without that, and his job as a mediocre clerk in the Hotel de Ville, he would doubtless not have seduced nor married Mathilde Maute, the little bourgeoise of sixteen who declared how much she loved poets. The apparent realization of the 'familiar dream' of the *Poèmes saturniens* (1866), and the happiness which he praised too affably in *La Bonne Chanson* (1871), soon

C. CARRIERE *Portrait of Paul Verlaine*. 1896

vanished into thin air. The meeting with Rimbaud, in September 1871, finished what had been started by the war, the siege of Paris, the Commune, the visits to the Bohemians and the absinthe shops. One knows how they set out, their effort to live together, the misunderstandings on which this was founded, their quarrel after the Brussels incident in July 1873.

Imprisoned in Brussels and then for two years in Mons, Verlaine felt that everything in and around him was wavering. His very beautiful sonnet, *Sagesse*, suggested this loss of equilibrium, in which, however, hope was not abandoned; nor was the certainty of one day finding a more stable course.

Hope gleams like a blade of straw in the stable,
What fear you from the drunk wasp in its mad flight?
See, the sun always rises in dust from some hole.
Why do you not sleep, with your elbow on the table?
Poor pale soul, at least drink this chilled water from
    the well.

Then sleep afterwards. Well, now, you see, I rest
And I will indulge the dreams of your siesta,
And you will hum like a rocked child.
Midday strikes. Pray go away, madame.
He is sleeping. It is astonishing how a woman's steps
Resound in the brain of poor unfortunates.
Midday strikes. I have sprinkled water in the room.
Go, sleep! Hope gleams like a pebble in a hollow.
Ah! when will the roses of September flower again!

He believed, after the visit from the almoner of the prison, and after a conversion to the Catholic faith about which he also wrote at length, that Catholicism would provide him with this course. But without doubt, his return to the faith was more dreamed about than lived. When he came out of prison, Verlaine strove for some time to lead a correct and ordered life: he became a farmer in north France, a teacher in England, in Stickney and Bournemouth of which he was admirably able to evoke, in a poem he wrote in January 1877, included in *Amour* (1888), the 'atmosphere of pearl and the sea of tarnished gold'. But he went back to drinking, he lost his protégé, Lucien Létinois, his former pupil who died of typhoid in 1883, and soon he was floundering again: he had bought a little farm in the north, but it was to be able to hide his drinking and the 'galopins aux yeux tribades' which he brought from Paris; he was arrested and imprisoned for having beaten his mother; ill, and without a penny in the world he wandered from hospital to hospital, from hovel to hovel, passing from Philomène Boudin to Eugénie Krantz, two women of easy virtue, two 'Eumenides' rather, who took it in turns to exploit him.

It was at this moment, however, that the poets of the new generation recognized the genius of this almost finished man. He showed them the 'poètes maudits' (first generation: Tristan Corbière, Arthur Rimbaud, Stéphanie Mallarmé; second generation: Marceline Desbordes-Valmore, Villiers de l'Isle-Adam, and the 'pauvre Lélian', who was of course himself) in which he rediscovered the 'pure, stubborn outline...which translate so well, through material structure, the incompressible ideal'. He gave pledges to 'decadentism', 'a literature shining through a time of decadence, not to walk in the steps of the period but very much 'against the grain', to rise up against, react through the delicate, the lofty, the refined'. It seemed as if he was going the direction of the Symbolists, and he acclaimed in René Ghil's book 'the effort of the most extraordinarily sympathetic art that had been attempted for a long time'.

Prefaces were wrung from him, he was made to go to meetings, but Verlaine remained independent, mistrusting labels, schools and theories. Having been asked by Viélé-Griffin in 1887 for a lecture on the principles concerning the art of verse, he vowed that the only conclusion he had been able to draw from his knowledge had been: 'Everything is beautiful and good from wherever it comes and by whatever process it is obtained. Classics, romantics, decadents, symbols, assonants, or how shall I put it? Purposely obscure, but provided that they give me the shivers or simply charm me, even, and perhaps above all without my knowing exactly why, that is all that matters to me' (Letter to Henri Régner, August 1887).

Let us ask nothing of Verlaine other than the example of a work, which is diverse, and, without doubt, uneven, but which is more continuous than has been realized, in spite of its ramblings and its occasional mistakes. *Les Fêtes Galantes* (1869) puts us into an atmosphere which is equivocal, bathed in moonlight, where the true and false simpletons mix in a perpetual game of dupes. *Les Romances sans Paroles* (1874) without doubt his most perfect masterpiece, raises insipidity to the level of an art. Jean-Pierre Richard showed it well: to conjure up the threat which faded sensation allows to lie heavily on the self and on things, the poet studies dissonance, trying to unite the 'vague' with the 'acute'. The series of *Ariettes oubliées* constitutes the best example of Verlaine's languor where the being exhausts and sickens himself to the point of passing from the personal to the impersonal:

> There is weeping in my heart
> As it rains on the town.
> What languor is this
> That pierces my heart?
> (Translated by Anthony Hartley, Penguin Book of French Verse, No.4 1957)

Sagesse, in 1881, brought in a new style, and his poetic conversion was perhaps more noticeable there than his religious conversion. Verlaine abandoned the neutrality where the self is lost, and attempted to 'recapture himself' and to 're-grasp things according to the practice of common sense' (Richard). From this came the evocation of 'the humble life of boring and easy tasks', the 'great towns', the sky above the roof, 'the icy blast which rushes through the black and green thickets', the spacing out of the hedges and the good wooden horses. In *Parallèlement* (1889), he even came to parody his own earlier style:

> Romances without words have,
> By an accord a discord together and fresh,
> Irritated this dull heart on purpose;
> Oh the sound, the shudder that they have.

Jadis et naguère: the title of the collection published in 1885 shows clearly that Verlaine had no intention whatsoever of making a sacrifice. If *Pierrot* brings us back to *Fêtes Galantes*, *Crimen amoris* displays the splendour of less subtle poetics in the service of 'the most beautiful of the angels', a young Satan who strangely resembles Rimbaud. *Kaleidoscope*, in the same collection, gives an important example of this Verlainian impression which became a school:

> In a street, in the heart of a dream town,
> It will be as if one has already lived:
> A moment which is both very vague and very sharp...
> Oh! this sunshine coming through the mist which is lifting!
>
> It will be like when one dreams and wakes up,
> And then goes back to sleep and dreams once more
> Of the same fairyland and the same scenery,
> The summer, in the grass in the watered sound of a bee's flight.

Religious inspiration is reborn in *Amour* (1888), *Bonheur* (1891), *Liturgies Intimes* (1892) which he composed like a 'trilogy of Grace'. The 'lamento' on Lucien Létinois recalls the Christian sonnets of *Sagesse*. But the hymn to carnal love and the celebration of lust rise up in their turn in *Parallèlement* (1889): in this last 'fête galante', although a different sort of gallantry this time, Verlaine invites us to embark, not for Cythera, but for 'Sodom and Gomorrah'. And in *Les Chansons pour elle* (1891) and *Les odes en son honneur* (1893) he is only concerned with living 'vigorously and verdantly'. Verlaine had not changed: he renewed at the time of *Les Amies*, the Sapphic evocations of his debuts. His desire, which had been continuous since his incarceration in Mons, to get away from the 'false impression', could not hide the permanence of his wavering between contradictory calls, the 'Voices' which can be heard in one poem in *Sagesse*, or of the very personal manner in which he turned 'the things which sing inside the head' into poetry. It is for this that poetry is 'music before anything else'.

VIELE-GRIFFIN Francis (Norfolk, Virginia 1864 — Bergerac 1937). A French poet who was born in the United States. He went to France at the age of eight, and visited Stanislaus college where he became the friend of Henri de Régnier. He went with him to Mallarmé, and wrote his first verse, *Cueille d'avril* (1886) following *Lendemain*. The preface to *Joies* (1889) stood up in defence of *vers libre* and 'personal rhythm'; his illustration of it was still rather timid, and it was in a whisper that he expressed his main statement:

> All is sadness of joys;
> What mourning fills the world?
> All is saddened by joys.

However, Viélé-Griffin was not going to remain the poet of 'deuil d'amour'. In his poems conceived in a parallel way to the *Jeux rustiques et divins* of Régnier, and put together in 1897 under the title *La Clarté de la vie*, he sings a hymn which praises nature, gaiety and sometimes even rapture. Without doubt life is only 'a smile on the lips of Death', but Viélé-Griffin understood the poetic faculty as forming part of the immense current of universal energy. His symbolism, in which there was nothing of Plato's theories, was very much concerned with the study of 'the form which dazzles from afar/From the great eternal sign, which turns to rejoin itself' (*Wieland le forgeron*, 900). That is why he drew from the sources of the Greek myths.

VILLIERS DE L'ISLE-ADAM Auguste (Saint-Brieuc 1838 — Paris 1889). A French writer.

He was less a representative of Symbolism than of 'supernaturalism'. He was nevertheless, the precursor of it, the 'Chateaubriand of Symbolism' as Remy de Gourmont called him, and his death was felt by the young people of the Symbolist generation. Mallarmé paid him homage in these terms: 'A genius! That is how we understood him. In this touching conclave which, at the start of each generation, in order to maintain at the very least a reflection of the sacred fame, assembles the young people in case one of them should reveal himself as one of the chosen, it could instantly be felt present among the commotion which they were all undergoing equally'.

His destiny was harsh, like his stories. Born into an old family of Breton nobility, he was a legitimist, and as hostile to democracy as he was to positivism. But the Villiers lost their money and from 1871 onwards, their descendant could no longer count on being able to live other than by his pen. He dreamed of a rich marriage with Anna Eyre, but had to be content to live with a char-woman. In his literary career he also went from failure to failure. His *Premières Poésies* passed unnoticed, even though the feeling of mystery which is so characteristic of Symbolism can be found in them:

In face of the Night with its sublime depths
Do you not feel, O mortals, — O victimized people,
Giddiness in looking at the Sky?

The theatre held nothing but disappointment for him (*Axël* was not successfully performed until after his death). He had more success with the short story, which was easier to place in a paper or periodical, and especially with those which he grouped into the collection *Contes cruels* in 1883. *L'Amour suprême* (1886), *Tribulat Bonhomet* (1887), *Les Histoires insolites* (1888) and *Les Nouveaux Contes cruels* (1888) followed soon after. Contrary to his scapegoat character of Turc Tribulat Bonhomet, the bourgeois positivist, who asked the writer to say 'true things! — things which really happen! things which everyone knows by heart! — things which are, have been and will be the talk of the town — in short, serious things! he wanted to make 'intense, unknown and sublime impressions' and to prove that man was 'related to a superior world'.

Thus Villiers brusquely tore himself away from reality. He believed in 'intersigns', those coincidences which suggested the existence of relations between the world and the beyond, such as the nightmare which warned Baron Xavier de la V... of the approaching death of his old friend the abbot Maucombe in one of his *Contes cruels*. The rationalism of Tribulat Bonhomet himself is ruined, since the scholar is frightened of wind, of the shadow of a bird passing over, and since he is tempted to look for the meaning of this 'caravanserai of apparitions' which makes up our world. Villiers, for his part, yielded without hesitation to this temptation. For him, beings, things and events were certainly a 'forest of symbols'. In *L'Amour suprême*, the last glance of Lysiane d'Aubelleyne, before his consecration, appears to him as the promise of an eternal rendezvous in that ideal world to which he aspires, and for which the price is the renouncement of this world. How to attain it? By the path of esotericism, like Tullia Fabriana, in *Isis*? By suicide, like *Axël* and Sara? By Christian detachment, like Lysiane d'Aubelleyne himself? Villiers hesitated, by reason of his multiple heritage and the contradictions which it brought with it: he was Catholic by tradition, hegelian by occasion, and very taken with the occult science.

Axël, the largest part of which was written after 1872, and published in 1885 thanks to a little review, *La Jeune France*, is a kind of spiritual testament of Villiers. Sara, in the silence of the convent, undergoes the Temptation of the Earth; Axël, in comparison with Maître Janus, suffers the Temptation of the Spirit. Both of them symbolically come down to Life, by the underground passages of Auersperg Castle, and crash into the mountain of gold. To take their love away from the degradation of life, they call on Death, the resurrection of the spirit. This work had an extremely marked influence on the Symbolist generation. It has even been thought of the as 'Bible of Symbolism'.

WILDE Oscar (Dublin 1854 — Paris 1900). An English writer.

If it is not correct to call him a Symbolist, he could be considered as 'the soul of decadence'. He was born in Ireland, but his literary career unfolded in England. He went to the University of Oxford in 1874, where he became known as a champion of art for art's sake, and for his eccentricity of dress. Four years later, armed with his degree and a prize for poetry, he arrived in London, where he visited the celebrities of the moment, especially Whistler. He became an apostle of beauty and of aesthetic revival; he published poems, undertook a lecture tour of the United States, and went to France (see Ernest Raynaud on 'Oscar Wilde in Paris' and his historic meeting with Moréas, in *La Mêlée symboliste*). When he returned to London, he was dreaming less of astounding the bourgeois than of extending his work in the sphere of criticism; he also wanted to establish himself as a writer. His *Poems* of 1881 were rather too full of his reminiscences, and lacked true originality. In 1885, he declared that the poet was the greatest of the artists, 'master of form, of colour, of music, king and sovereign of life and all the arts, guardian of all the secrets'. He applied himself to the school of Gautier, and of

Portrait of Oscar Wilde

the Flaubert of *La Tentation de saint Antoine*. A poem such as *The Harlot's House*, which appeared in the *Dramatic Review* on April 11, 1885, strikes the imagination like a Hoffmannesque vision, with the final evocation of the goddess who comes to chase away the shades of night:

> Then suddenly the tune went false,
> The dancers weared of the waltz,
> The shadows ceased to wheel and whirl.
> And down the long and silent street,
> The dawn, with silver-sandalled feet
> Crept like a frightened girl.

In 1887 Wilde became editor of a women's magazine, and wrote works of fiction including *The Crime of Lord Arthur Savile*, *The Phantom of Canterville*, and *The Sphinx without a Secret*. He was an excellent story-teller, and an equally brilliant dramatist with four plays of sparkling dialogue which had a triumphal success: *Lady Windermere's Fan* (1892), *A Woman of no Importance* (1893), *The Importance of Being Earnest* (1894) and *An Ideal Husband* (1895). His paradoxes were developed in his essays which were grouped in 1891 under the title of *Intentions*. He judged, for instance, that 'no essential incompatibility need exist between crime and culture', that 'art is a veil rather than a mirror', that the artist makes up for the deficiencies of

nature, and repairs her mistakes, and that the critic is superior to the creative artist.

In 1890 his masterpiece appeared, *The Portrait of Dorian Gray*. This was not just a repeat of *A Rebours* (which is, although not quite completely, the little yellow book which exercises such a decisive and deleterious influence on the hero) nor a tale of fantasy (in stabbing his double, Dorian Gray kills himself). It was also a handbook of dandyism, a collection of paradoxes (together with those expressed by Lord Henry Wotton), the gospel of a new hedonism and, for Wilde, a mirror or a game of anticipation. Indeed, at the height of his glory, Wilde was himself involved in a grave scandal. Accused of homosexuality by the Marquis of Queensbury, he brought an action for defamation of character against him. Having lost it, he was himself accused, and condemned to two years' hard labour. When he came out of prison in 1897 he was broken, exhausted, ruined. He went to Paris to hide, and died there three years later. During his seclusion he wrote a long letter to his alleged victim, Lord Alfred Douglas, *De profundis*: he poured out all his bitterness into it, drawing nevertheless from his suffering a new reason for hope. *The Ballad of Reading Gaol*, which was written in exile, in a little village near Dieppe, is one of the most beautiful poems in the English language. 'I have put all my genius into my life,' he said, 'and have only put my talent into my work'. One has made him a legend — the other has never ceased to fascinate succeeding generations.

WYSPIANSKI Stanislav (Cracow 1869 — Cracow 1907). A Polish playwright who was born at the foot of the Wawel. He discovered vivid sources of inspiration in popular tradition, legends, history and the poetry of the bards. Son of a modest sculptor, he studied painting and history, travelled abroad, and stayed particularly in Paris where he visited Gauguin. On his return to Poland he was appointed professor at the School of Fine Arts in Warsaw, and contributed to the review *Life*. From 1898 he devoted himself feverishly to the theatre all the more because he knew he was the victim of an incurable illness: in ten years he entirely revolutionized the Polish theatre, realizing, as M. Herman said, 'a synthesis where Classicism and Romanticism, Naturalism and Symbolism were united, as were archaic or popular language and language which was suggestive in the manner of Maeterlinck'.

Heir to the great Polish Romantics, he considered dramatic creation to be governed by a fundamental problem: the function of literature in society, and its capacity to save the nation. But he was at the same time the adversary of these Romantics: he took exception to the Messianic message and the empty formulas which, according to him, served as a lofty alibi to a society which was living in ignorance of true liberty. This critic of dead forms, this satire of tyrannic idols, this call to the reawakening of spiritual energies can be found in *The Legion* (1900), *The Wedding* (1902), *Liberation* (1903) and *Acropolis* (1904). Wyspianski's style is particularly characteristic in *The Wedding*, the comedy which made him famous in one evening and which moves smoothly from the simple evocation of a wedding to the phantasmagoria of the dreams and obsessions of the guests. Wyspianski hoped to create a monumental theatre like those in Athens and Bayreuth. He made use of the full panoply of art forms, becoming in turn painter, decorator, architect, stage designer and, of course, poet. He used the symbol to exteriorize the inner conflicts of his heroes, or to confront principles, great moments of history and his reflections on events.

Blending the pessimism of a world haunted by the meaning of death with the joy of the painter in love with beautiful forms and colours, as he blended the truth of reality with the suggestions of the dream, the everyday with the strange, the familiar with the fantastic, he composed plays charged with incantatory power as is evidenced in *The Warsaw Woman* (1898), *The Achilleides* (1903) and *The Return of Ulysses* (1907). Although he himself has been described as 'the slave of a single thought', his creative work was complete and diverse.

YEATS William Butler (Sandymount, near Dublin 1865 — Roquebrune-Cap-Martin 1939). An Irish writer. According to M.L. Cazamian, he was the 'most impersonal and the most personal, the most aware and the most inspired of the modern poets', exercising a scholarly double game of the mask and the symbol. The mask allowed him to divide himself into two: Yeats was both the indecisive John Sherman and the Reverend William Howard, Michael Robartes, the deluded occultist or Owen Aherme, the enlightened mystic. Convinced that 'every passionate man is linked in some way to another epoch, either historic or imaginary, and that there alone he can find the images which awake his strength', he was able also to impersonate those mythical heroes of Ireland which he loved to praise in his poetry and set into his plays: Cuchulain, Emer and Conchubar. The symbol was, as he himself explained, 'the only possible expression of some invisible essence, a diaphanous lamp around a spiritual flame'.

Such a definition came from a strict Symbolism. Yeats had indeed been formed in a good school; even if he had never visited Mallarmé, he revered him and frequently vowed that he owed to him the refined form of his book of verse *The Wind among the Reeds* (1889). Nourished by Blake (whom he defined elsewhere as 'the first writer of modern

times to demonstrate the insoluble marriage of all great art with the symbol') and by Shelley (among whose works he admired *Prometheus Unbound*), he had been very impressed by Romanticism, and had even come to describe himself as the last of the Romantics. But he was also the initiator in 1891 of the Rhymers' Club, where the latest French literature was admired. In 1894, aged twenty-nine years, he went to Paris and, with Arthur Symons, he paid a visit to Verlaine. The future playwright had been impressed by *Axël*, by Villiers de l'Isle-Adam. In 1914, when he was making a speech during a banquet of the review *Poetry* in the United States, he again praised French Symbolism, expressing reserve only on the use of *vers libre*.

Nevertheless it would be difficult to describe Years as a descendant of the French Symbolists. He distinguishes himself from them immediately by his links to his native country and his powerful Celticism. It is not necessary to recall that, when

I. OPFFER *Portrait of W.B. Yeats*. 1935

Yeats was starting to write, the Irish question was already burning. Very soon, therefore, he made up his mind to write about almost nothing except Irish subjects. He explained himself in the following manner: 'In the decadence of an age sworn to the cult of wealth, we find ourselves the priests of an almost forgotten religion. In order to keep their sacred capacity, the poets must no longer serve a vague and abstract internationalism, but espouse the characteristics of the surrounding nature, the dominant feelings of a race and a people. Ireland, who has stood aloof from an industrial and depersonalized civilization, is, by the circumstance of her history, excessively conscious of her national originality. She offers privileged themes to the artist: the love of the supernatural, and a passion for her independence — and thus she creates between her poets and her people a communion which makes the Irish race a chosen race, and one of the pillars which hold up the world'.

He used the Gaelic legends in *The Wanderings of Usheen* (1889): three journeys which were made not only through the geography of the myth, but through the inner geography of the poet as well. The first is based on the nautical memories of his childhood in Sligo. The second reflects the hostility against England. The third corresponds to a personal attempt to escape the fatality of life:

> I would die like a small withered leaf in the autumn, for breast unto breast
> We shall mingle no more, nor our gazes empty their sweetness alone
> In the isles of the farthest seas where only the spirits come.
> Were the winds less soft than the breath of a pigeon who sleeps on her nest,
> Nor lost in the star-fires and odours the sound of the sea's vague drum?
> O flaming lion of the world, O when will you turn to your rest?

Sometimes he described the bareness of the Irish landscape, for instance in *The Lake Isle of Innisfree* (1890) and sometimes he called up the fairies who haunt the Irish countryside, 'following the leafy paths with their crowns of pearl, their spindles of wool and their secret smiles' ('The Withering of the Boughs' in the collection *In the Seven Woods*, 1904). In this respect the theatre was a privileged instrument of expression, all the more so when the Abbey Theatre, founded in Dublin in 1899 by Yeats and Lady Gregory, put itself to the service of the cause of the Irish Renaissance. *On the Shore of Baile* (1904), *Deirdre* (1907), *The Green Helmet* (1910), *The Only Jealousy of Emer* (1919) and *The Death of Cuchulain* (1939) constituted a vast Celtic cycle corresponding to Yeat's dream, explained in *The Autobiography*, of a 'new *Prometheus Unbound* with

Patrick or Columbkil, Oisin or Finn, in the place of Prometheus, and Gro Patrick or Ben Bulben in place of the Caucasus', and to his desire to show that 'all races at first drew their unity from a mythology which blended them with their rocks and their hills'. It would be impossible to study the complex symbolism of Yeats without recalling the figure of Maud Gonne. A supporter of the patriotic cause since her childhood, this lovely girl of twenty-two came into Yeats' life in 1889 and dazzled him: he saw in her the incarnation of spring, and linked her with the image of the rose, the traditional symbol of spiritual love and supreme beauty. Whether it concerned the poems which appeared in 1897 under the title of *The Rose*, or the collected stories of 1897 called *The Secret Rose*, the same symbol was used to express the fervour of his love, of the patriotic cause, and of the cult of eternal Beauty. To this was added the occultism which interested the writer early in his life, and which shows particularly in the poem entitled *The Mountain Tomb*; this was a transparent homage to Rosenkreutz, founder of the order of the Rose + Croix:

> Bring roses if the rose be yet in bloom;
> The cataract smokes upon the mountain side,
> Our Father Rosicross is in his tomb.

Yeats has often been reproached for his obscurity, his liking for theosophy, his borrowings from the mystic of Jacob Boehme and from Hindu thought, and even the 'no' of his later pieces. The gyres, those spirals which climb and with which the poet composed the system in *A Vision* (1937), give an idea of this Symbolism which was of rare complexity, but also of rare richness and supported by a powerful lyrical movement. Yeats, who had reproached Mallarmé with isolating the artist's work, did not in fact imagine that drama or poetry could be cut off from life. Since 1900 he had established a distinction between intellectual symbols and those, the only true ones, which were charged with feeling. His life and work are there to show that, for him, this was not a vain distinction, but that he was devoted to that superhuman dream, constructed, nevertheless, by man; his poem *The Tower* which, since 1926, has appeared as his testament, proclaims this to be true.

Music

The musical aspects

Symbolism does not exist in the history of music, at least if one is to believe several illustrious works which are called *The Groves Dictionary of Music and Musicians, Die Musik in Geschichte und Gegenwart*, and *Le Dictionnaire de la musique*! Silence on this subject need not be disturbing: if, for example, one takes, as Cassirer did, the study of symbolic forms on a philosophical level, it is obvious that the symbol, 'the sensible vehicle of spiritual content', finds its most appropriate language in music; music seen in this perspective would be the symbolic art above all others. If, on the contrary, one thinks of Symbolism from a historical point of view, that is to say a movement which was of literary and French origins, as Jean Moréas first defined it in *Le Figaro* on September 18, 1886, then it is also quite obvious that music formed an integral part of this movement, whether one thinks of Mallarmé's Wagnerism or of Verlaine's poetry set to music by Debussy. Why, then, is there this omission and this disdain among the musicologists? The matter becomes further complicated if one enquires into the music personalities who were involved with the Symbolists: the chapter 'Debussy' always, unfailingly, conveys the Impressionism of this composer, which adds to the problem; while the chapter 'Wagner' is content to evoke Romanticism in a very general sense which leaves us dissatisfied. Did Symbolism really exist only for the aestheticians, the literary historians and the art critics? It is precisely one of the aims of this work to show the wide range of Symbolism, and the interpenetration of the arts which constituted it.

The music of the Symbolists: a Symbolist Music?
The 'Wagner Case'

Although it is difficult to establish at once the existence of Symbolist music, nevertheless it cannot be denied that there were musicians who aroused the enthusiasm of the Symbolists. Wagner was the most important of these composers, and the story of his renown in France leads us progressively to conceive the idea of Symbolism in the art of music.

The first Wagnerian outpouring took place during 1860-61, in Paris. While he was staying in the capital, Wagner organized three concerts of his works, on January 25, February 1 and 8, 1860. Excerpts were played from *The Flying Dutchman, Tannhäuser* and *Lohengrin*, and the prelude to *Tristan*. The following year his creation *Tannhäuser* was performed at the Opera, and produced the scandal which is well-known. The important thing to us was the immediate enlist-

Concert held to celebrate the foundation of the Festival Theatre at Bayreuth. On May 22, 1872, in the old Opera House of Bayreuth, Wagner conducted Beethoven's Ninth Symphony.

ment of several writers on behalf of the Wagnerian cause. Champfleury, in his booklet of January 27, 1860, entitled *Richard Wagner*, stated precisely that the music of Wagner aimed more at the expression of sentiments than at their description; thus Wagner's art appears as the start of play as opposed to the Romantic and Realist tendencies of the time; it truly was a 'music of the future' which was in question. More accurate still was Baudelaire, a direct ancestor of literary Symbolism, who evoked in *Richard Wagner et Tannhäuser à Paris* (April 1861) the impressions which so happily characterized the newborn aestheticism. In the prelude to *Lohengrin*, Baudelaire had the 'revelation' of 'space and depth, both material and spiritual'; – it was a 'volupté' – so powerful and so terrible'! And is that not the exact translation of the feelings which the same Baudelaire's poetry and the ambiguous figures of Gustave Moreau arouse in us?

Did these three artists not aim to express, as one critic said, 'mysterious intentions' through the 'repetition of the same melodic phrases'? Further on again, Baudelaire recalled judiciously that the function of music was to express 'the undefined part of a feeling which the word is too exact to be able to render'. Did not Symbolism, from then on, and in all the arts, consist of '*speaking* the feeling', as Wagner was the first to teach us in *Tannhäuser* and *Lohengrin*? On the other hand, these arguments brought back to favour a legendary and medieval character which, twenty years later, served only too easily to caricature the Symbolists' art.· The true hallmark of Wagner was the ambition of his projects and the grandeur of their conception: 'the nervous intensity, the violence of passions and of will' which allowed Baudelaire to conclude, with infinite justice: 'by the impassioned energy of his expression, he is currently the most faithful representative of modern nature.' Here, indeed, was the consecration of a new aesthetics, here indeed, inaugurated and analyzed by the Baudelairian criticism, the necessary support for future Symbolist music.

But it was not Baudelaire alone who felt Wagner's importance during these years of the Second Empire. Catulle Mendès, and the ephemeral *Revue Fantaisiste*, emphasized the aesthetic rupture favoured by Wagnerism: 'We long to know how the French public, faced with this serious work which has to be followed with sustained interest, will welcome the boldness of the innovator.' Later on, *La Théorie wagnérienne* recalled that Wagner had been the first to understand 'the duality of poetry and music, harmoniously absorbed into the unity of drama', and that his originality came from having shown that 'musical drama had been desired and foreseen in France by a large number of eminent and clear minds.' Perhaps drama was the only genre where art nouveau in music was clearly defined; nonetheless, Wagnerism was still synonymous with modernism for the first Symbolists, and it was in the work of this composer that the first musical expression could be found of a sensibility which only slowly became redefined. But there we are touching on the second wave of Symbolist Wagnerophilia.

If the first Parisian performances of Wagner's early works made some think that the language of music had been completely renewed, the creation of *Tristan* and the first two parts of *The Ring* allowed the connoisseurs to define more precisely that which it was becoming necessary to call the authentic music of the Symbolist art. Between 1862 and 1870, a group of writers and artists went to Tribschen and Munich to try to find a kind of confirmation of the value of their ambition and their studies. It should also be noted that the official reason for the journey of Catulle Mendès, Judith Gautier, and Villiers de l'Isle-Adam was to visit the international Fine Arts Exhibition in Munich (April 1869): it was thus quite naturally that Wagnerian art became associated with the convergent interests of the Schwabing painters.

This visit made it obvious that *Tristan* and *Das Rheingold* seemed to the French to be the first works to realize completely the aesthetic ambitions of Symbolism. For what reasons? Mèndes put it well, in *L'Oeuvre wagnérienne*, some years after his trip: *Tristan* is 'of all the Wagnerian masterpieces, the one which will most directly and most thoroughly conquer the French spirit...the most miraculous love drama which has ever been written by a human being...the supreme marriage of love and death'. In other words, *Tristan* is a *total* work, and Symbolism, in consequence, in music as in the other arts, an extraordinary voice, an incantatory language. Indeed, *Tristan* was the first 'integrally Wagnerian' work because it staged a myth which was common to the whole western world, and because it systematically came back to chromatism

Tristan and Isolde by Wagner, drawing by W. Gause after the first performance at the Vienna Opera House, October 4, 1883

and the use of the leitmotiv. It has often been said that Symbolism called itself an art, quint-essential and magical, and it gratifies in us the double desire for Eros and Thanatos; it is there-fore an aesthetics of the vague and the imprecise which, by the fact of its diversity, officially established these qualities on a par with individual artistic techniques. In this way Wagnerism formed an integral part of Symbolism, and Tristan demonstrated it admirably.

The last phase of Wagnerism in France was also the most obviously linked to the blossoming of the new aesthetics. It was a moment of great clarity when the triumph of *Parsifal*, in particular, gathered together in *La Revue wagnérienne*, in 1885, all the Symbolist authorities. As an example let us recall that Dujardin's prospectus announced among the contributors to the journal: Elémir Bourges, Villiers de l'Isle-Adam, Mallarmé, Verlaine, Laforgue, Moréas, Verhaeren, Viélé-Griffin, Henri de Régnier and Maeterlinck for the writers; Fantin-Latour, Jacques-Emile Blanche and Renoir for the painters; and Chabrier, Chausson, Vincent d'Indy and Dukas for the musicians. Certainly it could be confirmed that Symbolism, because of its huge ambitions, had been like a vast nebula, but nonetheless the paternity which the move-ment claimed, as well as its musical expression, were to be found in Wagner!

Debussy, far from complacent as far as Bayreuth was concerned, had himself realized that *Parsifal* was the work on which hinged, well beyond Symbolism, all the revolutions of the twentieth century: 'In *Parsifal*, the last effort of a genius in front of which we must bow down, Wgner tried to be less rigidly authoritarian towards the music: this time it could breathe more freely...not the nervous breathlessness from pursuing the sickly passion of Tristan, nor the furious animal cries of Isolde; nor was it the grandiloquent commentary on inhumanity of Wotan. Nothing in Wagner's music reaches a more serene beauty than the prelude to the third act of *Parsifal* and the whole episode of Good Friday...The decorative part of *Parsifal* is of an absolutely supreme beauty. One can hear orchestral sonorities which are unique and unex-pected, noble and strong. This is one of the most lovely monuments which has ever been raised to the serene glory of music.' (article in *Gil Blas* on April 6, 1903, reprinted in *Monsieur Croche et autres écrits*).

In other words he was again concerned with the emphasis on enchantment and spellbinding which Baudelaire had been the first to recognize. This quality appeared more clearly in *Parsifal* by reason of the mythical, even esoteric, character of the libretto: the action, even more than in *Tristan*, is purely interior, and throws the spectator back on to the single evocative power of sound, of harmony, of chromatism. There is no more audacious writing in *Parsifal* than in *The Ring* or *Die Meistersinger*, it is only the context which confers on the music the privilege, this time, of truly being 'before anything else' on that blurry frontier where the 'Indecisive is joined to the Precise'. It is undeniable that this imprecision of touch, this vague or confused pleasure, of sound for the sake of sound, acts upon the soul, even more so when the subject of the drama marries eroticism to mysticism. Beyond its grand and sonorous appearance, therefore, pointed out by Debussy, *Parsifal* bequeaths to Symbolism a special rhetoric and thematic.

The influence of literature on musical forms

The approach, which has until now necessarily been literary and historic, must not disguise that there existed, all the same Symbolist forms in music. If one prefers to continue thinking of the question from the chronological angle, one would say that Wagnerism inaugurated several musical fashions, or that it accelerated the diffusion of certain processes. Thus the universal blossoming of the symphonic poem, the birth of French melody, on another plane the misuse of chromatism, the hyper-refined treatment of sound, were to register as an equal number of formal characteristics of Symbolism in music, but it is honest to recognize that they owed their existence to the initial claims of Wagnerism and literature for a proud art.

The symphonic poem, heritage of Romantic music, and, even more precisely, of the '*musique à programme*', obviously owed its fortune to the literary origins of Symbolism. Considered in this way, it was a genre which lent itself directly to the translation of states of soul, and this all the better because the music, by its vague expressionism, suited the unutterable, the half-aware, the incantatory. Let it even be said that the symphonic poem of the Symbolists rested always on an anti-narrative scheme; thus one can distinguish better Saint-Saëns from Franck, Smetana from Scriabin, Dukas from Schönberg or Strauss. Nonetheless, the common reference in the matter is found in the music of Liszt: *Mazeppa* and *Hamlet* are dramatic theatrical works; the score appears as a narrative in which one can follow the thread; on the contrary, *Orpheus* and the *Preludes* (both of 1854) are of Symbolist inspiration because the theme remains vague; impressions and not descriptions place the discourse in the category of poetry rather than drama. One of Liszt's last works, *From the Cradle to the Grave* ('Von der Wiege bis zum Grabe') fully justifies this point of view: the choice of theme is clearly contemplative and philosophic, the instrumentation rich and well-finished, the discourse of virtuosity and sophistication — every element of this work, dated 1882, makes it one of the most perfect illustrations of the Symbolist symphonic poem; even the colouring, which offers in harmony the exact equivalent of chiaroscuro in painting, or the Verlainian 'imprecision', comes from Liszt: 'Since I have made the acquaintance of Liszt's works, I have become a new man from the harmonic point of view', confessed Wagner to Richard Pohl! In this way one can understand better the extraordinary German success of this musical form: it was under the double support of Liszt and Wagner that the symphonic poems of Strauss must be recorded, in particular *Death and Transfiguration* ('Tod und Verklarung'), *Thus spake Zarathustra* ('Also Sprach Zarathustra'), *Ein Heldenleben*, and the early works of Schönberg (*Die verklärte Nacht, Pelléas et Mélisande*). But it must still be seen that other compositions, although quite different in aspect, (*Poème* by Chausson, 1913; *Pelléas et Mélisande* by Fauré, 1898; *Psyche* by Franck, 1887) or even apparently revolutionary (the two *Poèmes* of Scriabin, those of Debussy, especially *Nocturnes*, 1899) are situated in this perspective. The music of the orchestra of Symbolism originated from the symphonic poem of Liszt; in his later illustrations he subscribed perfectly to the aesthetic programme worked out by the literary men.

Melody was another genre which, in France, demonstrated the existence of Symbolism in music. There, also, literary support was doubly evident since this type of composition leant on a poetic text, and the fact that it was the Symbolist poets who provided the opportunity for it. It is even that way that one can best distinguish the French melody in the German Lied: in Germany very few composers drew their inspiration from authors who were actually Symbolists; Baudelaire, Rilke and George hardly ever produced texts for Berg or Schönberg, who anyway treated them in a style which was too bold to have anything to do with Symbolism. As to the other musicians who, by their post-Wagnerian style, had rapports with the French movement, they indulged in the *fin de siècle* poetry (R. Strauss), or the exotic and folkloric (Wolf and Mahler).

There is above all a typical spirit of melody which illustrates wonderfully well the famous *Art Poètique* of Verlaine:

Prends l'éloquence et tords lui son cou!	Take eloquence and wring its neck!
De la musique encore et toujours!	Once again and always music!
Que ton vers soit la chose envolée	Let your line be the soaring thing
Qu'on sent qui fuit d'une âme en allée	Which we feel fleeing from a soul going
Vers d'autres cieux à d'autres amours	Towards other skies and other loves.

(Translated by Anthony Hartley, Penguin Book of French Verse, Volume 3, 1957)

This disqualifies all narrative, dramatic, or intellectual poetry, and all music which is too eloquent. However, in this perspective must be recognized that the Lied is almost always dramatic (even when Wolf becomes the interpreter of Morike!) and that the richness of the musical part constantly draws the Lied towards the symphony, as with Mahler. On the other hand, is it not significant that Strauss did not feel inspired by a single poem of Hofmannsthal, who was perhaps, in respect of poetry, the German author who was nearest to the French Symbolists? 'The truth? One cannot say. Do you want to know? Good. It is that in fact, the musicians who understand nothing about poetry would not put it into music. They can only spoil it', wrote Debussy ironically (*Monsieur Croche*: Musica, March 1911) and the paradox is profoundly illuminating; French melody is a Symbolist form because it calls itself a 'chanson grise' — to use the title of Verlaine's verses which Reynaldo Hahn set to music.

Such a statement does not mean that this was a minor art form, or that it was a form reserved for minor authors: certainly Reynaldo Hahn, Henri Rabaud, Charles Tournemire, and even Fauré could be found lacking in stature, if not in ability; but the spirit of Verlaine's precept must be remembered: here it is concerned with enchanting and bewitching, and not only with attracting and suggesting. In this case, the melody wears a somewhat blurred charm, but achieves a radiance which is completely analogous, although differently composed, to the most beautiful of Schumann's or Brahms' Lieder. Nevertheless, there are criteria of style which are more accurate. The first concerns the purity of the melody and the motif. All the French composers conformed to this: thus Franck, although usually preoccupied with polyphony, was the first to achieve an unaccustomed charm and simplicity in the 'beautiful music' he wrote for the voice: *L'Ange et l'enfant*, *Le Mariage des roses*, *Le Vase brisé*, *Les Cloches du soir*, *Le Premier Sourire de mai* border on 'drawing-room music'; the texts, often borrowed from the Parnassians, prevent these melodies from being of totally Symbolist construction; but the general meaning is not misleading, and it is certainly to Franck that must first be attributed the qualities which are praised more in his pupils, Duparc and Chausson, or in Fauré. *Chanson triste* and *Extase* (on texts of J. Lahors), *L'Invitation au voyage*, *La Vie antérieure* (on poems of Baudelaire) are masterpieces which are well enough known to put Duparc on a par with the most able masters of the Lied. Ernest Chausson, who put Maeterlinck's collection of poetry, *Serres Chaudes*, to music, also made himself famous, even though a little less brilliantly, by the same pursuit of purity. But the most exceptional powers of enchantment belong to Fauré. If one were selecting the most notable compositions from his melodic work, which is not considerable in quantity — in comparison with that of Schumann, for example, with which it has often been compared — one would choose the second collection of *Melodies* (*Le Voyageur*, *Adieu*, *Les Berceaux*, *Clair de lune*), the third (*Au Cimetière*, *Spleen*, *En sourdine*, *C'est l'extase*, *Le Parfum impérissable*, *Soir*) and *La Bonnes Chanson* (nine melodies on poems by Verlaine). Here the composer has full control of his art, he is master of his writing and his style; with the greatest discretion of ability, with the most evident concern for the magic formula, he translates quite freely the finest shades of sensibility, the most original inspirations of his imagination. The simplicity of the melodies enhances the distinction, the design of the accompaniments is of an intended moderation which brings out the precision. The harmonies and the chords are linked together in a sequence of rich and delicate sounds. In these melodies, of which the most beautiful could be classed as states of soul — which is typically Symbolist! — the poems preserve all their expression, and all their beauty; the music respects the turns, the resonances, the emphasis; at the same time, it creates an atmosphere of sound where they take an added value, where they spread out and echo more profoundly. Yes, the melodies of Fauré are certainly in the spirit of Verlaine, 'music before anything else'!

The second criterion of Symbolist melody is the harmonic boldness. Here Debussy distinguishes himself and, in a lesser measure, Ravel. Certain German composers like Strauss and Mahler seem to be equally engrossed, but in a different spirit: they aspire to colour, to exterior iridescence, like Strauss, or they subordinate harmony to an expressionism of the soul, like Mahler. Nothing like this with Debussy: he was concerned with experimentation, and purely technical study, which gave rise to the modernism, sometimes the most revolutionary, of his language. Debussy borrowed, for his texts, from all the poetic trends of his era: from the Parnassus of Banville (*Nuit d'étoiles*, *Pierrot*) and Leconte de Lisle (*La Fille aux cheveux de lin*, voice-piano version 1880, *Jane*) from Paul Bourget (*Beau Soir*, *Voici que le printemps*, *Paysage sentimental*, *Silence ineffable*, *Regret*, *Romance d'Ariel*, *Les Cloches*); but the most accurate illustrations of this discussion are not to be found here; these compositions all felt the effects of Russian and German influence on the word, on its sound, and on its relationship to the music, even in cases where the composer seemed to be well aware of it. On the contrary, while he measured his ability with the poetry of Baudelaire and Verlaine, or Mallarmé, Debussy did not put shackles on his imagination which he left free to complete, with his music, the sense which was implicit in the words; 'the music starts where the word is powerless to explain', he was in the habit of saying.

The problems set by Mallarmé's poems were manifold: it was important to lose none of his harmony, to transpose his tight syntax, and his elaborate vocabulary. Debussy dared to attack these difficulties, at least in the texts which deviated least from the traditional form: *Apparition, Placet futile, Soupir, Eventail de Mademoiselle Mallarmé*. The first, *Apparition*, set to music in 1885 — when the composer was twenty-two! — already showed the boldness of the Debussy language. The atmosphere suggested by the poet was imprinted with Pre-Raphaelism; like the whole Symbolist school, he had a liking for it:

> La lune s'attristait. Des Séraphins en pleurs
> Rêvant, l'archet aux doigts, dans le calme des fleurs
> Vaporeuses, tiraient de mourantes violes
> De blancs sanglots glissant sur l'azur des corolles.

> The moon is sad. Seraphins in tears
> dreaming, their bows in their fingers, in the calm of the vaporous
> flowers, pluck from the dying viols
> white sobs sliding over the azure of the corollas.

How was he to translate this text, which is so subtle and so modern, and in fact of which the skills taught by the Conservatoire were of such limited effectiveness? In the melody there is the comparison of a great vocal range (almost two octaves) and a range which is reduced almost to recitative; to this is added a principle of chord construction which differs from the traditional: the connection of their functions remains suspended, sometimes because of the superimposition of semitones, sometimes by the use of unexpected and very expressive modulations, sometimes even by the introduction of successive non-functional chords. This was a treatment of melodic form which was used fully in *Pelléas*, in which Symbolism and modernism had no need to be recalled! Debussy himself wrote in a very explicit fashion from the Villa Medici in 1885: 'I do not believe that I shall ever enclose my music in too correct a mould...I am not speaking of musical form, it is simply in a literary respect. I shall always prefer something where, in some way, the action is sacrified to the long-pursued expression of the soul's feelings. It seems to me in that way music can become more human, more lived, and that one can examine and refine the means of expression.'

The melodies after Verlaine (*Fêtes Galantes*, 1891; *Six ariettes oubliées*, all rest integrally on a new way of treating sound: the superimposition of many tonalities without modulation or transition (*Mandoline*), replacement of the tonal unity by a strict construction of themes (in *Fantoches*), or a melodic line of complete rhythmic and harmonic originality (in *Clair de lune*); there is a complete grammatical revolution. But it is unquestionable that the most decisive turning point came in the melodies composed for Baudelaire's texts. There one can fully grasp how, on one hand, Symbolist music was obligatorily defined through literary reference and formal standards, and how, on the other hand, they both originated from Wagnerism. In the *Cinq Poèmes de Charles Baudelaire* Debussy detached himself from the past and from Wagner; he revived the function and the character of former methods. These melodies were conceived under the influence of Baudelaire who was the initiator of the Symbolist movement and a Wagnerian enthusiast. During the sixteen months which separated the first (*La Mort des amants*, 1887) from the last (*Jet d'eau*, 1889), Debussy arrived at his own aestheticism and his own vocabulary.

All this goes to show that Symbolism in music at first only existed properly in regard to French literature, which contributed to the constitution of the Wagnerian phenomenon, through which all the revivals as well as all the revolutions in musical aesthetics can be explained. It enabled also to distinguish the genres which only blossomed because they were, like the symphonic poem and the melody, more or less attached to literature. Was that all? Was that clear enough? Quite obviously not: opera, because it is by its nature a mixed genre, a bastard placed at the cross-roads of music, literature and the plastic arts, saw the birth of works which were truly Symbolist from every point of view: but this was at the price of more aesthetic confusion, which should now be mentioned.

The ambiguities of Symbolism

In literature, as in painting, Symbolism was born from mystery and strangeness. In October

1864 Mallarmé wrote to H. Cazalis: 'I have at last begun my Hérodiade. With terror, for I am inventing a language which will necessarily erupt from a very new poetry.' Twenty years later, on August 14, 1888, Gauguin exhorted his friend Schuffenecker: 'Do not paint too much from life. Art is an abstraction. Take it from nature while dreaming about it...look for the suggestion more than the description, as music has also done.' It is tempting to enter Symbolism between these two dates, between these two somewhat connected programmes; in fact it is more honest and more illuminating to refer only to the desire for novelty which the progress of any art always involves. This affected music in the 1880s, especially in France; it concerned harmony, which is the language of music, just as colour is the language of painting, and emphasis that of literature. This rebirth, therefore, united with the thinking of Mallarmé and Gauguin; but did it mean that musical Symbolism was the entire renaissance? Certainly not: it was only one of its aspects; more — it contributed to giving to musical Symbolism those indefinite frontiers and those ambiguities which its literary and pictorial counterparts could hardly have.

Two facts of harmonic order characterized the evolution of music in western Europe at the end of the nineteenth century — one was the impoverishment of the tonal system, and the other was the revival of modality. One particularly affected German music, which is understandable since modern harmony can be traced back to Johann Sebastian Bach; the other was more noticeable in French music which came from modal harmony, still known as 'sentiment', as Rameau labelled it at a different time. If a more modern light on the problem is required, Wagner can be compared to Berlioz, the Tristanian chromatism to the modality of *L'Enfance du Christ* (1854). Both systems were expressive: during the years with which we are concerned, they even enjoyed a heightened expressivity, and it was this which was, inaccurately called Symbolism. It had certainly been seen before, when it concerned the fascination of the writers with Wagner; it is important to note it again in the context which concerns the introduction to modality in French music at the end of the last century. In other words, in both cases a purely technical evolution was linked to poetic preoccupations, a harmonic problem was likened to a question of a literary and pictorial order. It is true, nevertheless, that the best French musicians' use of modality often doubled with a great aesthetic sense, sometimes even an affectation, which approved this assimilation: here one can meditate on the affinities between Ravel and Valéry!

It has been said many times that it was Franck, with *Rebecca*, *Hulda* and *La Chausseur maudit* who inaugurated these processes. In fact it was Chabrier, in his operetta *L'Etoile* (1877) who integrated modality with the harmonic language of the French school: well before the discovery of the Javanese *gamelan* at the Universal Exhibition of 1889, French music had discovered the pentatonic (five-toned) scale. Chabrier and the young Debussy used it because, exempt from the demitone, the pentatonic scale eliminated the elements of tension which the sensible note and its modulation reserved for the diatonic regime (proceeding by tones and semitones). *Les Trois Valses romantiques* by Chabrier use, with a happy insistence, the scale of five full tones. The harmony of the musician is as free as air, with 'nothing (in it) which weighs or pitches.'

Debussy was, in truth, the first composer for whom the 'image' was essential in sound. In his letters and articles, it is always a question of 'la mise en place sonore' and from his early works this concern had its effect. Thus *La Damoiselle élue*, a lyric poem for female voices, *soli*, choir and orchestra, begun in Rome in 1884, distinguished itself by the distant, seraphic character of the harmony. The chosen maiden is in Paradise, where she hopes for her well-beloved; the exquisite simplicity of the angel choir, 'the gentle music of the stars' is remarkable for its treatment which is already 'stereophonic' and agogic. It is the exact equivalent of the verbal refinement of the poets of the period for whom, since Baudelaire, the word was also, before anything else, a resonant material. *Le Prélude à l'après-midi d'un faune* (1892) was Symbolist also, but independently of its Mallarmian context. In fact it is noticeable that the composer had not put the well-known poem into music, but had written a 'prelude' to the text; in it he certainly found sensuality and grace, but by the harmonic treatment which came back completely to the aphorism expressed by Mallarmé in *La Musique et les Lettres* ('Music and letters are alternating faces, here widening towards the obscure, there sparkling with the certainty of that phenomenon, which I have called the Idea.') In fact Mallarmé, an habitué and lover of Wagner, only knew tones which were too rich, too brilliant, at the limit even without poetry — and on this subject Debussy attacked particularly the orchestral 'pedals' — 'a kind of multicoloured putty which is uniformly spread out and in which one cannot distinguish the sound of a violin from that of a trombone!' In *Le Prélude*, on the contrary, a sound is a sound; the principal theme, stated by the flute, has an enveloping sweetness which gives its colour to the piece, the call of the faun in the clarity of the day; but it is a call 'widening towards the obscure', with a diffuse, insidious sensuality, not crushing like that of Alberich in *Das Rheingold*. There is still more innovation. We are used to the linear interpretation of harmony. It is the mode of thematic thought from which even Schönberg was hardly liberated. On the contrary Debussy, because the sound alone of his chords mattered to him, and not their connections, truly achieved a 'melodie des accords' (*Klangfarbenmelodie*, said Schönberg) which is closely linked to the famous 'pure poetry' towards which the whole of Symbolism was silently moving. At the bottom, the use of the tone scale and consequently the absolute pre-eminence of pure sound values, perhaps forms the common denominator which most surely permits the confirmation of the existence of Symbolist harmony in music, and this in a fashion all the more satisfactory because there is, in this case, no possible literary influence on the music. By modality and the cult of sound it was the musicians who, by a perfect technical expedient, took from Poetry what was theirs! In this respect, Chabrier, Debussy and even Ravel, with his *Concerto pour la main gauche*, or the *Chansons madécasses*, are all certainly Symbolist composers.

Symbolism and Impressionism

Let us return to the quotation from Mallarmé which was used to illustrate a previous ambiguity in Symbolism. The poet said exactly this: 'I have at last begun my *Hérodiade*. With terror because I am inventing a language which will necessarily erupt in a very new poetry, which I could define in these two words: do not paint the thing, but the effect it produces.' It is easy to see the early links of Mallarmês poetics with the aesthetics of the Impressionists. One thinks of the effort by the Proustian Elstir who aspired 'not to show things as he knows they are, but according to those optical illusions from which our vision is first made'; or again: 'If God the Father created things by naming them, it is by depriving them of their names, or by giving them others, that Elstir has recreated them. The names which designate things always correspond to an idea of intelligence, which is foreign to our impressions which are always true.' It is also tempting to reconcile these effeorts with the aspirations of the young Debussy who, when he was studying at the Villa Medici, declared: 'I wish to see some Manet!' There is certainly, in some way, the possibility of likening Symbolism to Impressionism; the main thing is to specify its limits and to evoke the reasons for it.

On the face of it, Symbolism and Impressionism are partially linked. The statements just made authorize us to say so; that is why musicology evokes the musical innovations of the end of the nineteenth century only under the title 'Impressionist'. Justifications for this are usually thematic or aesthetic. For example, the constant and varied link between some authors and nature is often noted. The same applies to Debussy whose scores are entitled *La Mer, Nocturnes, Jardins sous la pluie, Brouillards, Voiles, Le Vent dans la plaine, Bruyères, Feuilles mortes* and remind us of so many paintings which have similar or identical names. There is also Ravel with *Noctuelles, Jeux d'eau, Ondine, Schéhérazade, La Cloche engloutie*; finally there are isolated works of other composers: *Siegfried Idyll, L'Enchantement du Vendredi saint* by Wagner, *Dans les bois, Feux follets, Jeux d'eau de la Villa d'Este, Nuages Gris* by Liszt, the *Scènes de la fôret* by Schumann. It certainly seems as if, in these scores, the composers had received rhythmic and harmonic suggestions from nature; as Debussy said, in 1911: 'All the noises you hear around you can be interpreted. One can represent musically everything which a fine ear can perceive in the rhythm of the surrounding world. Some people at first want to conform to the rules; I myself only want to interpret what I hear.' In other words, the bearing of the musician is, in many cases, analogous to that of the Impressionist painter: based on a finesse and a subjectivity developed from what he has heard, it interprets the nuance, the iridescence of perception.

To this end the musician uses certain procedures which are the structural justification for the identification of Symbolism with Impressionism. To go back to a Debussy score already evoked for its sound values, the *Prélude à l'après-midi d'un faune*: one first notices the tonal liberty which is replaced by a modal coherence (a meeting, for the theme of the faun and its reply, of two distant tones, which are nevertheless united by the identity in harmony of A sharp and B flat). By its chromatic appearance the harmony only produces a sound which is drowned, pure, charged with mysterious feeling. To this is added the finesse and the excellence of the instrumentation: the song of the solo flute which modulates the theme of the faun, the harp arpeggios, the elaborate tones of the horns, the staccato of the woodwinds and brass which murmur like troubled water. Mallarmé aptly wrote to the musician after the first hearing of the *Prélude*: 'Your illustration of the *Prélude à l'après-midi d'un faune* would show no dissonance with my text, except that it really goes much further into nostalgia and light, with finesse, with uneasiness, with richness.' Surely that is the equivalent of the incantation in pure poetry, and the counterpart of the little spots which turn into sparkling light. Impressionism can sometimes be confused with Symbolism through the actual intention of the musician.

Nevertheless, if the treatment of the nuance and the cult of suggestion, in their principle and their means, sanctions aesthetic confusion, this confusion, like the nuance and the suggestion, does not last more than a moment. Those categories of beauty, those poetic systems foreign to music, deceived the artists themselves to start with. Debussy was the first who consciously defended, in front of C. Malherbe, the specific mystery of music: 'Who knows the secret of musical composition? The sound of the sea, the curve of the horizon, the song of a bird, leave us with many impressions. And, suddenly, without our least consent, one of these memories spills out of us and expresses itself in musical language. It carries its own harmony in itself...I abominate doctrines and their impertinences. That is why I want to write my musical dream with the most complete detachment from myself. I want to sing my inner landscape with the unaffected candour of a child' (Interview given to *L'Excelsior*, February 11, 1911, concerning the *Martyre de saint Sebastien*). And did he not refuse Berlioz the quality of musician because, precisely, he gave 'the illusion of music with processes borrowed from literature and painting'? Thus one must guard against applying to music principles which explain nothing to do with it.

Take, for example, the main conception, in Impressionism, of instantaneousness, which Monet tried to realize: this notion, to express the changes which intervene on the surface of things at different hours of the day, cannot be applied to music which is the 'instantaneous' art par excellence. 'The music of this prelude is a *very free* illustration of the lovely poem of Stéphane Mallarmé' wrote Debussy privately about this ambiguous and too famous *Prélude à l'après-midi d'un faune*! The reference to nature by which Impressionism could be defined on an equal footing with Symbolism, is a deceptive guarantee: in any music nature can only ever play a secondary role; it is *a posteriori* that the listener, and even the composer, identify it with the nature which is described by the literature and painting of the period. 'More expression of emotion than painting', said Beethoven privately about his *Pastoral Symphony*! One should not be concerned with saying in what way the 'jeux d'eau' of Ravel differ from those of Liszt, when musicology wishes to see in both a musical equivalent of Impressionism.

It is wrong to look at Debussy as the central figure of Impressionist music. It was the Impressionist spirit which suggested to him the titles of his works, with their 'natural' references, but it must be agreed that the period was under the sign of Symbolism rather than Impressionism, which was twenty years earlier. Besides, does a title make the style of the piece? Does the title of the *Préludes* not come at the end of the score rather than at the beginning? In Debussy's dislike of developments, in the moderation which he imposed on his melodic invention, could be seen the effect of a sensualism at a time when, on the contrary, his musical thinking — this has already been mentioned concerning modality — was at the opposite extreme of the anecdote, and the 'Wagnerized' music. Has it not been noted that when Debussy became a painter it was solely of immaterial bodies, without form or substance? Certainly one could interpret the procession of fifths and thirds in the third part of *La Mer* as a 'calm and white procession which slides across the night sky', like the 'play of the light on the sea'; nevertheless, this image leads us to a different dimension: in spite of oneself, one is overtaken by the nostalgia of another world, of a universe such as only the Symbolists could feel. Should a pictorial reference be absolutely essential, it would be appropriate to liken Turner rather than Monet to our composer. For Monet's sea is never terrifying. One can participate in the contemplation of the

The martyrdom of St. Sebastian, by Claude Debussy, with Ida Rubinstein, drawing by Léon Bakst

painter, himself in pantheist accordance with nature. On the other hand, in Debussy's *La Mer*, everything seems to happen — as with Turner — on a cosmic scale. In the last part of this polyrhythmic symphony, *Le Dialogue du vent et de la mer*, apart from the fact that the wind does not evoke a corresponding picture, the baneful sound of the hurricane seems to announce death and destruction. The public has been deceived by the critics and the musicologists who suggested a superficial analogy with Impressionist painting. Debussy makes us aware of what the Romantics made us forget: true music does not speak to the individuality of man, but to what is most profound in him.

Symbolism and national renaissance at the end of the nineteenth century

Every artistic renaissance, every new emphasis has, at the limit, been confused with Symbolism. On the single basis of a rather vague framework of time (the years 1875 to 1905), Russia, Spain and Scandinavia all in turn experienced Symbolism in music. Perhaps it was Norway and Finland which, of the Scandinavian countries, enabled the music of Grieg and Sibelius most justly to be called Symbolist. In fact these two countries had preserved the ancient liturgical forms in music better than their neighbours; they therefore benefited most, according to the musicologists, from the credit which attached to this use of the tone scale. On the other hand, the folklore of the Kalevala, like the literature of Ibsen and Bjornson, provided the composers of these countries with themes similar to those of which the French and German Symbolists were so fond. Hence the *Swan of Tuonela* by Jean Sibelius: the empire of death is Tuonela, or Manala, encircled by a dismal river down which Death sends the souls of the dead. The funereal swan glides down the gloomy waters of eternity, and sings its perpetual dirge through the voice of the tenor oboe above an ethereal background of muted strings: like that of Lohengrin, the barge of Tuoni (Death) gradually appears in front of our eyes. Grieg deserves the appellation Symbolist by reason of his own harmonic processes: a floating tonality, passing notes, chromatics and so many elements which finally converge, albeit less perfectly, with the Debussyist doctrine of sound values. When, in addition, in a subject such as *Peer Gynt*, borrowed from folklore and Ibsen, the kobold is evoked by certain modal forms, one is very close to an extremely and authentically Symbolist work.

There was in Russia an original Symbolist literature — but did it have a musical counterpart? Apparently not. Assuredly some aspects of Borodin's work, all of Scriabin's, seem to conform to Symbolist principles; but in fact their compositions have not the same quality as those of their poetic compatriots; above all, the widespread German influence, intensified by that of Tchaikowsky, on the whole of Russian music, prevented it from being really affected by the wave of Symbolism.

At the other side of Europe, the Spaniard Isaac Albeniz showed the characteristics which often linked him with Debussy. His visit to Paris in 1893 had also made him aware of the true meaning of Symbolist music: in his work, in his numerous *Pièces caractéristiques*, can be found his interest in folklore, and the original rhythms which at first served to articulate musically these new principles. He also had a literary taste which, curiously, in his three part opera *King Arthur*, led him into the nordic mists. But Albeniz's most personal work, and perhaps his most innovatory, was *Spanish Images*: it was the fruit of a very individual imagination which produced a Spain completely denuded of realism, and of all facile pictorial beauty; but it was a Spain seen, above all, through the wonderful world of music, painting and poetry which was the Symbolist Paris, the fertile Paris of the last years of the nineteenth and the first ten of the twentieth centuries.

Opera — the corner-stone of Symbolism

If there was, first of all, a music of the Symbolists, that is to say, Wagner's music; if there was, in a lesser measure, a Symbolist music represented by the very different aspects of the works of a great number of composers of all countries; it then follows easily that opera is, in the main, the one sphere which truly makes the art in question illustrious. It is easy to understand this and to define, at the same time, the characteristics of the genre.

Opera, being a complete spectacle (libretto plus music plus staging plus scenery) must, to establish its Symbolist inspiration, rely on a similar treatment for each of the parts which form its whole. For each of its parts? Assuredly, but nevertheless not in the same measure: Symbolist opera must first admit a libretto, or theme, more or less accurately borrowed from the Symbolist writers. It is this pre-eminence of the 'literary' which seems to characterize its existence most accurately; in fact, if one can say for example that romantic opera defines itself, to start with, by a musical writing (vocal for the Italians, orchestral for the Germans) and that baroque opera singles itself out by a world-wide aesthetic project (the desire to go back to Greek tragedy, especially noticeable in Monteverdi), it is the reference to the personalities or the themes of Symbolist literature which makes the opera of the same name. In this sense the lyric theatre of this trend is the fruit of a vast double influence: first that of the poets and the playwrights, especially Wagner who contributed, as we have seen, to the definition of Symbolist aesthetics. There is thus a thematic commonly shared by dramatic and lyric scenes: this could be the myth, which in its Symbolist 'reading' passes from theatre to opera, or vice versa (Ariadne, for example, chosen by Mendès for Massenet, and by Hofmannsthal for Strauss); or it could be the legend: Bluebeard, which inspired first Maeterlinck, then Paul Dukas, Reznicek and Bartók (with libretto by B. Balázs); there are, more subtly, convergent psychological or philosophic schemata: thus it is noticeable that the heroines in both theatre and opera, over a long period (from Wagner to Berg) are conceived as *femmes-enfants* or *femmes fatales* (Kundry in *Parsifal*, Lulu of Wedekind and Berg, and all the Salomés and Mélisandes); and it is also noticeable that a large number of works in all registers of art expresses both the horror and the ecstasy of life, the temptation of plenitude and the vertigo of the abyss (*Tristan*, *Electra*, both the *Manons*, and also *Le Roi d'Ys* and *Gwendoline*, who all share these characteristics with the plays of Claudel, Hofmannsthal, Ibsen and Blok); finally, one comes across cases of exemplary good fortune: that of Wilde who inspired Strauss (*Salomé*), Schreker (*The Infanta's Birthday*: 'Der Geburtstag der Infantin') and Semlinsky (*The Dwarf*: 'Der Zwerg'), that of Ibsen who provided Grieg and Egk with the subject of *Peer Gynt*, of Wolf (*The Feast at Solhaug*: 'Das Fest auf Solhaug') and above all that of Maeterlinck who gave Debussy and Schönberg the theme for their *Pelléas*.

Because opera, on an inspirational level, comes under the direct patronage of literature, and often, from the technical point of view, into the Wagnerian and post-Wagnerian tenure, it is truly the genre which is most charcteristic — and therefore also the most imprecise! — of Symbolism in music. Let it also be said that it was like a temptation to which all the turn-of-the-century musical schools, conservative or revolutionary, yielded.

The Symbolist temptation in the different musical schools

Verism is often thought of as a neatly defined and easily understood phenomenon. However, there are Symbolist aspects in opera which make use of this equivalent of Naturalism. The ambiguity, on a psychological level, of Puccini's heroines, has already been discussed: Butterfly, Liu (in *Turandot*) even Mimi, all have something in common with the characters of Maeterlinck and Debussy; what really matters, however, is not to be found there, but on the musical level. It is known to what extent Mascagni's *Cavalleria Rusticana* or Leoncavallo's *Pagliacci* depend on the aesthetics of the 'slice of life'; the brutality, the sordidness which came out in the scores of composers such as Puccini is also known. However, certain intentions of these composers, certain passages, and certain solutions, make us think of Symbolism. Moreover, the composers themselves were tempted by this school: D'Annunzio had put one of his dramatic poems, *The Crusade of the Innocents* at the disposal of the young Puccini, and Mascagni had also been attracted to the same author. It is *Pagliacci* which shows the greatest affinity with Symbolism: Leoncavallo took a great deal of trouble with his harmony, thus following the cult of sound values which was as characteristic of the poets as of a musician like Debussy. Three leitmotifs (Pagliaccio's unhappy laughter, love and jealousy) are introduced from the prologue on, and consequently cover the important dramatic and structural functions. This is surely a Wagnerian recipe, but besides the fact that Wagnerism was at the root of Symbolist aesthetics, Leoncavallo gives proof, in his use of this process, of an economy which lends the writing a truly persuasive and incantatory character. Thus the motif of the sad laughter is both the most important factor in the work and that which we hear the least: in fact it only occurs three times in the whole piece (it is true that these appearances are at the most noticeable moments); the first time is at the start of the prologue, with *messo-forte* horns alone; the second time is in Canio's great lament which ends the first act; this time it is heard *forte* in the unison of singer and orchestra, an octave higher than the first time. Here one wonders why the composer does not repeat the motif during the orchestral postlude which accompanies the lowering of the curtain; it is in order to keep the possibility of a real culminating point, for the third appearance of the motif, marked *fff*, an unleashed *tutti*, once again an octave higher, on the last page of the score. Such a dramatic progression founded on an absolute economy of musical means could only be the work of a composer influenced by Symbolism. Associated with a subtle art in the use of the chorus, it gives the whole end of the work a prodigious power of enchantment.

Besides verism, all the national schools who had tried to free themselves from the traditional influences in opera (that is to say German and Italian above all), in order to achieve an authentic and personal expressivity, had come across, objectively, the Symbolist preoccupations. Consider, for example, *La Vida breve* by Manuel de Falla: apparently it is a purely 'Spanish' work where folklore plays a preponderant role the whole time, and on all planes (subject, melody and rhythm), and yet the score reveals a certain 'compositional' attitude which is like that of Debussy (who was admired and known by de Falla). The composer knew all the problems of writing and expression posed first by Wagner, and later Debussy, from whom came the use of the tone scale (for example in the first intervention of the 'distant voices') and the harmonies which resulted; from him too came the general structure which, despite a certain subdivision of the acts, managed to resolve the problem of the unity of the whole by the continuity of an extremely varied discourse full of dramatic power.

As in *Parsifal*, the role of ensuring the transition from one scene to the next, and of guaranteeing the unity of the contrasting and independent sections falls heavily on to the chorus. Falla was therefore using a certain technique acquired from Symbolist music.

At the other side of Europe there was a certain Symbolist levelling-out in the works of Russians such as Rimsky-Korsakov: the choice of subjects, always taken from folklore, showed a taste for fairyland, for magic, and for the supernatural which also came from Wagner and the Scandinavian playwrights: one can already tell something about these works from their titles: *Sadko*, *The Golden Cockerel*, and particularly *The Little Snowflake* and *The Legend of the invisible Town of Kitesch*; is it not the same state of mind which made Debussy write *Children's Corner* and so many preludes with equally bewitching titles? It is true that Rimsky-Korsakov was sometimes a little too like Wagner, but in his best works, (*The Golden Cockerel*, for example) the national rhythms, the exotic quality of some of the melodies, again remind us of the basic innovation of style which represented, as has been said, the modality of musical Symbolism. It would not be hard to discover traces of this melodic nationalism, which in this case was mingled with Symbolist interests, in the works of Borodin, Mussorgski and Prokoviev, or the Czech composers. But we shall not go as far as that, because the encounter is rather too accidental. Symbolism, like all aesthetics, came as much from technique as from a state of mind or the personal taste of its authors; it is evident that, while in this respect, de Falla and the Slavs were far removed from the final metamorphosis of Romanticism, the Symbolists in painting and particularly literature were at first heirs to a very weighty tradition. The national renaissance was not in the order of their preoccupations.

On the other hand, seen from that angle, the German composers Schönberg and Berg, the Hungarian Bartók, were originally authentic Symbolists. Let us even say that their subsequent modernity only came out more precisely because it had been at first confronted with the temptation of the indescribable and the incantatory. As in poetry, 'purity' explained the development of music from post-Romanticism to dodecaphony and modality.

Waiting ('Erwartung' 1909) and *The Happy Hand* ('Die Glückliche Hand' 1913) by Schönberg were the first operas written in the revolutionary athematic style of the Viennese school, but they could also be considered, in the extension of the *Gurre-Lieder*, as works of transition marked by Symbolism. Expressionism has also been mentioned in connection with these two works: in fact the arguments, themes, characters and the sensual, spiritual atmosphere were more reminiscent of the early works of Hofmannsthal and Blok. And in truth, it seems that it was Expressionism which liked and took these subjects from Symbolist dramas and not the reverse! This was confirmed by Wedekind who inspired Berg to write *Lulu*, constructed on an analogous basis. Although, in their musical structure these two pieces are extremely different from each other, they nevertheless state a common characteristic which was essential to the Symbolist theatre: Schönberg wanted to give a musical expression to mythical ideas. It was very much the same problem as confronted Wilde in *Salomé*, and Maeterlinck in *Pelléas*; it was also very much that which, in the lyric theatre, distinguished Wagner from Meyerbeer or Verdi, and Debussy and Strauss, in some of their productions, from Puccini or Stravinsky. This implies the total rejection of normal everyday reality, to the advantage of the dream, and of an unreality stripped of conventional taboos. It implies also unique musical means of great suggestive power, like Mallarmé's 'essential word'.

The discovery of these works is important, because it places Symbolism both historically and aesthetically; apart from these problems and their individual solutions, all the composers of opera who were tempted by this state of mind were led to reflect on the possibility and the nature of a new mixture. Symbolism thus characterized itself on the lyric scene at least as much by the questions it stirred up in the mind of the composer as by the choice of a given response. In this spirit and by these two operas, Schönberg pinpointed the frontier between Symbolism, which is basically an apotheosis of romantic sensibility, and all the purely technical but revolutionary formalisms which characterized the different arts of the twentieth century. In comparison with this true leader of a school, the other turn of the century opera composers seem to be in retreat. Nevertheless, they are, perhaps, for this reason, more truly Symbolist than Schönberg: only Debussy in *Pelléas*, Strauss in *Salomé*, and Bartók in *Bluebeard's Castle* really created the theatre of which, perhaps, Mallarmé dreamed. Why?

The three masterpieces: Bluebeard, Salomé, Pelléas

Salomé perhaps is the most 'Symbolist' of the three in the historic meaning of the term. Chronologically *Pelléas* preceded it (*Pelléas* was composed in 1902 while *Salomé* in 1905), but while Debussy's work, in its originality, went beyond Symbolism to a fundamental modernity which made Debussy the equal and the rival of Schönberg and Stravinsky, Strauss in *Salomé* found the perfect expression of his time: he summarized all the new aspirations but also the old notions of Symbolism.

This has already been proved by his choice of a much more richly diversified theme than those of Maeterlinck and Debussy. *Salomé's* loves were well-known through literature (Flaubert, Wilde, Huysmans), through painting (Moreau, Klimt, Beardsley), and through other composers, (apart from Strauss there was Massenet with *Hérodiade*, F. Schmitt with *The Tragedy of Salomé*). And the dates, ranging from 1877 (Flaubert) to 1909 (Klimt), are in themselves evidence of the authentic Symbolism of the subject. In the wave which engulfed Europe, Strauss' work holds a far more central place than Debussy's. Why? Because the horror of the drama, the eroticism which forms its basis and the quality of the characters are infinitely more decadent than their eventual equivalents in *Pelléas*. There is no place for pity in the realm of Salome and Herod, and therefore no possibility of revolt, and no *catharsis* in the mind of the spectator. On the other hand there is no gratuitous cruelty, and no depraved deliquescence in Debussy's work. Thus *Salomé* is the only work to realize the double postulation of Baudelaire which has been said, concerning Wagnerism, to constitute the spirit of Symbolism: terror and ecstasy, 'the phosphorescence of putrescence'.

In particular it is the psychological and dramaturgical nature of this heroine which accurately shows the distance separating *Salomé* from *Pelléas*. Leiris spoke, a propos Salome, of the female praying mantis which destroys the object of its love after having enjoyed it. And she holds the stage from the beginning to the end of the work. Mélisande, obviously, is a totally different type! However, Electra, Lulu, the leading characters in Dujardin's and Huysmans' novels, and the characters of Wilde, Ibsen and D'Annunzio are all on the same side as Strauss.

Youth and morbidity, innocence and depravity, are interpreted through a colour: white; through a style: orchestral and vocal magnificence. The bodies of Jokanaan and Salome are white, as white as innocence and as white as death, as white as make-up and as white as fright. The whole vocabulary of the librettist reveals a predilection for the words which conjure up the cold, the static, the lunary, the flat, the chaste, the constrained. These epithets show by their nature the ambiguity of the atmosphere and the psychology: like the love of Hebe or Artemis in Greece, the love of Salome for Jokanaan is chaste and mortiferous. Not monstrous, but extra-natural.

We have the musical equivalent of this in the scholarly delirium, the controlled abandon of the composer. It certainly does not concern the scandal, aroused in former times, by the 'dance of the seven veils' (although recently the production of Wieland Wagner and the interpretation of Anja Silja have re-established this connection with the past), but several facts, several precise passages. For example, the two scenes where Salome is in the presence of Jokanaan, alive to start with, and then an executed criminal: the intoxicated love of the antithetic tensions is expressed in long sweeping melodies, in repetitions (almost leitmotifs) by Salome while the orchestral part, rich and diversified, bursts into Dionysiac delirium. There is truly a 'derangement of all the senses', but, properly, systematic and therefore artful. The Straussian word in *Salomé* is equally as incantatory, because controlled, as the equivalent in Mallarmé or Rimbaud. The vocal originality of Salomé's part could also be mentioned; the difficulty here comes from the necessarily artifical colour of the voice, which is often toneless, chaste and depraved at the same time. Fascination could be the key word for *Salomé*: it sums up both our attitude to the work and its actual substance, and it indicates at what point this opera proceeds from aesthetics to the most authentic Symbolism. *Salomé* is, in every sense of the word, the product of its era.

Enchantment would be a better word to define *Pelléas et Mélisande*. What first attracted Debussy to this play by Maeterlinck was in fact 'an evocative language whose sensibility could find an extension in music and orchestral décor' (*Comoedia*, interview of April 1902). Thus is measured the distance between Debussy and Strauss; it is approximately the same as that between Verlaine and Rimbaud. But it is not only a question of the language — Maeterlinck's art corresponds exactly to Debussy's dramatic ideal: characters 'for whom history and abode belong to no place and no time' (another difference from Strauss and Wilde), who 'do not discuss but yield to life and fate'. In fact, Debussy rejected the traditional manner of differentiating between his characters (a style still used by Strauss), which consisted of contrasting the characters and the situations. To situate a hero was not of interest to Debussy; he wanted to create a work which would lead us to the heart of consciousness, which would situate destinies in the pulses of man himself rather than in exterior events (and on this point Debussy recognizes with Strauss the spirit of Freudian psychology). Maeterlinck's theatre responded to the desire shared by all the Symbolists; the drama was played on two planes at the same time: one was apparent, composed of words and actions; the other was interior, where the real action took place, and it was this which determined the action on the stage. The words and the actions were only important inasmuch as they disclosed the unavoidable rules. The heroes were dreamlike characters: they knew neither whence they came nor whither they went.

By what means did Debussy succeed in giving life to these phantoms? By simple means: most often he used the recitative, which respects the particular inflexions of the French language, but he did not become a slave to this formula. To grasp and transmit the hidden meaning of the words, he made of recitative an infinitely supple instrument, never hesitating to use the methods discovered by others. For example, it is often said that Debussy made use of the leitmotif, which he had mocked Wagner for using. But with Wagner, in fact, the leitmotif had a vigorous character: it served to inter-unite the orchestral masses, and it was also used in narration. In Debussy, the motifs were static, often fragmentary, and they changed according to the situation, the atmosphere or the state of mind of the heroes. Why the difference? To avoid the clarity which Wagner wished to infuse into his work, and to avoid driving away the obscure, ambiguous meaning of things by too transparent musical symbols. At the very beginning of the first scene of the second act, the flutes announce Pelléas; but this motif does not recur in the same form, nor in a similar context, any more than the motifs of Mélisande, Golaud, or the fountain in the park, and so on. One of the variants of Golaud's motif is identified with the one of the ring which Mélisande drops into the water. Other motifs interchange, change colour and composition; this suggests reality, sometimes only the idea of reality. It is far removed from Strauss' world of beautiful appearances. Debussy's Symbolism is not that of refinement or of splendour, but that of impression and chiaroscuro.

The composer turned aside from romantic models, particularly those involving the conventional subjects of love and death. Strauss did too, but in the sense of the bizarre which led him to reinforce the expression by all sorts of means. Debussy was the first to dare to refuse an emphasis without weakening the expressive value. In the first scene of the third act, the great

Pelléas et Mélisande by Claude Debussy, scenography by Jusseaume

scene between Pelléas and Mélisande who is leaning out of the window of the castle tower, is played throughout, in spite of the enormous emotional tension, to a *pianissimo* orchestra accompaniment. One can imagine what the German composers would have made of their orchestras in such a situation! In the scene of the fountain, Debussy goes even further: at the moment that Pelléas and Mélisande speak their love, the orchestra, which until then has been playing *forte*, becomes silent, and then reappears *ppp* as if leaving the shadows to accompany Pelléas' recitative. In *Pelléas* respect for the incantation blossoms; fundamental to Symbolism since the time of Verlaine, it rested on an art made of silences and nuances; but at the same time it escaped, at least with Debussy, from all tradition. This prophetic sense of sound values took our author away from Symbolism and placed him in the camp of the greatest innovators of the twentieth century: *Pelléas* is a key work.

The Castle of Bluebeard by Bartók (1911), on a libretto by Béla Balázs, represented an outpost of Symbolism. At first because this work marked the end of a line: since Perrault, the theme had been treated successively by Grétry, Offenbach and Dukas; and the actual libretto, initially destined for Kodaly, owed a lot to Maeterlinck; but musically the score was obviously inspired by the experience of Debussy. *Bluebeard* is very much the end of the line.

The opera remains a hermetic work, like Maeterlinck's play, because of two essential elements: in the libretto Bluebeard's wives are not dead, but only imprisoned, and the last, far from being a victim, tries to play the part of a liberator who brings light into the heart of darkness. But Bluebeard carries her off, and she remains a prisoner with the others. Balázs emphasized the interior aspect, in a manner more metaphysical and psychological.

Basically, the story of Bluebeard has always expressed the confrontation of man and woman: it is the conflict between the creative, the rational and intuition; or again, the allegory of solitude and incomprehension, as it is in the text of Rimbaud and Claudel. But the most distinct meaning is that woman, who insists on knowing everything about the man she loves, kills love in trying to deepen it. It was already the theme of Lohengrin, so highly esteemed by the Symbolist writers. Bluebeard is a work which ends this trend, because it stages for the last time, in the opera, the parable of the forbidden fruit in the garden of Eden.

The dramatic tension and the atmosphere of cruelty are evoked by the first name of the heroine, who Balázs called Judith (in Maeterlinck's work her name was Ariadne). Thus Holopherne is superimposed on Bluebeard, and the heroic adversary on to the figure of the curious friend. If man is a danger to woman, woman is also a threat to man. This idea gradually imposes itself and, as in *Salomé*, better even than in *Salomé*, the blood which is present throughout the work is virtually spilt on both sides. Here sacrifice is potential and reciprocal.

On the plane of dramaturgy the elements in *Bluebeard* which marked the final blossoming of the processes of Symbolist art are clearly defined; no interval, but a single act of an hour, a bass and a soprano, as in *Salomé*; the minimum of voice, rather a dialogue somewhat as in *Waiting*. No action, unless psychological, and no scenery except the interior of a Gothic castle, dark and bare as a cave. Static opera, heavy with meaning and silence, like *Pelléas*. That the story may have symbolic value, the prologue tells us through the voice of the soloist:

'Voici monter les premiers mots.	Here are the first words rising.
Nous, nous regardons; le rideau	We...we are watching; the curtain,
Frangé de nos yeux, s'est ouvert.	fringed by our eyes has opened.
Mais où est la scène? Mystère!	But where is the stage? A mystery!
Dehors, dedans? Qui peut le dire?'	Without, within? Who can say?

In comparison with his predecessors, the composer established himself in a musical level by a more ample, more vigorous, more radical handling of the innovations which they had introduced. A Debussyist score? Without doubt, but more violent and more percussive. The opening of the prison gates is marked by frequent taps on the kettle drums, and the xylophone underlines the moments of tension. Janacek's influence has also been mentioned; it seems more apt to mention Schönberg for the freedom of his dramatic recitative: Bartók moreover had been acquainted since 1910 with the work of the Viennese composer. But the most noticeable thing of all is the impact of the music of folklore which is happily united here with the general Symbolism of the whole, and which reinforces it: the melodic line is often that of the Hungarian *parlando rubato*, and sometimes takes on the appearance of a sad litany in the repeated notes and the descending phrases (a little like the suppliant entreaties of Salome). The basses are marked by pentatones (five tones). Finally, as in Debussy, an arch-shaped construction is noticeable (Bartók afterwards used it frequently): the intensity of sound rises and then falls, and the subtle play of the tonalities is based on the same pattern of F sharp to C followed by a return to F sharp (it is this three-toned interval which Debussy in 1901 put between the tonalities of his two nocturnes *Nuages* and *Fêtes*). *Bluebeard*, by its origins, its philosophy, and by its writing, can be seen as the final opera of Symbolism.

We started by wondering if it was legitimate to speak of the musical aspects of Symbolism. The reply to this question is affirmative, but at the price of how many paradoxes! There is, first of all, a music of Symbolist writers: that of Wagner and several others who, more or less influenced by him, became involved in the discussions of the poets and painters: Chabrier, Fauré, Scriabin for the most notable. Afterwards there was other music which, cultivating in the sphere of letters the genre of the poem and the melody, discovered, in so doing, a new meaning of sound values: in this respect the great Symbolist musician was Debussy, and the best represented national school was in France. A phenomenon of influence and therefore a French phenomenon? Not only: Symbolist music which called itself newly and vigorously expressive, became confused, in this perspective, with other aesthetics: Impressionism in particular, but also all those which in one way or another advanced the national or folklore inspirations. In other words, there were only two criteria for defining Symbolism in music: its more or less explicit, more or less conscious, link with literature (that is to say with the authors who became known between 1870 and 1910), and its ability to draw inspiration, even by adapting them, from the harmonic innovations brought about by the reaction to Wagnerism. In this respect opera saw the triumph of musical Symbolism, and particularly in the closely-linked but distinct masterpieces which were *Salomé* by Strauss, *Pelléas et Mélisande* by Debussy, and *The Castle of Bluebeard* by Bartók.

BARTOK Béla (Nagyszentmiklós, Hungary 1881 — New York 1945). Béla Bartók started his musical studies with his mother, at a very early age. He then became a pupil of Erkel, who was son of the famous composer of opera in

ANDREAS BECK *Portrait of Béla Bartók*

Bratislava (which was then called Presburg and was one of the former capitals of Hungary); he finished his musical studies in Budapest in 1903. He was a remarkable pianist, and became in 1907 a professor in the Conservatoire of that city. In 1905 he met Kodály: they became friends and in 1906 travelled across the ancient, vast Hungary, in order to collect Hungarian, Slav, Roumanian, Bulgarian, Serbo-Croat and Turkish folk songs they recorded almost ten thousand!).

At the end of the First World War, Bartók was an active participant in the first people's republic of Béla Kun; then, worried and watched, he eventually left Hungary under the regent Horthy in 1940, and took refuge in the United States where he died in poverty in 1945.

The works which could give rise to speculation about Bartók's appurtenance to Symbolism are: *Kossuth*, the symphonic poem of 1903, two orchestral suites (1905-1907), the first string quartet (1908), various piano pieces, including *L'Allegro barbaro* of 1911, and stage music: *The Prince of the Woods* (1914), the *Marvellous Mandarin*, ballet (1919), and the opera *Bluebeard* (1911). Bartók crossed the path of Symbolism by reason of his temporary Debussysism (from 1907 to about 1918). Debussy taught him the meaning of chords in themselves,

freed from the constraints of tonal structure: he suggested to him the idea of a harmony which was arranged in a modal perspective accorded in advance to modalism and the monody of folklore. But it was folklore, on the other hand, which persuaded Bartók to leave Symbolism, with its arabesques and its arhythmia. His art is the art of effort and tension (in which he was strongly influenced by Beethoven, especially in his quartets): by his melodies of lively angles, he rejected sound which was too refined, fluid or persuasive.

Blue Beard by Béla Bartók, the castle

The novelty of Bartók's folklore was to be its definitive style — Symbolism on the contrary, had only been an experiment.

CHAUSSON Ernest (Paris 1865 — Limay 1904). He was a rich, bourgeois, non-professional musician, and he belonged quite naturally to Symbolism.

Having passed his law degree, he went to the Conservatoire where he joined Massenet's composition class. Having failed there, he went back to the teaching of Franck. In the wake of the latter he met Duparc, d'Indy, Fauré, and even Debussy, whose debut he commended. For a period of about ten years Chausson was secretary to the National Society of Music, an important semi-official organization for the protection of French music.

He had been fond of and visited the Impressionists, Renoir, Degas and Carrière, but was himself a Symbolist. He was Symbolist to start with because of his master, César Franck; he was situated very much among the heirs of that old-fashioned Wagnerism which had been Symbolist music; later, by his own very personal inspiration,

A. BESNARD *Portrait of Ernest Chausson and his wife.* 1892

he belonged to this special movement. The result was a profoundly original discourse, cast in the mould of the Wagnero-Franckists, but in which the particular emphasis suggested to C. Du Bos one of his most celebrated *Approximations.* The epigraph for this was, significantly, borrowed from Baudelaire: 'Music often takes me like a sea'. In the course of these pages, Du Bos teaches us why, and in what way, Chausson was a Symbolist. First his *Concert,* heard in 1913 in the house of Jacques-Emile Blanche, evokes the *Nuptial Sleep* of the painter Rossetti; then *Le Poème,* which brought to their full expression the studies of his predecessors: 'The first (Franck) thickened the smooth flow of I know not what priceless honey of feeling; the second (Chausson) was sometimes a collection of luminous aspirations, of rays already captive of the beyond, sometimes a beating of wings, the actual murmuring of joy...A universal balm where perhaps virtue, above all, lives, is the efficacy of Chausson's music...a balm which does not allow the wound to show through. So permeated with Wagner — especially the Wagner

of *Parsifal* — is Chausson...he is as distant a possible — I do not mean at all in his technique (that is for others to decide) but in his spiritual climate — from the paroxism of *Tristan,* from that world where "the soaring of love towards death is let loose with an astonishing vehemence, where insatiable longing is carried to the rapture of destruction" (D'Annunzio: *The Triumph of Death*)...here the only rapture is that of feeling. The true Symbolist inspiration of Chausson can be felt, can be seen, beyond the affectations of criticism, in its reappearance in these two major works.

Other titles tell of their own accord the same aesthetic appurtenance: the symphonic poem *Viviane,* which recalls the myth of 'la Belle Dame sans Merci', two lyric dramas: *La légende de saint Cecile* and *Le roi Arthus,* and the multiple melodies on Maeterlinck's *Serres Chaudes,* especially the third (*Lassitude*) and the fifth (*Oraisons*).

Those are the signs which are not mistaken, even if it is regrettable, from one point of view, that the evolution of a musical language was never brought, on account of its brutal death, to conclusion. Much more reliable is the judgement of Debussy, elsewhere so strict: 'Ernest Chausson on whom weighed the Flemish influence of Franck, was one of the most delicate of artists. Although it is undeniable that the influence of the master of Liège was of service to some contemporary musicians, it seems to have been a disservice to Chausson in that it placed the sentimental strictness which is the basis of Franck's aesthetics in the way of his natural gifts of elegance and clarity...*Le Poème* for violin and orchestra contains his best qualities...nothing is more moving than the dreamy sweetness of the end of the poem, where the music leaves all description and all anecdote on one side, and becomes the actual feeling which inspires emotion'. (SIM review, January 1013). Du Bos or Debussy? It does not matter: Chausson could well be, by the very fact of his contradictions, the most perfect example of the Symbolist musician.

DEBUSSY Claude (Saint-Germain-en-Laye 186— Paris 1918). It would be possible to prove the Symbolism as well as the Impressionism of Claude Debussy: German musicology and certain French musicology, now a little out of date, incline towards Impressionism; on the other hand, certain informed spirits such as W. Jankelevitch and S. Jarokinsky defend the Symbolist argument. There could well be other classifications. For example, J. Combarieu, in his colossal *Histoire de la Musique* (1919-1923), distinguished a Symbolist side (*La Demoiselle élue, Prélude à l'après-midi d'un faune, Pelléas*) and a Naturalist side (*La Mer, Images, Nocturnes*). Which, in fact, is he?

STEINLEN *Portrait of Claude Debussy*

It seems appropriate to recollect that the epoch of Debussy — but was it, in this respect, different from the other great epochs? — had witnessed the simultaneous coexistence of several streams. In fact, Symbolism in literature and Impressionism in painting had been, at the turn of the century, the strongest expressions of modernity in art. Debussy was the product of his era, and he demanded of music that it should reproduce that which he loved in both Symbolist poetry (including the Pre-Raphaelites) and Impressionist painting, which was even more revolutionary than Symbolist painting. ('I want to see some Manet', was the cry of the student at the Villa Medici).

Debussy established himself as the leader of the Symbolist school, and the Symbolist school was pre-eminently French. Siding with Wagnerism and Russian music, as well as becoming infatuated, at a later stage, with Indonesian music, Debussy drew his aesthetic ideal from these three sources. Between Indonesian music and Wagnerism, as between Wagnerism and Debussyism, there were some strange affinities: all three belonged to an art form which used enchantment to the full; the dispute between Debussy and Wagner solely concerned certain means of operation: like Mallarmé and Verlaine, Debussy leaned towards the quality and economy of these methods. Afterwards his aim was totally melodic: because of this, and although he appeared so liberated from tonality, he stopped short of atonality. On the contrary he borrowed from other tone scales, ancient or exotic, melodic material which they already had. Finally, and by way of conclusion, Debussy realized that which was his ideal for all the arts: to arrive at a *harmony* which consisted purely of timbres and fundamental values — sound in music and in poetry, colour in painting.

In the general introduction we tried to define musical Symbolism in a threefold manner: as a movement with a strongly literary foundation,

influenced by Verlaine, Mallarmé and Baudelaire; as a modal language; and finally as the application of certain privileged forms (the symphonic poem, the melody, the opera, and music for the stage).

In this spirit we have analysed the immense masterpieces of *Pelléas*, the *Mélodies*, *La Mer*, *Le Prélude*. It is fitting to mention here others which could have been included. *Le Martyre de saint Sébastien* (1911), stage music on a text by D'Annunzio, composed for the Russian Ballet, was a curious work. Reading this play by the Italian, written in French, one can find many passages reserved for music of which Debussy did not take note. He preferred only those situations which were best suited to a style which had already formed in his mind. The progression from one act to the next is sensitive, without any haste. Although each act has its own characters, there is a unity in the whole work which did not exist similarly in *Pelléas*. Assuredly Debussy was touched by the strangeness of the text and by the religious subject. The composer admired *Parsifal*; he made no secret of it, even if he did not like the libretto, and reproached certain children's voices with having 'such weird sounds that it could have contained childish candour'. On a subject much more suspect than that of Wagner, Debussy arrived at this synthesis. The score keeps a uniformly high tone. The two occasions on which the figure of Christ is musically evoked, that of the Passion and that of the Good Shepherd, the opening of the gates of Paradise and the celestial chants which follow, will live on among the most beautiful examples of religious music. The stringency which Debussy had applied to his style since *Iberia* had borne fruit: thanks to a lightening of the symphonic body and the harmonic substance, as well as subtle instrumentation, he obtained the clearness of a stained glass window. Music for the stage, or music for the spirit — what they both require is clear to see: self-denial and a great application on the part of the author, analogous to the most profound efforts of Mallarmé and Valéry.

Debussy's last works were all composed in 1915. *La Suite en blanc et noir* for two pianos used the same limpid and spaced-out material as *Le Martyre*, *Douze Etudes* for the piano, whilst scaling the different degrees of instrumental virtuosity, obey the scheme which *Jeux* had already accomplished in the realm of the symphonic poem: to realize a music of pure sound values. Debussy knew that he had written into this score a range reserved for the 'non-entendu', daring to write: 'the most meticulous of the Japanese prints is child's play beside the writing of certain pages'. It was a surprising conclusion to his whole piano work, and it can be explained retrospectively: it was on the keyboard that Debussy tried his very first experiments in 'musical chemistry'.

That term naturally makes us think of Rimbaud's *Alchimie du Verbe*. That, in music as in poetry, is Symbolism: it wants to rediscover the original prosody of the language. Debussy arrived at it in his sphere, just as Rimbaud, Mallarmé and Valéry did in theirs.

DUKAS Paul (Paris 1865 — Paris 1935). Is it serious to try to include Dukas among the Symbolists? At first glance it would seem not: the nature of his work, its guiding spirit and the development of the composer all seem to put Dukas into the conservative camp, indeed even that of the musical academicism of his era. This musician has been praised for 'the need to distinguish himself which is indivisible from existence itself', as if this did not, by the same token, signify that he remained impervious to all the newest, most seductive elements in the language of his time.

A Parisian all his life, Dukas began to study the piano at the age of five, but did not really feel his vocation until he was fourteen. In 1881, he joined Dubois' harmony class at the Conservatoire, and then studied composition with Guiraud in 1885, when he became friends with Debussy. He won the second prize in the Prix de Rome with *Velléda*, a

ANUQUET *Portrait of Paul Dukas*

cantata which has remained unpublished, and in 1888 he left the Conservatoire to work alone.

Dukas had the privilege of being the friend of Saint-Saëns, Debussy, Fauré and D'Indy. He did some work as a critic, the results of which formed his *Ecrits sur la musique*.

He was fed on a diet of Beethoven, Berlioz and Gluck; he lived with them for long and sever years; it was through them that he first discovered himself with *La Symphonie en ut*, and the over famous *L'Apprenti sorcier* (1897). The literary taste and extra-musical sources of inspiration, th critical thought of Dukas, did not show a trace o the least interest in Symbolism. Goethe, Corneille Shakespeare, and Balzac were the poetic world to which he referred, and where on occasion he sought his inspiration and creative ideas: h planned a *Roi Lear* and a *Goetz von Berlichingen* an his first composition was an overture for *Polyeucte* Dukas loved to imitate these strong characters in his style of composition, and his music dis tinguishes itself by the force of its themes, th beating of its rhythms, and also a tone of strang melancholy, as if held back by modesty or a sens of understatement.

Nevertheless...would Symbolism not have been a temptation, and would Dukas not have tried t resist it? Take, to start with, the forms cultivate by his preferences — the overture, the symphoni poem, the opera and the 'dramatic scene' — the were those in which the force of Symbolism was strongest, even if, in this case it did not refe to the poets who were 'accursed' (Baudelaire Verlaine) or affected (Mallarmé). Moreover ther was, in the thread of Dukas' discourse, an accurat indication of a Symbolist way of thinking: even i the works of 'pure music', like *La Sonate pour pian* (1901), one finds an undeniable sense of contrasts of progress, always an ascending movement from darkness into light, which evidences how dear ha been the acquisition of logic and clarity. These ar values of reference, and not natural values! T put it better: vigorous brightness was only con structed in Dukas' work from a rejection of *gri aille*, of chiaroscura, which he found depressing.

Nothing shows this insidious but slightly Mani chean Symbolism better than the lyric vein of thi composer. *Ariane et Barbe Bleu* and *La Péri* cu through symphonic productions and chambe music. Dukas explained the new character, so clos to that of fashionable aesthetics, of his works: 'N one wants to be liberated, it is better to libera oneself. Ariane triumphs over the pity which he poor passive sisters (Bluebeard's wives) inspire i her and leaves them very calmly and very sadly a is befitting after a victory of that sort': thus th symbol of Ariane is that of the inanity of all effor to free those beings who are prisoners of love. I *La Péri*, a choreographic poem, the symbol is tha of the renunciation of man when he has accom plished his desire so that the desired woman ma go to her destiny: that of a semi-fairylike bein whose sole weapon is seduction and purity th ultimate aim. These two plays with extreme! Symbolist subjects have great charm and aston ishing richness. In listening to them, one ca measure to what extent Dukas had a reserved vei of Symbolism.

ELGAR Edward (Worcester 1857 — Worcester 1934). Of all the British turn-of-the-century composers, Sir Edward Elgar is perhaps the one who has most affinity with Symbolism. This was actually so because of the inner struggle he fought, like all Symbolist musicians, to find an originality away from the German Wagnerian influence. Thus Elgar developed along the same pattern as Debussy, to compare him with the greatest of the Symbolists. He was brought up at first by his father on the violin and the organ. But his upbringing was not very scholarly; he only took a few lessons from Pollitzer in London in

Portrait of Edward Elgar

1879. In 1885 he succeeded his father as choir master of St. George's Chapel where he stayed until he became in 1924 Master of the King's Music. Elgar singled himself out by his individualism: he did not adhere to the musical reforms of Stanford or Parry who tried to raise the standard of English music, nor to the nationalism of Vaughan Williams.

In 1896 this self-taught conductor, then composer, came to write an oratorio with a highly significant title, *The Light of Life*, and then a great cantata of Nordic inspiration, *King Olaf*. Amongst his works note should be taken of the *Enigma Variations* and the *Sea Pictures*: the reference, literary in the first case and pictorial in the second, indicates in some measure the very 'Debussyist' spirit of these compositions: like the Frenchman, Elgar also tried to achieve a new orchestral language. The influence of Richard Strauss has been mentioned, but this seems incorrect; or rather, if

one can reconcile extremes, Strauss, with Debussy, and Elgar after them, rejected the language of Wagner; these composers all had in common a concern for purity and refinement in music, a respect for sound values, and a feeling for a gradual lessening of colour; this was the basis of the Symbolism in their music.

In comparison with these, Elgar's other works do not really come into our perspective: neither the Cockaigne score, which illustrated the bustle of the London streets, nor *In the South*, are very close to Symbolism: on the contrary their modernism brings Elgar closer to Apollinaire in literture or Stravinsky in music. An astonishing Englishman who summed up all the trends, however attenuated, of contemporary art.

Perhaps it is *The Dream of Gerontius*, an oratorio of austere mysticism, which is basically the most historically Symbolist of Elgar's work. In fact, taking the term here in its most retrograde and disused sense, which was often, with some reason, his, one can deduce from the religiosity of the style, from the dullness of the libretto, from the calculated pallor of the whole, that it is a work which is very close to the spirit of Maurice Denis' paintings, or the poems of Rilke's *Stundenbuch*. Here Symbolism is no longer, as in Debussy's case, synonymous with new research, but on the contrary, with the *fin de siècle* decadentism. To give a further example: Gerontius has a vision: he is on his deathbed, mingling his prayers with the confession of his faults; his friends and a priest are beside him. His soul, comforted by the angel, rises towards the realm of the blessed, while in the distance can be heard the clamour of Hell. The sky opens and the soul goes to appear before the supreme Judge. Little did Elgar study the exceptional effects of the instrumentation, but the choral writing was powerful, bursting out when he described the demons, emotive when Gerontius appeals to the God of mercy. The first part is the more expressive. In the whole can be found, precisely on account of a certain lack of warmth, a resemblance to *Le Martyre de saint Sebastien* by Debussy-D'Annunzio.

FALLA Manuel de (Cadiz 1876 — Alta Gracia, Argentine 1946). In his musical traditions (zarzuela, tonadilla, cante flamenco, cante jondo), he seems to belong completely to Spain; however, his stay in Paris at the beginning of the twentieth century allowed him to familiarize himself with the musicians and the problems of Symbolism. It was Paul Dukas, with whom he revised the orchestration for *La Vida breve*, who put him in touch with the circle of innovators. Falla remained faithful to Debussy, Ravel, Schmitt and Dukas, whom he admired, all his life. His *Quatro Piezas españolas* (1908) and *Tres Melodias de Teofilo Gautier* (1909) were very indicative of the impression which this avant-garde milieu produced on him.

This influence contributed to the development of his new style, as was shown definitely in *Noches en los jardines de España*. In this work the harmonic,

Portrait of Manuel de Falla

melodic and orchestral language appeared more dependant on the general poetic idea than others of his pieces which were equally famous but very Andalusian, such as *El Amor brujo* and *El Sombrero de tres picos*. It is only with this work that Falla could be said to belong to the Symbolist movement. He did, however, illustrate wonderfully well many of the coincidences which existed between the different national schools and Symbolism.

FAURE Gabriel (Pamiers, Ariège 1845 — Paris 1924). 'Unless I am mistaken, the most important intellectual manifestation to follow the 1870 war was Naturalism, in literature as well as in the plastic arts; after which appeared (perhaps as a kind of reaction) a literary and artistic movement which music did not escape, and which seemed to have its principal source in Wagner's *Parsifal*, which it envisaged from a philosophic, dramatic and musical point of view: whence came the Rose + Cross, occultism, Pre-Raphaelitism, and all the things which one could put together under these two titles: asceticism and immobility...the fearful tempest through which we are passing will restore

J.S. SARGENT *Portrait of Gabriel Fauré*

us to ourselves by giving us back our common sense, that is to say a taste for clarity of thought, moderation and purity in form, sincerity, and a dislike of coarse effect!' (Interview in *Soleil du Midi* of April 30, 1915). This affirmation of Gabriel Fauré shows a clear understanding of the Symbolist phenomenon, but at the same time it looks as if he kept his distance from this movement. On the whole, Fauré was a Symbolist, but without the party spirit and without a systematic desire. In this he distinguished himself from Debussy, and even his pupil, Ravel. He was a baffling and unusual personality in his intractable simplicity; indifferent to doctrines, regulations, fashions, he let nothing turn him away from being first and foremost faithful to himself, without bothering about his neighbour's business. In doing this, he showed a harmonic genius which, although it never felt the difference between the pleasure of composition and the luxury of modulation, was nevertheless well inside the fundamental line of Symbolism: to experience the primordial respect for sound values. In this spirit Fauré is often compared with Schumann, and this seems reasonable: both of them showed an exceptional sense of poetry which appeared as much in the choice of the texts which they set to music as in the scores themselves, always on that delicate borderline where 'the imprecise is joined to the precise'. This is music which always remains, if one dare call it so 'musical' and never *musique à programme*, in spite of the fact that it rested upon the most beautiful poems; it was music which loved the forms of the Symbolist era (melody, opera, stage music poetry), above all it was incantatory music. Fauré's works can be classified in the following manner *Pièces* for piano, comprising five impromptus eleven barcarolles, eleven nocturnes, four waltz-caprices, nine preludes; *Le Thème et variation*; melodies for piano and voice (which have been analysed above): three *Recueils* of twenty melodies each; *La Bonne Chanson* (on verses by Verlaine), *La Chanson d'Eve* (on verses by Charles van Lerberghe); chamber music; two sonatas for violin and piano, *La Romance*, *La Berceuse*, also for piano and violin; two quartets for piano and strings, the quintet in D minor for piano and strings, *Elégie*, *Papillon*, *Sicilienne*, sonata for piano and cello; symphonic music: *Ballade* for piano and orchestra, *Allégro symphonique*, *Pelléas et Mélisande* (suite after Maeterlinck); dramatic music: stage music for *Caligula* (by Dumas), for *Shylock*, for *Le Voile du bonheur* (play by Clemenceau), *Prométhée*, lyric drama (libretto by Jean Lorrain), *Pénélope*, lyric poem, and finally *La Messe de Requiem*.

A composer of pure music, a poet musician, Fauré must have been impressed by exterior things, but he preferred to express feelings, emotions, and his music remains essentially subjective and delicate. It is in this respect that Fauré belongs to the Symbolist movement.

LEKEU Guillaume (Verviers 1870 — Angers 1894). He did not have enough time, in such a short life, to realize the whole programme of Symbolist music. He is usually shown as the disciple par excellence of César Franck, and thus Vincent d'Indy wrote in his book entitled *César Franck*: 'The principal disciples who had the good fortune to receive tuition directly from Franck were, in chronological order: H. Duparc, A. Coquard,...V. d'Indy, E. Chausson,...C. Bordes, Guy Ropartz, and finally the unfortunate Guillaume Lekeu, who died at twenty-four, leaving behind him a considerable wealth of compositions of a poignantly expressive intensity'. In actual fact Lekeu, who had started by studying music and composition almost on his own, who read Beethoven's quartets with assiduity, only had time for about twenty lessons with Franck! The generalized finesse of Lekeu's melodic study was sufficient to class him among all those artists who saw in Symbolism an ideal of purity and beauty. The influence of Franck in fact only anchored him more surely in the way which would have naturally been his own. It has never been stated, for example, to what extent Lekeu was an aesthete and a complete 'poet' who realized in his multiform creation the old dream of a total masterpiece. When he was nineteen years old, he composed a symphonic piece, *Le Chant de triomphale délivrance*, before he had received a single lesson. His cantata *Andromède*, which won him the Belgian Prix de Rome, perfectly expressed all the trends which composed decadentism. In 1892 he wrote *Trois Poèmes* on his own verses: *Sur une tombe*, *Ronde*,

and especially *Nocturne*, of which the title as well as the composition seemed like the most interesting work of Debussy. In 1893, with *L'Ombre plus dense*, he relapsed into the style of its title. Lekeu thus characterized himself by the richness of his gifts, by the virtuosity of his means, and by the depth of his resolution; the remarkable inflexions of his work appeared suspended, unfinished, even 'pointillist' (for example the phrasing of the cellos which announce Ravel in *Fantaisie*, and the use of the pentatonic scale). It was quite natural that an artist as gifted as he should be spontaneously welcomed by Mallarmé to the 'Tuesdays' in the Rue de Rome, by Gabriel Séailles, by Wyzewa (who valued highly his *Etude symphonique* of 1889). Guillaume Lekeu practised with equal success all the Symbolist genres: chamber music with a trio, in 1890, sonatas for piano and violincello, melody, the symphonic poem, and opera. He seemed to

Portrait of Guillaume Lekeu

blossom best in two works: *La Deuxième étude symphonique* (1890), and *La Sonate pour piano et violon* (1892).

The first movement of *L'Etude symphonique*, entitled *Hamlet*, had as inscription a quotation from Shakespeare's play: 'To die: to sleep; to sleep: perchance to dream...Thy commandment all alone shall live within the book and volume of my brain'. Franck saw the first part finished, and according to Lekeu, announced himself 'flabbergasted' by it. The second part, entitled *Ophélie*, started with a quotation from Goethe's second *Faust*: 'The eternal feminine draws us towards the heights'. The more Wagnerian — or Franckist — of these two movements is the first; one can perceive the most skilful and attractive echoes from *Parsifal* and *Psyche*. In the second, it is the unknown personal originality of Lekeu which manifests itself both in the melodic invention and in the harmony: the post-Wagnerian style is here lit up from within by a polyphony which had been heralded by Debussy.

Dedicated to Eugène Ysaye, who had suggested it to the composer, the *Sonate en sol*, for violin and piano (1892) is rather more of a rhapsody. Without doubt a certain moderation, a slightly stressed virtuosity, betray the style of a musician who was still rather young, but even so the exceptional richness of the melody and the impassioned emphasis recall this musician who was 'almost a genius'. The principal motif is a descending octave and a figure in triplets which opens the sonata. After multiple transformations the motif reappears in its original form at the end of the last movement. The cyclic form is very sharply perceptible. Composed only six years later than that of Franck, Guillaume Lekeu's *Sonate* allows us to be conscious of very new and very beautiful accents in music.

MAHLER Gustave (Kalischt, Moravia 1860 — Vienna 1911). Mahler was the exact contemporary of Debussy. Is that to say that he could be compared with the Frenchman in connection with Symbolism in music? It would seem not; an anecdote may serve to illustrate the contradiction of their conceptions. In April 1910, Mahler went to Paris to conduct, at le Châtelet, his second symphony. The success was great, but in the middle of the second movement Debussy, Dukas and Pierné got up and left the room, thus making a protest against 'Slav' music with overtones of Schubert. Debussy, the anti-dilettante, had certainly been irritated by the melodic naiveties of the second movement, the traditional methods of the development of the initial allegro, and the explosions of sentimentality as opposed to the allusive discretion of *Pelléas*. Indeed, if Symbolism was synonymous with discretion and understatement with regard to scales and sound values, then Mahler had nothing to do with this movement! But things are not so simple. Rimbaud and Mallarmé also, at first sight, seem completely different!

In fact Mahler, through all his extremely varied enterprises, shows, by his diverse studies, several objective convergences with the world of the Symbolists. At first he frequented the Symbolist milieu of the *Jung Wien*, which was receptive to Symbolism, thanks to Anna Mildenburg, his interpreter, who became the wife of the literary critic and essayist Hermann Bahr. Later on Mahler

collaborated lengthily, for his staging, with Alfred Roller, a decorator who was particularly clever with lighting effects and atmosphere. For example, for the performance of *Der Freischutz* on October 21, 1898, the scene in the Gorge of the Wolves was only effected by 'ghostly lighting', a very typical and very new process which was taken up later by the Expressionists.

A performance of *Das Rheingold* and one of *Don Giovanni* in the same year also used similar effects.

RODIN *Portrait of Gustav Mahler*

Mahler, who was a very cultured spirit, deeply imbued with the most modern literature, battled for a long time — and in vain — to include *Salome* in the repertoire of the Opera in Vienna. This shows that he was not unaware of the aesthetic values of Symbolism.

More curious still in a composer who remained faithful always to tonality were the harmonic 'equivocacies' which were the equivalent of modality: thus in the *Song of Sadness* (Das 'Klagende Lied') the extreme variety of the tonalities results in a feeling of uneasiness. *The Song of the Earth* ('Das Lied von der Erde'), which was almost his last work, uses, in its numerous repeats, the pentatonic scale and an exotic instrumentation which are the equal of similar processes found in the works of Debussy. Sometimes used for its pictorial value such as in *Of Youth* ('Von der Jugend') and *Of Beauty* ('Von der Schönheit'), sometimes, and in a particularly convincing fashion as in the last movement of *The Farewell* ('Abschied'), uniquely incantatory in its transparent instrumentation, this pentatonality shows an alliance between the composer and the values of the 'essential word'. Similar also to Mallarmé is the way in which the last words 'ewig...ewig' gradually fade away, and the work ends in mystery and silence.

The most remarkable characteristic of Mahler's symphonies is the mixture of the grotesque with the sentimental; the impression of surrealism is born from this juxtaposition of two feelings. It could be said to be as paradoxical a marriage as that which can be found in the most beautiful of Rimbaud's writings. *L'Alchimie du Verbe, Les Illuminations* thus bring together the most vulgar and the most delicate registers; these two extremes are paired forcibly in *Wunderhorn* and in the first and seventh symphonies. Mahler has been praised for his intense and attractive interpretation of nature: fantastic and familiar, bewitching and calming in the *Lieder aus der Jugendzeit*, is not interpretation very close to the forest and the dawn of Rimbaud?

Mahler was a composer who cannot be classified. Deprecated and flattered in turn by a variety of musicians, he remained entirely himself; it is only on a few points that his aesthetic values differ from those of Symbolism.

RAVEL Maurice

RAVEL Maurice (Ciboure, Basses-Pyrénées 1875 — Paris 1937). One first thinks of Ravel in relation to the Symbolist movement in the name of the influences which were exercised on him. In 1889 he was admitted to the Conservatoire; there he met Ricardo Vinès, who was the most prestigious interpreter of Symbolist piano music (Debussy, Chabrier, Satie and Ravel). In 1902 he received flattering approval from Debussy for his *Quator en fa*, but not from the jury of the Prix de Rome who considered it only second-class. In 1905, thanks to his friends the Godebskis, Ravel met some artists who, although from varied backgrounds, had one factor in common: they had all, at one time or another, and in one work or another, belonged to the Symbolist movement. They were Léon-Paul Fargue, Maurice Delage, Roland-Manuel, D.E. Ingelbrecht, Déodat de Séverac, Fall, Florent Schmitt, Cocteau, Valéry Larbaud, Diaghilev, Nijinsky and Stravinsky. After that, Ravel followed his own path, marked by works which were, most of the time, immediate successes: *Rhapsodie espagnole* (1908), which used modal melodies very cleverly and very suggestively; *Daphnis and Chloé* (1912), a ballet commissioned from Ravel by Diaghilev on a theme of Fokine; the Alexandrine subject alone would have merited Ravel a diploma of Symbolism: it makes one think of the religious and aesthetic syncretism of the poets, of the portraits of the 'child-woman'. Also, by the 'trompe l'œil' effect which he adopted at that time ('My intention in writing *Daphnis and Chloé* was to compose a vast

OUVRE *Portrait of Maurice Ravel*

musical fresco, with less concern for the archaic than *for the fidelity to the Greece of my dreams*, which is extremely like that which the French artists at the end of the eighteenth century imagined and painted'), Ravel placed himself in the aestheticism of suggestion and imprecision and not in that of archaeological realism; he had the same attitude towards the Ancient world as Mallarmé and D'Annunzio. 1913 saw the birth of the *Trois poèmes de Stéphane Mallarmé*, and 1915 that of the *Trois Chansons* for mixed choir on poems by Ravel; here is *Ronde*, of which one can appreciate the spirit: 'Do not go into the wood, young girls, do not go into the wood. It is full of satyrs, of centaurs, of wicked magicians, of hobgoblins, of nightmares, of ogres, of sprites, of fauns, of will-o'-the-wisps, of lamias, devils, little devils, imps, gnomes, of demons, of werewolves, of elves, of myrmidons, of enchanters, of magi, of vampires, of sylphs and of churlish monks, of cyclops, of djinns, of leprechauns, necromancers and kobolds...Ah!' Is this not a clever imitation of the poetry of Verlaine or Maeterlinck? 1917 saw *Le Tombeau de Couperin*; 1920, *La Valse*; 1925 the creation of *L'Enfant et les sortilèges*; 1929-31, the composition of the two concertos; 1932, *Don Quichotte à Dulcinée* (texts by Paul Morand): and 1937 the death of Ravel.

Only certain works show the Symbolist vein in Ravel's art. In a more general fashion it could be said that the influence of Chabrier and Debussy on his piano, of Liszt on his orchestral work, and finally a taste for the picturesque and the suggestive which he shared with the Russians (e.g. the *Schéhérazade* by Ravel on Rimsky-Korsakov's model) denoted the impact of Symbolism on Ravel. More than the company he kept, or the importance of certain meetings (that with Satie for example, who was a friend of the great decadent Sâr Péladan, around 1911 in the Chat Noir), the mark of it shows in his musical writing: subtle sounds, partially suggested by his use of modality, an exaggerated baroquism, similar to that of Mallarmé, in his expression (a constantly 'appoggiatura' style, with passing notes, the basses a little too strained, both hands singing at intervals of many octaves) and older methods; Ravel always had an excellent sense of style, and a rigour which was almost the magic formula of pure poetry. It has often been called 'cerebral' art, and in this case it is that of Valéry to which Ravel is the closest; basically this is not a bad description: they both shared in a neo-Symbolism which blossomed during the Great War or very close to it: *La Jeune parque* is very like *Daphnis et Chloé*.

SATIE Erik (Honfleur 1866 — Paris 1925). Did this composer, considered a humorist, and certainly an iconoclast, have any links with Symbolism? His initial Wagnerism which was soon abandoned, his stylization, and the stripped style of his later compositions, place this musician rather in the camp of Stravinsky or Schönberg, and the great revolutionaries of the twentieth century. But on closer inspection things are not as

J. Cocteau *Portrait of Erik Satie*

simple as they seem. If, in order to understand Satie better, his work is broken down into periods, the first would be that of mysticism and Symbolist influences. This was the period when Satie was 'sponging' off the Chat Noir, and when he made

the acquaintance of Sâr Péladan, and it was also the time of the composition of *Ogives* and *Danses Gothiques*; does this not point towards decadentism? 'May the righteous indignation of the gods crush both the arrogant and the indecent' was the final point of the 'Dedication' which he inscribed at the top of his 'Wagnérie Kaldéenne' and which indicated his state of mind at that time.

His music during those years gives a better understanding of the impact which Symbolism had on Satie. The three *Préludes du Fils des étoiles* (1891), the three *Sonneries de la Rose + Croix* (1892) and the *Prélude de la Porte Héroïque du ciel* are the most meaningful examples. In this latter piece a succession of static sounds, treated by hollow chords in the manner of a rudimentary plainsong, provide the habitual character of Satie's avowal, according to the basis of Puvis de Chavannes' distances which he painted in attenuated colours and vaguely defined lines. This was music whose only ambition was to be decorative, and it can thus be called 'hermaphrodite' in the same way as one sees those strange and dual creations in the paintings of the era. *Le Saint Sébastien* of Debussy-D'Annunzio reflects, in places, the same singular poetry, and an identically mystical ethereality. From 1897 to 1915 the series of humorous pieces, which were soon remembered only for their unusual and provocative presentation, appeared at regular intervals. In fact Satie's sense of sound values and his desire for refinement on both the level of inspiration and of writing make him a stylist who was imprinted with Symbolism: should one read *La Manière de commencement* (borrowed from a gnostic) which is linked to all the nostalgia of the East by a persuasive exoticism, and later *La Prolongation* in which there is a caressing trio inspired by the 'sonoriel' principles of Debussy; should one entertain oneself by evoking the delicate melodic contours of *L'En plus*, or the tender modesty suggested in the brief *Redite*, then one can understand the validity of this discourse. Satie, in his compositions, because of his concern with linear accuracy and his disdain for colour, is absolutely related to Maurice Denis or Gide. There is a renounced Symbolism in the works of Satie; this can be understood in the examination of his next works, from 1911 to 1915: *Préludes flasques*, *Embryons déséchés* and others, which have all too often been considered apart from Satie's development, and which, for this reason, mask what was perhaps the true inclination of the composer. Nevertheless, in the twenty sketches published in 1914 under the title *Sports et Divertissements*, a certain number of open-air recreations offer the equivalent of the 'Haïs-Kaïs' in music, which have all the 'Mallarmian' conciseness of the Japanese poem, and the value of a couplet in sound in which is inscribed, with the line of an engraving-tool, the pictorial and precious synthesis of a feeling or a journey. Dare one say, in testimony of that, that Satie had nothing to do with Symbolism? Assuredly the proclamations of Satie himself, especially those of his latter period when he claimed to compose only 'wallpaper music' have too often been abused by us; it is essential to discover, in him, the hidden vein, the climate of the period, in order to understand to what extent Satie really comes into this discussion.

SCHMITT Florent (Blamont, Meurthe-et-Moselle 1870 — Neuilly-sur-Seine 1958). A thread of Symbolism ran right through the life of Florent

Portrait of Florent Schmitt

Schmitt: in 1900 he was awarded the Grand Prix de Rome for a cantato of which the name alone spoke the aesthetics: *Sémiramis*. He always had a fondness — in his music! — for *femmes fatales*, and it is in fact his most *fin de siècle* characteristic: in the theatre, he evoked the magnificence and splendour of Eastern refinement in his *Tragédie de Salomé* (1907), a 'silent drama', the martial powers of Rome in *Antoine et Cléopatre*, a much later work (1920), which proved, by the way, the strength and duration of Symbolist trends in music. In the same perspective, he wrote a musical score for a film taken from *Salammbô*.

Le Chant Elégiaque for cello, the *Quintette*, the *Psaume XLVII*, all date from the time the composer spent at the Villa Medici. The latter work is perhaps, in the field of religious music, one of the masterpieces of Symbolism. It was given a first hearing on December 27, 1906; Léon-Paul Fargue cried out: 'A crater of music is opening!...Florent

Schmitt had the time to open the door, and to enclose his psalm with a thunderous noise'. Time confirmed this prediction, and it is possible to affirm that the *Psaume* was, in the new musical order of those years at the beginning of the century, and for the form of oratorio, the same as that which *Pelléas* had represented in the lyric genre sometime previously: music which was vibrant and sparkling, sometimes brutal, it is true, sometimes gentle, but always full of new emphasis, rich with leaps of enthusiasm that the composer had constructed on a Biblical text whose grandeur was equalled by its moderation. Schmitt was a colourist, but one preoccupied with the brilliance of his discourse, and it is without doubt in this that he comes close to the Symbolist poets, those virtuosos of language. Whether he was writing for the brass and the woodwinds (*Sélamik*, *Les Dionysiaques*), for the orchestra (*Le Palais hanté*, *Mirages*, *J'entends dans le lointain*, *Danse d'Abisag*), for the piano (*Reflets d'Allemagne*) or for arrangements of chamber music, the composer always showed great virtuosity and an interpretation of sound values which could similarly be noted in Debussy.

In Florent Schmitt there was, more than the expression of his time, more than a particularly gifted pupil, a conviction of the correctness of the aesthetics at the end of the century.

Portrait of Alexander Scriabin

SCRIABIN Alexander (Moscow 1972 — Moscow 1915). Scriabin is a composer of transition: whilst belonging to Symbolism through his philosophy of art, his harmonic language, his use of Symbolist forms such as the poem and the prelude, he accomplished all the virtuosity of Symbolism and turned it round towards modernity. Thus Scriabin, like Debussy and even more like Schönberg made Symbolism blossom by underlining its most revolutionary aspects.

Particularly memorable of Scriabin's works are a *Rêverie* for piano of 1898, two symphonies composed in 1900 and 1902, some symphonic poems: *Le Divin Poème* (1904), *Le Poème de l'extase* (1906-08), *Prométhée* of 1911, and above all the fantastic sonatas for piano (seven in all, appearing between 1906 and 1911).

After his early efforts under the influence of Chopin, Berlioz, and to a certain extent Wagner (whom he discovered in Moscow in the circle which had formed around Belaieff, a patron of the arts), Scriabin can be seen through his two symphonies and his fourth sonata progressively complicating his writing: he studied the combinations of strange notes prohibited by classical harmony. In the *Poème de l'extase* the system was practically discovered, although not yet explicitly formulated as was the case in *Prométhée*. Before Schönberg, Scriabin had the feeling that the atonal and incantatory harmony of which he dreamed should rest on tiers of fourths. Thus he constructed groups of six or seven notes, arranged in fourths, which corresponded to the modal scales of the same number of sounds of which they thus made all the notes heard. From this came the title of 'synthetic chords' which he proposed for these combinations.

To all this were added the mystic and idealist ideas of Scriabin: his art relied on the desire to study ecstasy and contemplation in his art. To this end he dreamed up a kind of new form of the masterpiece: it would be a 'mystery' in which music, poetry, mime, dancing, the play of colours, and scents would be united under a dome with a view to forming an aesthetico-religious celebration. It is easy to see in this the echo of the ideas of Wagner, or more exactly of that exaggerated Wagnerism which became the aesthetics of Symbolism. For example, Scriabin foresaw the idea of using a luminous keyboard in his orchestra which would project on to a screen colours changing according to the harmonic and instrumental changes. In this way he enrolled himself as an authentic member of the Symbolist line, which to him was truly 'scents, colours and sounds which corresponded to each other'.

STRAUSS Richard (Munich 1864 — Garmisch 1949). During the length of his tremendous career, Strauss found himself confronted with all sorts of aesthetics, and many musical revolutions; he was a contemporary of Brahms as well as Stockhausen who started at the time when Berlioz was writing his *Mémoires* and finished during the

years when concrete music was taking its first steps. Did Strauss have connections with Symbolism?

To start with, it should be noted that his native town, Munich, had been one of the birthplaces of German Symbolism, in the shape of the group which formed around Stefan George. In Berlin, Strauss made the acquaintance of the 'Verlainian', Impressionist trend of literary Symbolism: Karl Henckell, Richard Dahmel, Detlev von Liliencron, Otto-Julius Bierbaum provided the texts for the

Portrait of Richard Strauss

essential parts of the sixty Lieder which appeared between 1894 and about 1900. Finally, Strauss' collaboration with Hofmannsthal in Vienna was also fairly significant: the poet's neurotic Elektra could be added to the number of heroines who had been inspired by the psychology of decadentism. Thus it can be seen that Strauss, by his tastes and the company he kept, had access to most of the trends which composed the nebulous Symbolism.

What about his music? It has also been asked to what extent *Salomé's* characteristics make it one of the masterpieces of Symbolist music. Independently of this opera, it is noticeable that Strauss' language, taken from the purely technical angle, reveals nothing: there is no harmony or counterpoint which is peculiar to him, nor is there a period in which Strauss could be defined as closest to the language of Symbolist music as it was defined in the introduction. Or rather: Strauss touched Symbolism at certain irregular moments, and in certain of his works (for example the

chard Strauss conducting with Astruc the first performance of *Salomé*

eider, opus 67 to 69, of 1919), and through one
f his favourite musical forms, the symphonic
oem. It is useless to try to find, in the works of
is composer, a revolutionary style of writing
ch as Debussy's. He was capable of writing mo-
al or polytonal music (the fourth Lied of the
rämerspiegel, of 1918, or the quintet of the Jews in
lomé), but he never became involved either for or
gainst any particular aesthetic or any particular
riod. Strauss remained himself before anything
se. It could rather be said that Strauss is defined,
nong others, in relation to Symbolism, but
ither more nor less than in relation to Schön-
rg, Stravinsky, Debussy or Wagner. In what
ays? In the first place by his reflections on opera
d his calling into question the traditional form
acts and scenes; noticeable is his preference for
e shorter forms, for operas all in one piece with
single thread: *Feuersnot, Salomé, Elektra, Ariane,*
termezzo, Friedenstag, Daphne and *Capriccio* which
re accompanied at the same time by a doubt on
e durable possibilities of writing another opera
riane, Capriccio). Was it not a similar step which
spired Mallarmé's limited experiment in *Un Coup*
dés as well as the silence and then the pure poetic

technicality of Valéry? Later he made some curious attempts to resurrect old melodrama with
works such as *Enoch Arden* (1897) and *Das Schloss am*
Meere (1898): these efforts revealed in Strauss a
preoccupation with the powers and the limits
respectively of speech and music, of words and
sound. The same thing can be found in Schönberg's experiments such as *Sprechgesang* and in
Mallarmé's distinction between 'verbal speech' and
'essential speech'. It was a characteristic of the
period; so it is not surprising that the ideas of
'pure music' (in the Viennese school) or 'pure
poetry' (the abbot Bremond's circle) should be its
logical and chronological result. Finally Strauss
realized a double move with the liquidation of the
symphonic orchestra and the establishment of
chamber orchestration: this was a final parallel
equally applicable to the trajectory of Debussy or
of Verlaine; the return to a certain discretion, and
even to hermetism as opposed to the sonorous
rhetoric of Romanticism is one of the most lasting
and incontestable fruits of Symbolist aesthetics.

In short, Strauss was too great to belong to any
one school. Nevertheless, the spirit of the time
explains certain aspects of his works.

The Symbolist period

Can one speak of a Symbolist period? This view has often been contested by the French who have always been in favour of the idea of Symbolism as an essentially literary and French movement. Looked at in this perspective, it obviously did not last long enough to become an epoch. But instead of being limited to the years 1885-95, a period of diffusion for the French Symbolist poets, should it not encompass, from an international point of view, the whole *fin de siècle*, and even go as far as 1910 in eastern Europe? More and more do the critics who study, beyond merely aesthetic doctrines, the phenomena of civilization, the customs and foundations of society, include Symbolism in a movement of reactionary idealism which started from the heritage of Baudelaire, spread widely around 1880 with the rejection of Naturalism, and ended with the triumph of art nouveau.

This was a time, therefore, of change in custom, taste and fashion which affected all the European countries. Victor-Emile Michelet, recalling this development in 1933, did not hesitate to credit the young people of his generation with the same aspirations, in spite of the shades of difference between them: 'There was at that time an extensive and violent revolt against a sordidly materialistic knowledge, against a decaying literature and art, against despotic plutocracy. Some threw themselves into the study of forgotten secret sciences: one can label them, rather crudely, as the occultists. Others could see from afar — maybe too far — how the symbolic world exists: they were called the Symbolists. Others praised individual development: they were the anarchists. They all understood one another. They were all united against official teachings.'

A need for the spiritual

1885 to 1900 was a period rich in research, in trials in experiments of every kind. This was the dominant characteristic of the Symbolist era. 'Never more reasoning, never more study, never more boldness' wrote Valéry.

This search for novelty at any price stemmed from the discontent of the young intellectuals with a world which they felt to be dominated by the most vulgar realities. A sign of the power of this materialism was the establishment of the reign of the machine. While the bicycle, the railway and the car were all evolving, writers and artists were singing their nostalgia for the Unreal, the Ideal, the Spiritual.

In Paris, around Zola and his followers, Naturalism was still holding sway over the novel while in painting, with Puvis de Chavannes, Fantin-Latour and Carrière, it was already being run down. Later it can be seen that the pictures by these artists, along with the infatuation with the works of Wagner, were only the precursory signs of a metaphysical and mystical rebirth. Starting with the English Pre-Raphaelites, this escape from the reality of contemporary society, sometimes seen as the last convulsions of Romanticism, spread rapidly outwards to overwhelm Europe before reaching America and Japan.

This result was no more than a reasonable turn of events, for in France itself there were numerous foreign influences intermingling in the melting-pot of Symbolism. It has rightly been said that in comparison with the wave of nationalism which broke out in 1905, the French Symbolists were cosmopolitan spirits. It was not unusual to find amongst them or their circle writers of foreign origin (Stuart Merrill, Edward Rod, Francis Viélé-Griffin, Teodor de Wyzewa); they helped to give the French public some knowledge of authors who had hitherto remained practically unknown, such as the Russians and the Scandinavians.

On this subject, Gustave Kahn gives us an idea of what the reading matter and artistic preferences of his Symbolist friends might have been: 'They know Goethe, Heine, Hoffmann and other German writers. They have been strongly influenced by Poe, they know the mystic writers and the primitive painters, they have some knowledge of Walter Crane, Burne-Jones and other Pre-Raphaelites, painters as well as poets. They have found in French Romanticism some notable exceptions to the influence of Victor Hugo; they have become, because of the era in which they live, totally involved in the legendary and symbolic music of Wagner which has completely preoccupied them whether they have understood it or not. It is this gathering of influences which has generated the present movement, and this collection of earlier works which makes up the ideal library'.

A precursor: Edgar Allan Poe

Gustave Kahn insists most particularly on the influence of Edgar Allan Poe. In fact, this American author was partially responsible for the atmosphere of Symbolism, quite apart from a style of feminine clothing which emanated from the paintings of Burne-Jones. Translated by Baudelaire, by Mallarmé, by Emile Hennequin, a friend of Huysmans and Redon, nearly all Poe's works have been published in France since 1880. Not only was he the source of the revival of tales of fantasy, but his aesthetic theories have also been abundantly discussed. Did not Mallarmé go as far as claiming that he had learnt English in order to be better able to grasp the finer details of his talent and thought? At the age of twenty-two he swore by Edgar Allan Poe alone, and thought of the pages on *The Philosophy of Composition* as his bible.

Edgar Allan Poe, thanks principally to Baudelaire, was thus known and esteemed in Europe before his own country, which for some time refused to acknowledge his importance. The Symbolists took from him the rigorous spirit which dissected poetic invention (Mallarmé, later Valéry), while the decadents retained from his work the morbid, the macabre, the invitation to dream, and the pathological phenomena which they so adored. In 1928 Maeterlinck confessed: 'Edgar Allan Poe has exercised over me, together with the rest of my generation, a great, lasting and profound influence. I owe to him the birth in myself of a sense of mystery, and a passionate interest in the life beyond'.

But no one has explained better than Valéry this enthusiasm which the Symbolists felt for Edgar Allan Poe. Having insisted on the genius of 'this prodigious inventor' from whom came the novel of suspense and the detective story of today, he pointed out what it was that had attracted Baudelaire and, later, the Symbolist poets: a doctrine in which were strictly united 'a form of mathematics and a sort of mysticism'. In the wake of Poe the Symbolists started out on the path of 'absolute poetry', that is to say a language which was freed from all didactic, discursive or anecdotal elements for which prose, and not poetry, appeared to them to be the more appropriate vehicle.

Between 1880 and 1900, poets and painters alike drew from the *Tales of Fantasy* a whole imaginary world, a mystique, an awareness. And in 1882, Odilon Redon dedicated a series of lithographs to Edgar Allan Poe, as proof of his admiration for him.

An art for an intellectual élite

It is true that these new ideas pervaded mainly the circles restricted to the nonconformists, the aesthetes, the intellectual snobs, and not the wide public. The Symbolists voluntarily looked for the approval of an intellectual élite alone; they scorned the masses. In their eyes a work lost its entire artistic value as soon as it received popular acclaim. To enjoy Art was not compatible with plebeian enthusiasm: Art was above everything; it was sacred. Its experts must commune inside it as inside a religious sect.

Nevertheless, certain critics set themselves to supporting the art of the Symbolists and to publicising their studies, from Aurier, who wrote in the *Mercure de France*, to Georges Vanor who, in 1889 dedicated his first book to *The Symbolist Art*. Although there existed relatively few galleries in which the Symbolist paintings could be regularly shown, they were still well represented at the great Parisian art exhibitions.

It must be said that since 1870, thanks to the efforts of the Impressionists, the public exhibition of art and the sale of pictures had undergone a transformation. The rise of Symbolism exactly coincided with the growth of a rich and worldly clientele. This milieu of well-to-do aesthetes loved to visit the artists and exercise their patronage.

Apart from this, the official Salon was no longer the only setting in Paris for the sanction of painters. The Society of French Artists, which controlled it, had been the subject of a split in 1884, and this gave birth to a rival organization, the National Society of Fine Arts. This association, which numbered among its influential founders Puvis de Chavannes, Rodin and Carrière, always welcomed the Symbolists in its annual salons.

The Symbolist painters had, in addition, at their disposal, a privileged place in which to exhibit their works: the Rose + Croix Salons. These had been created by Joséphin Péladan, and took place between 1892 and 1897. All those in search of the Ideal had the possibility of showing their paintings there. The only restriction concerned portraits: the only portrait allowed had to be that of Joséphin Péladan himself. Having awarded himself the title of *Sâr*, that is to say of a Chaldean magus, this singular personage with the majestic beard, clothed in a doublet ornamented with lace, officiated at the fate of Art in the vapours of incense. 'Our Aim', he proclaimed, 'is to pull love out of the western soul, and to replace it with love of Beauty, love of the Idea, love of Mystery.'

The extravagances of the Sâr Péladan were profitable, since they attracted both artists and public. Today these are forgotten, while with the passing of time the Rose + Croix Salons have become the important events. In 1892, the French discovered Hodler, Toorop and Khnopff there. They gave numerous young people the chance to become known; amongst these were Rouault and Bourdelle, who rose fairly quickly to fame. Not only France had the privilege of being at the heart of the Symbolist activity. Belgium, the native land of Charles van Lerberghe, Maurice Maeterlinck, Emile Verhaeren, James Ensor, Félicien Rops and Fernand Khnopff, has often been considered the actual breeding-ground of Symbolism.

Started in Liège in 1886 by the poet Albert Mockel, the review *La Wallonie* was the hyphen between Belgium and France. It published Maeterlinck, Elskamp and Verhaeran as well as Verlaine and Mallarmé. In Brussels, the new trends crystallized around Octave Maus and his review, *L'Art moderne*. In October 1883 the Groupe des XX was born, with Ensor, van Rysselberghe and Khnopff. They were later joined by Félicien Rops, the Dutchman Toorop, and the Frenchmen Rodin and Signac. By organizing meetings and exhibitions, Octave Maus made Brussels into a centre of artistic renown. Although sometimes accompanied by scandals, the private views of the Groupe des XX brought together the best of the European artists, and all the 'snobs' met each other there.

Symbolism and Art Nouveau

In studying the period between 1880 and 1900, it is striking to note, through the history of the Groupe des XX, the way in which the so-called Symbolist trends mingled with what came to be called Art Nouveau. This phenomenon became even more noticeable with the birth of the society of the Libre Esthétique, which succeeded the Groupe des XX in 1893. Octave Maus was encouraging here, in effect, the industries of art: glasswork, ceramics, tapestry, furnishing. Henry van der Velde, who exhibited as a painter with the Groupe in 1889, showed Art Nouveau style furniture in the salon of the Libre Esthétique in 1896. Towards the end of Leopold II's reign Brussels had become, thanks to this society, the capital of Art Nouveau in Europe.

Symbolism and Art Nouveau did in fact experience a parallel development. The opening of Samuel Bing's gallery in Paris, at the sign of the Art Nouveau, took place in 1896. Gallé's first glassworks were created in Nancy in 1883, Gaudi undertook the construction of the *Sagrada Familia* (Church of the Holy Family) in 1885, and Walter Crane founded the *Arts and Crafts Society* in 1886. To use an expression of Bernard Champigneulle which seems altogether appropriate, there was at that time a kind of brotherhood between the Symbolist poets and the Art Nouveau painters: 'If it was not born of Symbolism, Art Nouveau was in accordance with it, and it was not at all surprising that its music had been sung among the hangings where climbed the vine, the crystal shimmering like water, and the convolvulus-shaped candelabra.'

There was actually one theme which obsessed the imagination of the era, and which appeared as much in the works of the writers and Symbolist painters as in those of the Art Nouveau protagonists: this was the theme of the vegetable. Through this theme was manifested the anti-Naturalist reaction of the years 1880 to 1900. It passed from the typically Symbolist anthropomorphism of Odilon Redon where, for example, a flower would take human form, to a vegetation which was imprinted with decadent sensuality in the works of Ferdinand Hodler, and then to the plants which proliferated in the decorative elements of Art Nouveau.

The profusion of leaves and flowers in Beardsley's illustrations, Mucha's posters and Gaudi's architecture was characteristic of a subjective ornamentation which deliberately seemed to want to compete with Nature. The principal from which it arose was idealism, a principle which was often expressed by the Symbolists and the decadents: 'The universe', as Teodor de Wyzewa wrote in 1887, 'is the work of our souls'.

Throughout the last years of the century, there was, therefore, a combined celebration of the artificial. In Symbolism as well as in Art Nouveau, the object represented was denaturalized. The multiplication of the details in the Symbolist paintings and the proliferation of the decorative elements in Art Nouveau, resulted in the same effect of strangeness and unreality.

A reform in the theatre

All too often, when talking about the Symbolist movement, one whole field is left on one side: that of theatre production and, more generally, of the art of show-business. The anti-Naturalism which has been mentioned was as manifest here as in poetry or painting. It was even, with Paul Fort and Lugné-Poe, the origin of modern theatre production in Europe.

To understand what took place, it is necessary to go back to the trends which were uppermost in the theatre at the end of the nineteenth century. On one hand there was a commercial, bourgeois theatre which still obeyed the most outworn conventions. On the other, attempts were being made at scenic renovation through the theories of Naturalism. It was in opposition to this double inclination, which it finally reduced to one only, that idealism outlined its reaction.

André Antoine was, at that time, the representative of Naturalism in the theatre. In March 1887, he found the Théâtre Libre in Paris. Following his example, a movement for liberation of the stage reached Germany with Otto Brahm, Russia with Constantin Stanislavski, as well as England and the Scandinavian countries. The free theatres or their equivalents were starting to open everywhere.

Taking into account those theatrical activities which were purely entertainment, Antoine and his followers were in favour of a transformation of scenic effects. For them, theatre signified exigencies of ethics. Nevertheless, the conceptions of the Naturalists led not only to giving the theatre a certain privileged social content, and thus more or less smothering the dream and the imagination, but equally to trying to reconstitute a 'milieu' in its authenticity. The stage became, through objects, accessories, lighting, and backgrounds no more than a copy of the real.

Between 1890 and 1910, these Naturalist performances were not enough for the young intellectuals. The pupils broke the links with their former masters: Lugné-Poe broke with Antoine in France, Meyerhold with Stanislavski in Russia, and Reinhardt with Brahm in Germany. The whole of Europe was teaching the process of Naturalism. Two men of the theatre became the theorists, albeit quite differently, and the spokesmen of the dispute: the Swiss Appia and the Englishman Craig. They wanted to restore imagination to its proper level. Instead of trying to dissimulate, in order to realize them, the conventions on which all art rests, they thought that these must be affirmed and emphasised even more, so that they might become, for the spectator, a springboard towards the Dream. They entreated a communion in the Ideal against the domination of the material world.

A different repertory

This current of opposition to Naturalism was directly linked to Symbolism. The idealist rebellion which, among Mallarmé's following, had principally penetrated poetry, also touched dramatic repertory. *Les Flaireurs*, by the Belgian Charles van Lerberghe appeared in 1889; *Axël*, the Wagnerian drama of Villiers de l'Isle-Adam dated from 1890, as did *La Princesse Maleine* and *Les Aveugles* by Maeterlinck. The first version of *La Dame à la faulx* by Saint-Pol Roux was published in 1895, and the complete cycle of Edouard Dujardin's *La Légende d'Antonia* in 1893. *Tête d'Or* and *La Ville* by Paul Claudel dated 1890 and 1910 respectively, should also be mentioned in spite of their weaker pulling power. Between 1890 and 1910, the whole repertory of European theatre started out on the path of Symbolism: Yeats in Ireland, D'Annunzio in Italy, Briussov and Remizov in Russia, and Hofmannsthal in Austria.

For and against Wagner

The Symbolists were in at the beginning of this infatuation with Wagner's art, this fashion which came to be called Wagnerism; one of them, Edouard Dujardin, even founded in February 1885 *La Revue wagnérienne*, which appeared for three years. It remains to be seen, in this contact with music, how much benefit Symbolist theatre drew from Wagnerian drama, and especially from its essential element: the synthesis of the arts.

Baudelaire discovered Wagner in 1861, which was before the beginning of the Symbolist movement, and, for him, this artistic synthesis meant the union of poetry and music, each one of them lacking effectiveness without the support of the other. This was also the interpretation of Edouard Schuré in 1875 in his *Drame musical*, which simply added dancing to the other two arts; this was an indispensable complement to finding again the unity of the three muses of Greek antiquity.

What could Mallarmé and his disciples, the orthodox Symbolists, have thought? Although the fascination with Wagner's operas was general, unanimity was far from existing in regard to the fusion of the arts. Some, such as Teodor de Wyzewa, deplored the omission of painting. Others, like Rémy de Gourmont, reproached Wagner for outwardly assembling different aesthetic means by adding them together, when it would have been preferable to have envisaged this assemblage at the start as a true union on the stage of creation itself. Charles Morice, for his part, established a hierarchy between the different disciplines, in which he accorded poetry supremacy over music. This was an opinion which was faithful to the thinking of Mallarmé, since, in 1885 in a *Rêverie sur Wagner*, he·had referred to 'the gathering of different arts sealed by poetry'.

This text of Mallarmé, used again in *Divagations* having initially been published in Dujardin's *La Revue wagnérienne*, was very much more than an appraisal of position towards the synthesis of arts. It also brought an explanation to the Symbolist dramatic theories. In Wagnerian drama,

Mallarmé was attracted by the idea of a theatre which became a place of worship. Besides, he was fascinated by the dance — this was a fascination which he felt again in 1893 when he saw the almost disembodied choreography of the American, Loïs Fuller. His homage to the magician of Bayreuth, however, stopped there. He considered that the feast of scenery distracted the attention of the spectator, and that the presence of actors hindered the poetic word from exercising to the full its magical power.

A simpler décor

From these few restrictions suggested by Mallarmé came precise guidelines: décor should be stripped so that it should not be a hindrance to the dream; less room should be given to the actor, who should become more of a narrator — the ideal being to arrive at a monologue in which speech would take the place of the cumbersome apparatus of traditional theatre. As a remark of Lucien Muhlfeld, in *La Revue d'art dramatique* of May 1891, shows, these conceptions became widespread: 'He blames the theatre', he wrote of Mallarmé, 'for lacking artistic concern, and for hindering, by too much precision in the characters and too much reality in the staging, those dream flights into the beyond which are so necessary to aesthetic joy.'

When Paul Fort, in November 1890, founded the Théâtre d'Art in Paris, he shared the opinion of Mallarmé. He was convinced that 'the word is the theatre' and that 'scenery does not exist'. His staging of a play by Pierre Quillard in 1891, *La Fille aux mains coupées*, demonstrated the importance of the new theories: against a painted background, signed by Paul Sérusier, which represented figures from icons and ingenuous angels in prayer in the tradition of the primitive painters of the Cologne school, the characters spoke in verse with a slow solemnity from behind a gauze veil, while a narrator, in a corner of the foreground, pronounced the prose passages which specified the action, the behaviour of the characters and the changes of setting.

The argument about staging was: 'We depend on speech to evoke the scenery and to make it materialize in the mind of the spectator, relying on obtaining, by the charm of the word, an entire illusion into which no inappropriate contingency can come to mar the abstraction.'

Décor in the theatre, therefore, was to be practically suppressed, schematically sketched in order to suggest. It was the first revolution that the Symbolists had brought to staging. Pierre Quillard himself, attacking Antoine and his handling of scrupulously exact scenery, with real fountains and real quarters of beef which bled, commanded that all elements foreign to the human voice should be, as far as possible, banished. 'Décor must be pure ornamental fiction which completes the illusion through analogies of colour and line with the drama. Usually a background and a few draperies will be enough to give the impression of an endless multiplicity of time and place. The spectator will not be distracted from the action by a noise in the wings, or by an inappropriate property; he will abandon himself completely to the will of the poet and will see, according to his mind, terrible or delightful figures and countries of illusion where none but he can go; the theatre will be what it must be — a pretext for the dream.'

The staging of Maeterlinck's play, *Pelléas et Mélisande*, in 1893, was directed by Lugné-Poe and put together according to these rules. The furnishing and props were suppressed because they were not necessary to the action. All the nuances of scenic arrangement were calculated to accord with the general atmosphere. The actors were costumed in relation to the whole, so that they harmonized with each other as in a musical composition. The backcloth represented a forest with a very sombre park, on which alternated the play of luminous clusters of different colours, according to the development of the play.

The review *Dix-Neuvième siècle*, in its number dated May 17, 1893, reported the result: 'The costumes themselves were assorted to fit this dream setting and these visionary characters. They were made of material in dead colours and modelled on those of characters of ancient legend. Mélisande, who represented radiant youth, cruel in its rapid forgetfulness, amused at the harm which she unknowingly effects, was the only one dressed in white. The other characters were clothed in material of faded colours. In the scene of the third act where

Golaud kills Pelléas, all the costumes and scenery are dark and attenuated to make the clear and hard note of the shining sword stand out better.'

The Symbolists' ideas on staging heralded a movement of general reform which broke out in Europe at the beginning of the century. Its representatives were Appia in Switzerland, Gordon Craig and Granville Barker in England, Meyerhold in Russia, Max Reinhardt in Austria and Germany, and Adria Gual in Spain. They were all different, but a common ideal inspired them. This was the ideal which gave birth to Symbolism — anti-Naturalism. Their desire for reform, so like that of Jacques Copeau when he founded the Vieux-Colombier in 1913, fed on the ideas which had obsessed the Symbolist milieus.

Gaston Baty and René Chavance, in a work on *La Vie de l'art théâtrical*, did not hesitate to write in 1932 that all modern staging has come from Symbolism: 'They restored this truth of pictorial order where the tones of the costumes had to agree with those of the scenery, a truth disregarded for some time, but, nevertheless, obvious. From an especially scenic angle, they had realized that it was sufficient to establish surroundings by broad indications in place of multiplying the details and the ornamental skills; they had discerned the part which could be played by a simplified décor, a harmonious colouring where a well-thought out amount created atmosphere in the suggestion of the spectacle.'

Symbolism was very much more a state of mind than the coherent system to which the writers, painters and men of the theatre referred. Of what did it consist? Essentially of giving priority to the subjective over the objective. This is why Symbolism has sometimes been qualified as an offshoot of German and English Romanticism. In 1889, in his work *La Littérature de tout à l'heure*, Charles Morice defined a guideline which was not dissimilar to that of Novalis: 'The aspect of things is only a symbol which it is the task of the artist to interpret. Their only truth is in him; they have only an inner truth.'

Urged to submit his opinion of the Symbolist writers, Rémy de Gourmont replied in almost the same way as the famous *Enquête sur l'évolution littéraire* of Jules Huret: 'If this new literature had been called Idealism, I would have understood better, and perhaps even completely. Idealism is that philosophy which, without rigorously denying the outside world, only thinks of it as an almost amorphous material, which only achieves form and real life in the brain; there, having submitted to the action of the thought, to mysterious manipulations, the feeling condenses or multiplies, refines or reinforces itself, and acquires, relative to the subject, a real existence. Therefore what surrounds us, what is outside us, only exists because we ourselves exist. Consequently, so many thinking brains — as many different arts.'

What then was a Symbolist? He was a writer who did not try to reproduce reality as it was, but who lent it a significance which came from his inner world. As Saint-Pol Roux said, Symbolism was not a straitjacket of rules, it was merely 'the end of the stick of which Naturalism was the other end' and he ironically specified: 'The physical saddles of Naturalism will compel the spirits to metaphysical witticisms in the same way as the final thorns of the dialectic of the Middle Ages inclined those souls towards mystical roses.'

It follows that, rejecting all attempt at the representation of objective reality, Symbolism carried in itself the implication of the means of representation themselves. It appealed for a return to the starting point where man finds himself alone looking the world in the face, and inventing again, for his own advantage, a system of signs. This attitude gave rise to many excesses, even to hermetism. In any case, in literature, the habitual ideas had been overthrown: the sound of a word was preferred to its meaning, traditional versification was shattered, the poem thenceforth was written in prose, and the prose of the story had to become poetic. No longer to wish to *say* something, but to *suggest* it, implied in fact a negation of the established languages. This was an important innovation which opened the way to the movements of the twentieth century.

ADAM Paul (Paris 1862 — Paris 1920). Born of an industrialist and military family originating in Artois, he completed his secondary education at the Lycée Henri IV in Paris, and then tried to live by his pen. His father, who had been Postmaster-General under Napoleon III, had died while he was still young, having contracted an illness during the siege of Paris in 1870. Paul Adam chose, therefore, to throw himself into literture at a very early age. Having contributed to *La Revue indépendante*, he published his first novel, *Chair Molle*, with a Belgian publisher. Its immorality led to a scandal; he was heavily fined and received a suspended sentence of fifteen days in prison. Later he progressed from Naturalism to Symbolism, associating with and even motivating certain Symbolist reviews (*Le Carcan*, founded with Paul Ajalbert, *Le Symboliste*, and *La Vogue*). In 1886 he published two books of fantasy in collaboration with Jean Moréas, *Le Thé chez Miranda* and *Les Demoiselles Goubert*, as well as a novel of intimist inspiration, *Soi*. In 1888, his novel *Etre* confirmed his notoriety and his quality as a Symbolist writer. He then became deeply involved, on behalf of General Boulanger, with the political scene, only to return speedily to literature, writing twenty or so novels in a few years. Countless other books followed, from travel chronicles to essays, and from short stories to novels. During the war, too old to fight, he participated actively in the wave of patriotism, moving around with the troops and starting the *Ligue intellectuelle de fraternité Latine*.

Paul Adam's name appeared first in the Naturalist current which was still uppermost when he started writing; then he turned to Symbolism and finally to the literature of ideas for which the inspiration was politically traditional and nationalist. This literary evocation corresponded to his political development, since he passed from socialist leanings to conservative patriotism, following somewhat the same route as Maurice Barrès.

APPIA Adolphe (Geneva 1862 — Nyon 1928). Together with Gordon Craig, he is numbered among the greatest reformers of stage design. He started in Wagnerian opera (*La Mise en scène du drame wagnérien*, 1895) and ended with theories on every aspect of the theatre. He considered staging essentially as a means for transposing music into the realm of space. The set was conceived from drawings and measurements, with a view to a symbolic organization of space which serves to translate the essential quality of the drama represented. In the structuring of this space, lighting is of fundamental importance. It can conjure up atmosphere and even dimensions, and can therefore replace painted backgrounds. Lighting can also define symbolically the relationships between different characters. Strictly speaking, Appia did not belong to the Symbolist movement, but he developed his theories at a time when the European intellectual climate was favourable to Symbolism. As with all the Symbolist artists, his ideas in the world of the theatre were opposed to the Naturalist concepts, and more generally to those of the Realists. They were notably used at the Jaques-Dalcroze Institute at Hellerau, near Dresden. From the time of his staging of Claudel's *L'Annonce faite à Marie* in 1913, Jaques-Dalcroze rejected all realism in his décor, and used projections of light in order to develop an imaginary space.

AURIER George-Albery (Chateauroux 1865 — Paris 1892). A frequent visitor to Alfred Vallette's circle, he was one of the founders of the *Mercure de France*. He also contributed to other reviews, especially with poetry, among them *Le Décadent* and *La Plume*. He also edited *Le Moderniste*. During his lifetime he published a collection of poems and a novel, *Vieux* (Published by Savine). His posthumous works were collected in 1893, and prefaced by Rémy de Gourmont, editor of the *Mercure de France*. These comprised, in one brief volume, poems, short stories, various unpublished fragments (including a novel entitled *Ailleurs*) and all his articles, which are of great interest: they supported, in fact, the painting of the period. Aurier was a great admirer of van Gogh and Gauguin whose originality he recognized at an early stage. Contrary to what has been written at various times, he left no books on Symbolist painting, but reports on art, scattered between *Le Mercure de France*, *La Revue indépendante* and *Le Moderniste*, which evidenced what was generally appreciated by the Symbolists in painting. Thus van Gogh and Gauguin appeared to him as precursors of Symbolism, while he distinguished others as isolated cases: Eugene Carrière, Henry de Groux, J.F. Henner, and eventually arrived at those whom he considered were properly called Symbolists: Puvis de Chavannes, Gustave Moreau, Odilon Redon, Sérusier, Vuillard, Willumsen.

Having described, in an article about Gauguin (*Le Mercure de France*, March 1891), the painting *La Lutte de Jacob avec l'ange*, he developed a theory according to which, in painting, the objects represented 'were only signs, words, having in themselves no other significance'. He rejected 'every false impression of nature which acts on the spectator like nature herself', and praised the art of suggestion and the symbol, which he called 'ideist'. This had to obey the necessities of the idea to be expressed: 'The strict duty of the ideist painter is, in consequence, to effect a reasoned selection from among the many elements which are combined in objectivity; to make use in his work only of the lines, the shapes, and the general and distinctive colours which serve to write accurately the ideist meaning of the object, and not the several partial symbols which corroborate the general symbol'. That way Aurier claimed that painting came back to the 'decorative' frescoes of the Egyptians, Greeks and primitives; he affirmed: 'Painting, having finally discovered the exigencies previously formulated by the Symbolist poets, could only have been created in order to *decorate* with thoughts, dreams and ideas the banal murals of human edifices'.

His art criticism seemed to be subjective, partial, and pivoted against positivism and science. For him, true art was that which asked least of reality and most of imagination. In an unpublished essay on 'a new method of criticism', he even laid claim to a new mysticism: 'The most noble faculties of our souls are in process of becoming atrophied. In a hundred years we shall be beasts, whose only ideal will be the convenient satisfaction of bodily functions; we shall have gone back, through positive science, to pure and simple animality. We must react. We must cultivate again in our selves the superior qualities of the soul. We must become mystics once more'.

BAHR Hermann (Linz 1863 — Munich 1934). This Austrian writer played a role of great influence through his articles on French literature and contemporary art. A successful novelist, author of plays for the theatre, he was always ahead of the German-speaking public by trying to forecast the new artistic forms or fashions before they were born. In this spirit he produced two volumes of essays in which he approached Symbolism and decadence: *Die Überwindung des Naturalismus* ('The Conquest of Naturalism', 1891) and *Studies for a Critic of Modernity* ('Studien zur Kritik der Moderne', 1894). Having visited the representatives of Naturalism during the three years which he spent in Berlin, from 1884 to 1887, he then spent ten months, from December 1888 to October 1889 in Paris, during which time he discovered the anti-Naturalist current. Thanks to him Germany and Austria were informed, fairly impartially, of what the Symbolists were and what they wanted to achieve. At first he showed the decadents and the decadent sensibility through Huysmans, Barrès and Péladan. He then strove to define clearly Symbolist technique as an art of suggestion. It was again thanks to him that Maeterlinck's theatre became known in Vienna: he devoted a meeting to his *L'Intruse* in 1892. From 1894, Bahr reacted against the decadence which Montesquiou and Wilde embodied; he reproached them in their search for pleasure and for their dilettantism, their exaltation of the artificial, and praised, instead, a reconciliation between art and life.

BARRES Maurice (Charmes, Vosges 1862 — Neuilly-sur-Seine 1923). Having completed his secondary studies in Nancy, he went to Paris in 1883, where he founded a short-lived little review

H. RONDEL *Portrait of Maurice Barrès*

of Symbolist inspiration, *Les Taches d'encre*; he then joined the editorial staff of another review *Chroniques* (1886-87). Barrès visited the Symbolist milieux before turning towards political activity in support of General Boulanger. later he became one of the representatives of conservative nationalism, of 'the earth and the dead'. He passed from *Le Culte du Moi* to *Roman de l'énergie nationale* explaining his own evolution in the following terms; 'Having thoroughly examined the idea of Self with the only means of poets and mystics through interior observation, I descended among the unresisting quicksands to find at the bottom and for support, collectivism'.

In all his early works he shared the Symbolist sensibility, or indulged in the themes of decadent literature (*Du Sang, de la volupté et de la mort* in 1894 and *La Mort de Venise* in 1902). *Sous l'œil des Barbares* published in 1888, could certainly be considered a Symbolist novel. It concerned the description of an inner world where the Self became the only reality. On the other hand the subject of the book was that of the struggle of an individual who attempted to escape those (the barbarians) who were trying to submit him to their own image; this is the theme, often treated by the Symbolists, of the rebellion of the individual, of the Self which rejects the vulgarity of the people.

BERNHARDT Sarah (Paris 1844 — Paris 1923). Her real name was Henriette Rosine Bernard. Having studied at the Conservatoire, she made her debut as an actress in 1862 at the Comédie Française, which she later left for the Odéon where she appeared in François Coppée's play

Le Passant. Having returned to the Comédie Franaise, she became famous in the classic plays such as *Phèdre* by Racine, *Hernani* and *Ruy Blas* by Victor Hugo. In 1915 she had to have a leg amputated, but she continued to act with a wooden leg. In the memory of those who saw her she has remained an actress with a voice of extreme musicality which transfigured everything by its power. A *diseuse* of poetry, she won the admiration of the Symbolist generation. For thirty years, from 1880 until about 1910, she represented Modern Woman in the eyes of this generation. She was the Hermaphrodite which obsessed the imagination of the *fin de siècle*; she was the Muse. In his book on *La Mêlée symboliste* from 1870 to 1890 (La Renaissance du Livre, Paris 1920), Ernest Raynaud emphasised the influence which she exercised on the evolution of Symbolism: 'Her image resembled Baudelaire's *La Madone* or Mallarmé's *Hérodiade*. She seemed to be the living illustration of all those poems, absolute and polychromous,...full of lilies, eaglets, moonlight, sphinxes and centaurs, and she captivated the riders of clouds and chimeras by the unexpected and disturbing grace of her disguises, which evoked a vision of the Androgyne, the sexual Superbeing, the unpolluted Angel, that which deserved the homage of a refined and affected poet, the judge of style, the new Petronius, one of the experts in new aesthetics, from whom Huysmans took the idea for his Des Esseintes: Count Robert de Montesquiou'.

. CLAIRIN *Portrait of Sarah Bernhardt*. 1876

BOURGET Paul (Amiens 1852 — Paris 1935). He started by publishing poetry in which the influence of Musset and Baudelaire was noticeable. He then wrote numerous articles and critical studies. These were collected in 1883 under the title *Essais de psychologie contemporaine*. More *Essais* appeared in 1889. The same year, after several attempts in this field (*Cruelle Enigme, Crime d'Amour, Mensonges, André*

P. CHABAS *Portrait of Paul Bourget*

Cornélis) he published a novel which brought him success and was widely discussed: *Le Disciple*. Bourget, moralizing, was addressing the young people born after the 1870 war by offering them an ideal in the shape of a philosopher, Adrien Sixte (for whom the model was Taine) and his disciple, Robert Greslou. He posed the problem of liberty, by interrogating his hero about the moral and metaphysical aspirations of man; these interrogations led to a single outcome: a spiritual rebirth is possible only in a return to the Christian religion. In religion, as in politics, Paul Bourget continued to develop along traditional lines.

He is generally considered as the representative of the novel of the worldly psychology and introspection, as well as the novel of thesis, of the end of the nineteenth century. It is not possible to make him a Symbolist to the letter. But he did popularize, through his articles and his essays, certain themes which had been latent during the years 1880 to 1890. According to Michel Mansuy (*Un moderne: Paul Bourget*, Les Belles-Lettres, published Paris 1960) he had drawn a meaningful portrait of the generation of intellectuals and students at the end of the century: 'His works (with his *Essais* to the forefront) have particularly contributed to give birth to the decadent movement around 1884'.

DUMONT-LINDEMANN Louise (Cologne 1862
— Düsseldorf 1932). Having begun her theatrical
career very young, she acted notably with Max
Reinhardt's company. When he created the
Kleines Theater in Berlin (1901-02), she worked
only with the company of Gustav Lindemann, who
became her husband, and with whom she founded
the Schauspielhaus in Düsseldorf in 1905. She
became famous through her poetic interpretations
of morally-tormented female characters such as
Ibsen's Hedda Gabler. Having broken with the
Naturalist interpretation, she tried to put across to
the spectators the depths of the personality of the
individual she was incarnating, and strove to make
the unconscious and the inexpressible understood.
In this way she was close to the Symbolist theories
through an art of suggestion.

In 1909, the company of Louise Dumont and
Gustav Lindemann was invited by Lugné-Poe to
act in his Théâtre de l'Oeuvre. One of the French
spectators at the performances given in Paris
(August Dupouy, *France et Allemagne*, Delaplane,
Paris 1913) saw there the Symbolist theories in
practice: 'German Symbolism, born partly of
French Symbolism, has pushed its principles to
their ultimate conclusions, like their Naturalism',
he said. 'In the theatre it has tried to reform the
scenery, making it suggestive and not descriptive,
reducing it to the minimum of material in order
to give it the maximum of meaning. A Viennese
critic had proposed playing *Hamlet* between three
cloth walls where the colour could be varied
according to the moral atmosphere of each scene.
In 1909, Madame Dumont-Lindemann, director
of the Schauspielhaus in Düsseldorf, came to the
Marigny theatre to give performances complying
with these new principles. In *La Vie de l'homme*, by
the Russian Andreiev, the décor was grey in the
first act, pink in the second, then white and gold,
then grey, then black: this was to describe successively birth, youth, maturity, old age and death'.

DUNCAN Isadora (San Francisco 1878 — Nice
1927). This American of Irish descent studied
classical dancing to start with, and then reacted
violently against the traditional techniques; she
undertook to liberate the body of the dancer from
all the conventions with which it had until then
been surrounded. Having become friends with
Loïs Fuller, she followed her to Germany in 1902.
What they both wanted was that the personality
should be able to express itself profoundly, with
no artificiality. With no shoes and no scenery, the
dancing was mainly out of doors with bare feet.

Living in Paris, Isadora Duncan did not really
leave a mark on the Symbolist period since it was
already over by the time she became famous, in
1910. But the survivors of the Symbolist generation greatly admired her. As Fernand Divoire
made clear in 1924 (*Décourvertes sur la danse*, Crès,
Paris) her art could be seen as very close to the

Symbolist ideal: 'Mime? No. Never. But
suggestion. No more props, no more motley, no
more anecdotes. Bare, bluish hangings remain
and one human being whose gestures say only
Sadness, Joy, Youth, Prayer, Ecstasy'. The words
which he found to summarize her talen recalled a
Symbolist formula: 'Manifestation by beautiful
and harmonious gestures of the eternal feelings of
the human soul'.

BOURDELLE *Isadora Duncan*

FENEON Félix (Turin 1861 — Châtenay-Malabry
1944). After his secondary studies at Cluny and
Mâcon, he became a journalist for a Mâcon
regional newspaper. He then did his military
service, and on his return passed an examination
to go into the Ministry of War, where he worked
for thirteen years, up until 1894, the time of the
process against the anarchist murder attempts in
which he was involved. From 1883 onwards he
contributed to many of the lesser reviews of the
period, and became editor in chief of *La Revue
blanche* in 1896; he followed this as a journalist on
the *Figaro* (1904-06) and *Le Matin*. In 1809 he
became artistic director of the Bernheim Jeune

SIGNAC *Portrait of Félix Fénéon*

Gallery, and it was he who, in 1912, organized the first Futurist exhibition in Paris.

Fénéon was part of the intellectual movement which, at the end of the nineteenth century, gave birth to Impressionism, Symbolism and anarchism at the same time. An extremely cultivated man, he was art critic (the only 'Symbolist' art critic, according to the reports of the time!) as well as literary critic and author of novels. He supported Matisse, giving him a contract which enabled him to leave his job as a bank official. He encouraged Bonnard, and look favourably on the Nabis, as well as numbering Paul Signac among his many artist friends.

FORT Paul (Rheims 1872 — Argenlieu, near Montléry 1960). At the age of eighteen he founded the Théâtre Mixte in Paris in 1890. To start with he just wanted to produce plays, regardless of schools or genres. He proposed simply to give performances 'of unpublished or forgotten works on the last Friday of every month'. After the first play on June 27, 1890, a three-act play called *Le Florentin* which at that time was believed to be by La Fontaine, the Théâtre Mixte amalgamated, under the same name, with the Théâtre Idéaliste of Louis Germain. This lasted only a little over a month. The Théâtre Mixte then became, under the direction of Paul Fort alone, the Théâtre d'Art.

His repertory included, to start with, two short plays by Victor Hugo (*Sur la lisière d'un bois* and *Les Gueux*) to which were added a 'mystery' by Jules Méry (*Morized*) and a one-act play by Rachilde (*La Voix du sang*). These performances on November 18 and 19, 1890, showed no sense of direction, nor any real originality. In June 1891, a literary masterpiece was chosen by Paul Fort for his stage:

Les Cenci by Shelley, in an adaptation by Félix Rabbe. Sadly, the acting was not very convincing and the performance, due to insufficient preparation, was a failure.

One month later the Théâtre d'Art was declared 'Symbolist' by Paul Fort, under the patronage of Mallarmé, Verlaine and Moréas. Its first success was *La Fille aux mains coupées* by Pierre Quillard, in March, with décor by Paul Sérusier. Symbolist stage design had been born: the characters were developed behind a muslin curtain, and everything depended on the diction. In *La Mercure de France* Alfred Vallette named the Théâtre d'Art as 'the most original dramatic undertaking'.

But by far the most important play which Paul Fort performed was *L'Intruse* by Maeterlinck, in May, with Lugné-Poe in the principal role. The critic Henry Bauër wrote in *La Plume*: 'Nowhere

A. OSBERT *Portrait of Paul Fort.* 1887

else has the impression of the reality of intangible sensations been rendered with such intensity'.

After this, financial difficulties started to accumulate. Nevertheless, the theatre had another success: *Les Aveugles* by Maeterlinck, which was staged by Adolphe Retté and Lugné-Poe in December 1891. The other plays they put on were not very favourably received, and considered as going too far into an esoteric Symbolism. This applied to the *Cantique des Cantiques* Paul-Napoléon Roinard, Rémy de Gourmont's *Théodat*, and Paul Fort's last performance where he grouped together *Les Noces de Sathan* by Jules Bois, *Le Premier Chant de l'Iliade* and two scenes from *Vercingetorix* by Edward Schuré. After this performance, at the end of March 1892, the *Mercure de France* which, until then, had supported the Théâtre d'Art, was not merciful towards Paul Fort, predicting that his enterprise, unless he found a remedy, would soon be only 'a sound box, a grotesque puppet show, devoted to sarcasm and peals of laughter from the Philistines alone'.

With this failure, the Théâtre d'Art closed its doors. But in fact the experiment had proved that it was possible to shake off the recipes of Naturalism. On top of this, Paul Fort had had the audacity to put forward at least two principles which characterized the Symbolist approach to the theatre: the priority of the spoken word over the movements of the characters, and collaboration with the artists (Henry Colas, Paul Sérusier, Pierre Bonnard, and Maurice Denis) in order to produce a décor of atmosphere, of suggestion, as opposed to the illustration of a society or an action as produced by the scenery specialists.

This was the direction that Lugné-Poe followed in his own theatre, the Théâtre de l'Oeuvre. Paul Fort's merit lay in having given him at least a glimpse, during their collaboration in the ephemeral Théâtre de l'Art, of which path of study he should follow.

FULLER Loïs (Fullersburg, near Chicago 1862 — Paris 1928). Having attempted to break into the theatre, this American tried a singing career (*Faust* at the Chicago Opera in 1885) in order to get on to the stage, and finally achieved fame in dancing. In Paris she appeared in *La Danse du Feu* in 1892 at the Folies-Bergère, and then took part, together with Isadora Duncan and Maud Allen, in a series of spectacles at the time of the Universal Exhibition in 1900.

The Symbolists admired her enormously. She used absolutely no décor, the setting being created by the play of electric lighting on veils of gauze in unison with the movements of her body. In this way the spectator was invited to dream, working out his own décor in his mind. On a stage which was unencumbered by any apparatus, material objects gave way to the projection of a spiritual reality.

In 1904, in a book on Loïs Fuller, Roger Marx suggested that she had found the realization of the ideal spectacle to which Mallarmé had aspired. He himself paid her a tribute through an article in the *National Observer* in March 1893, attracted by the shedding of what he called the 'traditional planting of permanent décors' on the stage.

Camille Mauclair expressed powerfully what this dancer represented, at the end of the century, to her generation: 'Loïs Fuller pulls us away from the sight of the heartrending conflicts of every day and leads us to the purifying countries of the dream by the great, wide, elastic rhythm of her wings of illuminated gauze'.

GRANVILLE-BARKER Harley (London 1877 — Paris 1946). He started in the theatre at the age of thirteen. From acting he turned to stage design and produced in London two of Maeterlinck's plays: *La Mort de Tintagiles* and *Intérieur* (1900). From 1904 to 1907 he directed the Court Theatre with J.E. Vedrenne, and he successfully introduced Maeterlinck and Ibsen to the great English public. After this he devoted himself entirely to the works of Shakespeare.

After the First World War, he settled in Paris. In 1937 he was appointed director of the British Institute (Paris University). Three years later he left Paris to take refuge in the United States, where he worked for the British Secret Service as well as teaching at Harvard University. He returned to Paris in 1946, and died in August of the same year.

He was one of those rare Englishmen at the beginning of the century who tried to reform the theatre in reaction to the flatly realistic conventions. In his ideals and in his repertoire he followed the direction of Lugné-Poe's studies, without really being part of the Symbolist movement.

He himself wrote several plays, and his activity as dramatic author is no doubt partially responsible for his work as a pioneer in stage design being largely forgotten. He left two theoretical works: *The Study of Drama* (1934) and *On Poetry in Drama* (1937).

HURET Jules (Boulogne-sur-Mer 1864 — Paris 1915). After some difficult years in his home town, he arrived in Paris in 1886, where he contributed to various journals: *L'Evénement*, *L'Estafette*, and, in 1889, *L'Echo de Paris*, where he achieved notoriety with a series of articles published from March 3 to July 5, 1891, and collected the same year under the title *Enquête sur l'évolution littéraire*. They were based on interviews which he had with sixty-four writers of the period. The reason for them had been the publication of the novels *Le Jardin de Bérénice* by Barrès and *Le Pèlerin passionné* by Jean Moréas: these two books served as a pretext to pinpoint the position of Naturalism in literature, and that of the opposing current, Symbolism. This series of interviews has survived as a very important document of the literary problems of the epoch.

Jules Huret published other books: reports on travel, various investigations into social matters, legal chronicles and newspaper reports.

HUYSMANS Joris-Karl (Paris 1848 — Paris 1907). His father, of Dutch extraction, belonged to a family of artists, and made a living from his painting as artist-illustrator of prayer-books and missals. A sick man, he died in 1856. Young George's mother (it was later that he decided to call himself Joris-Karl) married again, in 1857, the comfortably-off proprietor of a book-binding studio, by whom she had two daughters.

G. ROUAULT *Portrait of Joris-Karl Huysmans*

Having started his studies in a private boarding-school, Huysmans attended the courses of the Saint-Louis Lycée in Paris until 1865. He then decided not to go to school any longer. Thanks to his special courses, he obtained his baccalaureate in 1866. He then worked in the Ministry of the Interior, whilst following at the same time advanced studies in law and literature. In 1867 he collaborated on a periodical, *La Revue mensuelle*, which, in 1870 was taken over; he then went back to his work as a civil servant. But he kept writing, and visiting the literary circles. In 1873 his first book, *Le Drageoir aux épices*, appeared at his own expense, as he had not been able to find a publisher. Several novels followed, including *Sac au dos*, published in serial form in 1877, and *Les Sur Vatard*, in 1879. He also embarked on a career in art criticism.

In his early works Huysmans was an admirer of Zola, and one of the representatives of Naturalist literature. The turning-point came in 1882, after the publication of his novel *A Vau-l'eau*. By this time he was reacting against the simplist psychology of Zola, and *A Rebours* in 1884 consummated his break with the master. His later novels were marked by spiritual preoccupations (*Là-bas*, and then *En Route*, *La Cathédrale*, *L'Oblat*, which were three books devoted respectively to the purgative, contemplative and unitive life). Moreover, in 1901 he became a monk.

The work which Huysmans left adds great historic interest to the knowledge of intellectual life in France at the end of the nineteenth century. In fact, many of his novels are witness to a collective climate: *A vau-d'eau* interprets the pessimism which followed the war of 1870; *A Rebours* has been called 'the breviary of decadence'; *Là-bas* is an account of the outbreak of occultism and spiritism in the 1880s; *En Route* is inseparable from the great conversions of the period and the return to Catholicism of a certain number of intellectuals.

From the point of view of the Symbolist movement, it is *A Rebours* which attracts most attention. *La Grande Encyclopédie* of the nineteenth century announces, for example: '*A Rebours* caused a great sensation, and this was the first battleground of the idealists and public opinion'. Huysmans had actually wanted to reflect, through this book, the spirit of the times, and he indicated in a letter to Zola that he had striven to make it very accurate. At the same time he is without any shadow of doubt also his own hero, Des Esseintes (whose exterior behaviour he copied from Robert de Montesquiou): it is himself, a man sick with neurasthenia, who is the narrator. The result of this double perspective is a book which gives a portrait of the decadent type and crystallizes in him all the elements of the reaction of idealism against naturalism. He revealed in it the element which forms the basis of decadent sensibility: neurosis, which is described as a pathological phenomenon of the age. Paul Bourget wrote on this that the novel seemed to him 'the most complete monograph...of a neurosis in an intellectual head'. This explains how *A Rebours* could have been the basis of a fashion. From 1887, particularly, the term 'decadence' became almost popular, decadent sensibility engendering a double movement: acclaim (at that time in England Oscar Wilde was praising Huysmans' book in the *Portrait of Dorian Gray*) and violent reprobation. *La Grande Encyclopédie* was not slow to claim that the Symbolists had been revealed to the public by *A Rebours*, through the 'decadent' Des Esseintes, 'according to the ridiculous title with which the new school was being rigged out'.

JAMMES Francis (Tournay, High Pyrenees 1868 — Hasparren, Atlantic Pyrenees 1936). He was a poet, who extolled simplicity, a return to Catholicism, Christian and family virtues. He possessed a deep feeling for nature, which he praised through his numerous poems on the country (see the collection which was called *Georgiques chrétiennes*). He was influenced by Symbolism from which he retained certain affectation of expression. But his inspiration was beyond that of Symbolist themes, preferring the naive evocation of daily existence to that of the great myths. He also wrote a play for the theatre, *La Brébis egarée* which was performed for the first time by Lugné-Poe at the Théâtre de l'Oeuvre. It concerned two lovers who undergo a series of tests, until the moment comes where Mercy intervenes. Ten years later the Opéra Comique produced it with music by Darius Milhaud.

LARA Louise (1876 — 1951). Her real name was Louise-Victorine Charlotte Larapidie Delisle. She belonged by her family background to the artistic world: her aunt was a dancer at the Opéra and her father had been the founder of the Society of Dutch Painters. Having studied at the Conservatoire, she played many parts in Lugné-Poe's Théâtre de l'Oeuvre: *La Gardienne* by Henri de Régnier in 1894; *Le Volant* by Judith Cladel in 1895; and *L'Annonce faite à Marie* by Claudel, in which she played the character of Violaine, in 1911. Having joined l'Odéon in 1895, she became a member of the Comédie Française in 1896. She resigned, famous, in 1918, as much in consequence of political discord (she was a pacifist, and had been nicknamed Lara the Red) as for aesthetic reasons. With her husband, the architect Edouard Autant, she established in 1919 a very avant-garde theatre, the Laboratoire Art et Action.

This theatre devoted itself from 1919 to 1925 to a repertory and stage design which were widely inspired by the Symbolist endeavours. Edouard Autant had been particularly influenced by René Ghil's theories, according to which 'sound could be translated into colour' and 'colour can be translated into sound and forthwith into the timbre of an instrument'. From these he drew his principles which were founded on the play of correspondences, the mix and the synthesis of the arts. One Symbolist who had already experimented with synthesis in the theatre was Paul-Napoléon Roinard, who was also a member of the foundation committee of the Laboratoire Art et Action. Louise Lara, on the other hand, was an admirer of the Symbolist writers. Mallarmé gave a reading of his *Hérodiade* at the Théâtre de la Renaissance in November 1919, and in May 1920 it was *Un coup de dés* which served as a trial in an experiment in 'simultaneous polyphony'. Claudel, Laforgue, Wyspianski and René Ghil also belonged in the repertory of the Laboratoire Art et Action.

LORRAIN Jean (Fécamp 1855 — Paris 1906). His real name was Paul-Alexandre-Martin Duval. He was the son of a rich shipowner from Normandy. At the age of nine he arrived in Paris from his native town, and was sent to board in various scholastic establishments. Having completed his secondary studies, he at first tried to paint, like many young people of the time, and then went into literature and journalism. His articles on contemporary life in the Parisian papers became famous. He collected them in book form, *Poussières de Paris* (1899): they described the Tout-Paris of art exhibitions, of salons, and of society meetings. He also wrote poetry and novels. He was of Naturalist inspiration in some of these (*La Maison Philibert*, 1904) but others (*Monsieur de Phocas*, 1901) and *Le Vice errant*, 1902) are completely typical of the decadent outlook in their descriptions of sexual perversions and neurotic phenomena.

LUGNE-POE Aurélien Marie Lugné, called (Paris 1869 — Villeneuve-les-Avignon 1869). Lugné-Poe was not in any way related, as was believed for some time, and which he did nothing to contradict, to Edgar Allan Poe. On his father's side his family came from Champoly, near Roanne, and his mother was born at Le Havre. It is true, however, that he did have links with the Anglo-Saxon world, since his father, a bank official, started his career in the United States, and was for a long time deputy director of the London office of the Société Générale.

He was still a pupil at the Lycée Condorcet when he founded, in November 1886 with one of his friends, a theatre company: the Cercle des Escholiers. They performed several plays which showed very little originality in their repertory (Octave Feuillet, Ponsard, Alphonse Daudet, Musset). But Lugné-Poe had already found his path. In July 1887, having failed his baccalaureate, he decided to embark on a career in the theatre.

He took the Conservatoire examination, frequented the actors' milieu and had some minor roles in several plays. Just when he was accepted for the Conservatoire, in October 1888, he was also engaged for a year and a half as actor and manager at Antoine's Théâtre Libre. With his height and his austere countenance, he was given comic parts, and seemed to have a vocation for light comedy.

After his military service in Rheims he became involved with a group of painters in Paris, the Nabis (Vuillard, Bonnard and Sérusier) thanks to Maurice Denis whom he had known at the Condorcet and with whom he had remained friends. He then became propagandist of this new style of painting and may well have been influenced by their reaction against Naturalism and Impressionism. In any case, he was initiated into Symbolism by Maurice Denis and made the acquaintance of Albert Mockel, Stuart Merrill, Charles Morice and Adolphe Retté along with the Nabis. It was with them that he visited Paul Fort's Théâtre d'Art, and he made his debut there in May 1891 in the leading role of *L'Intruse*, a play by Maeterlinck in which he had an enormous success.

He then became more or less part of the company of the Théâtre d'Art (playing in *Les Aveugles* by Maeterlinck and *Théodat* by Rémy de Gourmont) and then went back to his former companions of the Cercle des Escholiers before leaving them again when Paul Fort suggested putting on Maeterlinck's *Pelléas et Mélisande* for which he and Camille Mauclair did the staging in May 1893.

It was again with Camille Mauclair that he founded the Théâtre de l'Oeuvre the same year. In presenting the programme for the new theatre they both insisted on the necessity of an unknown repertoire in order, as Mauclair wrote, 'to struggle, to create new waves of ideas and stimulate argument'. Their first performance was *Romersholm* by Henrik Ibsen, which Mauclair presented as a

by Symbolist writers (Maeterlinck, van Lerberghe, Quillard) and by that of Alfred Jarry's *Ubu Roi* in December 1896. At this time Lugné-Poe was trying to get the Symbolists' famous art of suggestion accepted into the theatre. The other phase stretched from 1900 to 1930, and it comprised performances of D'Annunzio, Crommelynck, Chekov, Salacrou, and above all Claudel from before 1918 (*L'Annonce faite à Marie* in December 1912 and *L'Otage* in June 1914).

It should also be emphasized that l'Oeuvre owed a great deal to Suzanne Després (1875-1951), who married Lugné-Poe in 1898 and became an actress of international renown. She made her debut at l'Oeuvre in January 1895 in *Chariot de terre cuite* by Victor Barucand, and afterwards specialized in Ibsen. 'If she had not been by my side', wrote Lugné-Poe 'I would not have known how to proceed, either for myself or for the others'.

Lugné-Poe left two books of recollections: *Sous les étoiles* (Gallimard, Paris, 1933) tells the story of l'Oeuvre up till 1912, and *Dernière Pirouette* (Le Sagittaire, 1946) continues it until the theatre was finally closed in 1930.

masterpiece of Symbolism'. After this, Lugné-Poe became the recognized designer for Ibsen in France, playing *An Enemy of the People* (November 1893), *The Master Builder* (April 1894), *Little Eyolf* (May 1895), *Brand* (June 1895), *The Pillars of Society* (June 1896), *Peer Gynt* (November 1896), and *Jean-Gabriel Borkman* (November 1897), all plays which are slanted towards Symbolism, and which made Ibsen, the realist, understood in France as a dramatic Symbolist author. It could be said, on this subject, that Lugné-Poe performed Ibsen in the same way as Maeterlinck. In 1897, he admitted this himself, agreeing that there was 'an evident contradiction' between 'Ibsen's theatre and the Symbolists' theories'. Other Scandinavians equally received his support: Bjornstjerne Bjornson (*Beyond Human Powers*, February 1894), Hermann Bang (*Brothers*, June 1894), August Strindberg (*Creditors* in June, and *Father* in December 1894). When one thinks of the collection of plays which were performed at the l'Oeuvre (by Gerhart Hauptmann, John Ford, Marlowe, Shakespeare, Oscar Wilde, the Indian Kalidasa, Gogol), it appears that Lugné-Poe was indeed a discoverer of foreign theatre. He tried to make l'Oeuvre the official theatre in Paris for international literature.

The history of l'Oeuvre is divided into two phases. The first, from 1893 to 1899, corresponded to Symbolism on the stage. It was especially marked by performances of numerous plays

MAUCLAIR Camille (Paris 1872 — Paris 1945). Under his real name, Camille Faust, he started writing at a very early age, beginning with poetry, and visited the literary circles in Paris. He was the co-founder of the Théâtre de l'Oeuvre with Lugné-Poe in 1893. Poet, novelist and critic, he left very many books and newspaper articles. He published accounts and memories of the Symbolist movement. One book in particular provides us with a balance-sheet of this period: *Servitude et grandeur littéraires*. Apart from this, he wrote many works on history of art, Impressionism, Rodin, and French painting from 1830 to 1900.

MAZEL Henri (Nîmes 1864 — Paris 1947). A contributor to the Symbolist reviews and the Mercure de France, he directed *L'Ermitage* with Adolphe Retté. He was particularly interested in the theatre, and elaborated the theory of an 'idealist' theatre. He also wrote several dramas, and left a book of reminiscences on the Symbolist movement.

MENDES Catulle (Bordeaux 1841 — Saint-Germain-en-Laye 1909). He was not merely the son-in-law of José Maria de Hérédia, but also followed him in the poetic ideal of the Parnassus. This descendant of Théophile Gautier and Théodore de Banville was actually one of the instigators of Parnassian art. A minor writer, he cultivated all the genres in adapting himself with a certain technical skill, to the fashions in force in the Parisian salons. Thus he produced a libertine and erotic literature, the themes of which came into

Portrait of Catulle Mendès

fashion at the end of the century. For example, the incest in his novel *Zo'har* (Paris 1886) and the sexual perversions in *Le Roi vierge* (Paris 1881). He also became involved in the spread of 'Wagnerism' in France. In the theatre he was successful in the fields of drama in verse, and opera libretto. Finally, he left a *Rapport sur le mouvement poétique en France de 1867 à 1900* (Paris 1902) where he accorded a place to the Symbolist poets in the biographical section, but without extolling or even praising Symbolism.

MEYERHOLD Vsevolod Emilievich (Penza 1874 — ? 1942). The eighth child of a German family, he was born in Russia, where his father owned an alcohol distillery. Until his Russian naturalization in 1895, he had the name Karl Theodor Kasimir Meiergold.

After his secondary studies at the lyceum in Penza, where he first went on the stage, he attended the faculty of law at Moscow University. But he soon lost his taste for it, and left to take up a theatrical career. In 1896 he passed the entrance examination for the musical and dramatic Institute of the Philharmonic Society which was at the time directed by Vladimir Nemirovitch-Dantchenko. Students promoted that year made up the first contingent of actors at the Artistic Theatre in Moscow, established in 1898 by Vladimir Nemirovitch-Dantchenko and Stanislavski, and he played various roles there, notably in *The Seagull* and *The Three Sisters* by Chekov, *The Solitary Souls* by Hauptmann and Shakespeare's *Merchant of Venice*.

In 1902 he left the Artistic Theatre in order to found his own company, the Brotherhood of New Drama. His repertory at the outset was hardly different from that of Stanislavski: he put on Chekov, Gorki, Hauptmann and Ibsen. He then became very taken with the anti-Naturalist plays (Maeterlinck's *Monna Vanna*, Przybyszewski's *The Snow*), his literary adviser being the Symbolist Alexis Remizov.

Established at the Tiflis Theatre in 1904-1905 he decided to prohibit, because of the social unrest, the performing of *An Enemy of the People* by Ibsen and *Les Estivants* by Gorki. On returning to Moscow, he founded with Stanislavski's support the first Studio of the Artistic Theatre. There he put on *La Mort de Tintagiles* by Maeterlinck. There was no public performance; the play was performed entirely for the painters, actors, writers and musicians. But the Théâtre-Studio had to close its doors and Meyerhold, after a stay in Petersburg, went back to Tiflis in 1906 where the Brotherhood of New Drama was established. He produced *La Mort de Tintagiles* again, and then put on plays by Hauptmann, Ibsen and Gorki. The great actress Vera Kommissarjevskaïa then asked him to come and work in her own theatre in Petersburg. He accepted, and in 1906-07 he showed, among others, Ibsen's *Hedda Gabler*, Maeterlinck's *Sur Béatrice*, Alexandre Blok's *The Fair Booth*, Wedekind's *Awakening of Spring*, Maeterlinck' *Pelléas et Mélisande* and Sologub's *The Conquest of Death*. But disagreements arose with Vera Kommissarjevskaïa in December 1907, as she became more and more opposed to the Symbolist style of his staging. With his company, Meyerhold then went to the Imperial theatres of Petersburg, the Alexandrinski and Marinski Theatres. His first play was *On the Threshold of the Realm* by Hamsun, in which he himself played the lead. He was also

Portrait of Meyerhold

interested in opera, and in 1909-10 he put on *Tristan and Isolde* by Wagner which had a tremendous success; in 1911 it was *Orpheus and Eurydice* by Gluck and in 1913 *Electra* by Richard Strauss.

In September 1910, he played at the Studio of the House of Interludes in Moscow, under the pseudonym Doctor Dappertutto, a pantomine by Arthur Schnitzler, *Colombine's Scarf*, in a style which synthesized the Commedia dell'Arte, the fairground theatre, the fantastic Romantic, and Symbolism. It was the period where he was striving to deepen the principle of the grotesque, a new process which he defined in 1911 as the effect produced on the audience by unexpected contrasts.

At the beginning of 1913, he published a work, *Of the Theatre*, in which he retraced his own route. The same year, in April, he took part in eight Russian seasons: he put on *Pisanello or Perfumed Death*, by D'Annunzio, written for Ida Rubinstein, with ballets by Fokine and scenery by Léon Bakst. This provided him with the opportunity to visit Parisian theatres and circuses. He was at a notable meeting between the Futurists Marinetti and Boccioni, and made the acquaintance of Paul Fort and Jacques Rouche.

In 1914, in a new Studio, he staged a spectacle entitled *The Love of Three Oranges*, which gave birth, under the same title, to a theatrical review in which, in 1916, he presented his conceptions.

With the October Revolution, a decisive change took place in his work. He became a member of the intellectuals who immediately placed themselves at the service of the revolution. He broke with the old artistic forms, and joined the futurist avant-garde, trying to renew the Russian stage. He at once secured political responsibilities, at first as political commissary in the ranks of the Red Army, and then in directing the theatrical sector of the State Commissariat for Public Instruction.

He announced the October Revolution of the theatre. And, in order to put it into practice, he created in Moscow the theatre RSFSR-1 in a ruined building where he put on Verhaeren's *Les Aubes* on November 7, 1920. This was a play which he and Valeri Bebutov had adapted to a perspective of political propaganda. Having been influenced by Constructivism, he produced, in this new style, *Le Cocu magnifique* by Crommelynck in April 1922. On this occasion he also brought in a technique which he had invented: biomechanics, through which all aspects of the acting were linked to cadences of the economic production, using the transformations of Soviet society as a model. The performers, clothed in working blue overalls, acted with movements of mechanical precision — luckily the burlesque and humour compensated for their robot-like appearance!

By 1923 he had his own theatre — the TIM, or Meyerhold Theatre. After Gogol's *Revizor* in 1926 and *Unhappiness in the Spirit* by Griboiedov in 1928, he put on two plays by Maiakovski, *The Bug* in 1930 and *The Baths* in 1931. His last two productions of note were *La Dame aux camélias* in 1934, after Alexandre Dumas the younger, and Tchaikowsky's opera *The Queen of Spades* in 1935.

His decline began in 1934, when socialist realism was officially praised. In 1936 he was violently attacked for his formalism, and he became his own critic. Two years later his theatre was closed. He was arrested in July 1939, and totally disappeared.

Although he remained all his life hostile towards Naturalism, and although he had always cultivated a certain stylization in his art of stage design, Meyerhold ceased to be attracted by proper Symbolism around 1914. Not only had he much frequented the Russian Symbolist writers between 1905 and 1913 (Alexis Remizov, Alexandre Blok, André Biely, Valeri Briussov), but he had been in agreement with them to allow a certain amount of mystery to remain in every creation, to suggest instead of to show clearly. The idea of a conventional theatre which he developed at that time came from Valeri Briussov. As all art, according to him, was made of conventions, these conventions should be used consciously and, in place of trying to reproduce the real as faithfully as possible, one should be satisfied with a stylization. This was also Meyerhold's principle. Convention was not to be stuck on but underlined. The effect of illusion made room for the affirmation of a generalization, a symbolization. From that time on, scenery was included as such, and not, as in the Naturalist theatre, as representing reality. Meyerhold had himself indicated that he would like, in place of the accumulation so dear to the Naturalist stage, a composition in which the harmony would come from the rhythmic movement of lines and musical consonance of colours. In this there was nothing different from the usual correspondences established by the Symbolist writers between painting and music, with the emphasis on the latter. It is thus understandable that he described Oulianov's scenery for *Schluck et Jau* by Gerhart Hauptmann, a play which he staged in 1905 at the Studio-Theatre, as a symphony in mother-of-pearl.

MONTESQUIOU Robert de (Paris 1855 — Menton 1921). His name, and sometimes even his portrait (he was painted by Whistler and by Boldini) crops up many a time in evocative anecdotes about the years 1890 to 1910. He usually appears as a rich extravagant who, attracted by art as much as by the young artists, devoted himself to an aristocratic and worldly aestheticism. It was he who served as model to Huysmans for the character Des Esseintes in his novel *A Rebours*, as he did to Proust for the Baron de Charlus in *A la recherche du temps perdu*. Through him passed more of the style of the Belle Epoque than that of the Symbolist generation itself.

However, it must not be forgotten that he

frequented the literary and artistic circles. He played a quite important role, at first, as a patron: D'Annunzio owed his launching on to the French scene to him, with the performance of *Martyre de saint Sébastien*. Also this aesthete was himself a writer: he produced art chronicles in the reviews *Les Arts* and *Les Arts et la Vie*, which were collected in 1897 in a work called *Les Roseaux pensants*; collections of poetry; novels (*La Petite Demoiselle*, which was extremely successful, and after 1918, *La Trépidation*). He also left his memoires: *Les Pas effacés*.

MORICE Charles (Saint-Etienne 1860 — Menton 1919). Having completed his secondary studies at Saint-Etienne, and then at Lyons, he went to Paris in 1882. At first he collaborated on the review *La Nouvelle Rive gauche*. He became friends with Verlaine, and met Mallarmé who considered him to be one of the literary hopes of the rising generation. In 1889 he published *La Littérature de tout à l'heure*, a book which appeared in the evidence of the epoch as the credo of a generation, the manifesto of Symbolism. In 1890, he was on the team of the *Mercure de France*. Then, thinking that life would be less difficult for him materially, he settled in Brussels in 1896. He tried to earn his living as a writer by various contributions to newspapers and reviews, but he and his family lived from hand to mouth in wretchedness. In 1901 he went back to Paris. He collaborated on the *Paris-Journal* from 1908 onwards, and was appointed literary and artistic director in 1911. During the First World War he became virulently anti-German and chauvinist.

PELADAN Joséphin, called le Sâr (Lyons 1859 — Neuilly-sur-Seine 1918). He came from a milieu which was passionately interested in the study of philosophy. His father, who was a doctor, initiated him into esoteric doctrines and eastern religions. He became infatuated with occultism and mysticism, and behaved as a magician during the whole of his life. It is this aspect which has been remembered of him essentially, and which made this character of theatrical appearance, with his boots and velvet doublet, the laughing-stock of many of his contemporaries. He was influenced by Wagner, and tried to become the moving spirit of the mystic order of the Rose + Croix. He was no more than the Sâr Péladan (Sâr meaning magician in ancient Persian). In the Parisian Symbolist milieu he appeared thenceforth under that name and attracted followers. In fact, he organized exhibitions of painting. The first Rose + Croix salon took place, under his aegis, at the Durand-Ruel Gallery in March 1892. Many of the Symbolist painters showed their works there, and the Sâr opened the private view dressed as a knight of the Middle Ages.

A. SEON *Portrait of the Sâr Péladan*

Péladan was a writer, and published a novel, *L Vice suprême*, in 1884. He publicly proclaimed tota chastity in it. His heroine, the princess of Este refuses sexual relations after having been roughly taken by her spouse. She decides to reveng herself on men by exciting their desire withou ever yielding to them. There is also a magician the Sâr Mérodak, who has destroyed all sexua temptation in himself and praises the rejection o carnal love.

Another novel by Péladan, *L'Androgyne* (1891 takes up one of the major themes of the *fin de sièc* literature: that of the hermaphrodite, which turn into the temptation, often more suggested tha affirmed, of homosexuality. In that way Pélada expressed his ideal of a humanity which wa freeing itself from the yoke of sexuality. He too refuge in the idea of a creature without sexua differentiation, embodying the two sexes.

He also left plays for the theatre which, in hi admiration for Wagner and with concern for th application of his theories, he called 'Wagneries' They were of mythical inspiration (*Le Fils des étoile Babylone, Oedipe et le Sphinx, La Prométhéide*), and wer evidence of the idealist theatre of which th Symbolists made themselves the propagandists.

PICA Vittorio (Naples 1864 — Milan 1930). H was one of the first journalists to present th French Symbolists and the decadents in Italy. A the time of *La Revue indépendante* he was visitin Edouard Dujardin and Félix Fénéon. In *La Ga zetta letteraria* (Turin), he published a series c articles on Verlaine in 1885. In 1898 he brough ut a collection of essays, *Letteratura d'eccezione* Milan): among them were studies on Verlaine, Mallarmé, Barrès, France, Poictevin and Huysmans. These essays were detailed, with quotations in French, and showed an interest in the most up-to-date French literature, but Pica did not hesitate to express his reserve. He particularly critized the hermetism of Mallarmé and the ultra-subjectivism of Huysmans, whilst nevertheless underlining his admiration for their respective works.

An art critic, Pica directed the review *Emporium* from 1900 onwards, and, having founded the Binnale in Venice in 1895, he became its secretary-general from 1910 to 1927. He also published numerous monographs on Italian and foreign artists.

QUILLARD Pierre (1864 — 1912). He was a poet, and founded the review *La Pléiade* with his friend Ephraïm Mikhaël. But his importance came above all from his activity as dramatic critic and theoretician of the Symbolist theatre. Apart from this, two of his plays were performed according to Symbolist staging: *La Fille aux mains coupées* in Paul Fort's Théâtre d'Art in 1891, and the dialogue poem *L'Errante* in the Théâtre de l'Oeuvre in May 896.

He was passionately interested in social and political problems all his life. He put most of his energies into the liberation of Dreyfus, and fought in the Ligue des Droits de l'Homme and, as a libertarian, spread the ideas of the Russian revolutionaries of the end of the century. In 1893 he went to Constantinople and taught there until 896. He went back in 1897 on behalf of *L'Illustation*, in order to follow the war between Greece and Turkey. He died at Neuilly, as Camille Mauclair said 'prematurely used up, having given to social action a life which one would have thought destined for the dream'.

As for his theatrical conceptions, they rested on the rejection of Naturalism and the suggestive power of the word. The theatre to him was a pretext for the dream and scenery was born from the Word. After the performance of *La Fille aux mains coupées*, Pierre Veber, in his criticism in *La Revue d'art dramatique*, ranked this play among the examples of 'Symbolism at its most hermetic', and summarized the theatrical ambition of Pierre Quillard as follows: 'Complete simplification of dramatic means; a narrator, placed at the corner of the proscenium, explains the scene, the scenery and the action. The emphasis is accorded to the lyric word. The theatre disappears in order for this to be spoken completely, to give place to a declamation in dialogue, a sort of poetic decoration. Maeterlinck did not go as far as this'.

RACHILDE (Chateau-Leveque 1860 — Paris 953). Her real name was Marguerite Eymery.

Born near Perigueux, on an estate worked by her maternal grandparents, she had a disturbed childhood. Her father was an officer, and she was tossed from garrison to garrison until he resigned from the army and devoted himself to the family estate. She was twelve at the time, and was already writing short stories. She adopted the pseudonym of Rachilde, and gradually published them in regional newspapers. But evidently this young provincial girl dreamed only of success in Paris, where she went in 1878. Two years later, her novel *Monsieur Nouveauté* brought her fame. She frequented the Symbolist circles, emancipated but independent and reserved, even though she was famous for her beauty. In 1889 she married Alfred Vallette, with whom she was also involved in the destiny of the *Mercure de France*.

She left numerous novels, short stories and plays for the theatre. Many writers of the period praised her talent. Francis Miomandre, for example, in 1903, in the review *L'Art moderne*, paid

H. BATAILLE *Portrait of Rachilde*

homage to the originality of her work: 'There is no doubt that one day people will recognize that *L'Animal* is an admirable book, that *La Tour d'Amour* is a success not very far from genius, that *Les Hors-nature* are true poetry, with mad bounds of lyricism, and that through *La Sanglante Ironie* passes the shudder of Death, ever more vibrant, more violent, more irresistible. And he added, emphasising implicitly the link between certain themes of these works and Symbolist literature: 'When she had signed these four books, and many others, and her theatre, and so many short stories of such fierce idealist irony, she could claim the right to occupy, among the literary preferences of the sensitive, a place of her own in the middle of all the writers who have cherished free will, the liberation of the soul, the dream, and death.'

REINHARDT Max (Baden, near Vienna 1873 — New York 1943). Having been interested in the theatre from a very early age, he became an actor at seventeen, and then met Otto Brahm, director of the *Deutsches Theater* in Berlin. Brahm engaged Reinhardt to play in his company (1892-93); Reinhardt reacted strongly against the influence which Naturalism had on his master, and changed to a career in theatre design. Having become, in his turn, a theatre director, he bought the *Deutsches Theater* in 1905, on to which he built in 1906 a hall for experiments, using Strindberg's idea of an intimate theatre, a *Kammerspiele*. After the war, he organized different premises in Berlin, which were enormous and suitable for crowd performances, and which had been built by the architect Hans Poelzig: this was the *Grosses Schauspielhaus*, which he opened in November 1919 with a performance of *Orestes* by Aeschylus, and where in February 1920 he put on *Le Danton* by Romain Rolland. However, disappointed by the results in Berlin, he abandoned his theatrical enterprises in order to return to Austria. In 1920 he established a festival in Salzburg which was to become famous with the performance of a play by Hofmannsthal in the outer sanctuary of the cathedral: *Everyman*. From 1932 to 1937 he took part in numerous excursions abroad. One of these took him to Paris in 1933, to the Pigalle Theatre with *Die Fledermaus* by Johann Strauss. In 1937 he settled finally in the United States where he continued to work in the theatre, and where he died.

He was called 'the magician of the stage'. And it is certain that he tried to use all the new techniques possible in the theatre, rather like an 'illusionist': he made use of the moving stage, and he totally altered the lighting and noise effects. On the other hand, it is difficult to classify him as belonging to one current or another. He himself resisted the system with all his might, judging that his sole aim was to give reality to dreams. In 1924 he said that those who loved the theatre, actors and spectators alike, were only looking for 'ecstasy, rapture, which only drugs could otherwise bring'.

He was a fervent supporter of the Symbolist theatre, or rather, according to the term which was generally adopted in the German-speaking countries, the neo-Romantic theatre. While still an actor in Otto Brahm's company, he took part in the activities of the *Sezessiontheater*, with Martin Zickel and Paul Martin, and in 1898 he acted in *Pelléas et Mélisande* by Maeterlinck, which they put on in 1898 in Berlin (Schiffbauerdamm). In 1903 he staged this play himself, after Oscar Wilde's *Salomé* in 1902. This was really the start of his enthusiasm for Hofmannsthal: in 1903 he did *Elektra*, which marked an exact stage in his involvement with Symbolism. In his work could be found several characteristics which corresponded to the ambitions of the Symbolist movement: the stylization of the actors' methods, especially in the use of pantomime; a desire to raise the anecdote to an abstract generality; the effort to reject the Naturalist 'slice of life'. Elektra's character became the symbol of bestiality — she was stripped of all human individuality, she became all hate and vengeance. The lighting effects were those which made the symbol conspicuous: for example, during certain appearances of Elektra, a red light fell from a fig tree in order to be directed on to the ground and appear like pools of blood.

The last initiative of totally neo-Romantic staging was *Oedipus and the Sphinx* by Hofmannsthal in 1906. After this, Max Reinhardt turned his efforts mostly towards performances of plays by the classic authors, particularly Shakespeare. Nevertheless, there were a number of authors belonging to the European Symbolist movement who continued to be favoured by him: always Maeterlinck (*Aglavaine et Selysette* in 1907, *L'Oiseau bleu* in 1912) and Hofmannsthal (*Der Tor und der Tod*) in 1908, and then *Jedermann* in 1911), but also August Strindberg and Knut Hamsun.

For a very long time, Max Reinhardt used the methods of staging recommended by the Symbolist authors. These included the power of suggestion of the poetic word and music, or the play of lighting in various colours in order to immerse the spectators in a universe of marvels, in the life of the soul, just as Maeterlinck and Hofmannsthal wished. In his fundamental intentions, which consisted of making the 'grisaille quotidienne' forgotten, the Symbolist aspirations of the unreal can be found, their aspirations of an ideal where social preoccupations did not intervene, their aspirations of pure aesthetic pleasure in the rapture of the senses.

ROINARD Paul-Napoleon (Neuchâtel-en-Bray 1856 — ?). He completed his secondary studies at the Rouen lyceum, and then enrolled at the School of Fine Arts in Paris, and in the School of Medicine. He was a poet and playwright who led a Bohemian life. In 1886 he published a collection of poems (*Nos plaies*) and then, while frequenting the wine-shop *Le Chat noir*, in Montmartre, he established the *La Butte* society. In the end he was editor of *La Revue septentrionale*, and took over the direction of *Essais d'art libre*. Suspected of anarchist activities, he left Paris to take refuge in Brussels in 1895. He remained there for two years. On his return, he published a collection of poetry: *La Mort du rêve* (Mercure de France, 1902).

SCHURE Edouard (Strasburg 1841 — Paris 1929) He was one of the first interpreters of Wagner's works in France with *Le Drame musical* (1875), since the first book specifically devoted to Wagner's works to appear after this essay was that of Judith Gautier in 1882. The whole Symbolist generation after Mallarmé was indebted to him for this work.

But he was not just a music historian. He also recorded, at that time, the trends in thought. In this way he was at the source of the revival of mystic studies. In 1889 he published *Les Grands Initiés* (Perrin, Paris) in which he tried, in reference to a spiritualist philosophy, to surmount the crisis of contemporary thought, with his opposition divided between Science and Religion. He also wrote poems, plays and novels. One of these, *L'Ange et la Sphinge* (Perrin, Paris 1897) brought to the fore a theme which ran right through Symbolist literature and painting: the dual personality of woman, who was both angel and temptress trying to make man surrender to her instincts.

SCHWOB Marcel (Chaville 1867 — Paris 1905). He was one of the most original and most cultured minds, one of the most subtle critics, and one of the most curious writers of the turn of the century. This learned man was capable of studying both slang (1889) and Greek courtesans, Christian legends or Anglo-Saxon literature (Shakespeare, Defoe, Poe, Stevenson). Humour, fantasy, scholarly depravity and irony run through his numerous tales (collected in *Le Coeur double, Le roi au masque d'or, Vies imaginaires*). A novel, *Le Livre de Monelle* 1894) has been considered a condensation of all the Symbolist characteristics, and exercised a profound influence over all the young intellectuals who visited the *Mercure de France*.

STANISLAVSKI Constantin (Moscow 1863 — Moscow 1938). His real name was Constantin Sergueievitch Alexeiev, and he was the fifth generation descended from a serf who had invented a system of weaving gold thread, and who having thus gained his freedom had made at the same time the fortune of his family. In the nineteenth century the Alexeievs were foremost in the weaving factories.

The young Constantin acted in several plays even while he was at school. In 1885 he passed the entrance examination for the Imperial Theatres school while he was working in an office in his father's factory. But he found the tuition in drama unbearable and he left at the end of three weeks. He made frequent visits to France on textile business, particularly to Lyons, and he visited theatres which gave him the idea of trying to get into the Conservatoire in Paris. Since the Conservatoire did not accept foreign students, he was allowed to go to classes as a free listener. But it was another disappointment. So he returned to Russia, where he acted with the company of the Society of Art and Literature. At the same time he made his debut in stage design: in 1891 he put on the new play by Tolstoy, *The Fruits of Instruction*.

A career in drama was now opening for Stanislavski, which was the pseudonym he had adopted. This was to lead him in 1898, with the successful

writer Vladimir Nemirovitch-Dantchenko, to the foundation of the Artistic Theatre in Moscow. At first, their repertoire was Naturalist and social (Chekov, Gorki). They then tackled Shakespeare with a performance of Julius Caesar in 1904. There followed three plays — *The Drama of Life* by Knut Hamsun and *Man's Life* by Leonid Andreiev in 1908, and *L'Oiseau bleu* by Maeterlinck in 1908 — which seemed to effect a rupture with the aesthetics in which Stanislavski had previously been involved. Through Isadora Duncan, who was often engaged to play in Russia, he also discovered the ideas of Gordon Craig, and he invited him to put on *Hamlet* in Moscow in 1908. Sadly, in consequence of various difficulties, Shakespeare's play was not performed until 1911, and Stanislavski realized that his ideas in the theatre were fairly distant from those of Gordon Craig. He worked principally on the formation of the actor, and on the elaboration of what has become known as the Stanislavski system. This mainly consisted in bringing real life on to the stage, the actor having to learn not to imitate outward appearances but to behave as a living being. He claimed to study real truth in place of mere verisimilitude. This preoccupation concerned him until his death.

The favours which he had enjoyed in the Soviet Union from 1932 onwards, notwithstanding his avant-garde experiments aimed at promoting a so-called realist art, have tended to mask the diversity of his earlier efforts. A label had definitely been stuck on him: that of a Naturalist or a realist. However, he did go through a Symbolist phase, as was shown, for example, by the performance of Maeterlinck's *L'Oiseau bleu*: he rejected paintings which were too detailed in order to look at sketches which suggested. Egorov, the painter, realized a stylized décor in order to interpret the world of fairyland. He made no attempt to reconstitute reality, but conjured up a world of unreality which corresponded to the atmosphere of the play. To achieve this aim, the staging used every new technical means: a revolving stage, mechanical and lighting devices.

Stanislavski himself said that he had paid his tribute to every fashion in stage design from Naturalist reproduction to suggestive stylization. But it would also be true to say that he had rapidly rejected the attraction of Symbolism as a mere concession which he had deigned to make to the taste of the period, and which did not really correspond to his own interior need. He was in alliance with Meyerhold, a former pupil of the Artistic Theatre, in 1905 when they established the Theatre-Studio which was a kind of laboratory adjacent to the Artistic Theatre, but he came to oppose him in the end by reason of differences which were too pronounced: he blamed the Studio for having adopted the idea that realism had had its day and that it was necessary to show the irrational on the stage.

For his part, Meyerhold explained extensively

what separated him from Stanislavski. In 1926, for example, he went back to the settings used in the Artistic Theatre from 1898 to 1908, and he laid the blame on the fundamental principle of his former master, according to whom all that was represented must be true, from the scenery to the style of the acting. The result was, according to him, that the proper rhythm of the play was forgotten, that the actor was allowed no illusion, and that all possibility of the dream was removed from the spectator. He wished to retain only Stanislavski's designs for Chekov, which, although he had not known how to turn this *nouveau ton* to advantage, had given the Artistic Theatre the reputation of a theatre of the spiritual state.

In spite of their dissensions, Stanislavski declared on his deathbed in 1938, when Meyerhold was in disgrace with certain of the Soviet authorities, that he was the only person in the theatre worthy of assuring its posterity.

WAGNER Richard (Leipzig 1813 — Venice 1883). It would be strange to claim that Wagner was a Symbolist musician. On the other hand it would be unreasonable to speak of Symbolism without evoking Wagner and Wagnerism. The obsession of Baudelaire, Verlaine, Mallarmé and many others for this German composer has already been mentioned. It is known that a review such as *La Revue wagnérienne* was one of the great platforms for Symbolism. But was there more? It appears that while Wagner, to start with, was defined by relation to the 'grand opera' of Meyerbeer, his evolution and his most remarkable contributions

Portrait of Richard Wagner from a painting by Lenbach

came from what he himself had chosen, from several great European myths, to put to music and to stage. As a natural consequence, Wagner's dramatic principles, together with his dream of a 'complete' theatre, became adopted later by the Symbolists: Bayreuth had taught them how to present a theatre of atmosphere, to avoid the direct representation of events in order to show an action which was interior. And so finally, the double postulation which is so charcteristic of Wagner's heroes — depravity and innocence fatality of sin and nostalgia for purity, itself a heritage of European romanticism — became progressively the distinctive mark of the character of the Symbolist theatre: Lulu and Mélisande are the descendants of Kundry.

Certainly Wagner, having become the recognized musician whom we know, would have been surprised to know his partisans, the Symbolists, had he not kept Baudelaire politely at a distance from the outset? But there was undoubtedly one Symbolist concern in which Wagner would have shared: the desire to give to art a purity and a strictness which Romanticism had lost.

WYZEWA Teodor de (Kalusik, Poland 1862 — Paris 1917). The son of a Polish doctor who emigrated to France from 1836 to 1859 in order to escape the Russian oppression, and then went back there in 1879, he received a French education. A pupil at Beauvais, he passed his baccalaureate in 1879 and prepared at the lycée Louis-le-Grand to take the entrance examination for the normal High School. He failed the oral tests in this examination, and then enrolled at the Douai faculty of letters, where he made the acquaintance of Paul Adam. In 1882 he was teaching philosophy in Châtellerault, and then went to Paris where he tried to make a living by giving private lessons. His meeting with Edouard Dujardin opened the doors of the literary world to him. Thanks to Dujardin, he collaborated on *La Revue indépendante* where he played an influential role from November 1886 to December 1887. He wrote innumerable articles for newspapers and magazines, published translations of the Russian and German authors, and became the power behind the throne of the Symbolist movement. He took French nationality in 1913, and was exposed to the attacks of Charles Maurras and *L'Action française* who did not accept that the literary press should submit to the tastes of a foreigner living in their country. Having used morphine on the recommendation of his doctor, he became addicted to it and died of an overdose on April 8, 1917.

In July 1886, he wrote an article on Mallarmé in *La Vogue*, in which he described his poetry as 'suggestive', and explained what made up the aesthetics of Symbolism: according to him it was 'to translate ideas, and to suggest at the same time the feeling of those ideas'.

Principal reviews and organizations

When a group is formed of young people who have more or less the same ideas about life, and who write without being able to find a paper which will publish their work, there is only one solution: start a new paper! This is what happened between 1885 and 1900 with the numerous literary groups of the Symbolist generation. Having reached the age of recognition, this generation saw ahead of it its elders who held the main positions, and who could not be shifted. It was necessary, therefore, for them to create their own means of expression. And the lesser reviews, often short-lived, flourished almost everywhere. It was they who gave the movement its life, even as far afield as Japan.

Dissimilar these reviews certainly were. They varied from the journal in page form, like *Le Décadent* was at the beginning, to a solid review like *Le Mercure de France*. But a state of mind kept most of them together: the rejection of accepted values, in politics as much as in literature. From this came a sympathy, not only in the circle of *La Revue blanche*, with anarchist ideas and an opposition to previously accepted literary and artistic currents, especially that of Naturalism. To science's claims to govern everything, the young people of France replied with their longing for a Soul, for spirituality. To the frivolities in which their parents had bathed them, they opposed the defiance of intellectual pleasures.

This resulted in a dangerous situation which they could not avoid — they even encouraged it: life in an enclosed community, cut off from the established institutions. All these publications rarely broke through to the audience of the great public. What the public gave them was, at best, the derision which accompanied its attitude regarding those eccentrics of the period who were the decadents! The public found derisory the authors they most admired — Verlaine, Mallarmé, Villiers de l'Isle-Adam. Whatever the country, the situation was the same, and such that the desire to affirm their originality at any price often led the Symbolists to a provocative aestheticism, to a dandyism, to an isolation which even became hermetism. It was not by chance that the cult of Beauty and the exaltation of mystic doctrines found so much support in Symbolist circles.

The immense value of these little reviews appears more clearly to us today; and it is particularly their disregard for the daily press of the time which seems so astonishing, especially as it was frequently denounced by the Symbolists as frivolous and venal. These reviews were certainly not lacking in excesses; their expression in both invective and admiration was frequently noisy, and their desire to be provocative and eccentric, a far cry from the prevailing standards, sometimes ended in a style which was pompous or completely artificial. But this was just froth! From the other point of view, what effervescence of ideas, and, between them, what a new approach to old ideas, what boldness! In fact, what came out of those ideas was rather what is known today as the avant-garde. In spite of their limited circulation, they are responsible for the autonomy of the literary and artistic reviews of today, reviews on which a group rely to be sure of their existence and the expression of their ideas.

Beside these publications, certain organizations (Groupe des XX, the Order of the Rose + Croix), also played a determining role in the broadcasting of Symbolism, especially in painting. Both groups are listed below.

APPOLLON. Published in St. Petersburg, this review appeared from 1909 to 1917. It was a monthly (ten numbers per year plus a supplement, *The Literary Almanach*) which devoted itself to all the arts, and included numerous illustrations. It was the spokesman of Russian Symbolism (having Briussov, Ivanov, Blok, Annenski, Tchoulkov as contributors). Before 1914 it slightly changed direction, and gave room to those trends which were opposed to Symbolism, especially acmeism.

BLÄTTER FÜR DIE KUNST die. This review, founded by Stefan George, first appeared in 1892. To start with it was not produced for commercial reasons, but only for the circle of Stefan George's friends. It lasted until 1919.

Among its contributors, especially of poetry, were Dauthendey, Gérardy, Gundolf and Hofmannsthal. It also included translations by Baudelaire.

Title page of *Le Septième Anneau*
published by *Blätter für die Kunst*. 1907

CENTAURE Le This review appeared as a literary quarterly in 1896. It was edited by its founder, Henri Albert, a member of the editorial board of *Mercure de France*. Contributors included Pierre Louÿs, Henri de Régnier, André Gide, Paul Valéry. Numerous illustrations (Jacques-Emile Blanche, Albert Besnard, Félicien Rops etc.).

CONQUE La Founded by Pierre Louÿs, this review only saw eleven numbers, from March 1891 to 1892. Contributors: André Gide, Maurice Maeterlinck, Camille Mauclair, Charles Morice, Paul Valéry etc. It published poetry and appeared on eight printed pages.

DECADENT Le This publication was at first called *Le Décadent littéraire et artistique* until December 1887, and appeared until 1889. It was started by Anatole Baju, who defined his programme in the first number of 1886. This was an anti-bourgeois programme which used the example of Des Esseintes in Huysmans' *A Rebours*; 'Modern man has become deadened. Refinements of taste, of sensations, of appetites, of luxury, of enjoyments; neurosis, hysteria, hypnotism, morphinomania, scientific charlatanism, Schopenhauerism to excess, these are the premonitory symptons of social evolution'. *Le Décadent* united the Parisian circles which, in a flashy Bohemia, were opposed to art and literature in place, cultivating originality at any price, in clothing as in speech.

ECRITS POUR L'ART Under the editorship of René Ghil and Gaston Dubedat, the first series of this review, which appeared from 1887 to 1906, bound together the Symbolist generation. A second series followed the movement of René Ghil towards the school which he named 'instrumentist'.

ENTRETIENS POLITIQUE ET LITTERAIRES Founded by Henri de Régnier, Paul Adam, Georges Vanor, Bernard Lazare and Francis Viélé-Griffin, this review appeared between 1890 and 1893 with Edmond Bailly as editor. An interest in mysticism and occultism could be found in it, but all aspects of Symbolism were represented with equal emphasis. Notable contributions by Saint-Pol Roux, Mallarmé, Dujardin.

ERMITAGE L' Established in April 1890, this review remained in existence until the end of 1906. It tried various directions. To start with, it had no real plan, but the Symbolists brought their active collaboration to it, and this Symbolist support remained with it until 1895. Henri Mazel had been appointed director in March 1891, and printed articles by Rémy de Gourmont, Rachilde, Gide, Maeterlinck, Valéry and Saint-Pol Roux. In 1895 he resigned, and the editorship was entrusted to Edouard Ducote. The change of direction was not established until 1897 however, when Jacques des Gachons became head of the editorial staff. The review was then no longer Symbolist, but laid claim, with a homogeneous team, to Naturalism.

IDEE LIBRE L' This review was mainly literary, and receptive to foreign literature (rediscovery of the German Romantics, articles on Shakespeare, on Keats, and on contemporary Russian literature). It appeared monthly from April 1892 to December 1895. It was edited by Emile Besnus, and among its contributors were Paul Adam, Hermann Bahr, Paul Claudel, Paul Fort, Jean Lorrain, Henri Mazel, Henri de Régnier and Edouard Schuré.

LITERATORUL A Rumanian review, established in 1880 by Macedonski, generally considered the foremost Symbolist in Rumania, which especially supported the poet Tudor Arghesi.

MERCURE DE FRANCE Le Started at the end of 1889 by Alfred Vallette and a group of writers (Jules Renard, Louis Dumur, and later Rémy de Gourmont, among others), this review at first was the continuation of *La Pléiade*, which had been founded in 1886 by Rodolphe Darzens. On the

back cover could be read: '*la Pléiade*, second year.'
It inclined towards Naturalism and consisted of
instalments of thirty-two pages. Then, as the
thickness of each issue increased, the support for
Symbolism became more established, to triumph
completely in 1895.

One year later, *Le Mercure de France* became a
publishing house and brought out *Aphrodite* by
Pierre Louÿs, which it followed with the translation of Nietzsche's works. This progress took *Le
Mercure de France*, with the exception of a break
during the Second World War, beyond 1945.

According to Rémy de Gourmont in his *Promenades Littéraires*, this review was for the Symbolist generation, among fifty other reviews
or magazines published at the same time, 'the
concentration if not the synthesis of the new
literature'.

MIR ISKUSSTVA (World of Art). In this Russian
review, which appeared from 1889 to 1904,
devoted mainly to painting but also to literature,
the Symbolist trends had an opportunity for
expression, although they were not dominant.
Diaghilev and Léon Bakst were the moving spirits
behind it and the initial aim consisted of bringing
the new trends together by establishing a link
between the worlds of the Moscow and the
Petersburg artists. The general inspiration was
favourable towards Art Nouveau.

MODERNISTE Le A weekly directed by Georges-
Albert Aurier. Eight issues were published in
1889. Contributions were received from writers
such as Saint-Pol Roux and Charles Morice, but
also from painters and art lovers (Gauguin,
Clément Bellenger, Julien Leclercq, Rambosson).

NIEUWE GIDS de (The New Guide). This review was Dutch, founded by Willem Kloos, and
exercised some influence on the spreading of
Symbolism. It was notable for having published
an article by Barrès in 1885 on the Flemish
movement around the Belgian review *Van Nu en
Straks*.

NOUVELLE RIVE GAUCHE La Appearing first
in November 1882, it took the name *Lutèce* in April
1883, and continued to be published until 1886.
Its format was that of the daily papers (four
pages), and it came out weekly. It saw two hundred and fifty-six numbers. Receptive towards all
trends, it took contributions from the Symbolists.
Apart from contributions from Paul Adam,
Rachilde, Henri de Régnier, Francis Viélé-Griffin,
it also published *Les Complaintes* by Jules Laforgue.
It was directed by Léo Trézenik and the secretary
of the editorial staff was Georges Rall.

NYUGAT (Occident). This Hungarian review
appeared between 1910 and 1914, and brought
together the new trends. Among its influential
contributors were the two most remarkable poets
of the epoch: Endre Ady and Mihály Babits. Its
aim was to introduce into Hungary the most
contemporary and most lively western culture.

OEUVRE L' This was one of those rare Symbolist
reviews published in the country (Valence-sur-
Rhône). It appeared from 1897 to 1899. Contributions from Paul Adam, Edouard Ducote,
Francis Viélé-Griffin, Paul Fort, André Gide.

PAN This was one of the most attractive reviews
of the period. It last from 1895 to 1900. Among
those responsible were Julius Meier-Graefe for the
painting, and O.J. Bierbaum for the literature. Its
orientation was not very precise, but it promoted
the new trends in a general fashion, whence came
the publication of texts of neo-Romantic inspiration. Collaborators included: Dauthendy,
Dehmel, Flaischlen, Hofmannsthal, Liliencron,
Morgenstern, Schaukal.

PLUME La This review, of which the first number
came out on April 15, 1889, was not really Symbolist, although receptive to Symbolism as to other
trends. It remained in existence until 1914.

Special issue of the review *La Plume*. 1894

According to Ernest Raynaud, writing in the first volume of *La Melée symboliste* (La Renaissance du Livre, Paris 1920), it summarized all the smaller reviews of the time: 'It did even more than this, for, not content with literature alone, it was interested in all the arts; it organized special numbers for groups of poets from various provinces, and thus gave great impetus to the decentralizing movement which at that time was in the minds of so many people. It put on show the work of painters, sculptors, and craftsmen; it was involved with sociology, and music. It even gave some space to the theatre'.

PROMETEO This was a Spanish review started by Ramón Gómez de la Serna in 1908. *Prometeo* had altogether thirty-eight numbers. It published numerous Symbolist writers, as well as representatives of what was known as decadentism, (Rachilde, Oscar Wilde, Paul Fort, Maeterlinck, Camille Mauclair, Rémy de Gourmont, D'Annunzio, Saint-Pol Roux). It stopped appearing in 1913.

Poster for *La Revue Blanche* by Pierre Bonnard. 1894

LA REVUE BLANCHE La It was originally a Franco-Belgian review, published in Brussels, which bore this title, and appeared from 1889 to 1891. It was started by Paul Leclercq, Joé Hogge and August Jeunhomme, and was at first Naturalist in inclination and later entirely Symbolist.

In 1891, Alexandre Natanson founded, in Paris, another review with the same name, and it is generally to this one that reference is made. Lucien Muhlfeld was secretary of the editorial staff. This review played a most important role

from 1891 to 1900. With its anarchist tendency it reunited the whole of the Symbolist generation (Kahn, de Gourmont, Dujardin, Mallarmé, Viélé-Griffin), and was of general interest rather than specifically literary. It made Ibsen, Tolstoy, Strindberg and Hamsun known. The music reviews in it were managed by Claude Debussy.

REVUE CONTEMPORAINE La This review actually carried the title *Revue indépendante, politique, littéraire et artistique* on its twelve numbers which appeared between November 1884 and May 15, 1885. It was founded by Félix Fénéon who, twenty-three at the time, had been employed at the Ministry of War since 1881. In those days it was not a truly Symbolist publication. Many different signatures could be found there, and it accorded a certain amount of room to foreign literature. Two Germans were favoured by it: Schopenhauer and Wagner.

After this, the review disappeared for some time. Edouard Dujardin then decided to resurrect it, at the same time as he was publishing *La Revue wagnérienne*. He entrusted the direction, from 1886 to 1888, to Teodor de Wyzewa, and then, in January 1888 until 1889, this passed to Gustave Kahn. The whole period was marked by the support given by *La Revue indépendante* to the Symbolist movement.

Finally, at the beginning of 1889, a new slant was given to this publication with the direction of François de Nion and Georges Bonnamour: '*La Revue indépendante*' one could read, 'has just undergone a radical transformation to which we would like to draw your attention. Henceforth *La Revue indépendante* will strive to show no preference for any school. It will give an impartial welcome to all opinions and all talents.' In fact it was a case for a return to Realist inspiration. It was possible to admire Laforgue in it, as Camille Mauclair wrote, and to enjoy 'the literature which was bordering on occultism', but the 'Naturalist doctrines' were equally admitted. In 1892, this review disappeared completely.

REVUE WAGNERIENNE La This review appeared between 1885 and 1888, under the direction of Edouard Dujardin. Its aim was to make Wagner's works known in all their forms — musical, but also philosophical and political. It collected together the Symbolist generation.

ROSE + CROIX La Before the start of the seventeenth century, there is evidence of certain images where roses are associated with crosses. In 1614, a manifesto was published at Cassel, to which was added the life story of an alleged magician who had lived in the Orient and who had come back to Germany to start a monastery there: Christian

Poster for the *Salon de la Rose + Croix*. 1892

Rosenkreutzer. The Rosicrucian societies developed from this, like enclosed orders. This was still the case at the beginning of the eighteenth century. Born from a spiritual dispute with the Lutheran doctrine, they then inclined towards alchemy and esotericism.

In France, Stanislas de Guaîta founded, in 1888, the cabalistic order of the Rose + Croix. Joséphin Péladan belonged to it. But he broke away from this order to start another, the Rose + Croix of the Temple and the Grail, which was also called the Catholic Rose + Croix. This order was important for the arts of the period, since Péladan patronised, through its agency, the salons of painting. From 1892 to 1897, these annual salons, of which there were six in all, gathered together the young painters. The masters (Moreau, Puvis de Chavannes, Redon, Watts, Burne-Jones) did not take part in them, but Rouault showed there in 1897.

Among the Symbolists, this enthusiasm and sympathy for the order of the Rose + Croix were related to the contemporary fashion of mysticism. Péladan launched an appeal to the artists in these terms: 'Artists who believe in Leonardo and *The Victory of Samothrace*, you will be the Rose + Croix. Our aim is to tear love out of the western soul and replace it with the love of Beauty, the love of the Idea, the love of Mystery. We will combine in harmonious ecstasy the emotions of literature, the Louvre and Bayreuth'.

SIMBOLUL A Rumanian review founded in 1912, therefore belated in relation to the French Symbolist movement, but which still bore the traces of it. It was important, for one of its founders was a young poet, S. Samyro, who appeared later under the name of Tristan Tzara in French literature.

SYMBOLISTE Le This weekly, created on October 1, 1886, to argue against *Le Decadent*, had only four numbers. It was edited by Gustave Kahn, Jean Moréas and Paul Adam.

TACHES D'ENCRE Les This review was published from November 5, 1884, to February 1885, and was started by Maurice Barrès. It had four numbers with a circulation of only one thousand two hundred copies.

TOISON D'OR La The Symbolists of the second generation, in Alexandre Blok's circle, collaborated on this art review in Russia (Moscow), which also organized picture exhibitions. It lasted from 1906 to 1909, and was published by the art dealer and patron N.P. Riabuchinski. At the start of its career it included articles in both French and Russian.

VAN NU EN STRAKS By its title (Of Now and Later) this review placed itself in the Symbolist camp, since it recalled the work of Charles Morice, *La Littérature de tout à l'heure*. It was founded in 1893 by the Flemish writer Vermeylen. It was the origin of the development of Symbolism in Flemish literature in Belgium (with Karel van de Woestijne,

Prosper van Langendonck). It ceased to appear at the end of the year 1893-94, but was published again, with much more space given to foreign literature, from January 1, 1896, until 1901.

VER SACRUM The first number of this monthly review appeared in January 1898. It lived for two years, being published first in Vienna (1898) and then at Leipzig (1899). It printed mainly articles of art criticism. Among its contributors were Hugo von Hofmannsthal, Maurice Maeterlinck, Rainer Maria Rilke and Paul Scheerbart.

VESY This important Russian review spread Symbolism from 1904 to 1909, thanks to the influence which the poet Briussov exercised over it at that time. It was open to the whole of Europe and sent correspondents abroad. Thus it was that René Ghil provided it with about forty contributions in which he brought information on the development of Symbolism in France. It also published work by Maeterlinck and Verhaeren.

VIATA NOUA (The New Life). This was a Rumanian periodical started in 1905 by the poet Ovid Densusianu, and was extremely Symbolist in inclination. It remained in existence until 1925.

VINGT Les In 1883, Octave Maus and Edmond Picard established in Brussels a society which numbered — hence its name — twenty members, painters or sculptors. Thanks to them exhibitions were held each year from 1884 to 1893, the number of twenty exhibitors being adhered to by the artists who were invited. These artists were usually foreign. Thus Rodin, Monet, Renoir, Cézanne, Gauguin and van Gogh all showed under the auspices of the Groupe des XX. Among its regular adherents were James Ensor, Fernand Khnopff, Guillaume Vogels, Theo van Rysselberghe and Henry van de Velde. Octave Maus also started a periodical, *L'Art moderne*, which served as their medium of communication.

VOGUE La This weekly, which comprised thirty-six pages, appeared for the first time on April 11, 1886, with Leo d'Orfer as chief editor. Until 1887 (thirty-one issues) the first series published the writers of the period without partiality, but the second series, which was published until July 1889, showed a marked tendency towards the Symbolists with contributions from Henri de Régnier, Jean Lorrain, Adolphe Retté and Francis Viélé-Griffin.

VOLNE SMERY (Free Trends). This Czech review, established in 1897, was born of an artistic

association: the Alliance of Mànes Artists. It helped to widen Czech culture to include international artistic movements, especially Symbolism. In 1902 it organized a Rodin exhibition in Prague, and in 1905 an exhibition of the works of Munch.

WALLONIE La Among the many other Belgian reviews (*La Jeune Belgique, La Basoche, La Pléiade*) which were devoted to the Symbolists, this was the most important. It appeared in Liège from 1886 to 1892. With Albert Mockel as its moving spirit (he had in the past produced *L'Elan littéraire*, also in Liège), it was the assembly point for the Belgian and French Symbolists, a bridge between the same generations in Belgium and France.

Sketch for the title page of *The Yellow Book*. 1894

YELLOW BOOK The This was an English magazine with a yellow cover, the provocative colour which was also that of the cover of Huysmans' novel *A Rebours* and Anatole Baju's *Le Décadent* (Paris). Aubrey Beardsley brought it fame through his illustrations. It was representative of English aesthetics and the decadent movement in England, and came out from 1894 to 1897.

A few key words

There were certain terms which were in special usage between 1880 and 1900. This brief glossary intends purely to explain them, and is naturally limited to the meanings which they held at the time, without going into their semantic evolution. For this reason, priority has been given to the definitions used by the contemporaries of the Symbolist movement as opposed to the judgements of more modern critics.

AESTHETE, AESTHETICISM Like the *dandies* and the *snobs*, the aesthetes first originated in English fashion. Aestheticism was a notion which, overlapping that of 'decadence', ran its course in France from about 1885. It exalted the religion of Beauty, and its evolution continued until about 1900. In his *Etudes et Portraits*, Paul Bourget wrote: 'To compose life with impressions of art and art alone, that was in its ultimate simplicity the programme of the aesthetes'.

In 1892, aestheticism was embodied in Paris by Oscar Wilde. In *La Revue bleue*, Teodor de Wyzewa emphasised that, since his arrival in Paris, Oscar Wilde had been welcomed as the prince of aesthetes. And he added that the French were 'used to thinking of England as the last refuge of style, of intellectual refinement and that melancholy sensitivity which is always present in higher natures'.

This aestheticism necessitated a material independence, and it was therefore the prerogative of the refined who had a certain fortune at their command. It was characterized by an artificial way of life and was founded essentially on the appearance. In Oscar Wilde, it implied a moral and aesthetic need: it was necessary to make life into a work of art. In fact, while snobism only took up the superficial aspect of things, aestheticism implied a deep involvement, a sincerity.

DANDYISM Like snobism, it spread in France from 1880 onwards, and followed in consequence of Anglomania. After Baudelaire, who defined dandyism as 'an arrogant and provocative attitude of class', Paul Bourget was instrumental in its divulgation: from 1880 to 1883 he travelled in England, and published articles in the French magazines. Dandyism was manifested in ostentatious clothing, such as the velvet waistcoat and red gloves worn by Edouard Dujardin, and by a liking for the unusual and artificial, or a love of trinkets. All this testified to a horror of the vulgar or natural. This is why dandyism implied a pressing aesthetic and moral need which was shown by a cold impassiveness and an aristocratic haughtiness. This cult was professed in art and artifice.

In the *Portrait of Dorian Gray*, Oscar Wilde defined the dandy as one who scorned reality, which is mediocrity, and exalted Beauty.

DECADENCE Ever since the eighteenth century, there has been an argument between writers in France about decadence and the decline of taste. The general idea was one of a literary regression in relation to the examples of former times. Voltaire himself, in his book on the time of Louis XIV, espoused the cause of the classics, the Ancients, who were the source of good taste. Moreover, he wrote in a letter to La Harpe on April 23, 1770: 'My dear boy, there is no hope of being able to re-establish good taste. We are in every way in the age of the most horrible decadence'.

The belief that France was entering into a period of decline then developed above all after the Revolution of 1789. And it was around 1850 that works on the subject of decadence started to appear everywhere, together with the fashions of the decadent epochs, especially Latin decadence. Lengthy studies, claiming to be scientific, were also piling up in order to try to prove the physiological decline of the modern races. The contemporaries of the nineteenth century were the neurotics. Baudelaire, Théophile Gautier, Zola and the Goncourts claimed this decadence, this imbalance of nerves and sensitivity, to be a consequence of the times in which they lived. In *Mes Haines*, Zola wrote, in 1866: 'My taste, if you like, is depraved; I enjoy very spicy reading matter, decadent works in which a sort of sensitive sickliness replaces the abundant health of the classic epochs. I am a child of my times'. Two years later, Théophile Gautier analysed the style of decadence in his preface to *Les Fleurs du Mal* by Baudelaire: 'The poet of *Les Fleurs du Mal* liked what is inaccurately called the style of decadence, which is only art arrived at the point of extreme maturity which ageing civilizations discover in the rays of their setting suns: a style which is clever, complicated, scholarly, full of nuances and investigations, always drawing back the boundaries of language, borrowing from every technical vocabulary, taking colours from every palette, notes from every keyboard, striving to put back thought into that which is the most indescribable, the form in its vaguest and most fleeting contours, hearkening in order to translate them, to the most subtle confidences of neurosis, the avowals of ageing passion which becomes depraved, and the strange hallucinations of obsession turning into madness.'

With the defeat of 1870, the impression of decadence in France grew even greater. Paul Bourget more than any other contributed to the spreading of this concept with some of his articles. In *La Revue bleue* of June 6, 1885, a critic stated: 'This word *decadent* resounds in Monsieur Bourget's pages with such a loud flourish that it has aroused my curiosity. I have been inquiring and I have learnt, not without helpless amazement, that the sickness of pessimism does not only apply to a few eccentrics, but that it has become a mania, and infected a remarkable number of our youth.'

In other words, when Anatole Baju established the review *Le Décadent* in 1886, and people were speaking of a decadent 'school', the idea of decadence was already extremely widespread. Certain novels such as *Le Crépuscule des Dieux* by Elemir Bourges, *A Rebours* by Huysmanns, and *Le Vice suprême* by Joséphin Péladan, popularized it. Or else it was violently condemned because of the very relaxation of rules to which it had given rise: this was what Max Nordau did in *Entartung*, a work which was translated into French in 1894 under the title *Dégénérescence*. Sometimes it was praised and proclaimed with pleasure: numerous novels (Paul Adam, Jean Lorrain, and Rachilde in France, as well as Oscar Wilde and D'Annunzio abroad) and paintings showed up the artificiality and psychological refinements, with an appeal to several sexual perversions. One of the themes most often treated was that of the hermaphrodite. Homosexual love was no longer just imagined, the object of a theatre of the mind, but actually lived and paraded by the aesthetes.

DILETTANTISM The dilettante was in fashion at the end of the century: he played with all ideas and settled on none. In an article which appeared in *La Nouvelle Revue*, Paul Bourget defined it in this way, while proving that it was very prevalent: 'It is much less a doctrine than a state of mind, very intelligent and very voluptuous at the same time, which inclines us towards the various forms of life in turn and leads us to lend ourselves to all these forms without giving ourselves to any of them.'

IDEALISM It was through 'idealism' that the reaction against positivism (Auguste Comte,

Hippolyte Taine) and Naturalism (Zola) was manifested. The conscious was put forward as the creator of the world. In this respect the influence of Schopenhauer was determining. Under the title of idealism it was possible to distinguish two directions: either the dream and the imagination were exalted, as was the case with decadentism, or there was established, above the concrete world, a universe of abstract notions which allowed the essence of the real to be arrived at, and this ended in Symbolism as Mallarmé saw it. As Edouard Dujardin wrote, specifying what the Symbolists meant by idealism (*Mallarmé par un des siens*, Albert Messein, Paris 1936): 'The exterior world only existed for Mallarmé inasmuch as it was the symbol of the world of ideas; it did not exist for the young people who we were in 1885-86 except inasmuch as it was conceived through the mind. The outside world was a décor which was put together or dismantled according to the convenience of the poet.'

MYSTICISM The last twenty years of the century were marked, in the generation of the young intellectuals, by a return to the supernatural and a religious uneasiness which had disappeared with the Parnassian and Naturalist writers. At that time, the term mysticism usually meant, in an imprecise fashion, this reaction against science and positivism. Through mysticism the Soul was brought to the fore, but not in a strictly religious sense; it was rather to point out the mystery of the profound Self, an insoluble Unknowable. It is true, nevertheless, that this mysticism opened out after 1890 into what Charles Morice announced as a 'poetic restoration of Catholicism', and that it was interpreted, in the Symbolist and decadent generations, through effective conversions to the Catholic religion (Huysmans, Claudel).

NATURALISM A literary movement in reaction to Symbolism, of which the moving spirits were Maurice Le Blond and Saint-Georges de Bouhélier. The orientations of this movement were shown in a series of articles by Maurice Le Blond in *Les Documents sur le naturisme* from November 1895 to September 1896. For his part, Saint-Georges de Bouhélier published a manifesto in *Le Figaro* on January 10, 1897. In the main, the 'naturalists' sympathised with the Naturalist conceptions and Zola (Maurice Le Blond, incidentally, married Denise Zola), but they gave priority to emotion rather than observation. From March 1897 they published a review, *La Revue naturiste*. They also more or less heralded two other movements: unanimist and populism.

LE PARNASSE In 1886 the publisher Alfred Lemerre published in Paris a collection of poetry entitled *Le Parnasse contemporain*, which gathered together works by various poets. Catulle Mendès was the source of this regrouping. The principles which ruled it were borrowed from Théophile Gautier: strict formality, impersonality, the religion of *art for art's sake*. But it was only in 1876, with the third volume of the *Parnasse contemporain*, that the literary Parnassian movement was formed. Its most famous representatives were Leconte de Lisle and José Maria de Hérédia. They extolled the virtues of impassivity, the cult of the past, perfection of formality and the rejection of all personal emotion. Several of the Symbolist poets started out as Parnassians, including Verlaine (in the first collection of the *Parnasse contemporain*, which brought the poets of the moment quite simply together without insisting on a common aestheticism; Mallarmé was one of them). But in fact the Symbolist movement brought about a rupture with the Parnassian movement: in place of descriptive art, it brought invention to the fore; in place of set forms, it liberated versification.

PESSIMISM Pessimism was the characteristic of the *mal de jeunesse* at the end of the century, that is to say that nihilism was spreading, that no one believed in anything any more, that it was even possible to consider that nothing was real and that everything could be. This was a state of mind which followed the 1870 war, and the failure of the Commune. The philosophy of Schopenhauer became extremely fashionable. In the preface to his *Nouveaux Essais*, dated November 15, 1885, Paul Bourget emphasised: 'The existence of pessimism in the souls of contemporary youth is recognized today by those same people who find this state of negation and depression the most repugnant.' The use of the term 'depression' is important here, because this pessimism led to a current disorder of the period, and one with which Huysmans' Des Esseintes found himself afflicted in *A Rebours*: neurosis.

SNOBISM The snob type spread in France around 1880, as a result of English fashion. It represented the individual who frequented the society of aristocrats and claimed to be well up in the latest novelties. It concerned therefore a state of mind rather than outward behaviour. In 1884, Paul Bourget gave this definition of snobism: 'The malady of vanity which consists of a cultivated superstition of total social superiority through birth, fortune, or renown.'

SUGGESTION For Mallarmé, this was the foundation of Symbolist aesthetics. In 1891 he explained: '*To name* an object is to suppress three-quarters of the delight in the poem which is there to be found out little by little: to *suggest* it — there is the dream.' Two years earlier, in his work *La Littérature*

de tout à l'heure, Charles Morice defined what the Symbolists meant when they spoke of *suggesting* in place of *naming*: 'The suggestion is the language of correspondences, and of the affinities of the soul with nature. Instead of explaining the reflection of things, it pervades them and becomes their own voice. Suggestion is never indifferent and, in essence, is always new, because it is the hidden, the unexplained and the *inexpressible* in things which it speaks. It gives to an old word the illusion that one is reading it for the first time.'

SYMBOL In a book entitled *Origines du symbolisme* (published by Albert Messein, Paris, 1936), Gustave Kahn said: 'It was Mallarmé who above all spoke of the symbol, seeing in it an equivalent of the word synthesis, and conceiving that the symbol was a living and ornate synthesis, without critical comments.' What is to be understood from that? That Mallarmé saw poetry as a creative act which came straight from the poet's soul, and was not an attempt to describe the world.

In fact, the word 'symbol' had extremely varied definitions between 1885 and 1900, even on the part of the Symbolists. It was very often confused with, particularly, the allegory and the myth. However, in Mallarmé's mind they had to be distinguished. The allegory was the representation of predetermined abstract ideas, while the symbol depended on the obscure — it plunged into the mystery of the idea or the state of the soul which the poet tried to evoke from what was most profound in himself. Albert Mockel, at a meeting on Symbolism in 1927, perfectly translated this approach to the symbol: 'In the art of writing there is a symbol when an image or succession of images, when an alliance of words or a musical caress allows us to catch a glimpse of an idea, or permits us to discover it as if it were born in us.'

SYNTHESIS This concerned a union between the different sensations, with one calling and suggesting the other in order to elaborate a new and symbolic vision of reality. This unity to which poetry attained in a superior synthesis constituted the aestheticism which Baudelaire proposed in his sonnet called *Correspondances*. One verse summarizes it: 'The perfumes, the colours and the sounds correspond to each other.'

The syntheses were studied by the Symbolists. René Ghil approved them, they were experimented in the theatre (Roinard), and conjured up by Huysmans in *A Rebours*. But even more than Baudelaire's sonnet, it is Rimbaud's *Voyelles* which was especially invoked. In fact, if it was frequently a question of 'audition colorées' in the Symbolic circles, very little of it remained in the artistic productions of the period, and the various attempts at correspondences between the arts led to more failures than successes.

List of Illustrations

Index